PENGUIN BOOKS

SUPREME INEQUALITY

Adam Cohen, who served as a member of the *New York Times* editorial board and as a senior writer for *Time* magazine, is the author of *Imbeciles: The Supreme Court, American Eugenics, and the Sterilization of Carrie Buck* and *Nothing to Fear: FDR's Inner Circle and the Hundred Days That Created Modern America*. A graduate of Harvard Law School, he was president of volume 100 of the *Harvard Law Review*.

Also by Adam Cohen

Imbeciles

Nothing to Fear

The Perfect Store

American Pharaoh

Praise for *Supreme Inequality*

◆

"Cohen's sweeping review is impressive and necessary. . . . *Supreme Inequality* makes an important contribution to our understanding of both the Supreme Court and the law of poverty."

—*The New York Times Book Review*

"Meticulously researched and engagingly written, *Supreme Inequality* is a howl of progressive rage against the past half-century of American jurisprudence. Cohen . . . builds a comprehensive indictment of the court's rulings in areas ranging from campaign finance and voting rights to poverty law and criminal justice." —*Financial Times*

"[A] tour guide such as Mr. Cohen is invaluable. He understands both the 'what' and the 'why' of the court's past fifty years. Whereas the average citizen might feel that the Supreme Court 'ensures fairness for all,' Mr. Cohen's book demonstrates how it has become a 'court of the 1 percent, not the 99 percent.'" —*Pittsburgh Post-Gazette*

"Cohen's ambitious, well-written book makes a convincing case that the court has contributed to growing inequality through its rulings on everything from election law and education to corporate law and crime."

—*The Christian Science Monitor*

"Cohen persuasively argues that [the] Supreme Court helped to create the income inequality that has become a defining (and grotesque) feature of contemporary America. His trenchant, gripping, and surprisingly accessible account guides readers through a slew of ruinous rulings that warped the Constitution." —*The American Prospect*

"Cohen's lucid writing makes even the most difficult court cases understandable as he expertly details the evolution of the law in areas as diverse as the workplace, criminal law, campaign contributions, and the corporate boardroom. Cohen's greatest strength, however, is his ability to explain clearly and urgently how the court, supposedly the least political of the three branches of the government, has relentlessly pursued a political agenda that has made Americans less equal and less secure." —*BookPage*

"Weaving legal, political, and social history, Cohen creates a richly detailed, but accessible, account for all interested in the personalities and politics that have shaped and are continuing to shape not only the U.S. criminal justice system but also the fabric of American life. A must-read."

—*Library Journal* (starred review)

"With *Supreme Inequality*, Adam Cohen has built, brick by brick, an airtight case against the Supreme Court of the last half-century. With his trademark precision and broad sweep, Cohen proves that the high court has created one system of legal protections for America's wealthy corporate interests and a second for the poor and middle classes. By limiting the Warren Court's fledgling efforts to protect workers, schoolchildren, criminal defendants, and voting rights, while inventing new protections for millionaire donors, big businesses, and polluters, the court has steadily contributed to the tragic inequality that is hollowing out the American system of justice. Cohen's book is a closing statement in the case against an institution tasked with protecting the vulnerable, which has emboldened the rich and powerful instead." —Dahlia Lithwick, senior editor, *Slate*

"*Brown v. Board*? *Roe v. Wade*? Sure. But with *Supreme Inequality* you dig down and understand the real direction of the Court over the last five-plus decades. It's imperative. And you can't put it down—with not just the law but the stories behind the law. Don't miss it."

—Peter Edelman, Carmack Waterhouse professor of law and public policy, Georgetown University Law Center

SUPREME INEQUALITY

The Supreme Court's Fifty-Year Battle for a More Unjust America

ADAM COHEN

PENGUIN BOOKS

PENGUIN BOOKS
An imprint of Penguin Random House LLC
penguinrandomhouse.com

First published in the United States of America by Penguin Press,
an imprint of Penguin Random House LLC, 2020
Published in Penguin Books 2021

ISBN 9780735221529 (paperback)

THE LIBRARY OF CONGRESS HAS CATALOGED THE HARDCOVER EDITION AS FOLLOWS:
Names: Cohen, Adam (Adam Seth), author.
Title: Supreme inequality : the Supreme Court's fifty-year battle
for a more unjust America / Adam Cohen.
Description: 1st. | New York : Penguin Press, 2020. |
Includes bibliographical references and index.
Identifiers: LCCN 2019031002 (print) | LCCN 2019031003 (ebook) |
ISBN 9780735221505 (hardcover) | ISBN 9780735221512 (ebook)
Subjects: LCSH: United States. Supreme Court—History. |
Political questions and judicial power—United States. |
Equality before the law—United States. | Discrimination—Law and legislation—
United States. | Election law—United States.
Classification: LCC KF8748 .C549 2020 (print) | LCC KF8748 (ebook) |
DDC 347.73/26—dc23
LC record available at https://lccn.loc.gov/2019031002
LC ebook record available at https://lccn.loc.gov/2019031003

Printed in the United States of America

Book design by Daniel Lagin

For Dad

If our civilization is destroyed . . . it will not be by . . . barbarians from below. Our barbarians come from above.

—HENRY DEMAREST LLOYD

CONTENTS

INTRODUCTION

Maetta Vance, an African American catering assistant at Ball State University, came to the Supreme Court a few years ago with a case of on-the-job racial harassment. Vance said a white woman who directed her work on a daily basis used racist words around her, including "Buckwheat" and "Sambo," and laughed while her husband and daughter taunted Vance with racial epithets. The woman also slapped her for no reason, Vance said, and later asked her, "Are you scared?" Vance said a different woman in the department bragged about her family's connections to the Ku Klux Klan and called her a "porch monkey."

The Court threw out Vance's case, by a 5–4 vote. Vance's lawsuit against Ball State required her to show that the woman who harassed her was her supervisor, but the five conservative justices said she had not done so. As long as the woman could not do things like fire or demote her, the Court said, Ball State owed her nothing. The decision was a clear misreading of the law, and one that bore no relation to how workplaces operate in the real world. Justice Ruth Bader Ginsburg, writing for the liberal dissenters, said a worker who directs another worker's daily activities is, of course, a supervisor. She also warned that the Court's decision would make it harder to "prevent discrimination from infecting the nation's workplaces."

Jack Gross, an Iowa insurance executive, had a similar difficulty with the Court a few years earlier. He was one of a group of high-performing workers over the age of fifty who were demoted by his company on the same day. Gross was forced to hand his responsibilities over to a younger worker he supervised. A jury ruled that he had been a victim of age discrimination and awarded him damages.

The Court overturned the jury's verdict, again by a 5–4 vote. Gross met the standard of proof required in race and sex discrimination cases. The Court decided, however, that victims of age discrimination had a higher burden of proof, even though the federal laws against race, sex, and age discrimination used identical language. The dissenting liberal justices accused the majority of "unabashed . . . judicial lawmaking."

Then there was Lilly Ledbetter. Ledbetter was a manager at Goodyear Tire & Rubber's plant in Gadsden, Alabama, where for years she was paid far less than the male managers. She had no way of knowing she was underpaid, because the plant's salaries were secret, until one day she got an anonymous note telling her. Ledbetter sued for sex discrimination, and a jury ruled in her favor and awarded her damages.

The Court reversed the jury's verdict, again by a 5–4 vote, with the most irrational reasoning of all. It said Ledbetter had made her claim of discrimination too late. She would have had to file it, the Court said, within 180 days of when Goodyear decided to pay her a discriminatory wage. It did not matter that, at the time, she had no way of knowing how much male managers earned. Ginsburg, in dissent, pointed out that the Court was requiring women suing for pay discrimination to do the impossible. The ruling against Ledbetter was so obviously unfair that Congress overturned it with the Lilly Ledbetter Fair Pay Act, the first law Barack Obama signed as president.

If it seems that the Court's conservative majority has been twisting the law to rule against employment discrimination victims, there is a simple reason: it has. The Court's battle against victims of on-the-job discrimination is, however, part of a much larger war. For five decades, the Court has, with striking regularity, sided with the rich and powerful against the poor and weak, in virtually every area of the law.

In campaign finance law, it has opened the floodgates to money from wealthy individuals and corporations. In election law, it has upheld rules and practices designed to make it more difficult for the poor and racial minorities to vote, and struck down a key part of the Voting Rights Act. In corporate law, the Court has made it harder for employees and consumers to sue when they are injured. In criminal law, it has favored prosecutors so consistently that it has contributed significantly to the nation's mass incarceration crisis. And on a wide variety of issues, the Court has ruled, often cruelly, against the poor.

The financial and emotional toll on the losing parties in these cases has been considerable. Jack Gross was devastated when the Court manipulated age discrimination law to reject his case. "One of the things I have always counted on was the rule of law," he said. Gross was also upset that, in addition to losing the damages the jury had awarded him, he was out more than $30,000 in legal expenses. "That is money," he said, "that was intended to help my grandchildren get a college education so they wouldn't have to starve their way through like I did."

Ledbetter was crushed by her defeat, which she learned about when she was on the way to a church luncheon with her husband, who had been diagnosed with cancer. "I'd done what I could," she said. "Goodyear was simply a greater force than I could overcome. That was clear as day." Ledbetter had not only lost the damages the jury awarded her. It occurred to her that, because her pension and Social Security were tied to her salary, she would continue to be underpaid for the rest of her life.

As shattering as decisions like these have been for individuals, in the aggregate they add up to something much larger: a systematic rewriting of society's rules to favor those at the top and disadvantage those in the middle and at the bottom. The Supreme Court has played a critical role in building today's America, in which income inequality is the largest it has been in nearly a century. The Court's decisions have lifted up those who are already high and brought down those who are low, creating hundreds of millions of winners and losers.

IT DID NOT HAVE TO BE THIS WAY, AND THERE WAS A TIME WHEN IT WAS not. On October 5, 1953, Governor Earl Warren of California was sworn in as chief justice, and his arrival launched a progressive legal revolution. In his first year in office, Warren led the Court to a unanimous ruling in *Brown v. Board of Education,* which held segregated schools unconstitutional. When the South rose up in massive resistance, the Court did not back down, and it proceeded to integrate bus stations, restaurants, and other public spaces.

The drive for racial equality was only part of the Warren Court's "rights revolution." The Court also recognized new rights for criminal defendants, including the right to an appointed lawyer for those who could not afford one. It championed the rights of non-Christians by banning official state prayer in public schools. It expanded the rights of the poor in many ways, including by adopting new protections for welfare recipients.

The Warren Court was a powerful force for change, but a fragile one. There had been bitter opposition to its rulings every step of the way. The Court had many enemies, including an Alabama congressman who complained that "they put Negroes in the schools, and now they've driven God out," and right-wing groups whose IMPEACH EARL WARREN billboards dotted the rural landscape. By 1968, Richard Nixon was campaigning for president by running against the Warren Court, which he said in a *Reader's Digest* article had "weakened law and encouraged criminals."

During the 1968 campaign, Warren began to worry about the future of the Court. President Lyndon Johnson was not running for reelection, and in early June, the young and charismatic Robert Kennedy was assassinated. It looked increasingly as though Hubert Humphrey, Johnson's vice president, would be the Democratic nominee and that Nixon would be the Republican candidate. Warren, who was adept at reading the political landscape, thought there was a good chance Nixon would win.

If Nixon became president, it would pose a direct threat to everything Warren had built. Nixon was promising to appoint conservative justices, and Warren, who was seventy-seven, was afraid one of these could be the next chief justice, who would work to bring the Warren Court's accomplishments crashing down. Warren, however, had a plan for saving the Court, and American law, from Nixon.

On June 13, 1968, Warren went to the White House to tell the president he intended to resign. Warren asked Johnson to appoint a new chief justice who would keep the Court on its progressive path. Johnson was quick to agree. As a liberal Democrat, he did not want the Warren Court's legacy undone. Johnson also had a personal stake. As president, he had worked to build what he called the Great Society, by waging a "war on poverty," launching Medicare and Medicaid and other ambitious social programs. Many of these initiatives pushed the federal government into new areas, and were vulnerable to legal challenge. Johnson knew that a Court filled with Nixon appointees would be as much of a threat to his own legacy as to Warren's.

Johnson nominated Abe Fortas, a sitting justice who was a close friend and adviser, to be the next chief justice. Johnson, who as Senate majority leader had been the wily "master of the Senate," did not anticipate the trouble Fortas would have in being confirmed. Republicans attacked him for his close ties to Johnson—the word "crony" was used often—and southern Democrats defected over Fortas's pro-civil-rights record. In the end, Fortas could not win Senate confirmation, and the final months of Johnson's presidency ran out with no replacement for Warren confirmed. Johnson and Warren's plan had failed spectacularly.

Nixon won the presidential election in the fall of 1968, and when Warren retired, in mid-1969, Nixon replaced him with a conservative, Warren Burger.

The fabled Warren Court was now over, and the Court's new leader was an intellectually unimpressive jurist who shared Nixon's conservative ideology and hatred of the Warren Court.

The Court still had a liberal majority, however, which Nixon was intent on changing—by taking matters into his own hands. While he was waiting for Warren's retirement, Nixon decided to create another vacancy by targeting Fortas, who had been weakened by his Senate rejection. Nixon's Justice Department investigated the liberal justice and, even though it did not find that Fortas had broken any laws or court rules, Nixon's underlings still threatened Fortas into resigning. That gave Nixon his second appointment to the Court, and when two older justices retired for health reasons, Nixon was able to make two more appointments. These changes all unfolded quickly. In his first three years in office, Nixon named four justices, including a chief justice—one of the most intense periods of transformation in the Court's history.

The four Nixon justices, when added to two moderate conservatives who were already serving, killed off the liberal Warren Court and replaced it with a new conservative majority. The new Court was officially called the Burger Court, after Chief Justice Warren Burger. The role of one man had been so great in creating it, however, that journalists gave it a different name: the Nixon Court.

The Nixon Court has been extraordinarily durable. In the five decades since Burger arrived, there have been only conservative chief justices: Burger, William Rehnquist, and John Roberts. Since January 1972, when the last two Nixon justices arrived, these conservative chief justices have consistently had conservative majorities behind them.

There are many reasons the Court's conservative majority has endured for so long. Partly, it is simply that since 1969, Republicans have held the White House for more years than Democrats. That has given Republican presidents more time to appoint justices, and they have overwhelmingly chosen conservatives.

Conservative justices have also been more strategic in timing their retirements. Anthony Kennedy stepped down in the summer of 2018, when he was apparently in good health, while there was a Republican president and a Republican-controlled Senate, ensuring that his successor would be a conservative. Ruth Bader Ginsburg did not retire early in President Barack Obama's second term, when he could have replaced her with a younger liberal justice. In the aggregate, conservatives have done a much better job of handing their seats to justices who share their views than liberals have. An analysis conducted in 2014 found that all six of the most conservative justices who left the Court since the mid-1960s were replaced by Republican presidents, while of the six most liberal justices, only one was replaced by a Democratic president.

Republicans have also used hardball tactics. That was true in 1969, when Nixon drove Fortas off the Court. It was also true nearly fifty years later, when Antonin Scalia died and President Obama nominated Merrick Garland, a liberal federal appeals court judge in Washington, D.C., to replace him. If Garland had been confirmed, the Court would have had its first liberal majority since Nixon's presidency. Senate Republicans, however, refused to even consider Garland, insisting that the next president should fill the seat. When President Donald Trump took office, he nominated Neil Gorsuch, a conservative federal appeals court judge from Denver, who was quickly confirmed. Fortas's forced resignation and the Senate's refusal to consider Garland were bookends on a five-decade era on the Court: one disreputable move created a conservative majority and the other preserved it.

One of the main reasons for the conservatives' long-standing control of the Court, which has continued uninterrupted since Nixon's time, is that they simply seem to have wanted it more. Republicans have made the Court a focus of their politics in a way Democrats have not, and they have come to look on it with a sense of entitlement. As President Trump said on behalf of his fellow Republicans in a March 2018 tweet: "We . . . must ALWAYS hold the Supreme Court!"

WHEN EARL WARREN AND LYNDON JOHNSON MET AT THE WHITE HOUSE in June 1968, they hoped that after Warren retired the Court would continue on the path it was on. They wanted it to remain a champion of the poor, working people, and racial minorities and to keep building a more equal and inclusive America. They hoped that the Court would always play the role in society that it had in the Warren era. Instead, the Warren Court turned out to be a historical outlier. When it ended, the Court resumed its traditional role in national life: protector of the rich and powerful.

That is not, of course, the story the nation tells itself about the Supreme Court. In American history and civics classes, the Court is generally presented as the branch of government that looks out for vulnerable minorities and ensures fairness for all. The justices have often talked of themselves this way. In a 1940 case, the Court declared unanimously that courts are "havens of refuge for those who might otherwise suffer because they are helpless, weak, outnumbered, or because they are nonconforming victims of prejudice and public excitement."

Popular culture has reinforced this noble vision of the Supreme Court. There was a movie about *Brown v. Board of Education,* with Sidney Poitier as Thurgood Marshall, the lawyer for the black schoolchildren, and another one about *Gideon v. Wainwright,* with Henry Fonda as Clarence Gideon, the criminal defendant who won poor defendants the right to court-appointed counsel. Hollywood has yet to make a movie about *Citizens United v. Federal Election Commission,* in which the Court ruled that corporations have a First Amendment right to spend as much money as they want to influence elections.

Throughout the nation's history, the reality of the Supreme Court has been very different from the idealized version. Before the Civil War, the Court regularly sided with slaveholders, in cases like *Dred Scott v. Sandford,* the infamous decision rejecting an enslaved man's suit for his freedom. In the years after the war, the Court upheld racial segregation in the South against constitutional challenges.

In the Progressive Era, from the 1890s to the 1920s, when Congress and state legislatures passed laws protecting workers, the Court ruled that they violated the bosses' "liberty of contract." During the Great Depression, the Court struck down President Franklin Roosevelt's early New Deal programs, which were designed to provide emergency jobs to the unemployed and relief to destitute farmers. The Court gave in only after Roosevelt threatened to pack the Court with more sympathetic justices. During World War II, while the nation was fighting bigotry overseas, the Court endorsed the evacuation of Japanese Americans to internment camps.

The Warren Court was not only an exception to the Court's historical role; it was a brief one. It formally lasted nearly sixteen years, from Warren's arrival as chief justice, in 1953, to his retirement, in 1969. It was not until 1962, however, when President John F. Kennedy's two nominees arrived, that the Court had a strong liberal majority. Most of the Warren Court's best-known and most influential decisions came during its last seven years. When the Nixon justices arrived, the Court drastically reversed course from its Warren-era liberalism in a wide array of areas, including employment law, education law, campaign finance law, corporate law, and criminal law.

The post-1969 Court has not been conservative in all areas, and in some it has made the law more progressive. It recognized a constitutional right to abortion in 1973 in *Roe v. Wade*. It also struck down state laws that criminalized same-sex sexual activities in 2003, after initially upholding them in 1986, and it recognized a constitutional right to marry for same-sex couples. These more liberal rulings have generally been on social issues, and they have largely reflected the national consensus. The justices have also not always divided on ideological lines. Kennedy regularly voted in favor of gay rights, and John Paul Stevens, a liberal, wrote the Court's opinion upholding strict voter ID laws.

In the most important and controversial cases, however, the Court has generally broken down into conservative and liberal camps. In recent years, new justices have been selected for their clearly demonstrated conservative or liberal views and arrive with an ideological mission. When President Trump nominated Brett Kavanaugh, Vice President Mike Pence assured conservatives that they could count on his vote because he had a "proven judicial philosophy." The current Court, after years of being carefully constructed in this way, seems more like a political body than a legal one.

A half century after the end of the Warren era, the Court's politics are not merely conservative but in many ways extreme. One academic study that examined the Court's decisions from 1938 to 2010 concluded that 2010 was the most conservative year in that entire seventy-two-year period. The Court has moved even further to the right since 2010. Charles Fried, a conservative Harvard law professor who served in the Reagan Justice Department, said in a 2018 *Harvard Law Review* essay entitled "Not Conservative" that the Court's extremism can be seen not only in its positions, but in the reckless ways it has arrived at them. On important issues, it "has undermined or overturned precedents that embodied long-standing and difficult compromise settlements of sharply opposed interests and principles," Fried said. "These decisions are not the work of a conservative Court."

WHILE THE COURT MOVED TO THE RIGHT ON MANY SUBJECTS AFTER Earl Warren retired, there is no area in which it changed course more rapidly or more extremely than economic class. The Warren Court was one of the most powerful forces in American history for lifting up the poor. Poor people had always been seen through demeaning stereotypes—as lazy, immoral, dangerous, or biologically deficient—and they had often been victims of severe discrimination. There were, at various times, laws that allowed poor people to be consigned to poorhouses and laws making it a crime to transport a poor person over state lines.

These attitudes changed in the 1960s, when an increasingly affluent nation began to see the poor in a new light, and its leaders declared a "war on poverty." The Warren Court played a pivotal role in this new approach to the poor, interpreting the Constitution in ways that greatly expanded their rights. The Court significantly advanced poor people's political rights when it held that the poll tax was unconstitutional. Four years later, it greatly increased their economic rights when it ruled that welfare recipients were entitled to a hearing before their benefits were cut off.

The Warren Court also championed the middle class. Under Warren's leadership, the same Court that in the Progressive Era had reflexively sided with employers took an expansive view of the rights of working men and women. It defended their right to join unions and bargain collectively, and it showed a new understanding of the difficult lives they led. In one important case, the Court struck down a state wage garnishment law that made it too easy for creditors to seize workers' salaries. In its opinion, the Court underscored that the law "may impose tremendous hardship on wage earners with families to support."

For all of the progress poor people made in the Warren era, poverty lawyers still had a long list of rights they were hoping to win. There was a large and outspoken welfare rights movement that was calling for fairer rules, more privacy, and increased benefits for welfare recipients. Advocates for poor children were starting to focus on school finance, arguing that the Court should hold that all school districts in a state, whether rich or poor, should have equal levels of funding.

Most weighty of all was the question of whether poor people as a group should have special constitutional protection. Poverty lawyers argued that the poor deserved that status under the Equal Protection Clause of the Fourteenth Amendment, which was added after the Civil War to protect the rights of freed slaves and had become the main constitutional provision protecting equality for all Americans. The Court had developed an elaborate model that gave extra protections to groups it considered the most discriminated against and the least able to protect themselves through the political process. When a law imposed particular burdens on one of these "suspect classes," the Court applied "strict scrutiny"—or some other heightened level of review—and it was more likely to strike the law down. The Court had recognized racial and religious minorities as suspect classes, and advocates for the poor argued that poor people should also be recognized as a suspect class. In a number of rulings, the Warren Court came close to doing so.

When the Warren era ended, the Court quickly put a stop to the line of cases expanding the rights of the poor. The post-1969 Court changed direction almost immediately in welfare law cases, with a landmark decision rejecting a poor family's constitutional challenge to a cap on welfare benefits that pushed them far below the poverty level. It declared that the "intractable" problems presented by welfare programs "are not the business of this Court." It also decided that the poor would not be a suspect class.

Over the next few years, the Court ruled against the poor in other important cases, two of which were particularly pivotal. In 1973, it came within one vote of requiring all fifty states to equalize funding between rich and poor school districts. A year later, it was one vote away from requiring states to provide all children with a racially integrated education, even if it meant transporting students across the lines separating urban and suburban school districts. If Nixon had not driven Fortas off the Court, the plaintiff schoolchildren would almost certainly have prevailed in both of these cases—and poor and minority children would have far greater educational opportunity today.

The post-1969 Court has also reduced the rights of the middle class. It has eroded the rights of workers to bring lawsuits against their employers, whether for discrimination or wage theft. It has scaled back the rights of unions, most seriously in 2018, when it ruled that government workers in unionized work sites do not need to pay union dues or alternative fees to compensate the union for representing them. That decision is likely to greatly weaken public-sector unions, making them less able to defend workers.

The Court has also systematically diminished the political rights of lower-income Americans. It struck down a key part of the Voting Rights Act, one of the most important laws ever enacted to ensure that all Americans can participate in democracy on an equal basis. It upheld strict voter ID laws, which reduce the turnout of poor and minority voters, and strict voter roll purges.

The Court has also reduced the rights of criminal defendants, with poor and working-class people, and racial minorities in particular, bearing the brunt of the changes. Its rulings have made it easier for the government to win convictions and impose longer prison sentences. These decisions have contributed to making the United States' incarceration rate the highest in the world.

At the same time as it has reduced the rights of those at the bottom, the post-1969 Court has recognized important new rights for those at the top. The biggest freedom it gave the wealthy was the ability to use their money in unlimited amounts to support candidates for office, by equating money with speech. In recent years the Court has gone further and declared that corporations have the right to spend unlimited amounts of money to elect candidates to office. As a result of these rulings, wealthy individuals and corporations have an outsized influence on which candidates win elections—and on government policy.

The Court has expanded the rights of corporations in other areas, championing them in much the same way that the Warren Court showed special concern for the poor. It gave corporations new protections against being sued in class actions by their employees and customers. It also imposed limits on punitive damages when corporations harmed people, whether by selling defective products or polluting their land.

There is strong statistical evidence that the Court began a major pro-corporate transformation after the Warren Court ended. One study, conducted by two law professors and a federal judge, found that after the four Nixon justices arrived, the Court began to rule in favor of corporations more frequently and that its pro-business tilt has increased even more in recent years. The Burger and Rehnquist Courts were significantly more favorable to corporations than the Warren Court, the study found, and the Roberts Court even more so. A *New York Times* analysis, which reached similar conclusions, ran under the headline "Supreme Court Inc."

THE PAST FIFTY YEARS OF CONSERVATIVE RULINGS FROM THE SUPREME Court have coincided almost exactly with a period in which economic inequality in the United States has soared to near-historic levels. The Center on Budget and Policy Priorities, a leading expert on inequality, has observed that "the era of shared prosperity" in the United States "ended in the 1970s" and that since then there has been a sharp divergence between the wealthy and everyone else. By 2014, the top 1 percent earned more than 20 percent of all income in the United States, while the bottom 50 percent earned just 12.5 percent. The wealth gap that year was even larger. The richest 0.1 percent of families—just 160,000 families—owned about as much as the bottom 90 percent of Americans.

Many factors have contributed to this growing inequality, including some that are larger than any single country, such as globalization and job-destroying automation. There can be little doubt, however, that a major reason for our soaring income inequality is the choices that government has made over the past half century. According to Joseph Stiglitz, the Nobel Prize–winning Columbia University economist, "government policies have been central to the creation of inequality in the United States." To "reverse these trends in inequality," he said, "we will have to reverse some of the policies that have helped make America the most economically divided developed country."

The government choices that are most often associated with rising inequality are the ones made by presidents and Congress. The increase in wealth at the top is generally attributed to policies like the tax cuts for the rich championed by President George W. Bush and President Trump. The declines at the bottom are often said to be a result of policies like the welfare reform law of 1996, promoted by House Speaker Newt Gingrich and signed by President Bill Clinton, which ended "welfare as we have come to know it." The Supreme Court is rarely included in these analyses, even though it has been one of the most powerful drivers of income inequality over the past half century.

Many of the forces that are widening the gap between rich and poor—and leaving the middle class not far ahead of the poor—can be directly tied to choices made by the Court. The *World Inequality Report 2018*, which was prepared by Thomas Piketty and other economists, concluded that the income-inequality trajectory of the United States is largely due to two factors: "massive educational inequalities" and "a tax system that grew less progressive." The post-1969 Court has been a major contributor to each of these problems. When the Court refused to equalize funding between rich and poor school districts or to order racial integration across school district lines, it made extreme educational inequality inevitable. The Court's campaign finance decisions, which have given wealthy individuals and large corporations highly disproportionate influence over elections and government, are a major reason tax policy is so slanted in favor of the rich.

The Court has made many other choices that have increased economic inequality. By weakening labor unions, it has driven down workers' wages and benefits and allowed more corporate money to flow to top executives and shareholders. By making it harder to sue corporations, it has made the victims of corporate malfeasance poorer while expanding corporate profits. The Court's criminal law decisions, which have increased incarceration rates, have had a devastating economic impact on poor and working-class communities.

The Court has also contributed to the dismantling of the social safety net. One of the first ways in which the Court changed direction after the Warren Court ended was by abandoning welfare recipients. The Court gave a green light to the states to reduce welfare benefits as much as they wanted, or even to eliminate them entirely.

The nation's growing inequality hurts Americans on many levels. The media has extensively covered the "hollowing out" of the middle class, whose members are increasingly being pushed into poverty or near poverty. A Federal Reserve Board study in 2018 found that 40 percent of Americans could not come up with $400 in an emergency. Inequality is not only killing off the middle class—in some cases it is literally killing it. Life expectancy in the United States declined between 2014 and 2017, the longest such sustained decline since 1915 to 1918, a period that included a flu pandemic and World War I. American life expectancy is also declining relative to other nations—in 2018, the United States fell from forty-third place to sixty-fourth place globally. Public health experts connect these declines to "deaths of despair," including opioid-related fatalities and suicide, among working-class Americans.

The state of poor Americans is even worse. The nation is far wealthier than it was fifty years ago, but poverty has remained stubbornly persistent. In 1969, when the Nixon Court began forming, the poverty rate was 12.2 percent. In 2017, it was 12.3 percent. In a nation of more than 300 million, that means that tens of millions of Americans are still barely managing to survive. An estimated one in eight Americans is "food insecure," meaning they lack the funds for consistent access to sufficient food. That translates into more than forty million people, including more than twelve million children.

While the poor and the middle class are hurt most by increasing economic inequality, these trends hurt all Americans—because they threaten America itself. Extreme inequality puts democracy at risk: the concentration of wealth in the top 1 percent—and, to a striking degree, the top 0.1 percent—is pushing the nation toward plutocracy. Political scientists have long said that a healthy middle class is critical to warding off tyranny. In the sociologist Barrington Moore's classic formulation, "no bourgeoisie, no democracy." Legal scholars have observed that America's foundational document was drafted for a society with a strong middle class. "To function properly, the Constitution requires equality and solidarity," cautions Vanderbilt law professor Ganesh Sitaraman, author of *The Crisis of the Middle-Class Constitution*. "Once those are gone, it contains no mechanism to restore them."

Increased inequality also strikes at a fundamental aspect of America's identity. The United States has always seen itself as a nation where hard work and talent lead to success, and where each generation can expect to be better off than the last. That promise of upward mobility is unraveling as a growing share of the nation's wealth is arrogated by a small number of very wealthy people at the top. A study by a group of Harvard, Stanford, and University of California–Berkeley professors found that only half of thirty-year-olds born in 1984 earned more than their parents did at their age, holding inflation constant, compared to 92 percent of thirty-year-olds born in 1940. "Economic growth that is spread more broadly across the income distribution," the professors concluded, is necessary for "reviving the 'American Dream.'"

FIVE DECADES AFTER EARL WARREN VISITED LYNDON JOHNSON AT THE White House in an attempt to protect the Court from Nixon, that battle is ancient history—and Nixon won. The Warren Court's mission of uplifting the poor and the weak, and of building a more equal and inclusive society, has not only been stopped—it has been sharply reversed. The post-1969 Court has been working unrelentingly to protect the wealthy and powerful, and to make the nation more hierarchical and exclusionary—and it has been succeeding. When it comes to the law, and its many consequences for society, we are all living in Nixon's America now.

Increased inequality also strikes at a fundamental aspect of America's identity. The United States has always seen itself as a nation where hard work and talent lead to success, and where each generation can expect to be better off than the last. That promise of upward mobility is unraveling as a growing share of the nation's wealth is arrogated by a small number of very wealthy people at the top. A study by a group of Harvard, Stanford, and University of California–Berkeley professors found that only half of thirty-year-olds born in 1984 earned more than their parents did at their age, holding inflation constant, compared to 92 percent of thirty-year-olds born in 1940. "Economic growth that is spread more broadly across the income distribution," the professors concluded, is necessary for "reviving the American Dream."

FIVE DECADES AFTER EARL WARREN VISITED LYNDON JOHNSON AT THE White House in an attempt to protect the Court from Nixon, that battle is ancient history—and Nixon won. The Warren Court's mission of uplifting the poor and the weak, and of building a more equal and inclusive society has not only been stopped—it has been sharply reversed. The post-1969 Court has been working unrelentingly to protect the wealthy and powerful, and to make the nation more hierarchical and exclusionary—and it has been succeeding. When it comes to the law, and its many consequences for society, we are all living in Nixon's America now.

CHAPTER ◆ 1

PROTECTING THE POOR

In the spring of 1968, Sylvester Smith, of Selma, Alabama, asked the Supreme Court to restore her welfare benefits. The thirty-four-year-old Smith, a widow with four young children, worked from 3:30 a.m. until noon as a waitress and cook and picked cotton in her time off, but she earned only about $20 a week. She supplemented her wages with about $29 a month in Aid to Families with Dependent Children (AFDC), a federal cash assistance program for low-income families with children, jointly administered by the federal and state governments. When a tough new caseworker named Jacquelyn Stancil took over her case, Smith was told that she and her children were no longer eligible for benefits, because of information the state had received from an anonymous source. The problem, Stancil said, using the terminology of the day, was that there was a "man in the house."

Alabama was one of eighteen states with a "man in the house" rule, which denied welfare benefits to mothers who were having sex with a man on a regular basis. In Alabama, a man who visited frequently "for the purpose of cohabiting with" the mother, or met with her elsewhere for sex, was deemed a "substitute father" and obligated to support the family. The rule was meant to save the government money, but it also reflected the view that, as *The New York Times* put it, welfare was "an inducement to immoral behavior, especially among Negroes." Alabama's top welfare official defended the man-in-the-house rule by saying that a mother who lost her benefits could always choose "to give up her pleasure" and "act like a woman ought to" to get them back.

Stancil had received a tip that Smith had a boyfriend who visited her home—a shack on the outskirts of Selma—on weekends. Smith did have a boyfriend, a married man named William E. Williams, but, like many of the men who visited welfare mothers, he had little money, and he had a wife and nine children of his own. Williams gave Smith $4 or $5 a month, but he could not support her family, which Smith understood. "Ain't much he can do," she said. "You can't make a man take care of his own kids, much less take care of other people's kids."

Stancil told Smith that if she did not break off with Williams, she and her children would lose their AFDC benefits. Under Alabama law, Smith could defend against the charge that she had a boyfriend by providing evidence that she did not, including references from people considered to be in a position to know, such as clergymen, neighbors, or grocers. Welfare officials would ask the references if they believed she was having sexual relations. Smith, however, did not deny that she was seeing Williams. "If I end with him, I'm gonna make a relationship with somebody," she said. "If God had intended for me to be a nun, I'd be a nun."

Smith's situation was not unusual. Alabama adopted the man-in-the-house rule in 1964, and 15,000 children were removed from the AFDC rolls under it in the first year. Another 6,400 poor children were turned down when their mothers applied for AFDC. An analysis of the cases closed in Alabama because of the man-in-the-house rule found that 97 percent of the children were black. Nationwide, the numbers were far larger: it was estimated that more than 500,000 children were being denied benefits because of state man-in-the-house rules.

What was unusual about Smith's case was that she fought back. She challenged Alabama's rule in federal court. It was a courageous act for a poor African American widow and mother of four to take in 1960s Alabama, and it came at considerable personal cost. While the lawsuit proceeded, Smith's benefits were cut off, and the Selma power structure closed ranks against her. Stores refused to extend her credit to buy groceries, and at times her children went hungry. Smith also lost the minimal support she received from Williams, who stopped his visits after she filed suit.

Welfare recipients had many burdensome conditions imposed on them in the 1960s, but few were as despised as the man-in-the-house rule. It was widely understood that welfare officials saw it as a tool for removing people from the rolls, particularly black women and children. The man-in-the-house rule was, one analysis of Smith's case noted, the preferred tool for "an Alabama welfare official intent upon lopping off a lot of black bodies in a hurry." The rule also let caseworkers probe the most intimate aspects of their clients' lives. Two years earlier, the NAACP Legal Defense and Educational Fund had declared at a Washington, D.C., press conference that ending the man-in-the-house rule was one of its top priorities. The rule put the welfare mother in an "impossible dilemma," the group said, forcing her to choose between conducting "a secret relationship" while living "as if she were a criminal" or abandoning "her efforts to develop male friendships altogether."

Smith's case was taken up by northern lawyers, including ones from Columbia University's Center on Social Welfare Policy and Law. These lawyers thought Smith's challenge would be a strong national test case. Since Williams did not live in the home, was not the father of any of the children, and was too poor to support them, the state's claim that he should be considered a "substitute father" was weak. Alabama was also a good state to bring a challenge in. Governor George Wallace had stood in the schoolhouse door to resist integration at the University of Alabama just a few years earlier, and the state's close association with virulent racism meant there would be little sympathy for it if the case reached the Supreme Court.

Smith's lawyers argued that the man-in-the-house rule violated her rights under two parts of the Fourteenth Amendment: the Equal Protection Clause, which says the government cannot deny people "equal protection of the laws," and the Due Process Clause, which prohibits the government from denying life, liberty, or property without "due process of law." The lawyers also argued more narrowly that the rule violated the federal AFDC statute, because it denied welfare benefits to children who were entitled to them under the law. The statute required states that participated in the program to provide benefits to needy children if their father was dead, absent, or incapacitated, which Alabama was not doing for Smith's children.

The Supreme Court accepted the case, and it heard oral arguments on April 23, 1968, just weeks after Martin Luther King Jr. was assassinated. It was clear from the justices' questions that the man-in-the-house rule was in trouble. Warren expressed concern over whether welfare families like Smith's actually received support from the purported "substitute fathers" covered by the rule. Marshall, the first black justice, who earlier in his career had been director-counsel of the NAACP Legal Defense Fund, and William O. Douglas, the Court's most liberal member, questioned why the Smith children should be penalized for actions they had nothing to do with.

On June 17, 1968, in *King v. Smith,* the Court ruled for Smith by a 9–0 vote. It took a narrow approach, holding that the man-in-the-house rule violated the AFDC statute, and not reaching the larger equal protection and due process issues. Warren, who wrote the Court's opinion, said that under the statute, benefits had to be provided to every eligible "dependent child" deprived of "parental" support." Alabama's rule was invalid, Warren said, because poor children without fathers cannot be denied aid "on the transparent fiction that they have a substitute father."

The Court's narrow approach to the case was not surprising. Courts generally try to decide cases based on statutes rather than the Constitution whenever they can, a principle that is known as "constitutional avoidance." By ruling under the AFDC statute, the Court did not create any broad new constitutional rights for poor people that they could apply in other kinds of cases. Still, the decision's real-world impact was undeniably large. In addition to restoring the Smith family's benefits, it prevented about 500,000 children nationwide from losing benefits because of an irrational and cruel governmental dictate. The language Warren used in his opinion also highlighted the challenges faced by poor families like the Smiths. "All responsible government agencies in the Nation today," he declared, "recognize the enormity and pervasiveness of social ills caused by poverty."

Smith was pleased by the Court's ruling, and by the fact that it would help other AFDC recipients. "A lot of the ladies who got aid because of my case thank me," she said later. Legal commentators overwhelmingly praised the Court for striking down an invasive and mean-spirited rule and hoped the decision would be the first of many more like it. "The *King* decision is a salutary one," an article in the *North Carolina Law Review* declared, and it "very likely signifies a new role for the Supreme Court in protecting the rights of welfare recipients, though it is of small significance compared with the work yet to be done."

KING V. SMITH WAS THE CULMINATION OF A DECADES-LONG DRIVE TO establish greater legal rights for the poor. The origins of this campaign lay in the Great Depression, when the Court began to express a new concern for the disadvantaged. Starting in 1933, Franklin Roosevelt's New Dealers poured into Washington, D.C., on a mission to rescue the millions of Americans who had been driven into poverty, and some of that idealism eventually reached the Court. In 1938, in the obscure commercial case *United States v. Carolene Products,* the New Deal–inspired Court unveiled a new conception of the Equal Protection Clause that would systematically give special protection to the most vulnerable groups in society.

The Court set out its new vision for equal protection in footnote 4 of the *Carolene Products* decision, which has been called the most famous footnote in American law. The Court said that when it reviewed most laws, it would be highly deferential and rarely declare them unconstitutional. If a law imposed a special burden on "discrete and insular minorities," including religious, national, or racial minorities, however, the Court suggested it would apply a "more searching judicial inquiry." The Court's message was that it was highly likely that it would strike down laws that imposed special burdens on one of these vulnerable minority groups.

Footnote 4 marked a major new path for American constitutional law. To a degree it never had before, the Court was making a commitment to protect minorities who were too politically weak to protect themselves. It was not clear, however, which groups it considered to be "discrete and insular minorities" deserving of special protection. Footnote 4 expressly mentioned racial, religious, and national minorities, but it suggested that more groups might follow. One factor it said it would take into account was whether a group experienced prejudice that interfered with its ability to use "political processes ordinarily to be relied upon to protect minorities."

The Court did not raise the possibility that poor people would be one of these new protected classes, but there was a strong argument that they should be, based on the criteria in footnote 4. Poor people were a numerical minority. They were also a discrete and insular group: they were often physically segregated, in urban ghettos or on the "wrong" side of the tracks, and they were set apart socially by the stigma that attached to them in a nation that worshipped material success. Throughout American history, the poor had been a much reviled group, regarded as lazy, immoral, disease-carrying, and cursed by God. Poor people had also been unable to protect their rights through the political process. There had been a wide array of laws discriminating against them, including ones that consigned them to indentured servitude or poorhouses, and they had not been able to persuade the government to adopt welfare programs that would lift them out of poverty.

There was another factor working in favor of designating the poor a discrete and insular minority in the late 1930s. With so many formerly wealthy and middle-class Americans experiencing dramatic reversals of fortune during the Great Depression, there was a growing belief that poor people were not to blame for their misfortune. This new attitude came directly from the top. Roosevelt had declared at his inauguration on March 4, 1933, that poverty was a national problem that the government had an obligation to address. Later in his presidency, in his famous "Four Freedoms" speech, one of the freedoms Roosevelt argued for was "freedom from want."

There were also reasons, however, that the Court might be reluctant to designate the poor as a suspect class. Unlike racial and religious minorities, poor people were not yet recognized as a cohesive group that should be regarded as having collective rights. It also was not entirely clear what kinds of laws the Court would subject to heightened scrutiny if it decided that the poor were a suspect class. After all, even many of the most mundane government policies, like highway tolls and national park entrance fees, imposed a greater burden on the poor than the rich.

In 1941, in *Edwards v. California,* the Court had a chance to weigh in on the rights of the poor, and to use footnote 4 if it wanted to. The case was a challenge to a California law that made it a crime to transport a poor person into the state. Twenty-eight states had laws of this kind, which were known as anti-Okie laws, after the Oklahoma migrants immortalized in John Steinbeck's *The Grapes of Wrath,* who were the sort of people they were intended to keep out. The plaintiff in the case, Fred Edwards, had driven to Texas to pick up his brother-in-law, Frank Duncan, and Duncan's pregnant wife. He brought them back to his home, near Sacramento, and three weeks later Duncan's wife gave birth. Edwards was convicted of violating California's Welfare and Institutions Code, which barred "bringing into the state any indigent person who is not a resident of the state," and he was sentenced to six months in jail.

The Court struck down the law by a unanimous vote, though the justices disagreed on their legal rationales. The majority held that California's law violated the Commerce Clause, which limits the ability of states to interfere with exchanges between the states that have an economic impact, including the movement of people. *Edwards* was an important victory for the poor, since anti-Okie laws were so widespread and so stigmatizing. The majority opinion in *Edwards* also changed how the Court talked about poor people. Instead of calling them "paupers," "vagabonds," or a "moral pestilence," as it repeatedly had in past decisions, the Court went out of its way to humanize them. It was not true that "because a person is without employment and without funds, he constitutes a 'moral pestilence,'" the Court said. "Poverty and immorality are not synonymous."

The one thing the Court did not do for the poor in *Edwards* was hold that they had any special rights as a group, the way it could have if it had relied on the Equal Protection Clause and footnote 4. Roosevelt had nominated seven of the nine justices who decided *Edwards,* and he had elevated another, Harlan Fiske Stone, to be the chief justice. Still, the Court was not willing to expand the legal rights of the poor in the same way that Roosevelt had expanded their economic rights. By basing the decision on the right to travel across state lines, the Court did not give poor people a legal precedent they could use when they were discriminated against in other ways.

One justice, however, went further. In his concurring opinion, Robert Jackson, who had been Roosevelt's attorney general before he joined the Court, said the real problem with California's law was that it discriminated against the poor. Writing just weeks before America entered World War II to fight Nazism, Jackson insisted that the Court risked "denaturing human rights" by making the case about interstate commerce. "We should say now, and in no uncertain terms," he wrote, "that a man's mere property status, without more, cannot be used by a state to test, qualify, or limit his rights." In arguing that the case should have been decided under the Fourteenth Amendment's "Privileges and Immunities" clause, Jackson compared the poor to groups that footnote 4 had identified as "discrete and insular minorities." Lacking money was, he insisted, "constitutionally an irrelevance, like race, creed, or color." Jackson, however, had only his own vote for his views.

Not long after *Edwards,* the Court underwent a period of rapid turnover at the top. In 1946, the year after Roosevelt's death, Stone died. President Harry Truman nominated his treasury secretary, Fred Vinson, to be the next chief justice. Vinson was a political moderate and a legal mediocrity who, as a leading constitutional law expert said, "lacked both the taste for the complex work of the Court and the fine-tuned analytical skills to lead" it. While Vinson was chief justice, *Brown v. Board of Education* was headed to the Court. If *Brown* had been decided while Vinson was still in charge of the Court, he might have had trouble leading his colleagues to the unanimous decision they ultimately reached. In fact, some legal scholars wonder if the Court under Vinson might have upheld segregated schools. As it happened, though, Vinson died of a heart attack in 1953, at the age of sixty-three.

The decision about who would lead the Court next fell to Dwight Eisenhower, who nominated Earl Warren, the governor of California. The choice was a political payback. Warren had played a major role in steering his state's delegation to Eisenhower at the 1952 Republican National Convention and had gone on to provide important support in the general election. Eisenhower promised to nominate Warren to the next Supreme Court vacancy, and, nine months into his first year in office, he kept his word by making Warren the next chief justice.

President Dwight Eisenhower was not greatly concerned with Warren's views about the law. As part of the selection process, he asked his attorney general, Herbert Brownell Jr., to interview Warren and determine whether he was "generally sympathetic with the ideology . . . of the Eisenhower administration." Brownell's assessment was that Warren would have views about the law that were generally consistent with Eisenhower's. It was one of the great miscalculations in Supreme Court history.

The new chief justice was, as Brownell would learn, not easy to read. Warren had grown up in Southern California in modest circumstances. Both of his parents had immigrated as children, his father from Norway—the family name had been Varran—and his mother from Sweden. After meeting in Minneapolis, they moved to Los Angeles, where Methias Warren worked long hours at low pay for Southern Pacific Railroad. Warren worked for the railroad himself in his youth, and it left him, he said in his memoirs, with empathy for poorly treated workers and skepticism about corporations. "I saw every man on the railroad not essential for the operation of the trains laid off without . . . warning for weeks before the end of the fiscal year in order that the corporate stock might pay a higher dividend," he wrote. The experience taught him lasting lessons, he said, "about monopolistic power, political dominance, [and] corruption in government." Warren's hero was Hiram Johnson, the progressive California governor and U.S. senator who had been Theodore Roosevelt's Bull Moose Party running mate in 1912.

After earning undergraduate and law degrees from the University of California–Berkeley, Warren drifted from unsatisfying law jobs to service in World War I, and back to uninspiring legal work. His career took a new direction when he joined the Alameda County District Attorney's Office. As a deputy district attorney and, later, district attorney for California's third-largest county, Warren efficiently put criminals in prison. He went on to be elected state attorney general, a position from which he did battle with gambling interests and corrupt politicians. He was a crusading reformer, but very much a Republican one. When the Great Depression arrived, Warren did not support Roosevelt's New Deal. He warned that, with the government taking on greater powers to help the victims of the crisis, "the doctrines of individual freedom and personal property rights as laid down by our forefathers in the Constitution of the United States" were "under dangerous attack."

When Warren ran for governor in 1942, he began to show a more progressive side. In his campaign, he talked about the importance of schools and advocated government-funded pensions to help the elderly. When he became governor the following year, he promoted still more liberal ideas, including a universal health care program, funded by a payroll tax. Warren was not as liberal on other issues, however, including one that forever stained his progressive reputation. He was a driving force behind the internment of Japanese Americans during World War II, and he advocated it in crudely racist terms. At a 1943 governors' conference, Warren declared, "We don't propose to have the Japs back in California during this war, if there is any lawful means of preventing it."

Despite his politically ambiguous background and Brownell's intuition that he was a moderate Republican, when Warren arrived on the Court he immediately became a strong liberal voice. In 1954, a little more than seven months after he arrived, the Court decided *Brown*. The justices Warren joined were an ideological mix. There were liberals like former New Dealers Hugo Black and Douglas, both Roosevelt appointees. There were also moderates and conservatives, including Felix Frankfurter, who believed in judicial restraint, or declining to get involved in many legal disputes, and Stanley Reed, a Kentucky native who was initially inclined to uphold segregation. Warren was able, however, to persuade his colleagues to make the Court's ruling in *Brown* unanimous. The vote was an early indication that Warren would be a strong chief justice, who would be adept at forging majorities through a combination of political skill and personal charm. Potter Stewart, a moderate conservative also nominated by President Eisenhower, explained Warren's influence simply: "We all loved him."

With *Brown,* the Warren Court was off to a strong start. It acted powerfully, and in a single voice, to elevate African Americans, who had been profoundly oppressed since the founding of the republic, when the Constitution did not count them as full human beings. The Court did not hesitate to end a practice and a way of life firmly embedded in the history and culture of a large part of the country. It was not immediately clear whether the Warren Court would be equally bold in its approach to other issues—including the rights of the poor.

Two years after *Brown,* the Court was presented with a chance to hold that poor people as a class had special status under the Equal Protection Clause. *Griffin v. Illinois* was a challenge to an Illinois law that let defendants appeal their convictions only if they provided the appeals court with documents that required a trial transcript to prepare. Many poor defendants could not afford a transcript and as a result could not file an appeal. The Court struck down the law by a 5–4 vote, with Black writing an opinion for four of the justices. In criminal trials, Black said, a state "can no more discriminate on account of poverty than on account of religion, race, or color." With this opinion, which Warren joined, the Warren Court seemed to be moving toward recognizing the poor as a discrete and insular minority and providing them with the sort of special constitutional protection racial and religious minorities received. There were, however, only four votes for Black's opinion. The fifth justice in the majority, Frankfurter, joined in the result but not the reasoning. So Black's strong words about the rights of the poor did not have the force of law.

While the Court equivocated, a movement was forming in academia in favor of protecting poor people as a class. The leader was Jacobus tenBroek, a University of California–Berkeley constitutional law scholar and disability rights activist. TenBroek, who was blinded in a childhood bow-and-arrow accident, had founded the National Federation of the Blind. When he was appointed to California's Social Welfare Board, he championed blind poor people, and over time he expanded into advocacy for all poor people. In the 1950s, tenBroek began arguing for constitutional rights for the poor. In a 1955 paper, "The Constitution and the Right of Free Movement," he criticized laws that prevented people from receiving welfare benefits until they had lived in a state for a designated time period. TenBroek argued that these durational residency requirements, as they were known, which could be several years long, violated the right to travel.

TenBroek also argued that poor people as a group should have constitutional protection. In "California's Dual System of Family Law: Its Origin, Development, and Present Status," a three-part article that ran in the *Stanford Law Review* in 1964–65, he contended that California operated a two-track family law system, with one set of rules for the poor and another for everyone else. TenBroek suggested that poverty should "as a classifying trait be declared inherently discriminatory," citing Jackson's *Edwards v. California* dissent and its contention that lack of money should be "constitutionally an irrelevance, like race, creed, or color."

In the 1960s, the drive to increase poor people's rights was helped, as it had been in the Great Depression, by growing popular support. In 1962, Michael Harrington, a onetime editor of the left-wing *Catholic Worker*, published *The Other America*, one of the decade's most influential books. It revealed that as much as one-quarter of the nation lived "below those standards which we have been taught to regard as the decent minimums for food, housing, clothing, and health." President Kennedy embraced Harrington's call to arms, but he did not live long enough to put his ideas into action.

As the nation started paying more attention to poverty, the Court also became more interested. This new focus was helped along by significant changes in the Court's membership. In 1962, two Kennedy appointees joined—Byron White, who was deputy attorney general under Attorney General Robert F. Kennedy, and Arthur Goldberg, a prominent union lawyer. White and Goldberg joined four staunch liberals already on the Court: Black, Douglas, Warren, and William J. Brennan, who was, like Warren, an Eisenhower nominee. White was a centrist who often sided with the conservatives, but Goldberg and the four liberals already on the Court formed a solid liberal majority. For the first time since he became chief justice, Warren had a like-minded majority, and the Warren Court's heyday was about to begin.

The five strong liberals of the early Warren Court had something in common beyond their liberalism: all were born into poverty, or close to it. Warren's father was a low-paid railroad employee. Douglas was raised by a struggling single mother in various locations in the West. Brennan grew up in a hardscrabble Newark neighborhood, with a father who had a serious drinking problem. Black was one of eight children in a farm family in rural Alabama. Goldberg, one of eight children of a Russian Jewish immigrant peddler, grew up in a Chicago slum. All five understood from personal experience the issues the poor people who came to the Court were raising.

This newly constituted Warren Court almost immediately began to take a bolder approach to poverty cases. On the same day in 1963, it issued two decisions that revolutionized how poor people would be treated when they were accused of crimes. In the more famous one, *Gideon v. Wainwright,* the Court unanimously held that the Sixth Amendment, which guarantees the right to counsel, gives poor defendants the right to an appointed lawyer if they could not afford a lawyer on their own. The *Gideon* case had arrived at the Court in the form of a handwritten appeal from Clarence Earl Gideon, a fifty-one-year-old drifter who was in prison for the burglary of a Panama City, Florida, poolroom. In ruling for Gideon, who had no lawyer to represent him at trial, Black proclaimed the "obvious truth" that "any person haled into court, who is too poor to hire a lawyer, cannot be assured a fair trial unless counsel is provided for him."

In the second case, *Douglas v. California,* the Court ruled 6–3 that poor defendants also have a right to a lawyer on their first appeal. Rather than rely on the Sixth Amendment, which speaks of rights at trial, the Court in *Douglas* based its decision on the Fourteenth Amendment's Equal Protection and Due Process Clauses. More than *Gideon,* the *Douglas* decision continued the Court's talk of rights for the poor as a group. Douglas, writing for the majority, said that it violated the Fourteenth Amendment when a wealthy defendant "enjoys the benefit of counsel's examination into the record, research of the law, and marshalling of arguments on his behalf, while the indigent . . . is forced to shift for himself." Sounding like tenBroek, or Jackson in his *Edwards* concurrence, Douglas insisted that "an unconstitutional line has been drawn between rich and poor."

Support for combating poverty continued to grow at the national level. The civil rights movement, which was gaining force, had begun to place greater emphasis on economic rights. The 1963 March on Washington, at which Martin Luther King Jr. delivered his "I Have a Dream" speech, was officially billed as the March on Washington for Jobs and Freedom. In his famous address, King decried the fact that, one hundred years after emancipation, blacks still lived "on a lonely island of poverty in the midst of a vast ocean of material prosperity." The march's leaders later unveiled a "Freedom Budget for All Americans" that called for a federal jobs guarantee and a right to a basic income.

The president himself was speaking out. In his first State of the Union address, on January 8, 1964, less than two months after President Kennedy's assassination, President Johnson declared an "all-out war on human poverty . . . in these United States." In May, at the University of Michigan commencement, Johnson announced his plan to build a "Great Society" that would include "an end to poverty." Congress began passing laws establishing a wide array of antipoverty programs, including Head Start and Medicaid.

Law schools were also beginning to pay more attention to poverty, with new scholars following in tenBroek's footsteps. In 1964, Charles Reich, a young Yale law professor, published an article in *The Yale Law Journal* that set out a bold new theory of how the law should treat welfare benefits. In "The New Property," Reich argued that welfare benefits were a new kind of property, similar to land or physical possessions. He noted that the Fourteenth Amendment Due Process Clause says states cannot "deprive any person of life, liberty or property without due process of law." Since welfare benefits were a form of property, Reich argued, the government should not be able to cut them off without "scrupulous observance of fair procedures." Welfare recipients, he insisted, should be given a hearing, with a right to be heard and a right to appeal, before their benefits were taken away.

While Reich moved on to other subjects—a few years later he would write *The Greening of America*, a bestselling critique of modern society that became a counterculture bible—another academic, Edward Sparer, emerged as the "father of welfare law." Sparer, who was born in New York City, headed to the South after his first year at City College of New York to do fieldwork for Henry Wallace's left-wing 1948 presidential campaign. Sparer was "shaken to my core," he later said, by the conditions he saw, including "black poverty which surpassed my imagination." In 1963, after law school and a stint as a lawyer for the International Ladies' Garment Workers' Union, he helped found the Mobilization for Youth Legal Unit, the nation's first neighborhood legal services office, which was committed to "law as an instrument of social change."

Sparer established a Center on Social Welfare Policy and Law at Columbia University, where he became an influential voice in creating the emerging field of poverty law. In 1965, he published an article in the *UCLA Law Review* that included a welfare recipients' bill of rights, which he hoped would serve as a litigation agenda for poverty lawyers nationwide. Sparer's list included the right to privacy, the right to travel, and the right not to have the government's morality imposed in exchange for welfare benefits.

While academics were developing this theoretical framework, an army of poverty lawyers was forming to do battle in the courts. Community-based legal services offices were springing up across the country, many operating out of storefronts in poor neighborhoods. Universities began to house poverty law centers. Sparer's center at Columbia had nine staff lawyers, who provided training and backup to other lawyers and also brought direct litigation on behalf of the poor. New York University Law School established its own poverty law center. The mission of this new class of lawyer was, Sparer declared, nothing less than "to utilize the legal process . . . to help change the ground rules of American society."

Poverty lawyers used the law to confront institutions and individuals they saw as oppressing the poor, including welfare bureaucracies and abusive landlords. They were soon winning major victories all across the country. In Georgia, Sparer and his colleagues successfully challenged a state AFDC provision that allowed counties to cut benefits during the okra-harvesting season to force poor mothers out into the fields. Like the Supreme Court, lower courts began to talk about poor people and poverty in a new, more sympathetic way—and they began to chart a course toward group rights for the poor, up to and including some kind of a constitutional right to subsistence. In holding that New York State discriminated against some recipients of aid to the aged, blind, and disabled, a federal district court in Manhattan declared that the

Constitution incorporated "certain basic concepts of humanity and decency," including "the desire to insure that indigent, unemployable citizens will at least have the bare minimums required for existence."

In just a few years, poverty law had become a thriving field, and its potential seemed almost unlimited. It was a "heady time," recalled Patricia Wald, a poverty lawyer with the District of Columbia Neighborhood Legal Services Program who went on to become the chief judge of the U.S. Court of Appeals for the D.C. Circuit. Poverty lawyers "felt confident in 'going for it,' 'doing the right thing,' raising constitutional issues freely—almost profligately—seeking activist intervention from the courts, raising Cain with the welfare and the health care bureaucracies," Wald recalled. "We won the vast majority of issues we litigated."

Increasingly, poverty lawyers were interested in bringing their cases to the Supreme Court, where a win would have national impact. They were encouraged that there was finally a majority on the Court that was serious about expanding poor people's rights. In 1965, the Court's membership changed again, when President Johnson persuaded Goldberg to resign to become his ambassador to the United Nations. Johnson replaced him with Abe Fortas, a well-respected Washington lawyer who was also one of Johnson's closest friends and confidants. Fortas's views on the law were similar to Goldberg's, so the substitution left the Court's liberal majority intact.

In 1966, in *Harper v. Virginia Board of Elections,* the Warren Court issued another landmark ruling in favor of the poor. It held, by a 6–3 vote, that Virginia's poll tax of $1.50 a year discriminated against poor people, in violation of the Equal Protection Clause. The decision was an important victory for the political rights of poor people, but it was more than that. The Court went even further than it had in *Douglas* to suggest that the poor were a protected class. Requiring a payment to vote created an "invidious discrimination" between rich and poor, Douglas wrote for the majority. "Lines drawn on the basis of wealth or property," he said, "like those of race . . . are traditionally disfavored."

With those words, the Court appeared to be edging even closer to declaring the poor to be a suspect class, protected in the same way racial and religious minorities were—finally including poor people in the promise the Court had laid out in footnote 4 of *United States v. Carolene Products*. There was, however, a narrower way of reading *Harper* and the whole line of cases in which the Court had been expanding the legal rights of the poor. *Edwards v. California, Griffin v. Illinois, Gideon v. Wainwright, Douglas v. California,* and *Harper v. Virginia Board of Elections* all involved activities that had their own constitutional protection—interstate travel, criminal defense, and now voting. The Court was concerned about poor people's ability to fully participate in those activities on an equal basis, but it was not clear whether it was willing to take the larger step of holding that poor people were protected against discrimination more generally.

While the Court continued to consider that question, a grassroots poor people's movement was forming, focused on inadequacies in welfare programs. In New York, the City-Wide Coordinating Committee of Welfare Groups was demanding better treatment of recipients and higher benefits. Similar groups arose in other cities. On a single day of action, June 30, 1966, activists held twenty-five protests across the country. In Connecticut, welfare recipients descended on the state welfare office, while in Ohio there was a "Walk for Adequate Welfare" from Cleveland to Columbus, modeled on the Selma-to-Montgomery voting rights march that had occurred a year earlier.

At the national level, the National Welfare Rights Organization (NWRO) held its first convention in the summer of 1967. Under the leadership of George Wiley, a charismatic Syracuse University chemistry professor turned poverty rights activist, the NWRO adopted a platform calling for a welfare system that lifted all recipients out of poverty, ensured that they would be treated with dignity, respected their constitutional rights, and allowed them to participate in the decisions under which they had to live.

In 1967, Martin Luther King Jr. and the Southern Christian Leadership

Conference launched the Poor People's Campaign. With its economic-based calls for full employment, a guaranteed income, and access to decent housing and health care, the campaign represented a new phase for the civil rights movement. King described the Poor People's Campaign, which united blacks, whites, Puerto Ricans, Mexican Americans, and Native Americans, among others, as "a determination by poor people of all colors and backgrounds to assert and win their right to a decent life."

In the same year, President Johnson nominated a second justice, and, unlike the substitution of Fortas for Goldberg, this one did change the Court's ideological balance, making the Warren Court even more liberal. Johnson nominated Thurgood Marshall, who was serving as his solicitor general, to replace Tom Clark, a moderately conservative Truman appointee. Marshall became the first black justice, and with his arrival there was a solid bloc of six liberals—or there almost was. Hugo Black, the onetime New Deal liberal, was becoming more conservative in his old age, and as time went on he could be counted on less to join the other liberals in important votes. With Marshall's arrival, however, there were now five strongly liberal justices: Warren, Douglas, Brennan, Fortas, and Marshall. The other four justices were somewhere between centrist and conservative: Black; White, the moderate Kennedy nominee; Stewart, a moderately conservative Eisenhower nominee; and John Marshall Harlan II, another Eisenhower nominee, the most conservative member of the Court.

When Marshall took his seat, in October 1967, the Warren Court reached its liberal apex. The Court's liberalism extended to many areas, but none more than poverty law. It was during Marshall's first year, on June 17, 1968, that the Court unanimously struck down the "man in the house" rule in *King v. Smith*. That decision significantly expanded the rights of AFDC recipients, even if, as the *North Carolina Law Review* noted in its analysis of the case, it left considerable "work yet to be done" in vindicating the rights of the poor. The newly invigorated Warren Court seemed eager to do that additional work, but larger forces were rising up against it.

IN MID-1968, THE JOHNSON ADMINISTRATION, WHICH HAD PLAYED A large part in building up the Warren Court, was drawing to a close. Warren had his eye firmly on the fall election, and the possibility that Richard Nixon, an old enemy of his from California Republican politics, would be elected president. Warren, who was seventy-seven, worried not only for the country but for the Court—and he was thinking about how to keep the position of chief justice in liberal hands.

On June 13, 1968, just days before the *King v. Smith* ruling, Warren went to the White House to tell President Johnson that he planned to retire. Warren said he hoped Johnson would nominate a progressive to succeed him. Johnson would have to act quickly, since the election was just months away and he would be leaving office in January, but both men believed there was enough time. Johnson asked Warren his opinion about elevating Fortas to chief justice. Although Warren was not entirely enthusiastic, he said Fortas would be a good chief justice. Johnson did not ask whether nominating Fortas would be politically wise—a question that might have produced a different answer.

Fortas was a remarkable man, who in many ways embodied the American Dream. He was born in Memphis in 1910, to Orthodox Jewish immigrant parents, and grew up, he would later say, "as poor as you can imagine." Fortas walked the long distance to religious school because his family could not afford the streetcar fare. He also faced substantial non-economic challenges, including the bigotry of segregation-era Memphis. "As a Southerner—born and brought up in the Mississippi Delta," he said, "I recall the outrages of the Ku Klux Klan, directed against Jews, Catholics, and Negroes."

After attending a small local college on a scholarship, Fortas enrolled, on another scholarship, at Yale Law School, where he became editor in chief of *The Yale Law Journal* and won a reputation as perhaps the most brilliant student ever to attend the school. He graduated at the start of the Great Depression and felt the draw that many young people did to help Roosevelt with his plans for reviving the nation. Fortas accepted a teaching position at Yale

Law School and then took a series of prominent jobs with the federal government, including general counsel of the Public Works Administration, one of the most important New Deal agencies.

Fortas eventually helped to found a law firm, Arnold & Fortas, and became a consummate Washington insider. In 1948, when Johnson won the Democratic Senate primary in Texas by just eighty-seven votes, Fortas helped defend him against credible charges of irregularities in the vote counting. Johnson credited Fortas's legal advocacy, which included getting an order from the Supreme Court at a crucial moment, for his election to the Senate. In the 1950s and early '60s, Fortas was one of the nation's most respected and in-demand lawyers. During the McCarthy era, he helped prepare the playwright Lillian Hellman for her testimony before the House Un-American Activities Committee. When the Supreme Court needed a lawyer to represent Clarence Gideon in *Gideon v. Wainwright*, it appointed Fortas. Douglas would later say that Fortas's oral argument in *Gideon* was "the best single legal argument" he had seen in his time on the Court.

It was Fortas's ties to Johnson, however, that were pivotal to his rise. Fortas was a close adviser to Johnson in his years as a senator and as vice president. When Johnson became president, Fortas served as a "general handyman," as he put it, taking on large and small assignments, including recruiting Warren to head the commission that investigated the Kennedy assassination. In 1965, after Johnson moved Goldberg off the Court and over to the United Nations, he put Fortas in his seat. Fortas continued to advise Johnson after he joined the Court. *Time* magazine went so far as to call him "the true *eminence grise* of the Johnson Administration."

In his three years as a justice, Fortas was a key member of the liberal majority, and a strong supporter of civil rights and civil liberties. Fortas advanced student free speech rights considerably by writing a landmark decision holding that high school students had a First Amendment right to wear black armbands to school to protest the Vietnam War. Fortas's sympathies were invariably with underdogs, including the poor. One of his law clerks recalled that he was determined "to reduce the number of 'non-persons' in our society."

Within two weeks of his meeting with Warren, Johnson announced that he would nominate Fortas to be the next chief justice. To improve Fortas's chances of being confirmed by the Senate, Johnson at the same time named Homer Thornberry, a former Texas congressman who was on the New Orleans–based U.S. Court of Appeals for the Fifth Circuit, to fill Fortas's seat. Thornberry was another old friend, who had inherited Johnson's congressional seat when Johnson moved up to the Senate. Thornberry, a self-made son of two deaf parents, was well liked on Capitol Hill, and Johnson was counting on his personal charm and Texas lineage to appeal to southern senators who wanted another southerner on the Court.

Fortas's nomination ran into trouble immediately, much of it related to Johnson. Johnson was by now a lame duck, and a tired and unpopular one. He had alienated conservatives with the Great Society and liberals by escalating the Vietnam War. With his presidency winding down, he had little to offer wavering senators for their votes, and they risked little in disappointing him. Johnson, the onetime "Master of the Senate," had also lost his once unmatched ability to count votes in the Senate. He overestimated how many Democratic votes he could swing to Fortas and he underestimated how much Republicans wanted to stop the nomination of another liberal chief justice, particularly when there was a good chance there would soon be a Republican president who could fill the post with a conservative.

Fortas brought his own set of liabilities. Republican senators accused Johnson of cronyism, arguing that it was not appropriate for him to nominate a close adviser to lead the Court. Fortas's defenders pointed out that presidents had placed friends on the Court at least since Abraham Lincoln nominated his campaign manager, David Davis. They also noted that any conflict would be short-lived, since Johnson would be out of the White House in January. The cronyism charge was difficult to shake, however, and it caused the choice of Thornberry to backfire: critics called it double cronyism.

In their opposition to Fortas, Republican senators raised objections to his role on the Warren Court. They portrayed him as a wild-eyed integrationist, which hurt him with southern senators, who were a large part of the Democrats' Senate majority. The Republicans attacked Fortas's votes in favor of criminal defendants, an issue Nixon had exploited effectively in the 1968 presidential campaign. They also made a great deal of his role in the Court's obscenity cases, arguing that he was out of touch with Middle American values. Strom Thurmond, of South Carolina, invited his fellow senators to a screening of an X-rated movie, *Flaming Creatures,* that Fortas had said was not obscene. Patrick Buchanan, a top aide to President Nixon, dubbed the screening the "Fortas Film Festival" and tipped off a *Time* magazine reporter about the event and his nickname for it.

Another lurking problem for Fortas was resistance to confirming the first Jewish chief justice. The National Socialist White People's Party called him "this despicable Jew with a 'red' record that smells to high heaven," and other extremist groups were similarly vitriolic. Many senators understood, however, that the anti-Semitism was not limited to the political fringe, and it hurt Fortas, particularly with senators from the South. James Eastland of Mississippi was overheard saying that, after the confirmation of the first black justice, Marshall, "I could not go back to Mississippi if a Jewish Chief Justice swore in the next president."

Fortas did not help himself with his confirmation testimony, which was less than persuasive on some key points. Among other things, he told the Senate Judiciary Committee that since joining the Court he had made few policy or personnel recommendations to President Johnson. That struck many senators as implausible, even if they did not have the specifics to contradict it.

An issue that emerged at the last minute was Fortas's finances. The Senate learned that he had supplemented his Court salary with a lectureship at American University Law School, funded by contributions that his former law partner Paul Porter had raised from wealthy businessmen, including some of Fortas's former clients. Fortas was paid $15,000—more than $110,000 in 2019 dollars—to teach a weekly seminar over the summer. Other justices taught classes and were paid, but the amount of Fortas's stipend and the funding sources created an impression that he was unduly profiting from his current position and raised concerns about whether he would feel any debt to the wealthy people who had helped underwrite his position.

Despite the attacks, Fortas's nomination remained broadly popular. In a Harris poll in August, respondents favored his confirmation by a nearly two-to-one margin. When the nomination reached the Senate floor in September, Fortas appeared to have a majority of senators on his side. His opponents had decided to filibuster, however, and it soon became clear that he did not have the votes necessary to cut off debate. Johnson was forced to withdraw Fortas's name, the first time a Supreme Court nomination was defeated by a filibuster. With Fortas's seat not opening up, Thornberry remained on the Fifth Circuit. Nixon was quietly delighted by the outcome. He "wanted the Fortas nomination killed," Patrick Buchanan later recalled, but he "did not want our fingerprints on the murder weapon."

Johnson considered making another nomination in the final months of his presidency. He gave some thought to trying to bring Goldberg back from the United Nations. Johnson was convinced, however, that if he sent Goldberg's name to the Senate, "the same damned old snakes" would succeed in blocking him. In the end, Johnson did not make another nomination before leaving the White House. He would later call Fortas's rejection and everything that followed "the final blow to an unhappy, frustrating year."

On November 5, 1968, Nixon defeated Humphrey, edging him out by 0.7 percent in the popular vote but scoring a larger Electoral College win. In January, Nixon took office knowing that he would be naming a new chief justice. It was a rare opportunity: Nixon was the thirty-seventh president, but Warren was only the fourteenth chief justice. Nixon, however, was already eager for more vacancies so he could bring the Warren Court to an end and lock in a conservative majority. He obsessed over when the older justices would be gone. "From the time Nixon arrived at the White House he continually played his shuffle-the-people game with the Supreme Court," his chief domestic policy adviser, John Ehrlichman, recalled. "As I sat listening to him he would daydream about whom he might put on the Court in place of Black or Harlan or Douglas."

Not content to wait for the Court's membership to turn over on its own, Nixon went on the offensive. He used the resources of the White House and the Justice Department to try to threaten liberal justices into resigning. His first target was Fortas, who had been weakened by his Senate rejection. "Nixon cleared his desk of other work to focus on getting Fortas off the Court," according to Ehrlichman. William Lambert, a *Life* magazine reporter with ties to the White House, had been tipped off about Fortas's relationship with Louis Wolfson, a wealthy investor and supporter of liberal causes who was under investigation by the Securities and Exchange Commission. The Justice Department began "spreading rumors and leaking . . . information" to Lambert, recalled John Dean, a top Nixon Justice Department lawyer and future White House counsel.

Wolfson, a former client of Fortas's, had started a foundation to promote civil rights and religious liberty, and he asked Fortas to serve as a consultant. The justice agreed to work for the Wolfson Family Foundation while he served on the Court and accepted a stipend of $20,000 a year. Fortas told his law clerks that he had accepted Wolfson's offer because he believed he would be able to do good things and that it would not interfere with his work on the Court. There was no rule against justices and federal judges doing paid work for nonprofit foundations, and Fortas was not the only one to have an arrangement of this kind.

After Fortas learned that Wolfson was under investigation, he ended his ties to the foundation. Wolfson was indicted on charges relating to stock transactions, and a few months later Fortas returned the $20,000 he had already received. There were reports that Wolfson had dropped Fortas's name when he was under investigation, but Fortas had not authorized him to, and

Fortas did not offer Wolfson any advice or contact anyone on his behalf. There was nothing in Fortas's relationship with Wolfson that broke any law, nor had Fortas violated any Court ethics rule, since the Court had no ethics rules.

Nixon nevertheless saw an opening in Fortas's connections to Wolfson, and he put his attorney general, John Mitchell, in charge of the matter. Mitchell, who had been Nixon's campaign manager in 1968, played political hardball, and he was not averse to breaking the law to get what he wanted. He would later be convicted of perjury, obstruction of justice, and conspiracy in the Watergate scandal and become the first attorney general in history to serve prison time. Mitchell plotted against Fortas with Will Wilson, the head of the Justice Department's Criminal Division, who, in addition to being a loyal Mitchell lieutenant, held a grudge against Johnson, whom he blamed for destroying his political career back in Texas.

When *Life*'s investigation of Fortas stalled, the Justice Department told Lambert it had opened a criminal investigation into Fortas's ties to Wolfson. The leak was improper, since Justice Department investigations were supposed to remain confidential. It was also misleading, because the department had not done much investigating and had learned little of interest. The confirmation, however, encouraged Lambert to continue with his reporting.

There was clearly much about the investigation that was improper, but beyond that, there was a larger issue of whether the Justice Department should be investigating a sitting justice at all. The founders gave justices and federal judges life tenure and provided impeachment as a means to remove them from office. The question of whether the Justice Department had the authority to investigate Fortas was given to William Rehnquist, a highly political assistant attorney general, to research. Rehnquist prepared a memorandum for Mitchell reassuring him that there would be no constitutional problem with prosecuting Fortas while he was on the Court.

While *Life* and the Justice Department forged ahead, Nixon received constant updates in the Oval Office. Mitchell and Wilson raised the stakes for Fortas by reopening an old criminal investigation of his wife, Carolyn

Agger, who was a tax partner at his former law firm. Agger had previously been investigated over allegations that she improperly withheld documents in a case, but she was cleared of any charges. If the Nixon Justice Department prosecuted her and won a conviction, it would have been a felony and the punishment could have been considerable. Mitchell's pursuit of Agger was, Dean said, "purely a means to torture Fortas."

In early May 1969, *Life* published its exposé, "The Justice . . . and the Stock Manipulator." It described the $20,000 payment Fortas had accepted from the Wolfson foundation and indicated that Wolfson had dropped Fortas's name when he got in trouble, but it did not actually say that Fortas had done anything improper. Still, the piece prompted sharp criticism of Fortas, in Washington and on editorial pages across the country, and calls for him to step down. Some of his old Republican enemies in Congress began to talk about impeachment, and his onetime allies did not rush to his defense.

Nixon did not want Fortas impeached. He wanted something quicker and simpler: Fortas's resignation. He told congressional Republicans to hold off while his staff went to work. On May 7, Mitchell paid an extraordinary visit to Warren at the Court, bringing investigative documents with him. Although none were legally incriminating, one was a copy of Fortas's agreement with the Wolfson foundation, which showed that Fortas's annual retainer was to continue throughout his life and pass on to his wife after his death. As Mitchell anticipated, it was an arrangement Warren found troubling. Nixon and Mitchell knew that Warren was fiercely protective of the Court and of his own legacy. He would not want to end his tenure with a major ethics scandal, and he certainly would not want one of his justices charged with a federal crime.

Warren should have resisted Mitchell's overtures. He should have realized Nixon's only interest was in driving a liberal justice off the Court. He also should have refused, purely as a matter of ethics, to meet secretly with an attorney general to discuss an ongoing investigation. Nixon, however, had conducted a charm offensive to win Warren over, including a black-tie dinner in his honor in the East Room of the White House, which the chief justice called "the most thrilling social event of my half century of public life." Mitchell and Warren met for the first time at the dinner, and Dean said that when Mitchell visited the Court, "the glow of good feeling still radiated from that evening."

The Justice Department kept coming after Fortas. Wilson met with Wolfson at his federal prison in Florida and made him testify under oath about his relationship with the beleaguered justice. The Justice Department wanted Wolfson to say that Fortas had helped him with his legal problems, but Wolfson insisted he had not. For all of their effort, Nixon and his Justice Department never found any evidence that Fortas had committed a crime. John Dean later conceded that the administration was "not even close" to having "the goods on Fortas." According to Dean, "Mitchell's talk was pure bluff."

Fortas did what he could to resist the attacks. Even with impeachment talk on hold, he began planning a defense, asking a law clerk to prepare a memo on whether a sitting justice could be forced to testify before Congress. It was not clear how much danger Fortas was in. There was considerable ill will toward him in Congress, and it grew with each new revelation, but at the same time, there were large Democratic majorities in the House, which would have to impeach, and in the Senate, which would have to convict by a two-thirds vote. After the unpleasantness of his Senate rejection the previous fall, however, a congressional investigation was not something Fortas looked forward to.

The Nixon administration did not relent, and it continued to focus on Warren as the best way to remove Fortas. On May 12, the Justice Department delivered another packet to Warren, marked "Personal and Confidential: For Eyes Only of the Chief Justice," with documents that made clear that its investigation was still under way. At the same time, Mitchell spoke publicly about meeting with Warren and giving him "certain information known by me, which might be of aid to him," bringing vague allegations to a wide audience without having to produce any actual evidence of illegality. In an editorial, *The New York Times* chastised Mitchell for "slander by indirection" and declared that his machinations had "every aspect of an ugly squeeze play by the administration to force Justice Fortas off the bench."

The Nixon administration's courtship of Warren and the public pressure it exerted on him had their intended effect. On the morning of May 13, Warren called a meeting of the justices to discuss the Fortas matter. He laid out the evidence he had received against Fortas, and Fortas was forced to defend his actions in front of his colleagues. It was a painfully uncomfortable meeting, and it became clear as it proceeded that Fortas's time on the Court was coming to an end. The following day, May 14, Fortas wrote a letter of resignation to the president. In the end, Nixon's "ugly squeeze play" had worked.

Many factors came together to force Fortas's decision. The barrage of public attacks on him, prompted by the Nixon administration's constant leaks to the media, took their toll. So did his concern that he might have to testify before Congress and perhaps even face impeachment. Fortas also had to worry that the Justice Department would criminally prosecute him or his wife. Fortas told his former law partner Paul Porter that he had simply "had it." Of all of the sources of pressure on Fortas, however, the Nixon administration's shrewd use of Warren may have been the decisive factor. The members of Nixon's inner circle were certainly proudest of how they had manipulated a liberal chief justice to help drive a liberal justice off the Court. Warren did "the job well," Ehrlichman wrote in his memoirs. "He had persuaded Abe Fortas to resign, and suddenly we had *two* vacant seats on the court."

When the news of Fortas's resignation broke, there was an impromptu party in the attorney general's office. Mitchell gathered the staff members who had worked on the Fortas project and served celebratory drinks. Nixon called in to congratulate the team. The excitement over Fortas's departure was mixed with more than a little astonishment. "Mitchell's bluff had succeeded beyond his wildest expectations," Dean said.

Nearly two decades later, Pennsylvania State University political scientist Bruce Allen Murphy wrote an extensive study of Fortas's fall. He concluded that Fortas had been badly treated. Murphy acknowledged that Fortas had made mistakes, including being slow to return the foundation money after Wolfson was indicted, but his investigation confirmed that Fortas had not broken any laws. Murphy also found that, while Wolfson was a problematic figure, Fortas's contact with him "was limited and soon terminated." Murphy concluded that "Fortas paid a far greater price for his 'transgressions' than seems justified."

One of last votes Fortas cast was in a major welfare rights decision, *Shapiro v. Thompson*. The "Thompson" in the case was Vivian Thompson, a pregnant nineteen-year-old who had moved to Hartford, Connecticut, from Dorchester, Massachusetts, to be closer to her mother when she gave birth. When Thompson applied for AFDC, she was turned down under a Connecticut law that denied welfare benefits to anyone who had not lived in the state for a year.

Connecticut was one of forty states with "durational residency requirements" for welfare benefits. These restrictions were a modern version of English "Poor Laws," which required poor people to be "settled" in a community to be eligible for relief. In the old English model, care for the poor was done at the local level and communities were responsible for only "their" poor. American advocates for the poor had been campaigning against durational residency requirements since tenBroek argued against them in his article "The Constitution and the Right of Free Movement" in 1955. As the welfare rights movement gained force in the 1960s, opposition to the rule had grown.

Many poverty lawyers hoped *Shapiro v. Thompson* would be the case in which the Court finally handed down a sweeping ruling that gave the poor constitutional protection as a class. There were two obvious ways it could do that. The Court could designate the poor a suspect class, following on *Carolene Products* footnote 4, and hold that because the residency rule particularly burdened poor people it should be reviewed under strict scrutiny. Alternatively, the Court could declare that receiving welfare was a "fundamental interest." The Court had decided that in addition to the suspect classes of footnote 4, it would designate certain interests—such as travel or having children—as so fundamental that it would apply strict scrutiny to laws that interfered with them. If the Court decided that Thompson had a fundamental interest in receiving welfare as soon as she arrived in Connecticut, it could apply strict scrutiny to the durational residency rule.

When the Court applied strict scrutiny to a law, there was a very good chance it would hold it to be unconstitutional. The Court would uphold a law under strict scrutiny only if the government could show that it had a "compelling" interest in having the law, and that the law was "narrowly tailored" to achieve that interest. It was not clear that Connecticut would be able to show that it had a compelling interest in the durational residency rule, which did little more than save it money. If the Court took either route to applying strict scrutiny—finding the poor to be a suspect class or holding welfare to be a fundamental interest—it would not only make it likely that the durational residency rule would be struck down but would also give the poor a powerful new constitutional tool to use in future cases.

There were also more moderate courses available to the Court. Thompson's lawyer, Archibald Cox, the Harvard law professor who would later become Watergate special prosecutor, made these more modest arguments to the Court, because he thought they were more likely to prevail. Cox urged the justices to hold that the rule violated the Equal Protection Clause not because it discriminated against the poor more than the rich, but because it discriminated against new residents of the state more than longtime residents. Cox also argued that the rule infringed on the right to travel, the same rationale the Court had used in 1941 to strike down California's "anti-Okie" law. If the Court accepted either of these arguments, it could overturn Connecticut's residency rule without giving poor people as a class significant new rights.

Shapiro v. Thompson was argued before the 1968 presidential election, but by the time the Court decided it, on April 21, 1969, Nixon was president. He had not, however, been able to nominate any justices yet—Warren and Fortas had not yet stepped down, and there was still a solid majority of justices who were sympathetic to welfare recipients like Thompson. The Court struck down the Connecticut residency rule by a 6–3 vote, in an opinion written by Brennan.

It was no surprise that Brennan wrote the *Shapiro* opinion, or that he had become one of the Court's strongest advocates for the rights of the poor. Although he was an Eisenhower nominee, Brennan was a liberal Democrat who had known people like Vivian Thompson his whole life. His parents had been born into poverty in Ireland, and he grew up in a working-class part of Newark, New Jersey, in a large family in which money was tight.

Brennan escaped his neighborhood and a heavy-drinking father to attend Harvard Law School. He was serving on the New Jersey Supreme Court when President Eisenhower nominated him to the Supreme Court in 1956. Eisenhower chose Brennan for political reasons, not ideological ones: he thought it would help him in his reelection campaign to name a Catholic from the Northeast. As had happened with Warren, Eisenhower ended up appointing a crusading liberal to the Court without intending to. Brennan was a pious Catholic and a firm believer in "human dignity," a phrase he used often. He quickly became a pillar of the Warren Court's emerging liberal majority.

In his *Shapiro* opinion, Brennan took a narrow approach, holding that Connecticut's durational residency requirement violated Thompson's right to interstate travel. Limitations of this kind discourage a poor person "who desires to migrate, resettle, find a new job, and start a new life," he said, which was "constitutionally impermissible." Brennan's opinion did not recognize welfare as a fundamental interest, but he made a gesture in that direction. Connecticut's durational residency requirement, he noted, prevented poor people from receiving "the very means to subsist—food, shelter, and other necessities of life."

Shapiro was another important victory for the poor, removing a barrier to receiving welfare benefits in forty states, in a case that—despite the hopes of the poverty law community—could have gone either way. Durational residency requirements were a well-established part of the welfare system, and they did not incur the same level of animosity as the "man in the house" rule.

Court watchers also suspected that Warren, as a former governor and state attorney general, would sympathize with Connecticut and vote to uphold the rule. On that point they were right: Warren dissented in *Shapiro,* in a rare vote against the poor.

Although *Shapiro* was a clear victory for poor people, it was another limited one. As it had been doing since *Edwards v. California,* the Court had once again ruled for the poor in a way that did not expand their constitutional rights as a group. Two justices, Douglas and Fortas, told their colleagues that they were prepared to rule for Thompson on wealth discrimination grounds. Even if Marshall and Brennan agreed, however, there would not be five votes for such a bold position. With Warren voting against Thompson, Brennan had to win over Stewart, White, or Harlan to build a five-justice majority, and none of them would be likely to support a strong wealth discrimination holding. The result was a decision that helped the poor but once again did not elevate their status under the Constitution.

As narrow as the *Shapiro* decision was, there were indications in it that the Court was moving toward doing something more substantial for the poor—notably Brennan's reference to "the very means to subsist." It was a decision that left poverty lawyers with hope, and conservatives concerned. Philip Kurland, a University of Chicago law professor who was a Warren Court critic, argued in an essay entitled "The Judicial Road to Social Welfare" that the Court in *Shapiro* had actually come "close to creating a constitutional right to welfare assistance."

The Warren Court's liberal majority was not only helping those at the very bottom of the economy—it was also showing a newfound concern for working-class Americans. Throughout its history, the Court had favored employers over workers in a wide variety of disputes. In the Progressive Era, it had struck down state and federal laws establishing minimum wages and maximum hours and cracking down on child labor. During the New Deal, it held that major new laws designed to protect workers were unconstitutional, and it interpreted laws about unionization in ways that helped management.

The Warren Court, by contrast, had an inherent sympathy for workers and the difficulties they faced. In June 1969, the Court issued a strikingly pro-worker decision. *Sniadach v. Family Finance Corp.* was a challenge to a Wisconsin wage garnishment law that made it easy for companies to freeze the salaries of people they said owed them money. The creditors simply had to notify workers' employers to freeze their wages, and the workers would not receive their full paycheck until they paid what was owed or proved they did not owe it. The Court ruled, by a 7–1 vote, that letting workers' wages be garnished without first providing them with a hearing at which they could defend themselves "violates the fundamental principles of due process." Only eight justices voted, because Fortas was now gone.

The *Sniadach* decision was significant in its own right, but it was also important for the way the Court talked about working people. Douglas, writing for six justices, emphasized the power imbalance in the creditor-debtor relationship and noted that the debts that bill collectors tried to collect on were often "fraudulent." He also expressed concern that allowing wages to be garnished without a hearing could, "as a practical matter, drive a wage-earning family to the wall."

With *Shapiro* and *Sniadach,* which were decided within seven weeks of each other, the Warren Court's recognition of the rights of low-income Americans reached a new level. The Court did not merely bring important, substantive relief to welfare applicants and salaried workers. It also made clear that it understood the challenging lives that low-income Americans led, and it conveyed that it was troubled by laws that interfered with the ability of people to come up with the means of subsistence. The Court seemed to be moving, slowly but surely, toward finally taking a bolder stand on behalf of the poor. Then, very suddenly, the Warren Court collapsed—and the grand visions of advocates for the poor collapsed with it.

Warren retired in June 1969, the month after Fortas left, holding to his promise from a year earlier. Warren knew that, with Nixon now in the White House, his successor as chief justice would not be a liberal—and that ideological change was coming to the Court. As he stepped down, Warren declared somewhat wistfully that he hoped the Warren Court would be remembered as "the people's court."

Warren's departure marked the end of one of the Court's most consequential eras—and of one of the most controversial public service careers in American history. Warren had been a lightning rod from his first year on the Court, fifteen years earlier, when it decided *Brown v. Board of Education*. To civil rights and civil liberties supporters, the departing chief justice was a great hero. Many conservatives, however, believed that he had led the Court to impose dangerous social policies on the nation. Hubert Humphrey, speaking for many liberals, said that if President Eisenhower "had done nothing else other than appoint Warren Chief Justice, he would have earned a very important place in the history of the United States." Eisenhower himself had a different view. When asked what had been his biggest mistake as president, he replied, "The appointment of that S.O.B. Earl Warren."

Warren's successor was Warren Burger, a judge on the U.S. Court of Appeals for the D.C. Circuit. Burger was not known for his legal brilliance, but he had other qualities that appealed to Nixon. He "looked like a judge" and "talked like a judge," Ehrlichman said. He was also extremely conservative, he despised the Warren Court, and he was desperate to ingratiate himself to anyone who could help him fulfill his ambition of becoming a justice. Burger "wanted a seat on the Supreme Court so passionately," Ehrlichman recalled, that "he would have agreed to almost anything to get it."

Burger had strong midwestern Republican roots. He grew up on his family's farm in St. Paul, Minnesota, and spent two decades at a white-shoe law firm in his hometown. His rise, like Warren's, began as a reward for his role at the 1952 Republican National Convention. As floor manager for Minnesota favorite son Harold Stassen, Burger helped swing his delegation to Eisenhower. When Eisenhower won, he paid Burger back by naming him to head the Justice Department's Civil Division.

A few years later, President Eisenhower nominated Burger to the D.C. Circuit. In the 1960s, the D.C. Circuit, like the Warren Court, moved the law in a progressive direction on civil rights, criminal law, and other issues. Burger was one of the court's most resolute conservatives, regularly battling its liberal judges. Burger did not just disagree with them—he held them in contempt. "If I were to stand still for some of the idiocy that is put forth as legal and constitutional profundity I would, I am sure, want to shoot myself in later years," he told a colleague.

Burger made a strong impression on the Nixon administration when he came to the White House to swear in the economics team. Using the opportunity to campaign for a seat on the Court, he brought along a copy of a *U.S. News & World Report* reprint of a speech he had given at Ripon College, advocating a law-and-order approach to criminal justice. During the visit, Burger urged Nixon to appoint more strong conservatives to the D.C. Circuit, which he called the worst of all the federal appeals courts in the country.

Nixon nominated Burger on May 21, 1969, before Warren retired, and the Senate confirmed him just eighteen days later, by a 74–3 vote. Burger's arrival started an ideological realignment, but his vote alone would not transform the Court. When he arrived, there were still three solid liberals: Douglas, Brennan, and Marshall. There were four justices who were somewhere between centrist and conservative—Black, White, Stewart, and Harlan—and one vacant seat, Fortas's. Burger would need to hold on to all four centrist-to-conservative justices to form a five-justice conservative majority—something he could hardly count on. He had laid out his view of what was needed back in March, before his own nomination, in a letter to a fellow judge. "What can one man do to stop the nonsense?" he said. "RN can only straighten that place out if he gets four appointments."

With the ideology of the Court now murky, poverty lawyers still held out hope that it would expand the rights of poor people. Emboldened by its rulings striking down Connecticut's durational residency requirement for welfare and Wisconsin's wage garnishment law, they had begun promoting the boldest idea of all: that every American had a constitutional right to a minimum level of economic support. In September 1969, in a *New York Times* article headlined "Guarantee of 'Right to Live' Is Urged," Edward Sparer called on the Court to recognize a right to subsistence. Sparer argued that the rights enumerated in the Constitution presumed that people were alive and able to engage in them. "Speech, press and worship require speakers, writers and worshipers," he insisted. "Let the unemployed man lie starving . . . and you have killed off the speaker, the writer and the worshiper." As Sparer saw it, "no legislative majority ought to be able to vote in favor of taking away the right to live." Other progressive legal scholars agreed. Norman Dorsen, a New York University law professor and American Civil Liberties Union general counsel, endorsed a right to live as "sound legally as well as just in principle."

As the Court began its 1969–70 term, the *Harvard Law Review,* the nation's preeminent legal journal, published a high-profile argument for a constitutional right to subsistence. The first issue of the law review each year, which appeared in November, focused on the Supreme Court, and it began with a foreword that discussed the current state of the law. In the fall of 1969, Frank Michelman, a young Harvard law professor, wrote the foreword, which was entitled "On Protecting the Poor Through the Fourteenth Amendment." Michelman, who had served as a law clerk to Brennan before joining the Harvard faculty, suggested that the Equal Protection Clause could be read to guarantee a right to "minimum protection against economic hazard." That guarantee could include a right to food, housing, and other basic necessities for those who were without them.

There were other scholars who rejected the idea of a right to economic support. For many, it was an article of faith that the Constitution guaranteed almost exclusively "negative" rights, such as the right not to be prevented from speaking and the right not to be unreasonably searched, not "positive" rights to receive things from the government. Herbert Wechsler, an eminent constitutional law professor at Columbia Law School, flatly told *The New York Times* that a right to subsistence was "not valid as an interpretation of the Constitution."

Even at the height of the Warren Court, when it was still expanding the rights of the poor, it would have been difficult to persuade the justices to recognize a right to subsistence. Now that Burger was leading the Court and Nixon would be filling Fortas's vacant seat, it very clearly felt like an idea whose time had passed. The *New York Times* and *Harvard Law Review* articles, with their bold vision for taking the Warren Court's poverty law jurisprudence to a new level, seemed to be trying to persuade a Court that no longer existed.

When the new term began in the fall of 1969, with Burger presiding over an eight-justice Court, there was a major welfare case on the docket. *Goldberg v. Kelly* challenged the abrupt way in which welfare recipients were often thrown off the rolls, without notice or an opportunity to be heard. The issue was a high priority for the welfare rights movement because families whose benefits were taken away based on erroneous facts or arbitrary decisions by caseworkers often found themselves unable to afford rent, heat, or food until the denial could be reversed. Mobilization for Youth's Legal Unit, the legal organization founded by Sparer, and other legal services lawyers had carefully prepared *Goldberg v. Kelly,* assembling a class of plaintiffs with sympathetic stories that showed the harm done by cutting off welfare benefits without a hearing.

John Kelly, the lead plaintiff in the case, was a disabled New York City man who was unable to work because of injuries from a hit-and-run accident. He received $40.03 a week in state welfare payments, but his caseworker had made his benefits conditional on his moving into the Barbara Hotel. Kelly moved into the hotel but found that it was filled with drug addicts and unsafe, so he moved in with a friend instead. When the caseworker learned what Kelly had done, he abruptly cut off his benefits and took back a check he had been given to buy a winter coat.

Kelly argued that the Due Process Clause required the city to provide him with a "fair hearing" before his benefits were cut off. The claim followed directly from Charles Reich's 1964 *Yale Law Journal* article "The New Property," which read like a legal brief for Kelly. The city, for its part, argued that welfare recipients' interest in having a hearing before their benefits were cut off was outweighed by the government's interest in conserving administrative and fiscal resources.

On March 23, 1970, the Court ruled for Kelly by a 5–3 vote, with Brennan writing for the majority. Even though it was now the Burger Court and Fortas's reliable liberal vote was gone, Brennan managed to assemble a five-vote majority holding that the city had violated Kelly's due process rights. Brennan had been waiting for this day. After "The New Property" appeared, he had talked about it in a speech at George Washington University Law School. When he reviewed certiorari petitions, the papers filed by parties who wanted the Court to hear their appeals, Brennan had looked for a case raising the issues Reich had discussed. The Court found it in John Kelly's lawsuit.

Brennan's opinion closely followed the reasoning of "The New Property," which he cited in a footnote. Since welfare provides recipients with "the means to obtain essential food, clothing, housing, and medical care," he said, ending benefits when there was a question about eligibility could "deprive an eligible recipient of the very means by which to live while he waits." Brennan said the Due Process Clause required that, before welfare benefits were terminated, the recipient had to have "timely and adequate notice" and a hearing that included "minimum procedural safeguards."

Goldberg v. Kelly, which was reported on the front page of *The New York Times,* was a major triumph for the poor. The Court handed poverty lawyers across the country a powerful new tool to use in defending their clients against incompetent or vindictive welfare officials. With a single ruling, it had protected more than 8.4 million AFDC recipients from suddenly losing their benefits, giving them a new measure of economic security.

Goldberg also represented another advance in how the Court discussed poverty. Brennan said, in his opinion for the Court, that "we have come to recognize that forces not within the control of the poor contribute to their poverty." He also said that welfare, "by meeting the basic demands of subsistence, can help bring within the reach of the poor the same opportunities that are available to others to participate meaningfully in the life of the community." The Court had come a long way from the days when it referred to poor people as a "pestilence." It was now viewing poverty structurally and poor people as, to a significant extent, victims of a flawed economic and social order.

The Court did something else important in *Goldberg*: it tied the rights of the poor more closely than ever to the Constitution. It did not hold that poor people were a suspect class or recognize that receiving welfare was a fundamental interest. It did, however, hold that termination of welfare benefits required a level of due process that other government actions did not. The decision was a declaration that, in a case not related to travel, criminal prosecutions, voting, or any other protected right, a class of poor people were entitled to extra constitutional protection simply because of their vulnerable status.

In all of the excitement over *Goldberg,* there was little discussion of how precarious the ruling was. Brennan had to work hard, with Fortas gone, to cobble together a five-justice majority. He had the votes of the Court's three liberals, and the centrist White. Black, the onetime New Deal crusader, and the centrist conservative Stewart had joined Burger in siding with New York City. The fifth vote Brennan won over was Harlan, the Court's most conservative member until Burger arrived, who would hardly be a reliable ally of the poor in future cases.

Burger, in addition to refusing to join Brennan's majority opinion, wrote a dissent with a pointed message. He complained that *Goldberg* exhibited a "now familiar constitutionalizing syndrome." The way it worked, he said, was that "once some presumed flaw is observed, the Court then eagerly accepts the invitation to find a constitutionally 'rooted' remedy." If there is not an express constitutional provision governing the issue, he said, "it is then seen as 'implicit' or commanded by the vague and nebulous concept of 'fairness.'" In the midst of one of the greatest victories for poor people in the history of the Court, the new chief justice made one thing clear: he was intent on bringing an end to rulings like it as soon as he could get the votes.

CHAPTER ♦ 2

Turning Against the Poor

It did not take long for the dismantling of the Warren Court's approach to the poor to begin. Just two weeks after *Goldberg v. Kelly*, the landmark ruling recognizing a right to a hearing before welfare benefits were cut off, the Court decided another welfare case. In *Dandridge v. Williams*, a welfare recipient was seeking more than just the procedural rights the Court had recognized in *Goldberg*. She was asking the Court to hold that the amount of benefits her family received was unconstitutionally low. Poverty lawyers hoped *Dandridge* would be the case in which the Court finally began to recognize substantive economic rights. It was, instead, the case in which the Court began to turn against poor people.

Linda Williams, the lead plaintiff, was a single mother in Baltimore with a medical condition, whose husband had deserted her and their eight children. The family received AFDC benefits, but their benefits had been reduced sharply. Maryland had lowered its AFDC spending as part of an overall reduction in the state budget. Rather than cut benefits equally for all recipients, the state adopted a "maximum grant" rule that capped every family at $250 a month, regardless of how many children it had. The cap meant that small families received the same amount as before, while larger ones, like the Williams family, saw their checks shrink significantly.

Even before the cuts, Maryland's AFDC benefits were woefully inadequate. AFDC was created by the Social Security Act of 1935 to help children of widows, but over time it had become the nation's main program supporting the poor. AFDC was a federal-state partnership, in which the federal government set many of the ground rules but the states were allowed to set their own benefit levels. The federal government had recently established an official poverty level, which was deliberately set extremely low—the woman who created it conceded that it was "a level at which a nutritionally good diet, though possible, is hard to achieve." States were free to set their AFDC benefits below this already low federal poverty level, and they did. Nationally, the average AFDC benefits for a family of four in 1970 were $2,652 a year, just 66 percent of the poverty level.

More than one-third of the states had maximum grant rules, which made their already inadequate benefits particularly punitive for large families. The Williams family had initially received $3,553.80 a year, or 68 percent of the poverty level for a family of its size. When Maryland adopted its maximum grant rule, the Williams family's benefits fell to less than 58 percent of the poverty level, or a little more than half of the level at which federal poverty experts said good nutrition was "hard to achieve."

In February 1968, the Baltimore Legal Aid Bureau brought a class action challenge to Maryland's maximum grant rule, with Williams as the lead plaintiff. The bureau's lawyers argued that capping benefits for large families violated the Equal Protection Clause, because children in large families received less in AFDC benefits than children in small ones. The lawyers also said that Maryland was violating the Social Security Act, which required states in the AFDC program to provide aid to "all eligible individuals." The maximum grant cap, they said, meant that the younger children in large families were not receiving benefits at all.

Welfare lawyers had long wanted to take a challenge to maximum grant rules to the Supreme Court. When Sparer published an article listing the top ten issues that needed "social welfare law testing," he put maximum grant caps at number four. Sparer and other national poverty law litigators would have preferred, however, to bring the Court a case from the South. Family caps in southern states were considerably lower than those in the North, and it was not hard to find racist motives behind them. Advocates for the poor hoped the Court would hear a challenge from Mississippi, where the average monthly AFDC payment per recipient was $8.50, or Louisiana, where Senator Russell Long compared welfare mothers to "broodmares." The poverty law movement, however, had no centralized mechanism for deciding which cases would go up to the Court, something the civil rights movement did a better job of, and the Baltimore Legal Aid Bureau got there first.

There was a great deal riding on *Dandridge*. It had the potential to resolve more than just an important issue about benefit levels. It could also show that the Court cared not only about how welfare programs were administered, but about how much they paid in benefits. Even if the Court did not recognize a right to subsistence, the case gave it a chance to signal that it was troubled by the extremely low benefit levels many welfare families were forced to live on.

The Court that would decide Williams's case was far less favorable than the one that existed when it was filed. When Williams first challenged Maryland's maximum grant rule, Warren was the chief justice and Fortas was still on the Court, and it was not hard to imagine that the Warren Court's liberal majority would use the case to significantly expand the rights of welfare recipients. When the case was argued, in December 1969, with Burger presiding over a more conservative eight-justice Court, that prospect seemed less likely.

There were, however, ways the Court could rule for Williams narrowly that would get rid of the maximum cap without elevating poor people or welfare in constitutional law. It could apply simple "rational basis" review, the kind of review it gave to laws where no suspect class or fundamental interest was involved, and still strike down the maximum grant cap. Even under rational-basis review, the state had to show that it had rational reasons for acting as it had, related to legitimate government interests, and it was not clear how anyone gained by focusing the state's budget cuts on large families rather than spreading them across all welfare recipients. The Court could also avoid the constitutional questions and simply hold that the cap violated the Social Security Act's requirement that aid must be given "to all eligible individuals." That would have been similar to the cautious approach the Court took in *King v. Smith,* striking down the man-in-the-house rule based on its interpretation of "parental support" under the AFDC statute.

On April 6, 1970, the Court ruled against Williams by a 5–3 vote. The *Dandridge* majority was made up of the three *Goldberg* dissenters—Burger, Stewart, and Black—and Harlan and White, who had been in the *Goldberg* majority. On this new Burger Court, Harlan and White were in the center, and they showed it in this pair of welfare law cases, deciding that John Kelly would win his lawsuit and Linda Williams would lose hers.

The *Dandridge* decision was written by Stewart, a scion of the upper classes, whose path in life could hardly have been more different from that of Williams, the abandoned single mother of eight with serious health issues, living on welfare. Stewart grew up in a prominent Republican family in Cincinnati, where his father was mayor before serving on the Ohio Supreme Court. He described his Michigan-born mother, whose own father and grandfather were presidents of that state's oldest bank, as "kind of a small-town rich girl." Stewart attended Hotchkiss, the old-money Connecticut prep school; Yale College, where he was a member of the elite Skull and Bones secret society; Yale Law School; and Cambridge University. He practiced at white-shoe law firms and became a federal appeals court judge before he turned forty.

Stewart dispensed with Williams's equal protection claims tersely. He acknowledged that the case involved "the most basic economic needs of impoverished human beings," but he could "find no basis for applying" a heightened level of scrutiny. The maximum grant rule, he insisted, was nothing more than a "state regulation in the social and economic field." Therefore, he said, it should be subjected to mere rational-basis review.

Applying that lenient standard, Stewart said Maryland's rule had to be upheld. Even if it disadvantaged large families, he wrote, a classification is not unconstitutional merely because it was "not made with mathematical nicety or because in practice it results in some inequality." Maryland had adopted the rule to reduce costs, Stewart said, and it was within its rights to do so, even if it could have spread the cuts more evenly. "The problems of government are practical ones," he wrote, "and may justify, if they do not require, rough accommodations."

Stewart also rejected Williams's Social Security Act claim. He insisted that younger children in large families were not denied benefits in violation of the "all eligible individuals" requirement. As Stewart saw it, "a more realistic view is that the lot of the entire family is diminished," and he insisted that the act allowed states to make that kind of reduction.

Stewart went on to make a larger statement about government help for the poor that was sharply at odds with its recent sympathetic words in *Goldberg*. The Court did not care if it was "wise" to make a large family live on what a smaller family did, he said, or whether "a more just and humane system could . . . be devised." Using language that signaled a new hostility to welfare cases, Stewart declared that "the intractable economic, social, and even philosophical problems presented by public welfare assistance programs are not the business of this Court."

In dissent, Marshall, who as a lawyer represented people like Linda Williams, made an impassioned case for the Williams family. He argued that applying mere rational-basis review in this case constituted "emasculation of the Equal Protection Clause." It was wrong, he insisted, to apply a standard for a "gas company or an optical dispenser" to a claim "involving the literally vital interests of a powerless minority—poor families without breadwinners." Marshall said that Maryland had not sufficiently justified a rule that, for Williams and the class she represented, constituted "the denial of even a subsistence existence."

The contrast between *Dandridge* and *Goldberg* was striking: welfare recipients' greatest victory and greatest defeat in the Court had come just two weeks apart. The main reason for the different outcomes was no doubt what the plaintiffs were seeking. Kelly wanted only a hearing at which he could make the case for keeping his benefits, an easy thing for a court to order. Williams wanted her welfare benefits increased, the sort of financial decision courts are less comfortable making. Courts do issue rulings that affect government budgets, including *Gideon v. Wainwright*, which required cities and counties to provide lawyers to poor defendants. They are wary, however, of remedies that appear to be flatly redistributionist. Stewart alluded to this discomfort in his *Dandridge* opinion. "The Constitution may impose certain procedural safeguards upon systems of welfare administration," he wrote, citing *Goldberg*, but it "does not empower this Court to second-guess state officials charged with the difficult responsibility of allocating limited public welfare funds among the myriad of potential recipients."

Beyond the jurisprudential reasons for the Court's ruling in *Dandridge*, there was also one relating to personnel: Johnson's failure to fill Warren's seat. If he had selected a more easily confirmed nominee, there could have been a liberal chief justice instead of Burger. At the same time, if Fortas had not been weakened by his Senate rejection, *Life* magazine might not have investigated him, or he might have been able to survive the Nixon administration's onslaught. In that alternative version of history, there would almost certainly have been five justices on Williams's side: the new chief justice, Fortas, Brennan, Marshall, and Douglas. That Court might have struck down the maximum grant cap on narrow grounds, but it also might have been bolder, holding that poor people or welfare benefits had special constitutional status.

Dandridge's direct impact was significant, and it reached well beyond Maryland. The Court had given its approval to maximum grant caps that existed in more than one-third of the states, some with benefit levels that were well below Maryland's. As a result of the decision, many children in large families throughout the country grew up further below the poverty line than they otherwise would have.

Dandridge's deeper implications, however, went beyond maximum grant rules. The decision was an unmistakable turning point for poor people in American law. For decades, going back to Jacobus tenBroek's early writings, there had been a movement calling for special constitutional protection for the poor. The idea had gained traction with scholars like Charles Reich, Edward Sparer, and Frank Michelman and with a growing army of poverty lawyers who were working to devise new legal doctrines. In recent years, with its holdings and language, the Court had been starting to elevate the rights of the poor to a new level.

With *Dandridge*, however, it became clear that *Goldberg* would be the high-water mark for the poor in American law, at least for some time. After all of the talk about whether the poor as a class should receive heightened scrutiny, the Court had now made clear that they would not. Rather than recognizing welfare as a fundamental interest deserving of a higher level of review, the Court said just the opposite. The problems of welfare programs were "intractable," it insisted, and "not the business of this Court."

It would be hard to devise a more thorough rebuke to the ideals of the poverty law movement. *Dandridge* represented, as one scholar put it, the "deconstitutionalization" of poverty law. The following year, in another case involving the poor, Marshall described the new reality with an air of resignation. The Court had decided, he said, that laws that harmed poor people would receive "no scrutiny whatsoever." Sparer was crestfallen by the *Dandridge* ruling. If the Court had been willing to use the Equal Protection Clause more forcefully on behalf of the poor, he said, it "could have led to a different America."

AFTER MAKING BURGER CHIEF JUSTICE, NIXON HAD A SECOND SEAT TO fill, Fortas's, and he was eager to nominate a southerner. A key part of his presidential campaign had been his "Southern strategy," a blatantly racial appeal to white voters in the South. He hoped to use his next nomination to continue to stoke the politics of regional resentment. There was one southerner on the Court at the time, Alabama-born Hugo Black, but he had been in the majority in *Brown v. Board of Education* and supported later civil rights rulings. Nixon was looking to nominate a white southerner with an anti-civil-rights record—as Ehrlichman said, "a bona fide son of the Old South."

In August 1969, Nixon nominated Clement F. Haynsworth Jr., a judge on the Richmond, Virginia–based U.S. Court of Appeals for the Fourth Circuit who had unimpeachable southern credentials. Haynsworth, a native of Greenville, South Carolina, had spent his legal career representing textile mills and other monied interests. Rehnquist, the assistant attorney general who approved of prosecuting Fortas, got right to the point in an internal memorandum, vouching that Haynsworth "will not be favorably inclined toward claims of . . . civil rights plaintiffs."

There was opposition to Haynsworth in the Senate for his anti-civil-rights views and anti-labor rulings, and for his decision to preside over a case in which he had a financial interest. Democratic senators spoke against him, prodded by civil rights groups and unions and by lingering bad feelings over how the Senate had treated Fortas. Thinking the confirmation vote would be close, Nixon sent Vice President Spiro Agnew to the Senate in case he was needed to break a tie, but Haynsworth was rejected, 55–45.

Stung by the defeat, Nixon doubled down. He told an aide to "find a good federal judge further south and further to the right." His next choice, G. Harrold Carswell of the New Orleans–based U.S. Court of Appeals for the Fifth Circuit, met both criteria. Carswell, who was born in Georgia and lived in Florida, was even more steeped in Confederate values than Haynsworth. His family's plantation had been burned down in the Civil War when General William Tecumseh Sherman pillaged his way across Georgia. As a legislative candidate in 1948, Carswell declared that he yielded to no one in his "firm, vigorous belief in the principles of white supremacy." While Carswell's Confederate credentials were in order, his legal qualifications were weak. As a judge, he had an extraordinarily high reversal rate, and one commentator said his judicial opinions read "like plumbers' manuals." Carswell's unworthiness was underscored by the argument Senator Roman Hruska, a Nebraska Republican, made on his behalf. "There are a lot of mediocre judges and people and lawyers," Hruska said. "They are entitled to a little representation, aren't they?" Carswell was rejected by a 51–45 vote.

After his impressive success in getting Fortas off the Court and Burger on, Nixon's two failed nominations were painful setbacks. *Time*'s cover declared, "The Carswell Defeat—Nixon's Embattled White House," and Nixon's poll ratings fell. Nixon tried to exploit the defeats for his Southern strategy, insisting that Haynsworth and Carswell had been treated unfairly because "they had the misfortune of being born in the South." He was being forced, he said, to look outside the region for his next nominee.

Nixon turned next to Minnesotan Harry Blackmun, a judge on the St. Louis–based U.S. Court of Appeals for the Eighth Circuit, who was an old friend of Burger's. The two had attended the same St. Paul elementary school, and Blackmun was best man at the chief justice's wedding. Rehnquist reviewed Blackmun's record to ensure that he was sufficiently conservative. Top Justice Department lawyers questioned him in person, including about whether any of his three daughters, who were all in their twenties, were hippies—an interview Blackmun and his daughters passed.

The Senate was as exhausted from the last two nominations as Nixon was. There was little opposition to, or even curiosity about, Blackmun. After hearings marked by mild questioning, at which he insisted that he would not hesitate to vote differently than Burger, on May 12, 1970, Blackmun was confirmed by a 94–0 vote. Despite his protestations, when Blackmun first joined the Court, he was so close to Burger that the two justices were dubbed the "Minnesota Twins." The replacement of Fortas with Blackmun was another major step in the dismantling of the Warren Court.

Nixon, still intent on creating a conservative Court, turned next to two more liberal justices he thought could be driven off. One was Brennan, who represented everything Nixon opposed. The public attacks on Brennan began on May 15, 1969, the day after Fortas resigned. John Rarick, a segregationist Louisiana congressman, denounced Brennan for participating in an investment partnership with other judges and a real estate developer. He urged his colleagues not to be "pacified by the departure of one—Abe Fortas—while there remain in the federal judiciary others with similar interests damaging the solemnity of the judiciary." Rarick inserted purportedly incriminating documents into the *Congressional Record*.

The attacks lacked substance, but Brennan took them seriously. He liquidated all of his holdings, including AT&T stock his mother had left him. Brennan also withdrew from all outside activities, including teaching a seminar at New York University and serving on Harvard Law School's Visiting Committee. There was little left for his critics to complain about, and the attacks soon stopped.

Nixon's other target was Douglas, who was more vulnerable. The most liberal justice, Douglas was an iconoclast in law and life. At age seventy, he was married to his fourth wife, Cathy, a twenty-five-year-old law student—a union that attracted attention in legal circles and beyond. In his three decades on the Court, Douglas had sided with society's most marginalized members and staked out controversial positions. With the nation bitterly divided over Vietnam, he had been the only dissenter in *United States v. O'Brien*, a 1968 ruling upholding a young man's conviction for burning his draft card. In his dissent, Douglas went beyond the facts of the case to question whether, in the absence of a formal declaration of war, the draft itself was legal. Douglas, who was a committed environmentalist, later wrote a highly unconventional dissent arguing that trees and rivers should have legal standing to sue to protect themselves.

Nixon began his anti-Douglas campaign as soon as he took office. Within five days of his inauguration, the Internal Revenue Service was reportedly auditing Douglas's tax returns. The FBI investigated Douglas's ties to Albert Parvin, a Las Vegas casino magnate, on whose foundation board he served. Ehrlichman had a former New York police detective look for negative information on Douglas. FBI director J. Edgar Hoover, who was wiretapping Douglas's telephone, sent reports on the justice's phone calls directly to the White House.

While law enforcement worked behind the scenes, Nixon dispatched prominent people to attack Douglas publicly. Vice President Agnew, appearing on CBS News on April 9, 1970, said Douglas threatened national security. Ehrlichman told House minority leader Gerald Ford to lead an impeachment drive. The following week, Ford called for Douglas's impeachment in an impassioned speech on the House floor. He attacked Douglas for his ties to Parvin, who he said was in league with Mafia figures Bugsy Siegel and Meyer Lansky. Ford also called Douglas a radical, insisting that his book *Points of Rebellion* advocated revolution. Ford held up an issue of *Evergreen Review*, a magazine that had excerpted Douglas's book, and declared that it contained "perverted" and "downright filthy" content.

The campaign against Douglas did not go as Nixon had hoped. The *Detroit Free Press* said it would take Ford's claims more seriously if it "had greater faith in his objectivity." *The New York Times* editorialized that Nixon and Ford's "squalid campaign" threatened "the integrity and the independence of the Supreme Court." Ford was unable to generate enough support in the Democratic-controlled House to move forward with impeachment, and Douglas remained on the Court, with what John Dean called an "intractable resolve."

When the Brennan and Douglas campaigns failed, Nixon shifted to "easier ways," in Ehrlichman's words, of creating a conservative majority. He became intensely interested in the health of the justices, particularly Douglas, Black, Harlan, and Marshall, all of whom had medical issues. In private meetings, Nixon pressed Burger for updates on his colleagues' medical conditions. Nixon took comfort in the advanced ages of the liberal justices and in the notes Burger sent him suggesting possible health setbacks that could lead to new vacancies.

There was nothing subtle about Nixon's inquiries. Marshall, for one, understood that his health was a matter of intense interest to the president. When Marshall checked into the Bethesda Naval Hospital with pneumonia, Nixon asked for a status report. Marshall told a Navy officer, "Well, Admiral, you have my permission to give it to him only on one condition: that you put at the bottom of it, quote, 'Not yet.'"

THE SUPREME COURT IS A NEW COURT WITH EACH NEW JUSTICE WHO arrives. The arrival of two justices, including a new chief justice, was even more transformative. Burger and Blackmun started to shift the Court rightward, and in no area was that clearer than in cases involving poor people. Two of the greatest champions of the poor were gone, replaced by justices with very different outlooks. The first majority opinion Blackmun wrote for the Court was in a welfare case, and his and Burger's votes turned a decision that two years earlier would almost certainly have been a win for welfare families into a defeat.

Wyman v. James was a challenge to a New York law that allowed welfare caseworkers to inspect welfare recipients' homes on a regular basis and terminate the benefits of anyone who refused. Barbara James, a single mother in New York City who received AFDC benefits, attended meetings of a welfare rights organization and heard other mothers speak out against home visits. They did not want caseworkers rifling through their belongings and, as they said, "counting toothbrushes to see if there was a man in the house." James went to a neighborhood Mobilization for Youth legal office and told a lawyer that the city was insisting on a home visit before recertifying her and her two-year-old son, Maurice, for AFDC. James refused to allow her caseworker to make a home visit, but she made it clear that she would provide any information the city wanted. The city cut off James's benefits and the lawyer she spoke to filed a lawsuit on her behalf.

Welfare recipients and poverty lawyers had long objected to welfare programs that invaded recipients' homes. Sparer's welfare recipients' bill of rights in the *UCLA Law Review* called for protection against improper searches. James's lawsuit, which was filed as a class action, included affidavits from other AFDC recipients describing the impact of home visits, which were often conducted without notice. "It's very embarrassing to me if the caseworker comes when I have company," one welfare recipient said. The plaintiffs cooperated even when caseworkers questioned their guests or their children, because, as one said, "I cannot afford to have my caseworker angry at me because I am so dependent on him."

James's lawyers charged that the home visit law violated the Fourth Amendment. They argued that if welfare caseworkers did not have consent to enter a home, they should be required to get search warrants. The lawyers invoked a recent Supreme Court decision holding that inspectors were not allowed to conduct health and safety inspections in commercial properties without warrants. A three-judge federal district court that heard the case held that the home visits were unconstitutional.

On January 12, 1971, the Court ruled against James by a 6–3 vote. Nixon's two nominees, Burger and Blackmun, provided two of the votes to uphold warrantless home visits. Blackmun, in his majority opinion, said that home visits were not searches under the Fourth Amendment because they were not part of a criminal investigation. He also said they were conducted with consent, since welfare recipients were always free to refuse. If they did refuse, they were not criminally sanctioned, Blackmun said; their AFDC "merely ceases"—a flippant way to describe a family's loss of the money it depended on for food and shelter. In his first majority opinion, Blackmun came through strongly for Nixon and "demonstrated," as one news account noted, "that not all conservative jurists speak with a Southern accent."

Marshall, in dissent, pointed out the disturbing contrast between the Court's ruling and its recent decision holding that business owners had the right to turn away inspectors who did not have search warrants. In this case, he said, the Court was refusing to extend that same right to the "lowly poor" in their own homes. Marshall saw an ominous shift occurring. In the past, he said, the Court had "occasionally pushed beyond established constitutional contours to protect the vulnerable and to further basic human values." Now, with the steadily forming conservative majority, the Court was pushing the law not to *protect* vulnerable people like James but to take their rights away.

Even after *Dandridge v. Williams*, many advocates for the poor were not expecting to lose the *James* case. Barbara James was not asking for increased welfare benefits, as Linda Williams had been in *Dandridge*. She was only seeking basic procedural protections before welfare officials exerted authority over her, as John Kelly had been granted in *Goldberg v. Kelly*. A large part of the reason James lost where Kelly had prevailed, clearly, was the new composition of the Court. Warren and Fortas would almost certainly have voted in favor of James. Another part of the explanation was that the Court was simply turning against the poor.

On April 26, the Court handed poor people another defeat, in a new area: affordable housing. *James v. Valtierra* was a challenge to a provision of the California Constitution that prohibited the building of new public housing unless the voters in the surrounding community approved. The provision, Article 34, had been added to the constitution by referendum in 1950, with support from the California Real Estate Association.

The case arose out of fights over public housing in San Jose and nearby San Mateo County. Both the city and the county had long public housing waiting lists in 1968, and they wanted to apply for federal funds to build new housing. There was, however, strong community resistance. One San Jose city councilwoman declared that poor people can "drag the whole neighborhood down," bringing "piles of garbage" and "undisciplined children." The communities voted, as Article 34 required, and they rejected the proposed housing. Poor people eligible for public housing sued, arguing that Article 34 violated their rights under the Equal Protection Clause.

A three-judge district court ruled for the poor people, striking down Article 34. It relied on a recent case in which the Supreme Court had invalidated a voter-enacted amendment to Akron, Ohio's city charter. That amendment had required city laws that prohibited racial discrimination in housing to be approved by the voters. The Supreme Court said that imposing a higher threshold to enact laws aimed at racial discrimination violated the Equal Protection Clause. By the same logic, the district court said, Article 34 was unconstitutional because of the extra barrier it imposed to building housing for the poor.

The Supreme Court reversed the district court by a 5–3 vote and upheld Article 34. Black, writing for the majority, said the Akron case did not apply because it was about discrimination on the basis of race, not poverty. Requiring voter approval to let racial minorities into a community violated the Equal Protection Clause, he said, but requiring voter approval to let poor people in did not.

In dissent, Marshall argued that Article 34 should be struck down because it relied on "an explicit classification on the basis of poverty." Just a few years earlier, a majority of the Court might have seen the case the way Marshall did. That Court was striking down fees to appeal criminal convictions and the poll tax and comparing discrimination against the poor to racial discrimination. All of those opinions, however, came before May 14, 1969, when Fortas resigned.

Valtierra proved to be a serious setback to affordable housing in California. In the years since it was decided, Article 34 has reduced the supply of housing for poor people in a state where it is in short supply, and it has reinforced economic and racial segregation across the nation. Matthew Lassiter, a University of Michigan history professor, called *Valtierra* "one of the most important defeats in civil rights history in the last century," one that is "under-appreciated in how much it contributed to the stoppage of efforts to integrate communities across the country."

ON SEPTEMBER 17, 1971, NIXON FINALLY GOT THE NEWS HE WAS WAITING for. Black, who had been hospitalized since August, announced his retirement. Two days later he suffered a stroke, and later in the week he died. Black had drifted to the right over the years in many areas, including in cases involving the poor. He had, however, spent most of his career as one of the Court's great liberals, and that reputation persisted. John Dean said Black was "the epitome of a justice that Richard Nixon abhorred" and that Nixon was excited about replacing him.

As the White House prepared to replace Black, Nixon received more good news. Harlan, who was just seventy-two, had spinal cancer and did not have long to live. He waited to make his resignation public until September 23 so as not to upstage Black's announcement, but Burger informed Nixon confidentially. For much of the Warren Court, Harlan had been the most conservative justice, but he had become more liberal as Black became more conservative. In *Goldberg v. Kelly*, it was Harlan, not Black, who had provided the crucial fifth vote. The news that Harlan had late-stage cancer that would force him off the Court, Ehrlichman said, left Nixon "elated."

Suddenly, the conservative majority Nixon dreamed of was in sight. The Court was down to seven justices, with only three solid liberals left from the Warren era: Douglas, Brennan, and Marshall. There were two centrist conservatives, White and Stewart. If Nixon filled the two vacancies with conservatives, his four justices would form a powerful bloc. They would only need to attract Stewart or White to build a majority.

Nixon was more eager than ever to name a southerner, particularly after the departure of Black, the Court's only southern-born member. The first name he sent the American Bar Association to review was Virginia congressman Richard Poff, who had lobbied heavily for the position. Poff had, however, signed the "Southern Manifesto," a statement that 101 southern senators and representatives had placed in the *Congressional Record* in March 1956, declaring *Brown v. Board of Education* "contrary to the Constitution" and calling for the use of all "lawful means" to overturn it. He had also consistently voted against civil rights bills. Poff's supporters argued that if he had done anything differently he would have lost his seat in Congress. Still, his outright support for racial segregation caused considerable opposition to form against his nomination, and he withdrew.

Nixon eventually found his southerner. In a televised address on October 21, he announced that he would nominate Lewis F. Powell Jr., a corporate lawyer from Richmond, Virginia, to one of the vacancies—and William Rehnquist to the other. Powell, a former president of the American Bar Association, did not have the kind of inflammatory racial record that Nixon's previous two southern nominees had, and he had some moderate credentials, including having been a prominent supporter of legal services programs.

The media accepted the White House's portrayal of Powell as a courtly moderate. "In manners and polish, Mr. Powell fits comfortably into the image of the antebellum South," *The New York Times* reported. "But in the moderation of his ideas and his approach to integration, he appears to belong more to what has been called 'the new South.'" The paper presented Powell's service as chairman of the Richmond School Board in the post-*Brown* period positively, saying that "he quietly admitted Negroes to white schools in 1959."

In fact, Powell, who traced his family back to the first settlers at Jamestown, had connections to the Old South that went well beyond "manners and polish." He grew up in Jim Crow Richmond attending all-white schools and churches. As an adult, he lived in a world that had changed little. Powell was a member of private clubs that did not admit blacks, and there were reports that his law firm, which had no black lawyers, had a policy of not hiring any. Whether that was true or not, it seemed clear that, as one of his former law clerks observed, Powell had "never met a black as equal."

Powell, who knew his own record better than *The New York Times* did, told the White House that "there will be plenty of black leaders who will think that I was not active enough in [promoting] integration in Virginia." Powell had given them good reason for that belief. When *Brown v. Board of*

Education was decided, Powell opposed it as being wrong on the law and bad as policy. "I am not in favor of, and will never favor compulsory integration," he wrote at the time in a letter. As school board chairman, Powell was in no rush to desegregate Richmond's schools. When he resigned as chairman, in 1961, only two of Richmond's 23,000 black students went to school with whites.

Black leaders insisted that Powell's record should disqualify him. The all-black Old Dominion Bar Association said Powell had "consistently voted to resist or ignore the decisions of the Supreme Court requiring racial integration of public schools." Representative John Conyers Jr., speaking for the Congressional Black Caucus, opposed the nomination, saying Powell's lack of support for desegregation when he was head of the school board had "offended the constitutional rights of the black schoolchildren who were entrapped by Powell's policy decisions."

While Powell did little for civil rights, he strongly championed big business. In his law practice, he represented some of the nation's leading corporations, including United Virginia Bank, one of the largest in the state, and Philip Morris, the tobacco giant. He showed an unusual degree of loyalty to his clients, including the controversial ones. After the surgeon general's report linking cigarettes to cancer and early death was released in 1964, Powell stood by Philip Morris. In a show of allegiance, he took up smoking, or at least the appearance of it, and engaged in his new habit conspicuously, even smoking at Philip Morris board meetings, where he made himself available to be photographed with a cigarette in hand.

Many senators were eager to support Powell after rejecting Nixon's first two southern nominees. Powell also benefited from the fact that Democrats who had misgivings about him had greater concerns about Rehnquist. Despite the criticism from civil rights advocates, the Senate confirmed Powell by a vote of 89–1. The one vote against him came from Fred Harris, a populist Democrat from Oklahoma, who insisted that Powell was an elitist who lacked sympathy for the "little people."

Rehnquist, meanwhile, was a more unusual choice for the Court, and his confirmation did not go as smoothly. Presidents usually nominate federal appeals court judges and occasionally senators or high public officials. Rehnquist was none of these things, nor did he have the national stature Powell had as a former American Bar Association president. He was an obscure Justice Department lawyer. He did, however, have strong support at the highest levels of the Nixon administration, including from Deputy Attorney General Richard Kleindienst, an Arizonan who had recruited him to leave Phoenix to join the administration. Nixon came to see advantages to the choice. He liked that Rehnquist was just forty-seven and could be on the Court for thirty years or more, perhaps eventually as chief justice. Most important, Nixon liked Rehnquist's strongly held ideology, which he had proven in the attorney general's office and in Arizona. Barry Goldwater, the Arizona senator who had been the Republicans' far-right presidential nominee in 1964, said Rehnquist was the most conservative lawyer he had ever met.

Rehnquist's whole life had, in fact, been one of remarkable ideological purity. He grew up outside Milwaukee in what *The Washington Post* called a "village full of Republicans," where race relations were not an issue because "there were no blacks." His senior prom had a Harlem theme, and promgoers entered through a doorway festooned with "unique decorations in the form of Negro heads." After serving in World War II, Rehnquist attended Stanford on the G.I. Bill. He went on to Stanford Law School, where he graduated first in his class.

Rehnquist clerked for Robert Jackson and then settled in Phoenix. He worked on Goldwater's 1964 campaign and became part of his inner circle. When the civil rights movement reached Phoenix, Rehnquist testified against a proposed law to bar discrimination in stores and restaurants, which he insisted trampled on "a man's private property." After the law was enacted, Rehnquist complained in a letter to *The Arizona Republic* that, "unable to correct the source of the indignity to the Negro," the law "redresses the situation by placing a separate indignity on the proprietor." Rehnquist joined Nixon's Justice Department in 1969 as assistant attorney general for the

Office of Legal Counsel. In addition to his contributions to the effort to remove Fortas, Rehnquist worked on a variety of other politically charged matters, including monitoring student anti-war protesters, whom he called "the new barbarians."

There was considerable opposition to Rehnquist's nomination based on his hardline conservative views, particularly on race. His critics raised his opposition to Phoenix's civil rights law and presented witnesses who had seen him challenge minority voters at the polls as part of a Republican "ballot security" program. The program had used "harassment and intimidation," the critics said, to discourage blacks and Mexican Americans from voting. Rehnquist denied challenging voters, though it appears that he was lying. John Dean, Nixon's White House counsel, reviewed the testimony long after he left the White House and said that "the conclusion is inescapable that Rehnquist's statement . . . flatly denying that he had challenged voters . . . was false."

Just before the floor debate began, *Newsweek* dropped a bombshell. It reported on a confidential memorandum Rehnquist had prepared as a law clerk for Jackson, when the Court was deciding *Brown v. Board of Education.* He wrote, "I think *Plessy v. Ferguson*"—the 1896 decision upholding the separate-but-equal doctrine—"was right and should be reaffirmed." Rehnquist said in a letter to the Senate that the statement had simply been an attempt to capture Jackson's views, but Jackson's longtime secretary, Elsie Douglas, insisted that the memo in no way reflected the views of Jackson, who was a strong supporter of equality. Rehnquist had, she said, "smeared the reputation of a great justice." The weight of evidence was on her side. In *Simple Justice,* his monumental history of *Brown v. Board of Education,* Richard Kluger closely examined the memorandum's wording and history and concluded that Rehnquist was expressing his own view that racial segregation was constitutional.

Despite all of the objections, Rehnquist was confirmed by a vote of 68–26. When the news broke, Nixon called Rehnquist to offer his congratulations. He also gave Rehnquist some blunt advice that indicated what he expected from the Court he was creating: "Just be as mean and rough as they said you were, okay?"

Powell and Rehnquist were sworn in on January 7, 1972, becoming the third and fourth justices Nixon put on the Court in his first three years in office. When Harlan resigned, a White House official had understood exactly what it meant. "The next Court," he said, would not be known as the "Burger Court or the Warren Court"—it would be "the Nixon Court."

ON FEBRUARY 23, THE COURT DECIDED ANOTHER CASE ABOUT HOUSING for the poor, which the newly arrived Powell and Rehnquist did not participate in. Edna Lindsey and her husband, Donald, who was often confined to a wheelchair, lived with their three children, aged nine through fourteen, in a rented house that the Portland Bureau of Buildings found unfit for habitation. The house was, an expert witness said, "one of the worst" she had seen "that people are still living in." It had broken windows, missing back steps, porch supports that were tearing loose, exposed wires in a child's bedroom, and numerous other defects. The only repair the landlord was willing to make was nailing a single piece of plywood over one broken window. When it was clear she would not do any more, the Lindseys withheld their rent.

The landlord threatened to go to court to evict the Lindseys. If she did, there was an Oregon law that would prevent the Lindseys from raising as a defense the landlord's failure to maintain the property in habitable condition. As a result, the court that heard their case would treat them simply as renters who were delinquent with their payments, not people intentionally withholding rent to pressure a landlord to make urgently needed repairs. The Lindseys challenged the law, arguing that it violated their Fourteenth Amendment due process rights because it prevented them from raising every possible defense to a lawsuit brought against them. When they failed to persuade a three-judge district court in Oregon, they brought their case to the Supreme Court.

The Court in *Lindsey v. Normet* upheld the Oregon law by a 5–2 vote.

White, writing for the majority, said there was no due process right to defend against an eviction by asserting that a home was not habitable. If the Lindseys wanted to make that claim, he said, they could bring a separate lawsuit. White also firmly rejected the idea that shelter was a fundamental interest or that the Court should apply heightened scrutiny to the Oregon law because the Lindseys could lose their home. "We do not denigrate the importance of decent, safe, and sanitary housing," he said, "but the Constitution does not provide judicial remedies for every social and economic ill."

Lindsey represented yet another turning away from the rights of the poor. The Court could have declared that the Due Process Clause required government to meet basic elements of fairness before it removed people from their homes, much as it had ruled in *Goldberg v. Kelly* that there had to be a hearing before welfare benefits could be taken away. It also could have held that housing was a fundamental interest and imposed heightened scrutiny on any law that made it easier for landlords to take a family's home away. Instead, the Court made it clear that the details of eviction proceedings were largely not its concern, just as it had held in *Dandridge* that "the intractable . . . problems presented by" welfare programs were "not the business of this Court."

With the Nixon justices in increasingly firm control, the Court began to show a new meanspiritedness toward poor people. In January 1973, it decided *United States v. Kras,* a challenge to the mandatory fee that courts imposed on people who wanted to file for bankruptcy. Robert Kras, a New Yorker, was unemployed, heavily in debt, and the father of two, including an infant son with cystic fibrosis. He wanted to exercise his legal right to declare bankruptcy so he and his family could start over, but he could not afford the fee. He sued, arguing that preventing him from declaring bankruptcy because of his inability to pay a fee violated due process and equal protection.

Kras had strong precedents on his side. The Warren Court had ruled that poor people had a right to appeal their criminal case even if they could not afford to pay for a transcript, and it said that poor defendants had the right to an appointed lawyer at trial and on appeal. The Court had also held, in a case called *Boddie v. Connecticut*—decided in 1971, before Powell and Rehnquist joined the Court—that it violated due process for a state to deny poor people a divorce because they could not pay court fees.

In *Kras*, the Court ruled that there was no right to a waiver of a bankruptcy fee, by a 5–4 vote. Blackmun, writing for the four Nixon justices and White, said the fee should be subject only to rational-basis review, and under that lenient standard it had to be upheld. The *Boddie* precedent did not apply, he said, because marriages, and ending them, involved fundamental interests, but bankruptcy did not. Blackmun also insisted that, since Kras could pay in installments, he should not have a problem coming up with the fee. The weekly payments would be, he said, "little more than the cost of a pack or two of cigarettes."

Marshall, in dissent, chided the majority for being too cavalier about what the fee meant to a poor person, a result, he said, of the justices not understanding "how close to the margin of survival" the poor often were. For many poor people, he said, a pack or two of cigarettes might be "not a routine purchase, but a luxury indulged in only rarely." It was fine for judges to disagree about what the Constitution required, he said, but it was "disgraceful for an interpretation of the Constitution to be premised upon unfounded assumptions about how people live." Stewart, who was generally not a great supporter of the rights of the poor, was troubled by the obvious irony of the situation. "The Court today holds that Congress may say that some of the poor are too poor even to go bankrupt," he wrote in a separate dissent. "I cannot agree."

A few months later, the Court upheld another mandatory fee for the poor. In *Ortwein v. Schwab*, Raymond Ortwein, an elderly Oregonian, wanted to appeal when the state reduced his old-age benefits by $39 a month, but he could not afford the state court's filing fee. When the court refused to waive the fee, Ortwein argued that it violated his rights of due process and equal protection.

On March 5, 1973, the Court ruled against Ortwein by the same 5–4 vote as in *Kras*. In an unsigned opinion, the majority said it would not apply heightened scrutiny in its review of the fee, even though it prevented Ortwein from challenging a benefit reduction that pushed him further into poverty. Ortwein was not a member of a "suspect classification, such as race" or "nationality," the Court said, and there was no fundamental interest involved. Applying the lenient rational-basis standard of review, it accepted that the state court's desire to produce more revenue was enough reason not to allow a fee waiver.

The dissenting justices wrote four separate dissents, with Douglas most passionately channeling the old Warren Court spirit. The fee constituted "discrimination against the poverty-stricken," he insisted, and should have been struck down under the Equal Protection Clause. The Court's decision, he said, "upholds a scheme of judicial review whereby justice remains a luxury for the wealthy."

Something *Kras* and *Ortwein* had in common—besides holding that poor people could be too poor to use the legal system—was White. In both cases it was White, the Kennedy appointee, not Stewart, the Eisenhower nominee, who provided the Nixon justices with their fifth vote. White was a puzzle, and for liberals a great disappointment. He had been a friend of President Kennedy's before he served as the number-two lawyer to his brother, Attorney General Robert F. Kennedy. In that position, he played a leading role in the administration's civil rights efforts, including helping to protect the Freedom Riders, the protesters who traveled the South, starting in the early 1960s, challenging segregation in public facilities. When President Kennedy nominated White, he predicted that he would be "the ideal New Frontier judge."

If Kennedy's description suggested that White would be a solid liberal, that is not how it turned out. White was an often unpredictable centrist, who voted with the conservatives in some important cases, most famously in *Roe v. Wade,* the landmark 1973 decision establishing a right to abortion, in which White and Rehnquist were the only dissenters.

With the vote of White, or sometimes Stewart, the Nixon justices now dominated the Court. The liberals, who had once set the agenda, increasingly found themselves in dissent. In the 1972–73 term, Douglas, the most liberal justice, dissented in 50.7 percent of the cases, the highest dissent rate on the Court since 1795. The battle lines were drawn, and everyone acknowledged the new reality. When the elderly Douglas, whose vision and hearing were fading, was asked what he would do if he were no longer able to read the case briefs, he reportedly replied, "I'll listen and see how the Chief votes and vote the other way."

Even as the Court became more conservative, there were areas in which it remained liberal and even pushed the law in a more progressive direction. While it rejected claims from the poor, the Court was expanding the constitutional rights of noncitizens and women. In June 1971, in *Graham v. Richardson,* the Court struck down a law that restricted welfare benefits to citizens and people who had been United States residents for at least fifteen years. The challenge was brought by Carmen Richardson, a lawfully admitted resident noncitizen who had moved from Mexico to Arizona in 1956 and became permanently and totally disabled. The Court held that noncitizens were a suspect class under the Equal Protection Clause, and it applied strict scrutiny to the law. Comparing noncitizens to racial minorities, and invoking *Carolene Products* footnote 4, the Court said they "are a prime example of a 'discrete and insular' minority."

The Court also elevated the constitutional status of women. In November 1971, in *Reed v. Reed,* a woman challenged an Idaho law that gave men preference in becoming estate administrators, and the Court found that it violated equal protection. In May 1973, in *Frontiero v. Richardson,* Sharron Frontiero brought a challenge to an Air Force rule that gave male officers more generous benefits than female ones. Frontiero was supported by Ruth Bader Ginsburg, who, as a lawyer for the American Civil Liberties Union (ACLU), was making her first Supreme Court argument. The Court applied heightened scrutiny to strike down the Air Force rule. A few years later, it specified that women as a class were entitled to "intermediate scrutiny" under the Equal Protection Clause—not as demanding as the strict scrutiny standard the Court used for race, religion, and national origin, but still enough to strike down discriminatory laws.

The standards the Court had laid out in footnote 4 for a "discrete and insular minority" were generally a good fit for noncitizens and women, even if women were not actually a minority. Both groups had long histories of discriminatory treatment and had limited power in the political process to protect their rights. For poor people and poverty lawyers, however, the designations were a reminder that the Court was still creating new suspect classes—it just was not giving that designation to the poor, even though they arguably had just as strong a claim as women or noncitizens to being a "discrete and insular minority."

If the Court had recognized the poor as a suspect class and applied even intermediate scrutiny, many landmark poverty law decisions would probably have come out differently. The plaintiffs in *Dandridge v. Williams*, *Wyman v. James*, *James v. Valtierra*, and other cases would very likely have prevailed. As a result, millions of poor people nationwide would have had greater rights to welfare and housing.

There were many reasons the Court was unwilling to extend special constitutional protections to the poor. Some were inherent in the very idea of poor people's rights. Many of the rights the poor sought were not directly about money, as cases like the challenges to California's "anti-Okie" law and Oregon's law restricting defenses in eviction cases demonstrated. The poverty law movement was, however, increasingly focusing on creating a constitutional right to subsistence, which many justices had no interest in doing. The Court had made clear in *Dandridge* that it did not want to wade into the details of how the government funded social programs and the decisions government officials made about aid to the needy. Even putting aside the question of a right to subsistence, many of the issues raised by poverty law were in tension with capitalism, since so many government policies could be seen as discriminating against the poor in one way or another, even ones as simple as requiring passengers to pay a fare to ride the bus. It was, on the whole, far less complicated to tell the government not to discriminate against black people or women than to tell it not to discriminate against the poor.

Some of the reasons for the Court's reticence were more specifically tied to what was happening in America in the late 1960s and early 1970s. There was, of course, the enormous change in composition that the Court had just undergone. If Warren and Fortas had served longer, and even more so if Humphrey had won the 1968 election and appointed more liberals to the Court, the trajectory of poor people's rights would likely have been very different.

Also important was what was going on outside the walls of the Court, where the nation's economic and political climate was changing. The war on poverty had been launched in the early 1960s, at a time of optimism and growing prosperity. By the early 1970s, however, the economy was languishing, with both high unemployment and high inflation, which the press liked to call "stagflation." The nation's image of itself had also been badly wounded by Vietnam and Watergate. The idealism of the 1960s had been replaced by the cynicism and inward-looking focus of the 1970s, a national zeitgeist that was not favorable to expanding the rights of the poor.

Then there was what was happening within the poor people's movement, which had been such a powerful force demanding change in the 1960s. By the early 1970s, the movement was badly fraying, if not actively disintegrating. There was a growing schism between advocates for incremental reform and more radical elements, which was causing supporters to fall away and funding to dry up. The once fiery National Welfare Rights Organization ran out of money and laid off staff. After years of advocates for the poor complaining that welfare programs were badly underfunded, there was a growing countermovement of advocates arguing that welfare spending was excessive. When New York City teetered on the brink of bankruptcy in 1975, fiscal conservatives loudly put the blame on the burden imposed by its "overgenerous" social welfare spending.

Even in liberal circles, intellectuals began to turn against the poor. In the mid-1970s, the journalistic exploration of poverty talked about the most at New York dinner parties and in Washington salons was Susan Sheehan's "A Welfare Mother," a *New Yorker* article that was later published as a book. It took a very different approach from Michael Harrington's *The Other America,* which made such an impassioned case for rescuing the nation's poor. Sheehan presented her subject, a Puerto Rican mother in Brooklyn, with considerable detachment, drifting at times into disapproval. The book emphasized, one critic said, the welfare mother's "passivity, isolation, political apathy, and intellectual weakness." It was less a rallying cry than a cry of exhaustion.

In this new, less favorable national climate for the poor, the Court went from not expanding the rights of poor people to taking back rights it had already given them. In 1976, it decided *Mathews v. Eldridge,* a case that in every important way resembled *Goldberg v. Kelly.* George Eldridge, a Virginia father of six, had received Social Security disability benefits for diabetes, back strain, and chronic anxiety for four years when he was cut off without a pretermination hearing. He had no way to support his children without the benefits. Eldridge sued for the right to a hearing at which he could make a case for why he deserved to keep receiving benefits, relying on *Goldberg* as precedent.

The Court ruled against Eldridge by a 6–3 vote. Powell, writing for the four Nixon justices, Stewart, and White, conceded that Eldridge was seeking to protect the same interest John Kelly had: "the uninterrupted receipt of" his "source of income" until he had a chance to have his objections heard. Powell also admitted that disabled people generally had "modest resources" and that if Eldridge was cut off, it might take him a year or more to get the decision reversed, due to the "torpidity" of the review process. Still, Powell insisted that termination of disability benefits without a hearing was not as bad as the termination of welfare benefits at issue in *Goldberg*, because a disabled worker likely had access to more "private resources" or "other forms of government assistance."

It was a bizarre analysis. Eldridge was seeking the same kind of hearing Kelly was given and for the same reason, and the Court rejected him based on its conjecture that he would not be as affected by the cutoff of funds. In dissent, Brennan insisted that the Court's claim that disability recipients needed their benefits less than welfare recipients was purely "speculative." Brennan also noted that Eldridge actually did not have the sort of resources the majority assumed. The record showed, he noted, that after Eldridge's disability payments stopped, his home was foreclosed on, "and the family's furniture was repossessed, forcing Eldridge, his wife, and their children to sleep in one bed."

The Nixon Court's views about the rights of the poor were becoming unmistakable, and poverty lawyers began to avoid the federal courts. There was little chance, they understood, of winning another *Gideon v. Wainwright* or *Goldberg v. Kelly*. Now, a ruling from the Supreme Court was more likely to take rights away from their clients. From 1965 to 1974, lawyers from legal services programs, who did much of the nation's anti-poverty litigation, brought 164 cases to the Supreme Court, which accepted 119 of them. For the next decade and a half, legal services lawyers all but abandoned the federal courts. Patricia Wald, the onetime neighborhood legal services lawyer who went on to be chief judge of the U.S. Court of Appeals for the D.C. Circuit, said that in these years federal legal services litigation "in Alice in Wonderland fashion . . . got littler and littler until it almost disappeared altogether."

IN 1986, THE BURGER COURT ENDED, AFTER SEVENTEEN YEARS. BURGER announced that he was leaving to help organize ceremonies to mark the Constitution's bicentennial, the following year. The seventy-eight-year-old chief justice was healthy—he lived another nine years—and his new position was largely ceremonial. The timing suggested that, with Reagan's presidency winding down, Burger wanted to ensure that a Republican president filled his seat. If he was making a political calculation, it was an accurate one: had Burger remained in office until his death, in 1995, President Bill Clinton would have nominated the next chief justice.

At the time of Burger's announcement, the conservative Court that Nixon had created was intact, with a few changes in membership. In 1975, William O. Douglas had retired after suffering a stroke. Ford was in a difficult position, having inherited the presidency after Nixon resigned and facing an election in 1976. To succeed Douglas, Ford nominated a moderate Republican, Judge John Paul Stevens of the Chicago-based U.S. Court of Appeals for the Seventh Circuit, correctly assuming that he would be confirmed easily. Stevens quickly became one of the most liberal justices, which meant the replacement of the extremely liberal Douglas with Stevens shifted the Court only slightly to the right. In 1981, Potter Stewart retired and President Ronald Reagan nominated Sandra Day O'Connor to the seat. Her nomination was historic, in that she was the first woman justice, but her views were not substantially different from Stewart's.

In selecting a new chief justice to replace Burger, Reagan's main adviser was his attorney general, Edwin Meese. Meese was a hardline conservative, and no friend of poor Americans. A few years earlier, he had caused an uproar when he defended cuts to programs for the poor by saying, "We've had considerable information that people go to soup kitchens because the food is free and that's easier than paying for it."

Reagan, Meese, and the movement conservatives Meese surrounded himself with were eager to push the Court further to the right. They wanted justices who followed the "original intent" of the Constitution's framers, a fashionable conservative theory at the time, and ones who would be guided by "judicial restraint," by which they meant justices who would defer to the decisions made by the elected branches of government. Reagan quickly settled on Rehnquist, the Court's most conservative member, to be the next chief justice. To fill Rehnquist's seat, he chose Judge Antonin Scalia, of the U.S. Court of Appeals for the D.C. Circuit. Scalia, an Italian immigrant's son who grew up in Queens, New York, taught at the University of Chicago Law School before going on the bench. Reagan officials appreciated that Scalia was, as one news account reported, "a deeply conservative thinker whose views on major issues were quite compatible with the Administration's policy agenda."

At Rehnquist's confirmation hearing, Democrats raised the same issues they had at his first hearing—and one new one. "It now appears," said Senator Edward Kennedy, of Massachusetts, "that Mr. Rehnquist was less than candid . . . at his confirmation hearing in 1971." The Democrats presented witnesses who had seen Rehnquist harassing minority voters in Phoenix in the 1960s, including a former FBI agent, but Rehnquist continued to deny the charge. When Kennedy asked about the witnesses, Rehnquist responded, "I think they're mistaken. I just can't offer any other explanation."

Kennedy said the real issue was whether Rehnquist was "mainstream or too extreme," and he answered his own question. "He is too extreme on race, too extreme on women's rights, too extreme on freedom of speech, too extreme on separation of church and state, too extreme to be chief justice," Kennedy told his Senate colleagues. Rehnquist's critics were no more effective, however, than they had been in 1971. The Senate confirmed him by a 65–33 vote.

While the Senate focused on Rehnquist, Scalia sailed through to confirmation. He "declined to answer most of the questions in which the senators were most interested," *The New York Times* reported, but his uncooperativeness did not hurt him. Senators were reluctant to subject two nominees to tough questioning at the same time, or to oppose a nominee who would be the first Italian American justice. Scalia was confirmed by a vote of 98–0.

Rehnquist and Scalia were sworn into office on September 26, 1986. With Rehnquist replacing Burger and Scalia replacing Rehnquist, the number of conservatives remained the same, but there was still a shift. Rehnquist was a more forceful chief justice than Burger had been, and Scalia brought a new level of erudition and passion to the conservative bloc. As a result, the energy on the right of the Court increased significantly.

There would soon be more departures and arrivals. In June 1987, Lewis Powell retired. Reagan nominated Robert Bork, an archconservative judge on the U.S. Court of Appeals for the D.C. Circuit, who was defeated after a bitter confirmation battle that focused on his extreme views. Another nominee, Judge Douglas Ginsburg of the D.C. Circuit, was tripped up by a scandal over his having used marijuana years earlier. Reagan then turned to Anthony Kennedy, a conservative judge on the San Francisco–based U.S. Court of Appeals for the Ninth Circuit. Kennedy was confirmed, and when he took Powell's seat it was another roughly even exchange, ideologically speaking. In 1990, William Brennan retired, and President George H. W. Bush nominated Judge David Souter, of the Boston-based U.S. Court of Appeals for the First Circuit. Souter, a New Hampshire resident, was thought to be conservative, but he quickly joined the liberal bloc. It ended up being another change that did not significantly alter the Court's ideology. Liberals were surprised and delighted that Bush had ended up putting another liberal justice on the Court, while conservatives felt betrayed—and adopted the rallying cry "No more Souters!"

More changes followed, but the Court's ideological tilt remained roughly the same. In 1991, when Thurgood Marshall retired, Bush nominated Clarence Thomas, a conservative judge on the U.S. Court of Appeals for the D.C. Circuit. Thomas's nomination was nearly derailed when Anita Hill, his former employee at the Equal Employment Opportunity Commission, accused him of sexual harassment, but he was confirmed by a 52–48 vote. Marshall's replacement by Thomas moved the Court considerably to the right. In 1993, President Clinton nominated Ruth Bader Ginsburg for the seat of the retiring Byron White, shifting the Court to the left. The following year, Clinton nominated Stephen Breyer, a judge on the Boston-based U.S. Court of Appeals for the First Circuit, to replace Harry Blackmun. Blackmun, who wrote the majority opinion in *Roe v. Wade* in 1973, had undergone one of the most extreme ideological transitions of any member of the Court: the onetime conservative Nixon justice had ended up as one of the most liberal justices. As a result, when the pragmatic liberal Breyer replaced Blackmun, the Court's ideology did not change greatly. More than two decades after the Nixon justices arrived, the conservatives maintained their dominance.

IN THE MID-1990S, WHILE THE COURT CONTINUED TO SEE FEW POVERTY cases, the political branches moved aggressively into welfare policy. The war on poverty was now long-ago history, and there were growing calls for "welfare reform." In the 1994 election, Republicans released their "Contract with America," a set of promises for what they would do if they took control of Congress, including a commitment to make major changes in welfare programs. After Republicans won majorities in the House and Senate, Congress enacted the Personal Responsibility and Work Opportunity Reconciliation Act of 1996, an overhaul of federal welfare law. President Clinton, who had promised to be a new kind of Democrat when he ran for office in 1992, signed the bill into law.

The new law ended AFDC and replaced it with Temporary Assistance for Needy Families (TANF), dismantling a key part of the social safety net that had been building since the start of the New Deal. Under AFDC, there was a right to welfare for eligible recipients, even if the amounts were inadequate. TANF ended that right, allowing states to completely deny benefits to needy families. The new law also limited recipients to five years of aid over the course of a lifetime, with few exceptions. In another major change, TANF gave welfare funds to the states in block grants, allowing them to spend the money on programs that did not deliver cash directly to poor people. When Clinton signed the law, in the summer of 1996, two of his top welfare officials resigned in protest.

Under TANF, poor people's access to welfare was sharply reduced. Before the new law, about thirteen million people received cash benefits. By

2016, only about three million did. The amount of money states spent on cash assistance declined by two-thirds in inflation-adjusted dollars between 1997, when TANF took effect, and 2017. Arkansas spent only 4 percent of its TANF funds on direct cash assistance in 2017. States have shifted federal welfare money to an array of programs that do not help poor people pay for food and shelter. In some states, TANF funds have been used to promote "healthy marriage" programs or abstinence-only education. A national study found that the higher the percentage of black families in a state, the more likely it was to use TANF funds for these "family values" programs rather than give it to poor people to pay their bills.

The number of children in extreme poverty increased dramatically during these years. From 1995 to 2005, the percentage of children who were living below half the poverty level increased from 2.1 percent to 3 percent. By the end of those ten years, an additional 700,000 children were living in this kind of deep poverty, a level of deprivation that has been shown to have "lasting consequences on health, developmental, and educational outcomes, which can lead to persistent poverty across generations." The Center on Budget and Policy Priorities concluded that the 1996 welfare reform law had produced "a system that provides a safety net to very few families in need."

The unraveling of welfare was driven by Congress and the president, but it occurred against the backdrop of a Supreme Court that had made it clear that, as it said more than two decades earlier in *Dandridge v. Williams*, the "intractable . . . problems presented by public welfare assistance" were not its "business." Had the Court been more protective of the rights of poor people, advocates for the poor might have been able to defend the social safety net against the onslaught of the 1996 law.

If the Court had held that the poor were a suspect class, and applied strict scrutiny—or even the intermediate scrutiny given to laws that burden women—it would have provided a basis for challenging some of the harshest effects of welfare reform on poor Americans. Peter Edelman, a Georgetown law professor who was one of the two Clinton welfare officials to resign in protest, has argued that if the poor were a suspect class, major parts of the 1996 law could have been struck down. Government should have leeway in designing public benefits, Edelman said, but it should not be able to establish systems with outcomes as arbitrary as TANF, which provides no support to many Americans and highly inadequate amounts to many more.

TANF could have been challenged for the highly unequal way it operated nationwide. As a result of the broad discretion the law gave the states, coverage rates vary greatly. About a decade after TANF took effect, roughly 73 percent of poor families in California received benefits. In another nineteen states, fewer than 20 percent of poor families received benefits, including Wyoming, where just 4 percent did. Benefit levels are also highly unequal, ranging from about half the poverty level in Alaska to about 11 percent in Mississippi.

Another provision of TANF that would have been vulnerable to challenge if the poor had greater constitutional status was the lifetime limit on receiving benefits. This limit cut off assistance even if a beneficiary had no prospect of finding work or other income, and the impact was felt most by children, who were unable to work. TANF set a lifetime limit of five years, but it gave states discretion to set even shorter limits. In 2016, Arizona adopted a twelve-month lifetime limit. Benefit termination from hitting a lifetime limit is often devastating to poor people. One study of Maine families that were cut off after five years found that their median income was $3,120 a year, or about 16 percent of the federal poverty level.

After the Nixon Court's rulings, the poor had no legal recourse when the national welfare program was decimated. Congressional Republicans and President Clinton were free to do what they wanted in the 1996 law because, as Marshall observed at the start of the Burger Court with only slight exaggeration, laws harming the poor received "no scrutiny whatsoever."

IN SEPTEMBER 2005, WILLIAM REHNQUIST DIED OF CANCER, BRINGING another era to an end. The Court's ideology at the time of his death was still essentially the same as it had been in 1972, when the Nixon Court formed. Only the justices had changed. There were five conservatives: Rehnquist, Scalia, Thomas, Kennedy, and O'Connor. There were four liberals: Stevens, Souter, Ginsburg, and Breyer. The most centrist of the conservatives, O'Connor, was the swing justice, and her vote decided many of the most ideologically charged cases.

Since George W. Bush was president at the time of Rehnquist's death, the next chief justice would clearly be a conservative—unless there was a miscalculation, as there had been with the choice of Souter—and the Court's ideological balance would remain unchanged. There was, however, a complication: when Rehnquist died, President Bush was already in the process of choosing a new justice. In July 2005, Sandra Day O'Connor had announced plans to retire to spend more time with her husband, who was suffering from Alzheimer's disease. Bush announced that he was nominating John Roberts, a conservative judge on the U.S. Court of Appeals for the D.C. Circuit, to replace her. At the time of Rehnquist's death, Roberts was preparing for his confirmation hearings. The plans were changed, however, and Bush nominated Roberts to be the next chief justice.

The White House was excited about Roberts, the administration's first nominee to the Court. His record had been pored over by conservative activists, including the Federalist Society, the preeminent conservative legal organization. Conservatives were still bitter about the Souter nomination and were intent on avoiding another post-confirmation surprise. The ideological gatekeepers felt confident that Roberts would remain true to his conservative convictions.

There was a great deal in Roberts's background to reassure them. He was the son of a Bethlehem Steel plant manager and had spent most of his childhood in Long Beach, Indiana, a comfortable, largely white enclave near the poorer and blacker city of Gary. After graduating from Harvard College, where he attended Catholic Mass every Sunday, and Harvard Law School, Roberts served as a law clerk for Rehnquist. He then worked in the Reagan

Justice Department, where he argued for scaling back the reach of the Voting Rights Act, among other anti-civil-rights positions. Roberts went on to serve as a politically oriented deputy solicitor general in the George H. W. Bush administration and to advise George W. Bush's side on the Florida recount in the 2000 election. After Bush won Florida and the presidency, he named Roberts to the D.C. Circuit. When Roberts was not working for the federal government, he was a partner in a large Washington law firm, representing major corporations, including automakers and the National Mining Association. Roberts and his wife, a lawyer who served on the board of a right-to-life organization, were devout Catholics, described by one friend as "deeply religious."

Many Democrats were worried about Roberts's views about the law, but there was little in his record they could use to stop him. At his confirmation hearings, Roberts insisted that he would not come to the Court with an ideological agenda and that he believed in judicial restraint. In his testimony, he used what would become an oft-quoted metaphor to explain how restrained he intended to be. "I will remember," he said, "that it's my job to call balls and strikes, and not to pitch or bat." Roberts was confirmed by a 78–22 vote.

To fill O'Connor's seat, President Bush first nominated Harriet Miers, his White House counsel, who met with stiff resistance. Conservatives did not trust her ideological commitment, and a wider group of critics questioned whether she had appropriate qualifications to serve on the Court. In the face of this opposition, Miers withdrew.

Bush then nominated Judge Samuel Alito, of the Philadelphia-based U.S. Court of Appeals for the Third Circuit, who had strong backing from conservative activists. They "were as enthusiastic about Alito as they had been wary of Miers," Karl Rove, Bush's political adviser, recalled. Alito had a lengthy record of supporting conservative causes, including his membership in Concerned Alumni of Princeton, which had a variety of complaints involving coeducation, affirmative action, and other changes to Princeton's traditional ways. One of Alito's first political inspirations was the 1964

Goldwater presidential campaign, and his views on the law were shaped, he said, by "deep disagreement with Warren Court decisions."

Like Roberts, Alito had served in Reagan's Justice Department, helping with his right-leaning legal revolution. On the Third Circuit, Alito had been a reliable conservative vote, including in abortion and civil rights cases. He was sometimes called "Scalito," a nickname he disliked, because of his similarity to Scalia.

With the addition of Roberts and Alito, the ideological center of the Court shifted. Roberts and Rehnquist had roughly comparable ideologies. Alito, however, was considerably to the right of O'Connor. With O'Connor's departure, the new swing justice was Kennedy, who was now the most centrist of the conservative justices. O'Connor and Kennedy were not very far apart ideologically, but with Kennedy as the new swing justice, the center of the Court would undeniably be further to the right.

During the Obama presidency, the Court's membership continued to change, though its ideological balance still did not. In 2009, David Souter retired and President Obama nominated Sonia Sotomayor, a judge on the New York–based U.S. Court of Appeals for the Second Circuit, to fill his seat. Sotomayor, a Puerto Rican American raised by a single mother in a Bronx housing project, became the first Hispanic to serve on the Court. The following year, John Paul Stevens retired and Obama nominated Elena Kagan, his solicitor general, who had been the first woman dean of Harvard Law School. Sotomayor and Kagan, both liberals, replaced two departing justices who, though nominated by Republicans, had also been liberals. As a result, the Court maintained its 5–4 ideological split.

The Roberts Court continued scaling back the rights of the poor. In 2011, in *Turner v. Rogers*, it undermined *Gideon v. Wainwright*'s promise of a right to counsel for poor defendants. Michael Turner was an unemployed man from rural Oconee County, South Carolina, who fathered a child as a teenager. Turner, who was never married to the child's mother, was ordered to pay child support. The family court knew he was unemployed, but it still imputed an income to him and ordered him to make weekly payments. Turner fell behind on his child support obligations, and, with a disability, drug addiction issues, and few job prospects, he had little hope of catching up. He had already served a one-year jail sentence for failure to pay child support.

Turner had a hearing scheduled for failure to pay child support, and he did not have a lawyer. He told the judge he had already been sent to jail for being behind in his payments. "I've tried to find a job. I, honest to God, have tried this time," he said. "There's no work out there hardly for carpenters. I couldn't find anything, so I been putting in applications in grocery stores, you name it." The judge did not ask Turner about his disability or addiction, and there was no reference at the hearing to the fact that, with the Great Recession raging, unemployment in the area was above 13 percent. Turner was sentenced to six months in jail unless he could come up with a significant part of the money he owed.

Turner argued on appeal that a lawyer should have been appointed to represent him. The rule that emerged from *Gideon* and later cases was that poor defendants had the right to an appointed lawyer for felonies or misdemeanors that could result in imprisonment. Turner faced an obstacle, however: *Gideon*, which was decided under the Sixth Amendment, applied only to criminal cases, and child support hearings were civil proceedings. In his appeal, Turner argued that the Due Process Clause guaranteed a right to counsel to parties in civil proceedings who faced imprisonment. Turner contended that, civil or criminal, the principle was the same: that the state should not be able to sentence someone to prison because he could not afford to hire a lawyer to put on a competent defense.

When his case reached the Court, Turner had strong support in the legal profession. A former solicitor general represented him before the Court, and the National Legal Aid & Defender Association and the ACLU weighed in on his side. Turner could also point to twenty-two federal appeals courts or top-level state courts across the country that had ruled in favor of people in his position. Advocates for the poor were optimistic that Turner's case could be the one in which the Court finally extended *Gideon* to civil defendants facing jail time.

The Court, however, ruled against a right to counsel in civil proceedings, and its decision was unanimous. Breyer, writing for a five-justice majority, applied a due process balancing test to Turner's claim. In considering whether the civil proceeding was fundamentally fair under the Due Process Clause, the Court considered a number of factors: what Turner's interest was; the risk that he would be erroneously deprived of it; and the government's interest in not providing what Turner was seeking.

On the first prong, Breyer conceded that Turner's interest was very strong: staying out of jail. On the second prong, he insisted that there was not a great risk, because whether or not a parent is able to pay child support is not a complicated matter for a court to figure out if the right procedures are in place. On the third prong, Breyer said the government had a strong interest in not providing parents like Turner with lawyers, because to do so could mean that the delinquent parent would have a lawyer at a child support hearing but the parent seeking to recover child support would not.

Weighing all of these factors, Breyer said the balance came out against requiring an appointed lawyer, as long as there were "procedural safeguards" to protect Turner and others like him. Breyer listed the sorts of safeguards he had in mind. One safeguard was a requirement that the court conducting the hearing notify the defendant that his ability to pay was a critical issue in the proceeding. Another was the court using "a form (or the equivalent) to elicit relevant financial information" from the defendant, so it would be clear whether he had an ability to pay. A third was that the court should have to make an express finding that a defendant had the ability to pay before sentencing him to jail. The four dissenters would not have required even those safeguards.

The *Turner* decision was an indication of just how badly the Court's approach to the rights of the poor had degraded. In 1963, the Court ruled unanimously that a poor man facing burglary charges had the right to an appointed lawyer. In 2011, not a single justice voted that a poor, disabled parent who could not pay child support had the right to a lawyer for a proceeding that could put him behind bars for a year. Advocates for the poor insisted that the Court did not understand what it meant for someone like Turner to try to defend himself—and that it put too much faith in its vaunted "procedural safeguards." The executive director of the National Association of Criminal Defense Lawyers said the *Turner* decision "betrays naïve simplicity and a breathtaking disconnect from the real world."

A year later, in 2012, the Court handed the poor an even larger defeat, in a ruling widely hailed as a progressive victory. The case was *National Federation of Independent Business v. Sebelius,* the high-profile challenge to the Patient Protection and Affordable Care Act (ACA), better known as Obamacare. Many observers expected the Court to strike down the "individual mandate," which required most Americans to obtain health insurance or pay a penalty. The Court upheld the mandate, however, by a 5–4 vote, with Roberts joining the four liberal justices—Ginsburg, Breyer, Kagan, and Sotomayor—to create the majority. *The New York Times* hailed the ruling as "a victory for Mr. Obama and Congressional Democrats, affirming the central legislative achievement of Mr. Obama's presidency."

The news coverage focused on Roberts's vote to affirm the main provisions of the law, which came as something of a surprise. It was later reported that in the first vote after the oral argument, Roberts had been inclined to provide his fellow conservatives with the fifth vote to strike down the individual mandate, but that he later switched his position. Legal analysts debated Roberts's motives, weighing the possibility that he had acted out of a desire to protect the Court's reputation—or his own.

Far less attention was paid to the fact that the Court did strike down another part of the law, its Medicaid expansion provision, which was enacted to bring health care to millions of the poorest Americans. Medicaid expansion added to the categories of people that the states were required to provide with coverage if they wanted to remain in the program. It required states to cover all adults with incomes up to 133 percent of the federal poverty level, a significantly higher threshold than many had been using. It also filled another major gap. As originally conceived, Medicaid covered poor children and their parents but not poor adults without dependent children. Medicaid expansion required states to cover childless adults. If a state did not expand coverage as the ACA specified, it would lose all of its federal Medicaid funding.

The Court invalidated the ACA's mandatory Medicaid expansion by a 7–2 vote, holding that it violated the Constitution's Spending Clause. This decision was another surprise: Court watchers and legal scholars did not consider the Medicaid expansion to be in danger of being struck down, and the lower courts that had reviewed the ACA had no problem with it. The majority for striking down Medicaid expansion included the Court's five conservatives—Roberts, Thomas, Alito, Scalia, and Kennedy—and two liberals, Breyer and Kagan. A veteran Supreme Court journalist, in a biography of Roberts, reported that Breyer and Kagan were going to vote to uphold Medicaid expansion but instead made a pragmatic decision to join Roberts's opinion to help lock in his vote on the main parts of the ACA, which affected a much larger group of Americans. If that is what happened, no real harm was done: Roberts had the five votes to strike down Medicaid expansion without Breyer or Kagan.

Roberts said in his opinion that the Medicaid expansion provision, by requiring states to cover the new categories of beneficiaries if they wanted to remain in the program, was unduly coercive. The states spent so much on Medicaid, he said, and such a large percentage of the funds came from the federal government, that it would be nearly impossible for them to say no to the expansion. The pressure to accept Medicaid expansion was so great, Roberts insisted, that it amounted to "economic dragooning" and a "gun to the head" of the states.

To reach this holding, Roberts relied on the Constitution's Spending Clause, an obscure constitutional provision that had never been used in this way. Roberts cited a 1987 case in which South Dakota had tried to use the

Spending Clause to challenge the National Minimum Drinking Age Act, which docked states 5 percent of their federal highway funds if they did not raise their drinking age to twenty-one. The case, however, was weak support for Roberts's position. What Congress did with the National Minimum Drinking Age Act was far more coercive toward the states than Medicaid expansion. Congress was using highway funds to meddle in drinking ages, which had long been set by states, while Medicaid expansion was merely changing the qualifications for a program whose eligibility rules had always been set by Congress. There was another reason the South Dakota case was weak support for Roberts's argument: the Court in 1987 had rejected South Dakota's argument and upheld the National Minimum Drinking Age Act.

The two dissenters from the Medicaid expansion holding were Ginsburg and Sotomayor. It was no surprise that they were the two justices to vote in favor of the poor Americans who would lose health coverage. Ginsburg and Sotomayor were not only the two most liberal justices; more than any justice since Marshall, they had come to the Court with personal experiences that inclined them to look out for marginalized members of society, and both have said that their backgrounds helped shape their approach to the law.

Ginsburg grew up in working-class Brooklyn. Her father was a Russian Jewish immigrant, and her mother was born in America to an immigrant family. Neither of them had enough money to attend college. In her childhood, Ginsburg had been exposed to bigotry firsthand. At her confirmation hearing, she recalled driving through Pennsylvania with her parents and seeing a resort with a sign out front that read: NO DOGS OR JEWS ALLOWED. Ginsburg's formative years occurred while the Holocaust was unfolding. "We came to know more and more what was happening to the Jews in Europe," she said in an interview, and had "the sense of being an outsider—of being one of the people who had suffered oppression for no sensible reason."

She attended Cornell and Harvard Law School, where she was one of nine women in a class of more than five hundred. She then transferred to Columbia Law School to be in New York with her husband, who had taken a law firm job there, and graduated tied for first in her class. Ginsburg taught law at Rutgers and then at Columbia, but she made her name as co-founder of the ACLU's Women's Rights Project. One of her greatest victories came in 1973 in *Frontiero,* when the Court struck down the Air Force benefits rule that favored male officers over female officers.

Ginsburg was nominated to the U.S. Court of Appeals for the D.C. Circuit in 1980 by President Jimmy Carter and to the Supreme Court in 1993 by President Clinton. There had not been a public interest advocate like Ginsburg on the Court since Marshall left, and her background in working for equality was evident in her rulings. She also brought her childhood experiences with her. They made her, she said, "more empathetic to other people who are . . . outsiders."

Sotomayor, a self-proclaimed "Nuyorican," was also in many ways an outsider. She was born in the South Bronx to a father who was a factory worker and a mother who was a nurse, both of whom had relocated from Puerto Rico. Her father died when she was young and her mother raised her alone, in public housing, while working six days a week. Sotomayor was diagnosed with juvenile diabetes at the age of eight and had to inject herself with insulin throughout her childhood.

After graduating from Princeton and Yale Law School, Sotomayor worked in the Manhattan District Attorney's Office and in private practice and served on the board of the Puerto Rican Legal Defense and Education Fund. On the recommendation of Senator Daniel Patrick Moynihan, a Democrat, President George H. W. Bush appointed her to the federal district court in Manhattan in 1992. Six years later, President Clinton nominated her to the New York–based U.S. Court of Appeals for the Second Circuit, and in 2009 President Obama nominated her to the Supreme Court.

Sotomayor had talked about feeling different because of her Puerto Rican background and her challenging childhood, and about her sense of being "not completely a part of the worlds I inhabit." In a lecture at the University of California–Berkeley School of Law in 2001 entitled "A Latina Judge's

Voice," she said, "Personal experiences affect the facts that judges choose to see." Although she said she could not define exactly what difference they made in her judging, she accepted that "there will be some based on my gender and my Latina heritage."

In her opinion dissenting from the Medicaid expansion ruling, which Sotomayor joined her in, Ginsburg insisted that the issue was "simple" and the majority got it wrong. There was nothing unduly coercive about Medicaid expansion, she said. Congress created Medicaid with the idea that it would expand over time, and it set the eligibility rules for it each year. Adding new eligible individuals to the program was not "economic dragooning," she said. It was ordinary annual budgeting, and states were free to participate in that year's version of Medicaid or not. Many experts agreed with Ginsburg. One scholarly article said that, in its Medicaid expansion holding, the Court had "cut many corners on the actual history and facts of the Medicaid program, pounding many a square peg into round holes in order to fit a narrative of coercion."

Ginsburg also argued that the claim that Medicaid expansion would impose "very substantial costs" on the states was overstated. The Congressional Budget Office, she pointed out, projected that the expansion would increase states' Medicaid spending by just 0.8 percent. Later, the nonpartisan RAND Corporation issued a study concluding that Medicaid expansion was actually the best economic option for states when increased federal funding, reduced costs of uncompensated medical care, and other factors were taken into account.

Ginsburg did not point out one of the most troubling aspects of Roberts's opinion: the hypocrisy. At his confirmation hearings, Roberts had insisted that he saw his role as a judge as simply calling balls and strikes. For years, conservatives had criticized the Warren Court, and liberal judges generally, for their "judicial activism." They meant two things: that liberal judges were overruling decisions of the elected branches of government and that they were using vague constitutional provisions to implement their own policy preferences. Now that Roberts was on the bench, he was being a judicial activist by the standard conservative definition. He was striking down a mandate that Congress had adopted and the president had signed into law, and he was doing it based on a constitutional clause whose meaning was anything but clear.

With its Affordable Care Act ruling, the Court's evolution on the rights of the poor was complete. The days were long past when the Court was finding new ways to interpret the Constitution to ensure that no one was wrongly deprived of "the means to obtain essential food, clothing, housing, and medical care," as Brennan wrote in *Goldberg v. Kelly*. Now it was interpreting the Constitution to deny poor people medical care that Congress had provided them through legislation. The poor were no longer on the verge of being recognized as a "discrete and insular minority"—they were being branded as people who "dragooned" the states, gun in hand, to give them things they were not entitled to. The Court no longer saw poor people as a group to be protected but as one to be protected against.

THE COURT'S PAST FIVE DECADES OF RULINGS ON THE RIGHTS OF THE poor have been more than debates over legal doctrine: they have had a significant financial impact on Americans who live, as President Johnson said in his 1964 State of the Union address, "on the outskirts of hope." The Court wrestled, often at high levels of abstraction, with questions like whether the poor should be a suspect class and how to interpret the AFDC statute. On a practical level, its decisions in many cases determined whether poor families had enough money to pay the rent or buy food for the week.

The Warren Court's rulings provided low-income people with critical financial support. Until *King v. Smith* was decided, the man-in-the-house rule made about 500,000 poor children ineligible for AFDC benefits. Before the Court handed down *Shapiro v. Thompson*, durational residential requirements cut off at least another 100,000 people a year. The *Goldberg v. Kelly* decision prevented untold numbers of welfare recipients from being cut off from welfare at the whim of a caseworker. These decisions worked quietly: no poor person received a check signed by Earl Warren and the other justices, and many no doubt did not know who had saved them. In the aggregate, however, the Warren Court's poverty law rulings made an enormous difference in the lives of millions of low-income Americans.

When the Court reversed direction starting in 1970, the harm it did was also far-reaching. The impact of some of its rulings against the poor has been large but incalculable. There is no data on how many people have gone to jail, or for how long, since the Court held in *Turner v. Rogers* that they did not have the right to a lawyer at a child support hearing. There have certainly been many. Enough parents are going to jail for not paying child support that the Congressional Research Service did a report on it in 2012, concluding that they suffer a wide array of financial injuries. Similarly, the impact of *Lindsey v. Normet,* which denied tenants facing eviction strong due process rights, has also been unknowable but significant. If the Court had given poor tenants greater constitutional protections against unjustified evictions, it could have helped to prevent or alleviate the nation's eviction crisis. In a recent year, nearly one million Americans were evicted—an event that is often crushing for the finances and futures of the adults and children involved.

There is more evidence about the harm done by the 1970 decision *Dandridge v. Williams.* The Urban Institute did an analysis in 2006 of the impact of slightly different family caps than the one Maryland imposed on Linda Williams and her family, but ones that *Dandridge* had cleared the way for: caps that deny eligibility to children conceived and born while a family was receiving TANF. States began adopting them after the 1996 welfare reform law, and twenty-two enacted them at some point. Although the purported purpose was to discourage people on welfare from adding to the welfare rolls, an undeniable effect has been to ensure that some of the nation's poorest children, brought into the world through no fault of their own, grow up in severe poverty. The Urban Institute found that these family caps increased a state's "deep poverty" rate—those living below 50 percent of the poverty level—for children by 1.7 percentage points. As with the beneficiaries of the Warren Court's rulings, the families who are further impoverished likely do not know the role the Supreme Court played in their lives—or that if Nixon had not driven Fortas off the Court, they might well be receiving uncapped welfare benefits.

The impact of *Sebelius* is even clearer. It allowed states to continue denying Medicaid to groups that Congress had required to be covered. Under this "red state option," as the new legal landscape came to be known, by 2019 there were still fourteen states, mainly Republican-controlled ones in the Deep South and the middle of the country, that chose not to expand their Medicaid rolls. If the Court had not struck down Medicaid expansion, as many as 4.7 million more low-income Americans would have coverage.

The harm to those nearly five million poor Americans was enormous. The ruling hurt them financially: people without Medicaid have to pay more of their medical bills out of their own pockets. According to one study, low-income non-Medicaid families spend about five times as much on health care as Medicaid families. The study also found that low-income non-Medicaid households spent 19 percent of their budgets on food, as compared with 24 percent for low-income Medicaid households. That suggested that in non-Medicaid households, medical costs used up scarce household dollars that otherwise would have gone to putting food on the table.

Even more disturbing, striking down Medicaid expansion cost a significant number of poor Americans their lives. Poor people without Medicaid are less likely to see doctors and get preventive care and are more likely to die early. A study published by the National Bureau of Economic Research in 2019 estimated that about 15,600 people had died who would not have if all fifty states had expanded their Medicaid programs when the ACA first took effect.

There is no knowing how much better the economic conditions of poor people would be if the Court had recognized them as a protected class. If they had been accorded even the intermediate-level scrutiny that women were, the

Court might have struck down many aspects of the 1996 welfare reform law, which has drastically reduced the amount of welfare money available to the nation's poor. It might have invalidated arbitrary limits on years of eligibility and the large disparities between states, which would make a particular difference for poor people in places like Wyoming that have very low rates of enrollment.

The change from AFDC to TANF has had a devastating—and little appreciated—impact on the finances of the poor. The number of people receiving benefits fell 75 percent between 1996 and 2014. "TANF was meant to 'replace' AFDC," two academic experts said of the decline. "What it did in reality was essentially kill the U.S. cash welfare system." The collapse of cash assistance has plunged many families into deep poverty. A study from the University of Michigan's National Poverty Center found that from 1996 to 2011, the number of families living on less than $2 per person a day, a World Bank definition of poverty in developing nations, more than doubled, to nearly 1.5 million, including 2.8 million children. There have been questions surrounding estimates of how many Americans are living on less than $2 per day, but there is clearly a considerable amount of deep poverty in the post-AFDC era.

The Court's antagonistic approach to poor people has hurt in another way: it has sent a message about how they should be treated by the political branches and society in general. Political scientists have argued that the Court can create "policy legitimacy" when it puts its authority behind a marginalized group seeking mainstream acceptance. There is some evidence that the Court's decisions on such issues as school desegregation and abortion rights had a measurable impact on public opinion. The Court's rulings that the poor do not have the kinds of constitutional rights that racial minorities, women, and other groups have, and its insistence that Congress and the states must have broad leeway in designing welfare programs, helped to create an environment in which it was easier to end the right to welfare and keep benefit levels well below the poverty line.

In 2017, the United Nations special rapporteur on extreme poverty and human rights toured the United States to evaluate the state of poverty. The special rapporteur, Philip Alston, found that 40 million Americans were in poverty and, of those, 18.5 million were in extreme poverty. He concluded that although the United States was one of the world's richest nations, "neither its wealth nor its power nor its technology is being harnessed to address the situation in which 40 million people continue to live in poverty." An Urban Institute study the same year gave a snapshot of the impact that poverty has on the lives of Americans in a single year. It found, among other things, that about 10 percent were behind on their rent or mortgage, and more than 1 percent were evicted or otherwise forced to move.

Something very important happened to the nation in the two weeks between the Court's rulings in *Goldberg v. Kelly* and *Dandridge v. Williams* in the spring of 1970: the highest court in the land changed from one that expressed concern about poor people and their ability to survive to one that announced that such matters were "not the business of this Court." In saying this to Linda Williams, the Court sent the same message to all of the nation's poor—one it would repeat many times in the decades that followed. With the end of the Warren era and the rise of the Nixon era, the Court changed from being a force for equality for the poor to being a powerful driver of inequality. This would be true in areas that went well beyond poverty law.

CHAPTER ◆ 3

EDUCATION

In October 1972, the Supreme Court heard a case that, more than any since *Brown v. Board of Education*, had the potential to transform the nation's education system and create a more equal America. In *San Antonio Independent School District v. Rodriguez*, students from a poor school district in Texas challenged the state's system of financing its public schools. The plaintiffs argued that the wide disparities in funding that existed between Texas's wealthiest and poorest school districts violated the Fourteenth Amendment Equal Protection Clause.

For advocates of equal educational opportunity for all children, school finance reform was the next frontier. By the early 1970s, the nation had made considerable progress in implementing *Brown*'s mandate to dismantle segregation in schools all across the South. Even if the promise of *Brown* was fully realized, however, there would still be enormous differences in the quality of education available to the nation's children based on the wealth of the school district they lived in. The *Rodriguez* plaintiffs were asking the Court to rule that when the state provided public education, it should not be able to discriminate against poor children—or, more precisely, children in poor school districts—any more than it could against black children.

Rodriguez arrived at the Court at an inauspicious time for the plaintiffs. Though they had filed their lawsuit at the height of the Warren Court, just six weeks after it unanimously struck down the man-in-the-house rule in *King v. Smith*, by the time the case was argued in the Supreme Court, the Burger Court was three years old, and the Nixon justices were firmly in place. The case would be decided by a Court made up of the four Nixon justices, three liberal justices—Douglas, Brennan, and Marshall—and two moderate conservatives: Stewart and White. Although the plaintiffs had considerable momentum behind them, it was not clear whether they would be able to find five votes on the new Nixon Court.

THE *RODRIGUEZ* PLAINTIFFS' PATH TO THE COURT BEGAN ON MAY 16, 1968, when four hundred students at Edgewood High School in San Antonio, Texas, walked out of their classes to protest the quality of the education they were receiving. The Edgewood School District was an impoverished Mexican American ghetto carved out of wealthier, whiter San Antonio. Edgewood's schools were 90 percent Hispanic and 6 percent African American. The district's median annual family income was just $4,686.

The Edgewood students who walked out had a long list of complaints. Classes were overcrowded, and there was a shortage of textbooks. Many teachers were unqualified: 20 percent lacked college degrees, and 47 percent were working on emergency teaching permits. The district had decrepit, unsafe school buildings. At the elementary school, the second and third floors had been condemned but were still being used for classes, and the fire escapes were crumbling. "I'd be afraid to get on the fire escape," a school board official said. "That would be as much a hazard as the fire."

The nearby Alamo Heights School District was a world away in economics and demographics. It was the wealthiest district in the San Antonio metropolitan area, with a median family income of over $8,000. It was also considerably whiter than Edgewood—its students were just 18 percent Latino and less than 1 percent black. Property values in Alamo Heights were far higher than in Edgewood, which gave the district a strong tax base to pay for its schools.

The educational opportunities available in Alamo Heights reflected the district's greater resources. Its top teacher salaries were 25 percent higher than Edgewood's, which attracted more qualified teachers. Alamo Heights teachers all had college degrees, and only 11 percent worked on emergency permits. Alamo Heights' teacher-student ratio was significantly lower than Edgewood's, and it had more and newer textbooks. The facilities were also far superior. Alamo Heights' high school had an Olympic-size swimming pool and an air-conditioned clubhouse with a disco ball.

Edgewood's problem was its limited tax base. Alamo Heights, with its expensive homes and prosperous businesses, had $45,095 in taxable property per student, while Edgewood had just $5,429. There were state funds that were meant to equalize the finances of poor school districts, but because of flaws in the formula, the money failed to do that. Taking all revenue into account, Alamo Heights had $594 per student per year, while Edgewood had just $356, or about 40 percent less.

The gap in school funding between rich and poor districts across the state was even larger than the gap between Edgewood and Alamo Heights. A Syracuse University professor did an analysis of statewide school finance data and found that Texas's wealthiest districts spent an average of $815 per pupil annually. The poorest districts spent an average of just $305 per pupil.

After the Edgewood High School walkout, parents formed the Edgewood District Concerned Parents Association to work for better schools. It was clear, however, that there was little they could do locally. The state imposed a limit on local tax rates, and even if Edgewood reached that limit it would not be able to raise as much money per pupil as districts like Alamo Heights.

The Edgewood parents were also blocked at the state level, due to the legislature's unwillingness to support meaningful reform. Governor John

Connally had appointed a blue-ribbon commission that actually recommended increased state funding, with special attention to the needs of districts like Edgewood. Connally, however, would soon leave office and the commission's recommendations would go nowhere.

The only hope, it seemed, was the courts. The Edgewood parents met with Arthur Gochman, a local civil rights lawyer, to discuss their options. Gochman told them there was a good argument to be made that Texas's school finance system was unconstitutional. At the time, the Supreme Court had already issued many of its rulings expanding the rights of the poor, including *Gideon v. Wainwright*, recognizing a right to counsel, and *Harper v. Virginia Board of Elections*, striking down the poll tax.

While the Edgewood children and parents were rising up, a movement was forming in academia to establish that poor children had a right to equal educational opportunity. In 1965, three years before the parents' meeting with Gochman, Arthur Wise, a University of Chicago graduate student, began formulating an argument that disparities in funding between rich and poor school districts were unconstitutional. Three years later, he published his critique of school finance systems in a book, *Rich Schools, Poor Schools: The Promise of Equal Educational Opportunity*. Wise believed that school funding disparities could violate the Equal Protection Clause, and his argument was gaining adherents across the country.

Courts had also been moving in that direction. In 1967, Judge J. Skelly Wright, a leading liberal on the U.S. Court of Appeals for the D.C. Circuit, had ruled that disparities in educational opportunity among the schools in the Washington, D.C., school system were unconstitutional. The Equal Protection Clause did not permit "rich and poor" to be "consigned to separate schools" that were not "run on the basis of real equality" in "their objectively measurable aspects," he said, unless there were adequate justifications for the inequities.

On July 30, 1968, Gochman sued Texas on behalf of Edgewood parents and schoolchildren. The lead plaintiff in *Rodriguez v. San Antonio Independent School District* was Demetrio Rodriguez, a member of the Edgewood

District Concerned Parents Association. Rodriguez's own story reflected what was at stake. He was the son of farmworkers who had moved from the Rio Grande Valley to San Antonio when he was six, in search of a better education for their children. Rodriguez, who left school to serve in the Navy in World War II, became a sheet-metal worker on an Air Force base. He wanted a better future for his own children and did not believe that Edgewood's schools would provide it.

Rodriguez was assigned to a special three-judge federal district court in San Antonio. There were two distinct arguments for why the court should apply strict scrutiny to Texas's system of funding its schools. One was that the school finance system discriminated on the basis of wealth. At the time, when the Warren Court was still expanding the rights of the poor, it seemed like a promising argument. The other argument for why the district court should apply strict scrutiny was that education was a fundamental interest. The Supreme Court was establishing a list of fundamental interests under the Equal Protection Clause. It had not said that education was a fundamental interest, but it had described it in past cases in ways that suggested that it might one day. In *Brown v. Board of Education*, the Court had declared unanimously that "education is perhaps the most important function of state and local governments" and said that "where the state has undertaken to provide" children with a public school education, it "is a right which must be made available to all on equal terms."

If the district court accepted either of these arguments for strict scrutiny, the plaintiffs would have a strong chance of winning. If the court applied strict scrutiny, Texas would have to show that its highly unequal school finance system was necessary to advance a compelling state interest and that it was narrowly tailored to advance that interest. It would be extremely difficult for Texas to make that case on behalf of Texas's deeply flawed system.

About a month after *Rodriguez* was filed, a group of parents in California brought a challenge to that state's school finance system. The claims in *Serrano v. Priest* were similar to the ones raised by the Edgewood parents, but in addition to suing under the Fourteenth Amendment Equal Protection Clause, the plaintiffs also argued that the school finance system violated the California Constitution's own equal protection guarantee. That separate state constitutional claim would allow the California Supreme Court to strike down California's funding system even if the United States Supreme Court ruled that systems like California's and Texas's did not violate the federal Constitution.

While the Texas federal district court considered *Rodriguez* and the California state courts heard *Serrano,* the school finance reform movement kept growing. Wise's scholarship turned out to be the start of a wave of academic writing aimed at establishing a legal basis for challenging school funding disparities. In *Private Wealth and Public Education,* John Coons and Stephen Sugarman, two University of California–Berkeley law professors, and William Clune, a University of Wisconsin law professor, showed that there were large inequities in school budgets nationwide, and they explored how they could be shown to violate the Equal Protection Clause.

The court hearing *Rodriguez* put it on hold temporarily to give the Texas Legislature a chance to address the inequities the Edgewood parents and students were challenging. The legislature, however, adjourned its session in June 1971 without doing anything to equalize school funding or to direct more money to districts like Edgewood. When it was clear that the legislature had no intention of acting, the court held a trial.

On August 30, 1971, while the Texas federal district court was still considering *Rodriguez,* the California Supreme Court ruled that California's school finance system violated both the Fourteenth Amendment Equal Protection Clause and the California Constitution's equal protection provision. In doing so, the court held that wealth was a suspect classification, and that California was impermissibly favoring wealthy districts. It also held that education was a fundamental interest. *Serrano v. Priest* was a strong endorsement of the school finance reform movement from the highest court in the nation's most populous state. "By our holding today," the California Supreme

Court said, "we further the cherished idea of American education that in a democratic society free public schools shall make available to all children equally the abundant gifts of learning."

About six weeks later, a federal district court ruled for plaintiffs who were challenging Minnesota's school finance system under the federal Constitution. The district court in Minneapolis held that the state was denying students in poor school districts their rights under the Equal Protection Clause. The court said that education was a fundamental interest, noting that it had "a unique impact on the mind, personality, and future role of the individual child" and that it was "basic to the functioning of a free society." It also decided that the state's school finance system discriminated against the poor, and it said that the two factors "mutually reinforce" the poor students' challenge to the system.

The school finance reform momentum continued to grow. The Lawyers' Committee for Civil Rights became a clearinghouse for school finance challenges, backed by funding from the Ford Foundation. There would soon be more than fifty school finance lawsuits working their way through federal and state courts nationwide. A "chain of reactions" had been set off "in states throughout the country," *The Christian Science Monitor* reported. "At issue is the whole structure of the financing of American education."

On December 23, the federal district court in Texas handed the *Rodriguez* plaintiffs a sweeping victory. The three-judge court ruled unanimously that the state's school finance system violated the Equal Protection Clause. The court accepted both arguments for applying strict scrutiny. It said that Texas had divided children into districts that varied significantly by wealth, and it held, citing the 1966 decision striking down the poll tax, that "lines drawn on wealth are suspect" and required a higher standard of review. The district court also recognized that education was a fundamental interest. As support, it quoted *Brown v. Board of Education*'s statement that "today, education is perhaps the most important function of state and local governments."

The court held that Texas did not have a compelling interest that justified its unequal funding system. Texas had tried to justify the disparities in funding available to rich and poor school districts by invoking the principle of "local control," which held that important decisions about education should be made at the community level. The court noted, however, that the system did not actually promote local control, since there was nothing a district like Edgewood, with its low tax base, could do to have well-funded schools.

Having ruled that Texas's school finance system was unconstitutional, the district court had to come up with a way to bring it into compliance with the Equal Protection Clause. The court did not take control of the system or hand down specific directions for how it had to be structured. It also did not order the legislature to spend more money on education. It simply ordered the legislature to come up with a new system that provided equal educational opportunity to all of the children of Texas.

FEDERAL DISTRICT COURT RULINGS DO NOT OFTEN MAKE NATIONAL headlines, but the *Rodriguez* decision did. *The New York Times* reported it at the top of the front page, with a subheadline that declared, "Wide Impact Foreseen." *The Wall Street Journal* had its own front-page story, which advised that if the Supreme Court affirmed the ruling, it could be "the *Brown vs. Board of Education* of the 1970s." The *Rodriguez* plaintiffs wanted "to outlaw school discrimination based on wealth," the *Journal* said, the way *Brown* had "outlawed school discrimination based on race."

The newspapers had good reason to believe that *Rodriguez* could have a broad impact. Education spending was highly unequal in every state but Hawaii, which had a single statewide school district. In many places, the disparities were even wider than in Texas. Beverly Hills, California, had a tax base of $50,885 per pupil, while nearby Baldwin Park had just $3,706 in taxable property per pupil. Beverly Hills spent more than twice as much per student as Baldwin Park did.

The *Wall Street Journal* story on *Rodriguez* warned that the decision could reach beyond education to launch a broader "revolution" that "could reshape the face of America." The paper said that if the Supreme Court affirmed the ruling, it could lead to a "drastic revamping of property taxes to even out the school-tax burden." That, in turn, could inspire "similar challenges to a host of vital public services, like housing, welfare and health care," the *Journal* said. The Court might soon have to decide whether all citizens, regardless of the wealth of their community, were entitled to the same level of police protection or equally clean sidewalks, according to the paper. It quoted one lawyer who said that *Rodriguez* had opened "a very large door" to a "revolution in [public] services."

While *The Wall Street Journal* contemplated how far the revolution might go, education advocates remained focused on what *Rodriguez* could mean for schools in poor communities. The district court's ruling, they hoped, would be the start of a new, more egalitarian era in public education. Experts were already moving beyond the issue of liability—whether state school finance systems were unconstitutional—and on to remedy, or how the inequities could be eliminated. The days after the *Rodriguez* decision were heady ones for the education reform movement, as was reflected in the quote that John Coons, co-author of *Private Wealth and Public Education*, gave *The New York Times* about the ruling: "Hot diggity!"

Rodriguez was part of a rising tide of change that was sweeping the country. Two weeks before the federal district court ruled, the Wyoming Supreme Court issued its own ruling on equal school funding. A New Jersey superior court and the Michigan Supreme Court followed with decisions recognizing a constitutional requirement of equal funding. The momentum seemed almost unstoppable.

There were still holdouts resisting the idea that funds should be equalized across school districts. Wealthy districts argued that they were being unfairly penalized. The mayor of Beverly Hills, no admirer of the *Serrano* decision, insisted that "the way to lift the bottom isn't to drag down the top." Conservative education experts challenged the assumptions underlying the litigation. Chester E. Finn Jr., who would go on to become an assistant secretary of education in the Reagan administration, wrote an article in *Commentary* entitled "'Serrano' vs. the People." In it, he made an argument that critics of school finance litigation would come to rely on: that money is not important to student outcomes. "We now have enough evidence," he said, "to show that the kinds of expenditures" at issue in lawsuits like *Serrano* and *Rodriguez* "have very little bearing on what and how much the children actually learn."

Most commentators, however, were on the side of reform. Journalists and academic experts largely cheered on the courts as they ordered states to restructure their school finance systems so all children were treated equally. The reason *Serrano* was greeted so enthusiastically was probably "the growing public eagerness for its result," a legal scholar declared in the *University of Pennsylvania Law Review*. "Unlike many other societal problems in education and other areas," he said, "the concept of fiscal equality in education is perceived as unambiguously good."

THE SUPREME COURT DECIDED TO REVIEW THE DISTRICT COURT'S DECIsion in *Rodriguez v. San Antonio Independent School District*, and it heard arguments on October 12, 1972. This time, Gochman had the backing of an array of national organizations that submitted friend-of-the-court briefs, including the National Education Association, the AFL-CIO, and the NAACP Legal Defense and Educational Fund. Texas upgraded its legal team for the argument, retaining Charles Alan Wright, a prominent University of Texas constitutional law professor, to defend the school finance system. Wright was an outspoken conservative who, the following year, would represent Nixon in his efforts to prevent Watergate special prosecutor Archibald Cox from obtaining the White House tapes.

The Court that heard *Rodriguez* was very different from the one that existed when the case began. In July 1968, when Gochman filed the complaint, the Court had just struck down Alabama's man-in-the-house rule, and nine months later it would strike down Connecticut's durational residency requirement for receiving welfare. The Court appeared to be edging closer to recognizing the poor as a suspect class. By the time the *Rodriguez* case arrived, however, the Court had already decided *Dandridge v. Williams*, in which it made clear that it had little interest in the rights of the poor.

The membership of the Court had also changed considerably. When the case was filed, there were five justices who almost certainly would have voted for the Edgewood parents and children—Warren, Fortas, Douglas, Brennan, and Marshall—and possibly several more. It would have been hard back in the summer of 1968 to count more than two or three justices who could be expected to vote for the Texas defendants.

Now, a little more than four years later, only three of the Warren Court liberals remained—Douglas, Brennan, and Marshall. The Edgewood plaintiffs would almost certainly win the votes of those three, but it was not clear where they would find two more. The plaintiffs' greatest hopes lay with three of the remaining justices: White, Stewart, and Powell. White and Stewart were in the Court's center. Powell was the Nixon nominee who had come to the Court with a background as an educational leader in Virginia and purported moderate instincts.

Two weeks before the oral argument in *Rodriguez*, news broke that threw doubt on how sympathetic Powell would be. Jack Anderson, an investigative reporter and syndicated columnist, revealed a memorandum Powell had written for the U.S. Chamber of Commerce in the summer of 1971, just before his nomination. In "Attack on American Free Enterprise System," Powell wrote that American capitalism was under assault, not only from radicals but from "perfectly respectable elements of society," including the media, universities, organized religion—and the courts. The judiciary could be the "most important instrument for social, economic and political change," he advised, "especially with an activist-minded Supreme Court." Powell said that groups ranging "from 'liberal' to the far left" had been "perhaps the most active exploiters of the judicial system." He urged big business to use the courts in a similar way to promote its own agenda.

When the Senate voted on Powell's nomination, it did not know about the Powell Memorandum. Anderson noted in his column that the memorandum was stamped CONFIDENTIAL and that the FBI failed to turn it up when it investigated Powell. Anderson was blunt in his assessment of the memorandum and its author. It was "so militant," he said, "that it raises a question about his fitness to decide any case involving business interests."

The memorandum also raised questions about how Powell would approach *Rodriguez.* Its author sounded like a conservative ideologue who believed the nation was under assault from many of the groups that were backing the *Rodriguez* plaintiffs. Powell warned in the memo that "labor unions, civil rights groups and now the public interest law firms are extremely active in the judicial arena," and "their success" was "often at business' expense." Powell also seemed to be disturbed by the sort of equality claims that were at the heart of the plaintiffs' case. "This setting of the 'rich' against the 'poor,'" he wrote, "is the cheapest and most dangerous kind of politics."

At oral argument, Wright said the district court had been wrong to apply strict scrutiny to Texas's school finance system. Students in poor school districts were not a suspect class, he said, and education was not a fundamental interest. Wright urged the Court to look to *Dandridge v. Williams, Lindsey v. Normet,* and "cases of that kind." He asked the Court to apply rational-basis review to the school finance system and to hold that it was justified because of the importance of local control of education. If the Court upheld the district court's decision, he said, it would "impose a constitutional straitjacket on the public schools of fifty states." For the plaintiffs, Gochman argued that the district court had been right to apply strict scrutiny. He emphasized that the case was about discrimination—wealth discrimination. He also underscored the "constitutional importance of education." It was "preservative of other rights," he said, since Americans had to be educated properly to exercise rights that are expressly mentioned in the Constitution, including free speech, voting, and serving on juries.

It was hard to tell from the justices' questions and demeanor at oral argument how the Court would come out. The Edgewood parents and students were optimistic that the victory they had won in the lower court would be preserved and that change was coming. Demetrio Rodriguez told the Associated Press that he believed the Court would "rule in favor of all the people" and uphold the district court's decision. "They are fair men," Rodriguez said, "and I have faith in their judgment."

ON MARCH 21, 1973, THE COURT REVERSED THE DISTRICT COURT AND upheld Texas's school finance system, by a 5–4 vote. The majority was composed of the four Nixon justices—Burger, Blackmun, Rehnquist, and Powell—and Stewart. Powell wrote the majority opinion rejecting the Edgewood students' plea for greater equality of educational opportunity.

Powell said the district court in Texas had been wrong to apply heightened scrutiny. He rejected the idea that students in poor school districts were a suspect class. There was no reasonable way, he said, to define such a class, in part because the state's poorest people did not necessarily reside in the poorest school districts. The plaintiff class was, he said, too "large, diverse, and amorphous" to merit heightened scrutiny.

Powell also insisted, despite his time as a school board chairman, that education was not a fundamental interest. What mattered in making this determination, he said, was not the "relative societal significance" of education or whether it was as important as other fundamental interests the Court had recognized, such as travel. It was, he said, a matter of "assessing whether there is a right to education explicitly or implicitly guaranteed by the Constitution."

Once Powell rejected strict scrutiny, he had no trouble upholding the finance system under rational-basis review. He accepted Texas's argument that allowing variation in funding among school districts promoted "local control" in education. Texas's school finance system was, Powell insisted, an example of the noble American ideal of leaving "each locality . . . free to tailor local programs to local needs."

Powell offered weak words of consolation for children in poor school districts across the country. There was a need for "innovative thinking" about education, he said, "to assure both a higher level of quality and greater uniformity of opportunity." These changes should come, however, from "lawmakers and from the democratic pressures of those who elect them," he said. This, of course, was exactly what Texas's legislature refused to do, even after the district court held its school finance system unconstitutional. Powell said his opinion should not be "viewed as placing its judicial imprimatur on the *status quo*"—although, as a legal matter, that is precisely what it did.

In losing the case, the plaintiffs failed to win over not only Powell but Stewart. Stewart wrote a concurring opinion that went further than the majority in saying that the educational status quo was not ideal. Texas's school finance system, like almost every state's, had "resulted in a system of public education that can fairly be described as chaotic and unjust," he said. His sympathetic words, however, offered little to the Edgewood plaintiffs or to children in other poor school districts, since he provided the fifth vote to uphold the Texas system.

White wrote a narrow dissent, which Brennan and Douglas joined. He argued that it was not necessary to find that education was a fundamental interest or that wealth classifications were suspect. Even under rational review, he said, the Texas school finance system had to be struck down because it was not rational. It did not allow for true local control, he said, because districts like Edgewood, with impoverished tax bases, could not choose to fund their schools adequately.

Marshall wrote a more impassioned dissenting opinion, which Douglas signed, that reflected the personal history he brought to the Court. Marshall had grown up in segregated Baltimore, the son of a steward in an all-white club on the Chesapeake Bay. After graduating from Howard Law School, he became a leading civil rights lawyer in Baltimore and later director-counsel of the NAACP Legal Defense and Educational Fund. President Kennedy nominated Marshall to the New York–based U.S. Court of Appeals for the Second Circuit, and he was confirmed over heated opposition from southern senators. President Johnson appointed Marshall solicitor general and then nominated him to the Court.

Marshall was the preeminent civil rights lawyer of his time. He was the movement's chief legal strategist, and he argued many of the most important civil rights cases before the Court, including ones that invalidated racial restrictions in house deeds and ended all-white primary elections. Some of Marshall's most important cases involved discrimination in education, including, most famously, *Brown v. Board of Education.*

In his dissent in *Rodriguez,* Marshall said the district court had been right to apply heightened scrutiny. He agreed with Gochman that education was a fundamental interest, because of its "close relationship" with "some of our most basic constitutional values." He also argued that children in poor school districts were a class that was entitled to more than mere rational-basis review.

Marshall compared the students in poor school districts like Edgewood to the kinds of students he represented as a lawyer, who had been forced to attend all-black schools that had far fewer resources than the all-white schools. Just as his clients had not asked to attend these educationally impoverished all-black schools, he said, "it is difficult to believe that, if the children of Texas had a free choice, they would choose to be educated in districts with fewer resources." The Court's decision to uphold the Texas school finance system, he said, could "only be seen as a retreat from our historic commitment to equality of educational opportunity."

Marshall was not impressed by the majority's hope that legislatures would address the problem. He had a different suggestion about where reform might come from. He ended his dissent by noting that there was nothing in the Court's decision to prevent state courts from striking down campaign finance systems under their own state constitutions, as courts in California, New Jersey, and Michigan had done. If the Court would not provide children in the nation's poor school districts with equal educational opportunity, Marshall suggested, they should look for other courts that would.

The New York Times once again reported the *Rodriguez* decision on its front page. It emphasized how close the Court had come to ordering a revolution in American education. "If a single Justice had shifted his vote, reversing the Court's ruling, the school system of every state except that of Hawaii would have been materially affected," the *Times* noted, "with residents of richer districts paying more taxes to help support comparable standards in poorer districts."

To civil rights groups and anti-poverty advocates, the decision was "a crushing blow," the *Los Angeles Times* reported. As a result of the Court's ruling, a whole wave of lawsuits in lower courts around the country would be dismissed. The academic experts who for years had been doing the theoretical work underlying the litigation suddenly saw their visions for the future crushed. "It hurts," John Coons said, "especially because the vote was so close."

In the Texas Legislature, there was palpable relief. The chairman of the House Revenue and Taxation Committee told *The Austin Statesman* that he was "very surprised" by the outcome. The chairman of the House Education Committee expressed gratitude to the Court, which he credited with freeing the state from the "huge tax bill that probably would have resulted." Texas governor Dolph Briscoe said he was pleased that his state would not have to reform its education system "under the pressure of court edicts."

Edgewood, which had its hopes raised by the district court's decision, was despondent about its loss. *The Austin Statesman* reported that the school district was "depressed." Edgewood's deputy superintendent, Mauro Reyna, said the ruling meant that a bad financial situation would continue or quite possibly get even worse. "We're left holding the empty bag," he said.

The plaintiffs felt the loss most keenly of all. At the end of its story on the ruling, *The New York Times* appended a short report from San Antonio on Demetrio Rodriguez's reaction. He said he could not avoid "feeling deep and bitter resentment against the supreme jurists and the persons who nominated them to that high position." Rodriguez declared that "poor people have lost again, not only in Texas but in the United States." The *Times* ran the report under the headline "Plaintiff Is Bitter."

RODRIGUEZ WAS AN EDUCATION REVOLUTION THAT NEARLY OCCURRED, and there are many ways it could have. If the Edgewood plaintiffs had filed their lawsuit a few years earlier, the Warren Court would have decided it, and they would almost certainly have won. Alternatively, if President Johnson had succeeded in replacing Warren with a liberal chief justice, there would have been enough votes for the plaintiffs to prevail.

The real ghost haunting *Rodriguez,* however, was Abe Fortas. Fortas would have been on the Court in 1973 if Nixon had not misused the power of the presidency to drive him off. If Fortas had still been serving, he would doubtless have provided the plaintiffs with the fifth vote they needed to win. It is little appreciated how profoundly Nixon's lawless campaign against Fortas changed constitutional law and public education. Poor school districts and the children who attend school in them have paid the price ever since.

The movement to equalize school funding did not end after *Rodriguez.* As Marshall pointed out in his dissent, the Court's ruling was only an interpretation of the U.S. Constitution, and state courts were free to hold that their own state constitutions prohibited unequal school funding. These state claims were generally stronger than the federal constitutional claim as a matter of constitutional interpretation, since virtually every state constitution contained an express education provision in its text, something the U.S. Constitution does not have.

Coons advocated shifting the battle to state courts, though he said it would at best be a "consolation prize." The state court route had significant disadvantages, starting with the amount of work required. Rather than winning a single national victory, as the civil rights plaintiffs had in *Brown v. Board of Education*, advocates for poor children would have to bring a separate lawsuit in every state except Hawaii. Each would have to be brought under a different state constitution, which had its own text and history, and argued to a different state supreme court.

Even if some lawsuits prevailed, it was almost inevitable that others would not and that some schoolchildren would lose out. After *Brown*, the right to desegregated education was a national one, guaranteed to every child in America. As the state school finance cases proceeded, by contrast, the result would be a legal patchwork in which students in some states would have the right to an equally funded education while students in others would not.

In the decades that followed, some state challenges did succeed. From 1973 to 2019, plaintiffs won school finance lawsuits in twenty-five states, including California, New York, Ohio, and Pennsylvania. In the same period, lawsuits failed in twenty-one other states, including Illinois, Virginia, and Florida. The Louisiana Supreme Court, in rejecting a school finance equalization lawsuit, declared that, with only limited exceptions, "the legislature has control over the finances of the state."

In Texas, after *Rodriguez*, poor school districts moved into state court. They prevailed under the state constitution, and the court ordered Texas to direct more funds to districts like Edgewood. The system became less unequal, but, even after decades of litigation, court orders, and legislative plans, it fell short of actual equality. In 2016, the all-Republican Texas Supreme Court unanimously upheld a school finance system that still directed more funds to wealthy districts. A lawyer who represented a group of school districts called the ruling "a dark day for Texas school children."

In many other states where school funding lawsuits have prevailed, poor districts have had difficulty making the courts' orders a reality. In New York, a school finance lawsuit was settled in 2006, but in 2018 education advocates said the state was underfunding the schools that won the lawsuit by more than $4 billion. The fight to equalize school funding in New Jersey has gone on for nearly forty years.

If the Court had ruled for the Edgewood parents and students, school funding would be far more equal across the country today. It would have required all fifty states to adopt a school finance system that did not discriminate against some school districts. Even in states where state funding lawsuits have prevailed, a ruling from the Court would likely have been more effective in bringing about reform. If the Court had put its power and prestige behind equal school funding and not left equality up to the vagaries of individual state courts, it might well have been more difficult for state legislatures to resist making school finance formulas equal across districts. The Court would have had more vigorous enforcement tools at its disposal than state courts have, including the ability to order Congress to use federal education funding to compel states to equalize their school funding.

If the plaintiffs had prevailed in *Rodriguez,* there no doubt would have been more school finance lawsuits, and the Court could eventually have moved beyond equal funding across school districts. It could have held that the Equal Protection Clause requires "equitable" school funding, meaning funding formulas in which money is allocated based on the difficulty of the educational challenges a school district faces. The Court could have recognized that poor school districts that have students who are on average more expensive to educate, because they come to school less prepared to learn, needed more funding per student than districts in which students arrive with greater advantages.

In time, the Court might have gone further still and recognized a right to not only an equitable education but an adequate one. The Kentucky Supreme Court did this in 1989, when it declared the Kentucky school finance system unconstitutional. The court held that the Kentucky Constitution's mandate that the state "provide an efficient system of public schools" required it to operate schools that were adequately funded. The court also identified a set of educational "capacities" that Kentucky should have the goal of providing to every child. Unlike other rulings, the Kentucky decision addressed the kind of education that had to be provided, not merely how it should be funded.

The following year, the legislature adopted the Kentucky Education Reform Act of 1990, a major overhaul of school finance, curriculum, and other aspects of the state education system. The reforms were designed to provide equal educational opportunities for all schoolchildren and to ensure that education throughout the state met minimum standards of adequacy. The new law narrowed the funding gap between rich and poor school districts and produced substantial educational gains across the state. After the reforms took effect, reading and science scores increased significantly, the dropout rate declined, and Kentucky rose in the national educational rankings from forty-third, in 1992, to thirty-fourth, in 2005.

If the Supreme Court had ruled in favor of the *Rodriguez* plaintiffs on their equal funding claim, it could have been the start of a new and robust constitutional right to an education. Even if the Supreme Court had only equalized school funding within states, and steered clear of recognizing a right to an "equitable" or an "adequate" education, it would have dramatically changed the nation's education system and increased the quality of education for millions of students in poor school districts. It would also have sent an important message: that in the eyes of the government, all children are equal and entitled to the same opportunity to succeed in life.

THE YEAR AFTER *RODRIGUEZ*, THE COURT DECIDED ANOTHER LANDMARK case that had the potential to transform the nation's schools and equalize educational opportunity for all children. The issue in *Milliken v. Bradley* was not school funding but racial segregation. The Court heard the case at a time when significant progress was being made in desegregating schools in the South but schools in the North were becoming more segregated. A new racial geography was emerging in large metropolitan areas: the overwhelmingly black and Hispanic big-city school system surrounded by overwhelmingly white suburbs. The *Milliken* lawsuit was an attempt to bring integration to the North, in a place where segregation was particularly pronounced—the Detroit metropolitan area.

Milliken began, as *Rodriguez* had, with a school walkout. In 1966, more than two thousand students at Detroit's Northern High School left school to protest educational conditions. In another era, when it was overwhelmingly white, Northern High School had been highly regarded. By the mid-1960s it was an important black institution, whose alumni included Aretha Franklin and Smokey Robinson, but its academic quality had declined. To members of the black community, the issue was not only Northern High School's academic weaknesses but the disparities that existed between it and Detroit's majority-white high schools in resources, teacher quality, and college preparatory courses.

The walkout at Northern High School occurred at a time of growing frustration among blacks in the North, many of whom were beginning to feel that, in terms of education, they had it even worse than blacks in the South. By 1966 the South had made substantial progress in desegregating its schools. It had been slow going for a number of years after *Brown v. Board of Education:* in the 1962–63 school year, not a single black child in Alabama, Mississippi, or South Carolina attended an integrated school. In 1964, a decade after *Brown*, just 1.2 percent of black schoolchildren in the South attended school with whites. Congress, however, increased the pressure by passing the Civil Rights Act of 1964, which authorized the attorney general to file desegregation lawsuits and the secretary of education to collect data to monitor progress. The 1964 act brought about what one civil rights scholar called "the first serious implementation of *Brown*." In the decade after the law passed, school integration in the South increased so significantly that before long its schools would be more integrated than schools in other parts of the country.

While the South was combining all-white and all-black schools into integrated school systems, white and black students in the North were moving further apart. In the early twentieth century, schools in the North had been overwhelmingly white. That began to change with the Great Migration, in which millions of southern blacks fleeing racism and poverty moved to northern cities like Chicago, Cleveland, and Detroit. Whites kept their distance from the growing black population, either by working to keep their neighborhoods white or by leaving for the suburbs. White flight was helped by an array of government programs, including subsidized Federal Housing Administration (FHA) and Veterans Administration (VA) home loans, which favored whites moving into non-integrated areas, and large-scale highway construction, which spurred the growth of new suburbs.

Detroit was a textbook case of how school segregation emerged in the North. In 1910, it was overwhelmingly white, with just 5,741 blacks, who made up 1.2 percent of the population. In each successive census, blacks constituted a larger percentage of the city, increasing from 4.1 percent in 1920 to 28.9 percent in 1960. As more blacks arrived, whites used an array of methods to reinforce neighborhood racial boundaries, from restrictive covenants—which barred nonwhites from buying homes in certain areas, until the Supreme Court invalidated them in 1948—to physical barriers. The most well known of those was the Eight Mile Wall, a six-foot-tall concrete barrier built in 1941 along a black-white border on the north side of Detroit.

Many Detroit whites fled to the suburbs. From 1950 to 1960, the population of the Detroit suburbs soared by nearly 80 percent. White flight continued in the 1960s, particularly after the 1967 Detroit riot, four days of unrest that resulted in forty-three deaths, more than a thousand injuries, and $200 million in property damage. With the riot, a city history notes, "what had been a gradual white exodus turned into a stampede." By 1970, the black population in the city had increased to nearly 44 percent, and it was still rising.

Detroit's demographic changes were even more pronounced in its public schools, which were significantly more black than the city population as a whole. In 1970, Detroit's public schools were nearly 64 percent black. There was considerable racial segregation within the city school system, with white students concentrated in heavily white schools in white neighborhoods. The greatest racial disparity, however, was between the city and suburban schools. Some of the school districts in the Detroit suburbs were more than 98 percent white.

The 1966 Northern High School walkout was the start of a larger drive by the black community to demand greater educational opportunity. The next year, the newly formed Inner City Parents Council issued a report enumerating the shortcomings of the Detroit schools, which it charged were preparing blacks only for military service in Vietnam or welfare. In early 1968, the Detroit High School Study Commission, which was established after the Northern High School protest by prominent black and white leaders, declared that Detroit's schools, particularly the ones with majority-black student bodies, "are becoming symbols of society's neglect and indifference."

Similar conclusions were being drawn all across the country. In 1967, after riots broke out in major cities—and while the Detroit riot was still under way—President Johnson appointed a National Advisory Commission on Civil Disorders to investigate the causes of the violence and recommend responses. In February 1968, the commission, which was named for its chairman, Illinois governor Otto Kerner, released a bestselling report that made the famous declaration "Our nation is moving toward two societies, one black, one white—separate and unequal." One of the primary causes of the recent civil disorders, the Kerner Commission found, was the nation's highly segregated and deeply unequal education system, particularly in large cities. "The bleak record of public education for ghetto children is growing worse," the report declared. "In the critical skills—verbal and reading ability—Negro students are falling further behind whites with each year of school completed." The commission declared integrated education "essential to the future of American society."

The Kerner Commission increased pressure on the nation to confront the growing racial segregation in the schools. In March 1970, the Detroit School Board developed an integration plan that called for moving more blacks into majority-white schools and more whites into majority-black ones. When the newspapers wrote about the still confidential proposal, which they called a "sweeping integration plan," white parents organized to combat it. Despite strong white opposition, the school board adopted the plan at a contentious public meeting, which was followed by bomb scares and death threats against the school board president.

White parents had greater success with the state legislature. It enacted a law, Public Act 48, that nullified Detroit's integration plan and created a mechanism for white students in neighborhoods that were becoming more black to transfer to whiter schools. In the city, whites petitioned to recall the four school board members who voted for the integration plan. On Election Day, August 4, powered by heavy turnout in white neighborhoods, 60 percent of the voters supported recall. None of the new board members who replaced them supported integration.

Since the city and state had rejected desegregation, and the federal government was not working to combat school segregation in the North, supporters of integrated education had no choice but to go to court. On August 18, 1970, the NAACP sued the State of Michigan on behalf of Detroit students and parents, including Ronald and Richard Bradley and their mother, Vera. The lawsuit contended that Public Act 48, the state law designed to block integration, was unconstitutional and that Detroit's schoolchildren were being denied the right to a desegregated education. *Bradley v. Milliken,* which was named for Ronald Bradley and Michigan governor William Milliken, had the same goal as the school desegregation lawsuits in the South. The NAACP would, however, face significant legal challenges that did not exist when it sued for desegregation in the South.

The first problem concerned proof. In civil rights law, segregation came in two varieties. There was *de jure* ("by law") segregation, which resulted from laws and government actions that explicitly discriminated on the basis of race. In the South, where the law established separate school systems for whites and blacks, de jure discrimination was not hard to prove. There was also *de facto* ("in fact") segregation, which was racial separation that came about without direct government action, because of housing patterns and other factors. The writer James Baldwin said that de facto discrimination meant "Negroes are segregated, but nobody did it." Courts regularly ordered desegregation when they found de jure segregation, but not when they found de facto segregation. Unless the courts changed the law of de facto and de jure segregation, the NAACP would have to find a way to prove that the school segregation in Detroit was a product of explicit discriminatory government action.

The NAACP did have evidence that Detroit's school segregation was de jure. New schools had been built in locations designed to reinforce racial lines. Detroit also engaged in discriminatory school assignment practices, such as transporting blacks from overcrowded black schools to other black schools, going past closer white schools that had room for more students. The state's adoption of Public Act 48 was another official act designed to prevent racial integration. It was not as straightforward a case as the ones the NAACP regularly made in southern school districts, but it could be a winning one.

The NAACP's second problem concerned remedy. Even if the Detroit schoolchildren won, it was not clear how the court could provide them with an integrated education. With the percentage of black students in the public schools approaching 70 percent and rising, even if a court ordered black and white students to be distributed evenly in schools across the city, black students would still attend heavily black schools. Such an order would also almost certainly cause many white parents to take their children out of the Detroit school system, making integration even more elusive.

There was, however, a possible solution. Since the metropolitan area's student population was overwhelmingly white, a desegregation order that included both the Detroit and the suburban school systems could allow all of the students in the Detroit metropolitan area to attend integrated schools. That would, however, require the court to order busing of students among as many as eighty-six school districts, which were located not only in Wayne County, which contained Detroit, but nearby Macomb and Oakland Counties. A "metropolitan area" remedy of this kind, which moved students across the city-suburban line, would be new terrain for a desegregation case, and it was not clear that a judge would order it or that it would be upheld on appeal.

Bradley v. Milliken was assigned to Judge Stephen J. Roth, of the federal district court in Detroit, which was not particularly good news for the plaintiffs. Roth, who had been nominated to the bench by President Kennedy, was a former prosecutor and no great liberal. He had immigrated from Hungary as a child, and he grew up in an integrated neighborhood in Flint, where southern and northern whites, blacks, and immigrants all lived together. As a result of his upbringing, he said, he did not understand the idea of segregation. During the *Milliken* trial, which lasted three and a half months, the plaintiffs put on extensive evidence about the segregated education they were receiving and the roles Detroit and the State of Michigan had played in making it segregated. It made a strong impression on Roth, who later said that "all of us got an education during the trial."

On September 27, 1971, Roth ruled in favor of the plaintiffs, holding that they were being denied a racially integrated education, in violation of the Fourteenth Amendment Equal Protection Clause. Roth held that the NAACP had proven that Detroit and the State of Michigan had engaged in de jure segregation. In an array of ways, the government had, Roth said, "acted directly to control and maintain the pattern of segregation in the Detroit schools."

There was still the matter of coming up with a remedy. In June 1972, Roth issued a metropolitan remedy order that included Detroit and fifty-three districts in the surrounding suburbs. The Detroit schools could not be desegregated, he concluded, "within the corporate geographical limits of the city." Roth was not concerned about whether the suburban districts had engaged in affirmative acts of racial segregation. What mattered was that the students in Detroit were victims of de jure racial segregation by the State of Michigan, which oversaw all of the state's school districts. The Court had made clear since *Brown v. Board of Education,* he said, that the remedy for de jure segregation was "prompt and maximum actual desegregation of the public schools by all reasonable, feasible, and practicable means available." That, he insisted, required a metropolitan-area-wide remedy.

Roth did not impose a specific plan for desegregating Detroit and the fifty-three other suburban districts. Instead, he laid out general principles for the remedy. All of the schools and classrooms in the fifty-four school districts should be roughly reflective of the racial composition of the metropolitan area as a whole, which was about 70 to 80 percent white. Also, the plan should limit as much as possible the amount of time students spent on buses. Roth appointed a committee, with representatives of the state, the city, the suburbs, and the plaintiffs, among others, to work out the specifics.

Whites in the Detroit metropolitan area responded to Roth's ruling with outrage. Demonstrators converged on the federal courthouse to denounce what they regarded as forced integration. The protesters targeted Roth personally, with bumper stickers declaring ROTH IS A FOUR-LETTER WORD, as well as death threats. The response in the suburbs was similar to the South's massive resistance to *Brown v. Board of Education.* A Birmingham, Michigan, policeman was quoted in a newspaper story saying, "I'll go to jail before my kids go to Central High School in Detroit." In the state's May 1972 Democratic primary, voters shocked the nation when George Wallace, Alabama's segregationist governor, who was running on an anti-busing platform, coasted to victory, winning more votes than any candidate ever had in a Michigan presidential primary.

Michigan appealed the case to the Cincinnati-based U.S. Court of Appeals for the Sixth Circuit, which affirmed Roth's decision, including his order of a metropolitan-area remedy. District lines are not "sacrosanct," the appeals court said, and Roth had the power to "disregard such artificial barriers." Given the demographics of the Detroit metropolitan area, it said, a desegregation plan that included both Detroit and the suburbs was "essential to a solution of this problem."

Michigan asked the Supreme Court to review the Sixth Circuit's ruling, and the Court accepted the case. The Burger Court that would be deciding it, despite the changes in membership since the Warren era, had not abandoned school desegregation the way it had quickly turned against the poor. In a 1969 case, the first major desegregation ruling after Burger arrived as chief justice, the Court continued to insist that segregated school districts in the South integrate "at once." In 1971, in a case from North Carolina's Charlotte-Mecklenburg School District, the Court gave specific directions on how desegregation should proceed, including, for the first time, expressly endorsing school busing as part of a desegregation remedy.

Although the Court had not abandoned its commitment to enforcing *Brown v. Board of Education* across the South, at least so far, a critical question was how it would approach what civil rights leaders saw as the next phase of school desegregation: the drive to bring it north. The year before it heard the *Milliken* case, the Court ordered desegregation in Denver, a city that, like Detroit, had never had a school system that was segregated by law. The Court found enough official acts promoting segregation to support a desegregation order. That decision, which came on a 7–1 vote, seemed on the surface like an encouraging sign for the *Milliken* plaintiffs.

The Court's lopsided vote in the Denver case, however, was a misleading gauge of its enthusiasm for school desegregation in the North. Burger was in the majority, but he had nearly dissented, and he only concurred with the outcome, not with any of the majority's reasoning. Powell wrote a separate opinion that expressed his affection for neighborhood schools and his dislike of busing. Rehnquist went further, with a sharply worded solo dissent that confirmed civil rights groups' concerns about his confirmation. For years, going back to *Brown,* the Court had worked hard to be unanimous in its school desegregation rulings, to make clear to recalcitrant school boards that it was united in its commitment to racial equality. That consensus had now broken down. The real question, however, was what the Court would do when confronted with a large-scale urban-suburban desegregation order that, if accepted, would likely become the model for major metropolitan areas all across the country.

THE FOLLOWING YEAR, ON JULY 25, 1974, THE COURT OVERTURNED ROTH'S decision by a 5–4 vote, handing the Michigan defendants a sweeping victory. The Court broke down along the same lines as it had in *Rodriguez,* with the four Nixon justices—Burger, Blackmun, Powell, and Rehnquist—and Stewart in the majority. As he had in *Rodriguez,* Stewart wrote a concurring opinion that seemed to chart a more moderate course while still rejecting the plaintiffs' claims. *Milliken,* which was almost entirely the work of justices Nixon had placed on the Court, came down just two weeks before Nixon resigned the presidency in disgrace over Watergate.

Burger, writing for the majority, focused not on whether the Detroit schoolchildren's rights had been violated, but on whether the metropolitan-area remedy Roth had ordered was legal. He emphasized the importance of respecting school district lines. "No single tradition in public education is more deeply rooted than local control over the operation of schools," he wrote, echoing Powell's opinion in *Rodriguez.* While Roth had focused on the black children in Detroit, Burger was more moved by the plight of the white suburbs, which he viewed as innocent bystanders. Upholding Roth's order would impose a desegregation order on "outlying districts" that had not been "shown to have committed any constitutional violation," he said.

Burger, a proud son of Minnesota, rejected the civil rights movement's contention that school segregation in the North and the South were comparable. The South had dual school systems for white and black students in the same district, a clear equal protection violation, he said, while Michigan had not created separate schools for whites and blacks. Unless Michigan "drew the district lines in a discriminatory fashion, or arranged for white students residing in the Detroit District to attend schools in" the surrounding suburbs, Burger said, it was "under no constitutional duty to make provisions for Negro students to do so."

Stewart, in his concurrence, sounded more troubled that the Court was consigning black children in Detroit to a racially segregated education. He insisted, however, that despite what Roth and the court of appeals had said, the government was not in any way responsible for the de facto segregation they were living with. Stewart focused on the heavy concentration of blacks in Detroit schools, and he said it had been "caused by unknown and perhaps unknowable factors such as in-migration, birth rates, economic changes, or cumulative acts of private racial fears." It was a more elaborate way of saying what James Baldwin had: "but nobody did it."

There were several dissenting opinions, but Marshall wrote the most heartfelt one, which all four dissenters—Marshall, Douglas, Brennan, and White—joined. In his description of the underlying facts of the case, Marshall challenged the idea that "nobody did it." There was a great deal of evidence that affirmative steps had been taken to segregate black and white students in Detroit, Marshall said, and the responsibility for those acts lay with both the Detroit Board of Education and the State of Michigan. Since the state was partly responsible, he insisted, the remedy order could include all parts of the state—including the suburban school districts outside Detroit, which were part of the state school system.

The key point in the case for Marshall was that, because the Detroit school district was so heavily black, desegregation could not be achieved without including the suburban districts. That meant, he said, that there was no choice but to make the suburbs part of the remedy order. The Equal Protection Clause required, Marshall said, that when de jure segregation exists, "school authorities must, to the extent possible, take all practicable steps to ensure that Negro and white children, in fact, go to school together." That is, he said, "in the final analysis, what desegregation of the public schools is all about."

As Marshall saw it, the Court's reversal of Roth's order was nothing less than a betrayal of *Brown v. Board of Education.* It had been almost exactly twenty years since that civil rights landmark, and now, he said, the Court was taking "a giant step backwards." Marshall sounded an alarm about where the Court was leading the nation. "In the short run," he said, "it may seem to be the easier course to allow our great metropolitan areas to be divided up each into two cities—one white, the other black—but it is a course, I predict, our people will ultimately regret."

Milliken was to a striking degree a repeat of *Rodriguez.* The Court was once again reviewing a district court ruling that interpreted the Equal Protection Clause to require that all students receive equal educational opportunity, no matter where they lived. In both cases, the state asked the Court to reverse the district court and uphold a status quo in which disadvantaged students received worse educations than other students. The states' position in both cases was that better-off people had a right to separate themselves in zones of privilege, in part because of their right to "local control." The outcomes of the two cases were also the same: the four Nixon justices and Stewart provided the five votes to reverse the lower court.

There was one more important similarity: in *Milliken,* as in *Rodriguez,* had it not been for Nixon's having driven Fortas off the Court, the schoolchildren almost certainly would have won. There were now two monumental ways in which Nixon's abuse of the powers of his office to take control of the Court had hurt the nation's most disadvantaged schoolchildren: it denied them equally funded schools, and it prevented them from receiving a racially integrated education.

The heavily white school districts around Detroit celebrated their victory. "Joy Is Expressed in the Suburbs," declared one headline. "Many White Parents Now See Their Children as Safe," reported another. Conservative commentators lauded the ruling. *The Wall Street Journal,* in an editorial, praised the Court for resisting "the notion that a federal judge or bureaucrat could reach into a community . . . and overturn its local school system."

Civil rights advocates saw *Milliken* as not only wrong on the law, but an indication that the nation's resolve to address segregation was winding down.

A *New York Times* editorial declared that "in refusing to fashion a remedy sufficiently broad to correct the constitutional wrong which it found, the Court's majority has made us all, not just the black children of Detroit, the losers in the long run." Judge J. Skelly Wright, in Washington, D.C., who had issued his own ruling about unequal educational opportunity in that city's schools, lamented that the Court had "abandoned the ideals of *Brown* at the sign reading 'City Limits.'"

Detroit schoolchildren and their supporters felt abandoned. Vera Bradley, whose family gave their name to the lawsuit, said she was "in a state of shock for a few minutes" when she heard the news. William Serrin, a former *Detroit Free Press* reporter, wrote an op-ed in *The New York Times* attacking the Court's decision. "Integration is now a matter for Detroit only," he said. "Thus it will be of little concern to the people of wealth and power, who live elsewhere."

Milliken brought an end to the *Brown* era. As the South desegregated, the biggest obstacle to integrated education nationwide had become the district lines in the North that separated urban and suburban school districts. If the nation's schools were ever to become truly integrated—so that, as Marshall put it, "Negro and white children" would, "in fact, go to school together"—orders like Roth's would be necessary not only in Detroit but in Chicago, New York, and other large cities. The Court, however, had now declared that to be impossible.

If the Court had upheld Roth's order, there undoubtedly would have been resistance, as there had been to *Brown*. Roth, however, had crafted a remedy order that should have done a great deal to address the white community's concerns about busing. All of the schools and classrooms in the metropolitan region would have student bodies that were roughly reflective of the racial mix of the Detroit metropolitan area. So apprehensive white parents could be reassured that their children would, even after desegregation, attend schools that were 70 to 80 percent white. There would also be as little busing as possible. About 300,000 students in the area covered by the remedy order already took a school bus every day, and the order would have raised that to only about 310,000. The increase in actual busing was so minimal that it was hard to avoid the conclusion many blacks had already reached: that, as a saying in the black community went, "it's not the bus, it's us."

Had the Court upheld Roth's order, after the initial protests died down, the ruling might even have become popular over time. Busing to achieve racial integration was often met with outspoken opposition, but polls showed that the parents of the schoolchildren involved actually gave it high marks. A Harris poll in 1981 found that, among families whose children were bused to achieve racial integration, 54 percent of the parents said the experience was very satisfactory, 33 percent said it was partly satisfactory, and only 11 percent said it was not satisfactory. The highest levels of opposition were among people who did not have children who were bused. "It seems that the idea of busing to achieve racial balance is unpopular," poll taker Louis Harris said. "And yet, those whose children have experienced busing report that it was a satisfactory process that worked out well in the end."

Milliken and *Rodriguez* powerfully reinforced each other. Many of the nation's most disadvantaged students were victims of both rulings: they were trapped in highly racially segregated school districts that received less than their fair share of funding. The Court had rejected their claims to equal educational opportunity in two different ways in a period of a little more than a year, each time by a 5–4 vote. When it was done, the Court had condemned millions of American schoolchildren, as Marshall said, to a "separate and inherently unequal education."

In the following decade, the Court issued two rulings that helped disadvantaged students, both of them important but limited. In 1978, in *Regents of the University of California v. Bakke*, the Court upheld affirmative action in university admissions. The plaintiff, Allan Bakke, challenged a University of California–Davis Medical School admissions policy that designated places in the entering class for minority applicants. Powell, who wrote the controlling opinion for a fractured Court, said admissions policies that considered race were subject to heightened scrutiny under the Equal Protection Clause. While it was constitutional to consider race holistically as one of a group of factors, he said, setting aside specific positions for racial groups violated equal protection. Powell cited Harvard College's admissions policy as one that used race constitutionally.

The *Bakke* decision helped minority students by upholding admissions policies that were bringing them into selective schools in larger numbers. If the Court had invalidated those policies, it would have become significantly more difficult for black and Hispanic applicants to gain admission, and for many poor students as well, because of the correlation between race and wealth. *Bakke* did not, however, offer disadvantaged students anything new. It merely allowed voluntary affirmative action policies to continue, and it did not even fully do that. As a result of the decision, many policies that were in effect—including the one at University of California–Davis Medical School that Bakke challenged—were no longer constitutional.

In 1982, the Court issued a ruling that expanded the rights of immigrant students. In *Plyler v. Doe,* undocumented immigrants challenged a Texas law that denied state funds to school districts for students who were not "legally admitted" to the United States and that allowed districts not to enroll those students. As a result of the law, undocumented students were charged tuition, and many families could not afford to send their children to public school.

The Court struck down Texas's law, with Brennan writing for a 5–4 majority that again included Powell. The Court did not recognize undocumented immigrants as a suspect class, and it did not hold education to be a fundamental interest. It did say, however, that education was more important than most government benefits, because of its "pivotal role in maintaining the fabric of our society," and that Texas did not have sufficient basis for denying it to a class of children who were not responsible for their status. Brennan also noted the harm the law would do to society "by promoting the creation and perpetuation of a subclass of illiterates within our boundaries, surely adding to the problems and costs of unemployment, welfare, and crime."

The right the Court recognized in *Plyler*, of undocumented children to attend public school for free, has made an important difference in the lives of these children. Although Texas was at the time the only state with a law barring funds for their education, if it had prevailed, other states would likely have adopted similar ones. *Plyler* was also, however, a narrow decision, which expressly did not hold that children have a constitutional right to education.

It was not long, however, before the Court returned to rejecting claims of students seeking greater educational opportunity. In *Kadrmas v. Dickinson Public Schools*, a poor rural family challenged a North Dakota law that allowed school districts to charge for transportation to school. Sarita Kadrmas, who was nine years old, attended a school sixteen miles from the family's home. The district began to charge a $97 transportation fee for her school bus, which the Kadrmases had trouble paying. When the bus no longer stopped for Sarita, the family sued, arguing that the district's refusal to grant fee waivers violated the Equal Protection Clause.

On June 24, 1988, the Court ruled against the Kadrmases, by a 5–4 vote. It rejected their argument that the mandatory fee violated the Equal Protection Clause, either by interfering with access to education or because of its effect on poor students. The majority opinion rejecting the Kadrmases' claim was, to the surprise of some observers, written by Sandra Day O'Connor, the first woman to serve on the Court.

O'Connor had an unusual background for a justice. She had grown up on her family's Arizona ranch, driving tractors and branding cattle. When she reached school age, her parents sent her to live with her grandmother in El Paso. O'Connor went on to Stanford and Stanford Law School, where she graduated third in the class Rehnquist graduated first in. O'Connor, whose only law firm job offer was to be a secretary, joined a county attorney's office and then became an Army lawyer when her husband, John Jay O'Connor III, a Stanford classmate, did military service. The O'Connors settled in the Phoenix area, and Sandra was elected to the Arizona Senate, eventually rising to majority leader. She was elected Maricopa County trial court judge, running as a "law and order" candidate, and later appointed to the Arizona Court of Appeals.

O'Connor served eighteen months on that midlevel state court before she was nominated to the U.S. Supreme Court. In the 1980 campaign, Reagan had promised that one of his first nominees to the Court would be a woman, and when Stewart announced his intention to retire, Attorney General William French Smith assembled a list of four women. O'Connor had the most modest credentials, but she had the support of Barry Goldwater, still an influential conservative, and Rehnquist. She also charmed President Reagan at her White House interview, where she spoke about her childhood on the ranch. He announced her nomination on July 7, 1981, and the Senate confirmed her 99–0.

Although she was undeniably conservative, there were reasons to believe O'Connor might be sympathetic to the Kadrmases' case and might give the liberal justices the fifth vote they needed for a majority. O'Connor had faced obstacles the other justices had not, especially in her early career as a lawyer. Some scholars also expected that the first woman justice would be sympathetic to women, children, and marginalized people in general. Suzanna Sherry, who was then a University of Minnesota law professor, argued in a 1986 *Virginia Law Review* article that O'Connor brought a "feminine voice" to constitutional adjudication. Drawing on the writings of feminist psychologist Carol Gilligan, Sherry argued that O'Connor's discrimination rulings in her first few years revealed a "reluctance to accept conduct that condemns groups or individuals to outsider status."

In her *Kadrmas* opinion, O'Connor showed no such reluctance. She said the Court's previous rulings had made clear that poverty was not a suspect class and education was not a fundamental interest. The *Plyler* decision was of no help to the Kadrmases, she said, because the Court had limited it to its own "unique circumstances." There was therefore, she said, no reason to apply heightened scrutiny to North Dakota's law.

Like many justices who spent their entire lives in economic comfort,

O'Connor exhibited little sympathy for the plight of people struggling to survive. Mr. Kadrmas worked only "sporadically" in the North Dakota oil fields, and the family's income was around the official poverty level for a family of five. The Kadrmases were also heavily in debt. O'Connor said she had "no reason to doubt that genuine hardships were endured by the Kadrmas family when Sarita was denied access to the bus." It was still "difficult to imagine," she said, why the Constitution would require schools to offer transportation, even to the poorest students, "for free."

In dissent, Marshall said Sarita had a right to a fee waiver. Even if poverty was not a suspect classification, a battle that had been lost long ago, wealth classifications still had "a measure of special constitutional significance," he said. Similarly, even if education was not a fundamental interest, its "extraordinary nature," he insisted, "cannot be denied." Against these factors, Marshall argued, the district's interest in saving a little money by denying the Kadrmas family a waiver was minimal. The Fourteenth Amendment Equal Protection Clause had been adopted, he pointed out, "to abolish caste legislation." A law that erects barriers to education for the poor can trap them in "their current disadvantaged status," he said, and threatens to create "a discrete and permanent underclass."

The *Kadrmas* ruling was widely criticized as not only wrong, but cruel. *The Washington Post*'s Mary McGrory, in a column headlined "The Court Missed the Bus," said it made "the court and North Dakota look bad." Even North Dakota attorney general Nicholas Spaeth, the lawyer who won the case, had deep misgivings. "I wish the Court had never taken it," he said when the decision came out. "Now they have stated some conclusions I do not agree with. An awful precedent has been set."

At the time *Kadrmas* was decided, few school districts imposed transportation fees. In the years since, they have become more common. In at least thirteen states, including such large ones as California and Texas, school districts impose transportation fees, which in many cases were adopted in times when budgets were tight. A *Boston Globe* investigation found that in

Massachusetts, a number of districts imposed transportation fees after the Great Recession began, in 2008. In some parts of the country, the fees can be more than $500 per student each school year, and some districts do not allow waivers for poor families, although there is sparse data on the subject. When researchers for the Florida Legislature interviewed six school districts across the country that charged transportation fees to students who did not live within walking distance of their schools, they found that four gave waivers to poor families, one charged reduced fees, and one charged full fees. There is considerable anecdotal evidence that school districts are imposing fees on families that cannot afford them. In some states, schools use professional bill collectors to go after parents who cannot pay. One single father in San Diego told a local newspaper that he was nearly driven into bankruptcy when the school district referred a bill for his son's transportation to collections agents.

In the years that followed, the Court returned to the issue of school desegregation and it began to take a more aggressive stance against. Instead of merely refusing to extend *Brown v. Board of Education*'s principles to segregation in the North, it started to unravel the progress that had been made in integrating once segregated school systems. In 1991, in *Board of Education of Oklahoma City v. Dowell*, the Court made it easier for segregated school districts that had been ordered to desegregate to get their orders lifted. In a 5–3 decision, it said that desegregation orders could be dissolved as long as districts had taken all "practicable" steps to eliminate segregation—even if they remained segregated. The Court's opinion, written by Rehnquist, was an invitation to school districts nationwide to ask courts to lift the desegregation orders against them, and it helped usher in a new era of resegregation in the South. From 1990 to 2009, 45 percent of districts under court oversight were released from their desegregation orders. That included large districts like Miami-Dade County, whose obligation to desegregate ended in 2001. After the orders were lifted, racial segregation in these districts increased significantly.

In 2007, the Court delivered a new blow to school desegregation: it went after plans that school districts had adopted voluntarily. *Parents Involved in Community Schools v. Seattle School District No. 1* was a challenge to integration programs that Seattle and metropolitan Louisville, Kentucky, had put in place without any court ordering them to. Both programs used race as one factor in making school assignments, in order to promote diversity. This was not "court-ordered busing," which conservatives had long railed against. It was communities choosing diversity in education on their own.

Parents Involved arrived at the Court not long after Roberts became chief justice and Alito replaced O'Connor, who had been more moderate than he was in cases involving race. The Court ruled 5–4 that the voluntary plans violated the Equal Protection Clause. Roberts, writing an opinion signed only by the four most conservative justices, said that using race positively to promote diversity was essentially no different from using it negatively to create the segregated school systems that the Court had struck down in *Brown*. He ended by declaring that "the way to stop discrimination on the basis of race is to stop discriminating on the basis of race." Kennedy, who provided the necessary fifth vote for the conservative majority, wrote a concurring opinion allowing that race could be used in school assignment in limited circumstances, if the programs were sufficiently "narrowly tailored"—a test he said Seattle and Louisville had not met. Still, even with Kennedy's qualification, the ruling was a major setback to efforts by localities trying to voluntarily integrate their schools.

It was notable that in *Parents Involved* the Court had abandoned the reverence for local control of education that it had expressed in *Rodriguez* and *Milliken*. Breyer, writing for the four dissenters, reminded the Court that it had emphasized in those education-law landmarks "the importance of acknowledging that local school boards better understand their own communities and have a better knowledge of what in practice will best meet the educational needs of their pupils." Now that localities were using their control over education to promote integration rather than fight it, the Court no longer deferred to school district decisions.

Stevens, in a separate dissent, underscored just how extreme the majority's position was. He said it was his "firm conviction" that not a single "member of the Court that I joined in 1975 would have agreed with today's decision." It was a striking statement, given that Rehnquist and Burger—Nixon's idea of two extremely conservative justices—were on the Court that Stevens had joined.

It is remarkable, from today's vantage point, to realize how close the *Rodriguez* and *Milliken* plaintiffs came to winning. If they had filed their cases just a few years earlier, if Johnson had gotten his chief justice nominee confirmed, if Humphrey had won the 1968 election, or if Fortas had not resigned, the Court almost certainly would have ruled in favor of both sets of plaintiffs. If it had, American education would likely look very different.

If the Court had ruled for Demetrio Rodriguez and the other Edgewood parents and children, all fifty states would have been required to have equal funding across their school districts. Had they done so, students in poor school districts would have been considerably better off. The U.S. Department of Education has estimated that 6.6 million students nationwide are receiving less educational opportunity than they would if school funding were equalized. On average, wealthy districts across the country receive nearly 16 percent more state and local funding than poor districts to spend on teachers, facilities, and supplies. There are also profound differences by race: a recent study found that school districts that mainly serve students of color received $23 billion less a year than majority white districts, even though they served the same number of students.

There have been many studies describing the financial disparities that exist today between school districts within the same state, which are often quite large. In Connecticut, the average expenditures per student were recently $16,988, but on a district level, spending ranged from $12,828 in Danbury to $35,155 in Cornwall. In Pennsylvania, Bryn Athyn, a suburb of Philadelphia, recently spent $26,675 per student on school operations, more than three times the $8,660 spent by Mount Carmel, in the state's coal region.

As large as the differences in funding are, they understate the gap in educational opportunity. Districts with the least money to spend often have the most expensive students to educate. Poor children are less likely than other children to start school with the necessary skills. A Brookings Institution study found that 75 percent of children from high- and moderate-income backgrounds are ready for school at age five, as compared with just 48 percent of poor children. Poor districts generally also have greater needs for bilingual educators, social workers, and other expensive specialized personnel. If school district funding levels were adjusted for the additional cost of educating higher-need students, the disparities would in most cases be significantly larger.

Journalists have written compelling portraits of how finance gaps between school districts translate into differences in educational opportunity. One *Washington Post* investigation of Pennsylvania's schools, which it pronounced "the nation's most inequitable," found dramatic differences between a Philadelphia high school and a suburban one ten miles away. Martin Luther King High School, which is inside the city limits, had a textbook shortage. It solicited donations for music and dance classes, and only sixty of its twelve hundred students could take them. Although many students suffered from deprivation and trauma, there was no social worker. At suburban Lower Merion High School, which had 75 percent more funding, textbooks were not used much, since every student had a school-issued laptop. The arts program included photography, ceramics, and jewelry-making classes. Lower Merion also had a social worker, though the need for one was not as great.

There is evidence that school finance reform, when it does occur, has a measurable impact on student achievement and life outcomes. One study by economists at the University of California–Berkeley and Northwestern University compared test scores in twenty-six states that had increased funding for poor districts with twenty-three states that had not. It found that states that directed more money to poor districts showed significantly greater academic improvement. The impact was at least twice as much per dollar than from another popular reform, decreasing early-grade class sizes. Greater educational spending has also been shown to have a positive effect on students' futures. One study found that for students from low-income families, a 20 percent increase in per-pupil spending for all twelve school years was associated with nearly a year more of completed education and a 20-percentage-point reduction in the annual incidence of adult poverty.

If *Milliken* had come out differently, it might have changed the nation's racial trajectory. If Roth's remedy order had been implemented, it could have ended the widespread model of overwhelmingly minority urban school districts surrounded by largely white suburban ones. States would have been forced to draw up assignment plans that ensured that all children attended schools that reflected the racial composition of their overall metropolitan area. The result could have been decades of integrated education across the country.

The best evidence that a transformation of this kind could have been done successfully is that it has been. While Detroit's metropolitan-area plan was being overturned by the Court, there was a similar court-ordered plan for Louisville. The Louisville plan combined the city school system, which was about evenly divided between black and white students, with suburban schools that were overwhelmingly white. In the new urban-suburban school district, elementary schools were required to be between 12 and 40 percent black, and secondary schools to be between 12 and 35 percent black.

Louisville's plan, which was implemented in 1975, required 23,000 students to be bused to achieve racial balance. There was resistance, including protests by the Ku Klux Klan, but the plan was carried out. It worked the way its supporters had hoped, and black achievement increased substantially, by a wide variety of measures. From 1975 to 1977, black second graders' reading scores improved from the twenty-fifth to the thirty-fourth percentile and black fifth graders' scores rose from the twenty-fifth to the thirty-sixth percentile. The Louisville integration order set the Louisville schools up for success, particularly for the most disadvantaged students, while *Milliken* set the Detroit schools up for continued failure.

If the Court had upheld Roth's order, the whole country would have had to redraw school districts in the way Louisville did. It would have meant taking seriously the Constitution's promise of racial equality and applying Marshall's standard for success: that "Negro and white children, in fact, go to school together." The transformation would not have been easy, but it would have charted an alternative path for American public education.

The combination of *Milliken,* which prevented school desegregation litigation from moving north, and the Court's unraveling of desegregation in the South in cases like *Board of Education of Oklahoma City v. Dowell,* has helped to produce America's current reality: extremely high levels of school segregation. Racial isolation is higher, by some measures, than at the time of the civil rights movement. One study calculated that in 1970–71, the average black student was in a school that was 32.0 percent white. By 2009–10, the average black student was in a school that was 29.2 percent white.

There is evidence that school desegregation, like higher spending levels, affects student achievement. A study by University of California–Berkeley economist Rucker Johnson found that black students who were affected by court-ordered desegregation in all twelve of their school years had an increase in educational attainment of about a full year. They were also significantly more likely to graduate from high school. For black students, attending integrated schools was also associated with attending a higher-quality college, being in better health as an adult, and being less likely to end up in prison, among other positive outcomes. The study found that, by these same measures, desegregation has minimal to no negative effects on whites.

IN HIS *RODRIGUEZ* DISSENT, MARSHALL WARNED THAT THE COURT WAS taking the nation away from its "historic commitment to equality of educational opportunity" and toward a system that deprives children of "the chance to reach their full potential." Decades after *Rodriguez* and *Milliken,* the nation has ended up where he feared. American education today is marked by large disparities not just in educational opportunities, but also in outcomes.

The socioeconomic achievement gap, which the *Rodriguez* plaintiffs wanted to eliminate, remains large. Family income is still one of the strongest predictors of how well children do in school. Racial achievement gaps—which the *Milliken* plaintiffs hoped to end—have also persisted. These gaps exist by a wide array of measures. White children score significantly higher than black and Latino children on elementary and high school reading and math tests. They are also doing considerably better in one educational measure that is particularly critical to positive life outcomes: graduating from high school.

These socioeconomic and racial gaps carry over to college. In families with incomes in the top one-quarter, 58 percent of children earned bachelor's degrees by the age of twenty-four, according to a University of Pennsylvania study. In families in the bottom one-quarter, just 11 percent did. There are also large gaps by race, with blacks and Hispanics significantly less likely than whites to earn a bachelor's degree.

These large and growing educational disparities are helping to drive inequality in America. The *World Inequality Report 2018,* which was produced by a team that included Thomas Piketty, cited "massive educational inequalities" as one of the two primary causes of the United States' "income-inequality trajectory." Educational inequality is of particular concern because of the powerful impact it has not only on the present but on the future. In a study of the academic achievement gap between high- and low-income Americans, Stanford University education professor Sean Reardon identified a "feedback mechanism" that decreases intergenerational mobility. "As the children of the rich do better in school," he said, "and those who do better in school are more likely to become rich, we risk producing an even more unequal and economically polarized society."

CHAPTER • 4

CAMPAIGN FINANCE

In 1976, the Supreme Court decided a case that was as important to equality in elections as *San Antonio Independent School District v. Rodriguez* and *Milliken v. Bradley* were to equality in education. *Buckley v. Valeo* was a challenge to sweeping campaign finance reforms that Congress enacted in 1974, in response to public outrage over the Watergate scandal. The reforms included strict dollar limits on how much Americans could contribute to political campaigns or spend independently to affect the outcome of an election.

On the day the law took effect, a group led by New York senator James Buckley, brother of the conservative intellectual William F. Buckley, filed suit. The Buckley group argued that contributing to campaigns and spending money on elections were forms of speech and that putting limits on it violated the First Amendment. The Court's decision would profoundly shape the future of American politics and government. If it upheld the law, the role of money in politics would be sharply limited. If it struck down the law or critical parts of it, the floodgates would open, and wealthy individuals and special interests would have tremendous influence over who won elections and what policies they adopted.

THROUGHOUT AMERICAN HISTORY, CAMPAIGN FINANCE REFORM HAS been closely tied to political scandals over money in politics. In the late 1800s, with the rise of the large corporation, special-interest money poured into national politics. It was so influential that it became an object of cynical humor. "There are two things that are important in politics," Mark Hanna, the legendary Republican political boss, said at the time. "The first is money, and I can't remember what the second one is."

When the Progressive movement gained power and Theodore Roosevelt became president, Congress responded to the public's demands for reform. It passed the Tillman Act of 1907, which banned corporate campaign contributions in national elections. Other laws followed, including the Federal Corrupt Practices Act of 1910 and later amendments, which imposed campaign spending limits and disclosure requirements. Many of the rules were not observed, however, and few violators were prosecuted.

There was a new push for campaign finance regulation in the late 1960s and early 1970s. It was an era in which progressive reform swept across the country, transforming everything from university curriculums to mental hospitals. This reformist spirit reached politics, where it changed how legislative district lines were drawn, how Democratic National Convention delegates were selected, and how campaigns were funded. At the urging of good-government groups, including the newly formed Common Cause, Congress adopted the Federal Election Campaign Act of 1971 (FECA), which created the modern framework for regulating campaign finance, including tougher disclosure requirements. A related law allowed taxpayers to check a box on their tax form to contribute to a fund to provide candidates with public financing. There was no central office charged with enforcing the 1971 law, however, and violators were still rarely prosecuted.

Just a few years after that law was passed, Watergate broke. It was the biggest political scandal in American history, and it prompted the greatest reforms. Although it is best known for the burglary of the Democratic National Committee offices and a cover-up that reached all the way to the Oval Office, Watergate also included major campaign finance crimes. The Committee for the Re-election of the President, which was known by the evocative acronym CREEP, was caught accepting multi-million-dollar contributions from corporations, in violation of the Tillman Act.

Investigators found illegal contributions to CREEP from some of the nation's largest corporations, including DuPont and American Airlines. Many of them sought specific actions from the White House, including the milk industry, which pledged $2 million to CREEP while it was asking the administration to raise federal milk price supports. The chairman of American Airlines, George Spater, said his company contributed "in fear of what could happen" if it did not. Much of the money was funneled in questionable ways, including cash in bags.

Watergate created a groundswell of support for tougher laws regulating money in politics. *The Philadelphia Inquirer* spoke for much of the country when it called for a campaign finance law "revolution" to bring an end to "the need for money, in huge quantity, that corrupted the 1972 electoral process beyond the grimmest, most cynical limits of previous imagination." The general public was also demanding reform. After Watergate, more than 25 percent of all mail sent to members of Congress was about campaign finance regulation, according to one account, "far more than on any other issue." In a September 1973 Gallup poll, 65 percent of respondents favored public financing of federal campaigns and a total ban on private contributions.

In response to Watergate and the public's reaction to it, in 1974 Congress enacted a set of amendments to FECA—and these sweeping reforms were the ones challenged in *Buckley v. Valeo*. The 1974 amendments were the "revolution" *The Philadelphia Inquirer* and others demanded, strengthening campaign finance regulations in important ways. They established a $1,000 limit on contributions to candidates in federal elections. They also imposed a separate $1,000 limit on independent expenditures "relative to a clearly identified candidate." This category applied to spending during an election—such as taking out a newspaper advertisement—by anyone who was not part of a campaign and not coordinating with a campaign, that could be seen as promoting a specific candidate. The 1974 amendments also imposed new and more rigorous public disclosure requirements. To ensure that the regulations were actually followed, the new amendments established a Federal Election Commission to enforce the limits, oversee the disclosure, and manage the public financing system.

Buckley's group of plaintiffs charged that many provisions of the 1974 amendments, and even some parts of the original 1971 law, were unconstitutional. The most important challenges were to the newly established contribution and expenditure limits, which had the potential to greatly reduce the role of money, and particularly special-interest money, in elections. The plaintiffs argued that the restrictions infringed on the First Amendment free speech rights of people who wanted to contribute or spend more than the limits the law allowed.

The plaintiff class included some of the nation's most conservative elected officials and organizations, starting with Buckley, who had been elected senator from New York on the Conservative Party of New York line, in an electoral fluke, when the Democratic and Republican-Liberal candidates split the liberal vote. He was joined by the American Conservative Union and the Mississippi Republican Party. There were also, however, some prominent liberals and civil libertarians, including Eugene McCarthy, the 1968 anti-war Democratic presidential candidate, and the New York Civil Liberties Union. The liberals and civil libertarians believed that the limits on contributions and expenditures made it difficult for insurgent candidates to challenge entrenched incumbents.

THE FIRST COURT TO HEAR *BUCKLEY V. VALEO,* THE U.S. COURT OF APPEALS for the D.C. Circuit, upheld nearly all of FECA. The D.C. Circuit, which had a majority of judges nominated by Democratic presidents, held that spending money on campaigns was not pure speech. Since it was not, the court said, FECA's restrictions on campaign contributions and election spending did not violate the First Amendment.

To support its holding about money and speech, the D.C. Circuit drew a comparison to *United States v. O'Brien,* the Supreme Court's ruling from 1968 upholding a law that made it a crime to burn a draft card—the same case in which Douglas had been a lonely, and radical, dissenter. In *O'Brien,* the Supreme Court said that burning a draft card is partly speech and partly not speech. The burning of the card registered opposition to the war and to the draft, which was communication. It also, however, destroyed a military document that the government had reasons for preserving that had nothing to do with speech. The Court said the government had a legitimate interest in regulating that part of the burning of a draft card. In the same way, the D.C. Circuit held, the government had legitimate reasons for regulating money in politics that had nothing to do with suppressing speech.

The D.C. Circuit did something else that was important: it recognized that the government had several distinct interests in regulating money in politics. It was critical, the court said, to safeguard "the integrity of elections." The government also had an interest, however, in "avoiding the undue influence of wealth" on democracy. The D.C. Circuit expressly cited *Harper v. Virginia Board of Elections,* the decision striking down the poll tax, and it defended campaign finance regulations as a protection of the rights of non-rich Americans. "It would be strange indeed," the court said, "if . . . the wealthy few could claim a constitutional guarantee to a stronger political voice than the unwealthy [merely] because they are able to give and spend more money, and because the amounts they give and spend cannot be limited."

The Supreme Court heard arguments in *Buckley v. Valeo* on November 10, 1975. Two days later, Douglas, the most liberal justice, announced his retirement. His seat would be filled by President Gerald Ford, who a few years earlier, as House minority leader, had been a key part of Nixon's campaign to drive Douglas off the Court. Ford was in a weak position politically. His path to the White House had been highly unusual. Nixon appointed Ford vice president after Spiro Agnew resigned in disgrace, following his plea of no contest to a charge of tax evasion. Ford then became president when Nixon was forced to resign over Watergate. Once in office, Ford made the controversial decision to pardon Nixon, which still haunted him. Ford needed to nominate a justice who would be confirmed by a Senate with a large and unfriendly Democratic majority.

His choice was John Paul Stevens, a former antitrust lawyer who was a well-respected, moderate Republican judge on the Chicago-based U.S. Court of Appeals for the Seventh Circuit. As President Ford hoped, Stevens proved to be popular with senators from both parties: he was confirmed by a 98–0 vote. Stevens was sworn in on December 19, which was too late to participate in *Buckley v. Valeo.*

The ideological makeup of the Court that heard the case was very different from that of the liberal D.C. Circuit. Half of the eight justices were Nixon nominees, and only two had been put on the Court by Democrats. The Court was under pressure to rule quickly, with the 1976 presidential election fast approaching. In less than three months, it reversed the D.C. Circuit and invalidated key parts of FECA.

The Court insisted that spending money on elections is speech. It then established a key constitutional distinction that became the framework for all future campaign finance decisions. The Court upheld FECA's limits on direct contributions to campaigns, on the theory that financial contributions were not actual speech but rather a way of "associating" with a candidate or a party, making the First Amendment interests less compelling. At the same time, the Court struck down FECA's limits on independent expenditures, which it held were pure speech that deserved full First Amendment protection.

In its First Amendment analysis, the Court held that the government had only one legitimate interest in regulating campaign finance: limiting corruption or the appearance of corruption. It emphatically rejected the D.C.

Circuit's holding that the government had an interest in leveling the playing field between candidates with more money and ones with less. "The concept that government may restrict the speech of some elements of our society in order to enhance the relative voice of others," it said, "is wholly foreign to the First Amendment." By interpreting the government's interest in campaign finance regulations so narrowly, the Court made it easier to strike down the independent expenditure limits. It simply decided that there was not a great risk of corruption or the appearance of corruption when money does not pass through candidates or their campaigns. Therefore, it insisted, the government had no legitimate interest in preventing people from spending as much money as they wanted to get their preferred candidates elected.

The Court in *Buckley* upheld many other parts of FECA in addition to the contribution limits, so it almost appeared to be a victory for campaign finance reform. The Court's invalidation of limits on independent expenditures, however, was an enormous loss. It gave wealthy individuals and special interests a way to inject unlimited amounts of money into political campaigns.

The *Buckley* decision did not break down neatly on ideological lines. On the whole, the conservative justices were more opposed to the law than the liberal ones. Two of the Nixon nominees, Burger and Blackmun, voted to strike down both the contribution and expenditure limits. The most liberal justices, Brennan and Marshall, joined the majority of the Court in voting to uphold the campaign contribution limits and strike down the expenditure limits—although, according to the justices' internal notes, they came close to voting to uphold both kinds of limits. In time, a strong ideological division would develop, with liberals generally supporting campaign finance regulations and conservatives largely opposing them. In this first major campaign finance ruling of the modern era, however, it was possible to make out only the vague outlines of the ideological divide that would eventually emerge.

Buckley v. Valeo has been called "the Rosetta Stone of campaign finance jurisprudence." The pronouncements it laid down, some of which were highly damaging to American democracy, still profoundly shape the law governing money in politics decades later. *Buckley*'s most harmful holding was its most basic one: that money equals speech. The logic behind it was strained. Spending money is different from speaking in important ways. Money amplifies whatever speech it is put behind and it brings it to a larger audience, but it is not speech itself, any more than using a high-powered sound system to blast a political message on a street corner is speech. The Court's equation of money and speech was, as one critic has said, the "original sin" of campaign finance law, which was responsible for almost everything bad that followed.

Even if the Court was intent on recognizing money as speech, it should have at least recognized the wisdom of the D.C. Circuit's more nuanced analysis. Campaign finance regulations do not prevent people from saying whatever they want about politics. At most, they are a restriction on a combination of speech and non-speech elements, like the law against burning a draft card. If the Supreme Court had adopted the D.C. Circuit's approach, it would have been far easier for the government to defend reasonable campaign finance regulations.

The *Buckley* Court also reached another very damaging conclusion: its insistence that the government's only legitimate interest in campaign finance regulations is preventing corruption or the appearance of corruption. The Supreme Court's rejection of what the D.C. Circuit saw clearly—that the government has an interest in "avoiding the undue influence of wealth" in elections—has been a major obstacle to defending campaign finance laws. One commentator has said that the Court's dismissal of this interest—its holding that the government cannot "restrict the speech of some elements of our society in order to enhance the relative voice of others"—may be "the single most damaging sentence in the modern canon of constitutional law."

The Court's decision to strike down limits on independent expenditures opened the floodgates to vast amounts of money in politics. As long as wealthy people spent their money independently and did not give it to a candidate or a political party, they could use as much as they wanted to get their candidates elected. Francis Valeo, the secretary of the Senate, who was formally the defendant in the case, understood what the Court's ruling meant. "I knew the minute that they took off the limitations on personal expenditures that you were setting up a Senate of millionaires, or people who could rely on other people's money for their support," he said. "I thought that was a disaster in terms of what it would do to the Senate, and it is."

By opening these floodgates, *Buckley* did something else very harmful: it eroded the basic principles underlying American democracy. The First Amendment, many constitutional law scholars say, was enacted not merely to prevent government from limiting speech but, more broadly, to promote democratic values, including fair and inclusive political debate. Critics argue that in *Buckley* the Court instead embraced a form of "free market democracy" in which wealth is given almost completely free rein in elections. *Buckley* adopted, according to this critique, "an Ayn Rand–style libertarian" approach that treated money as a "placeholder for allocating political power."

The *Buckley* Court's interpretation of the First Amendment made it inevitable that the wealthy would have an outsized, and perhaps controlling, role in elections and in setting government policy. J. Skelly Wright, who was one of the judges in the majority in the D.C. Circuit's *Buckley* decision, wrote an article for the *Columbia Law Review* that looked back mournfully on the Court's decision to reverse the ruling he had signed on to and strike down the limit on campaign expenditures. In the article, entitled "Money and the Pollution of Politics," Wright criticized the Court's ruling as "tragically misguided." As a result of it, he said, "concentrated wealth" threatened to drown out the voices of individual Americans. If the trend of money in politics that it started continued, Wright warned, "the principle of one person, one vote could become nothing more than a pious fraud."

Two years later, the Court expanded on its free-market approach to money in politics. In *First National Bank of Boston v. Bellotti,* it struck down a Massachusetts law that barred corporations from making contributions or independent expenditures in favor of or against state referendums. The vote was 5–4, with Powell, whose memorandum for the Chamber of Commerce had argued that business should do more to influence politics and law, writing for the majority.

The Court did two important—and, for supporters of campaign finance law, troubling—things in *Bellotti.* It continued its skeptical approach toward campaign finance regulation, showing a clear willingness to strike down laws that reformers had put in place to make elections fairer. At the same time, it began to minimize the distinction between corporations and human speakers under the First Amendment, something it would do in more extreme form decades later, in *Citizens United v. Federal Election Commission.* "The inherent worth" of speech in "informing the public," Powell said, does not depend on "the identity of its source, whether corporation . . . or individual." The Court made clear that it was talking only about corporations speaking on ballot initiatives, and that it was not saying they could spend money to elect candidates for office. That would come later.

The breakdown on the Court was becoming more ideological, with the liberal justices gravitating toward supporting campaign finance regulations. In *Bellotti,* the Court's two strongest liberals, Brennan and Marshall, dissented, along with White, who was staking out a position as one of the Court's strongest defenders of campaign finance regulations. Their dissent, which White wrote, set out a strongly liberal, almost populist, defense of regulating campaign spending by corporations. It was a mistake, White said, to give corporations the same political speech rights as people, given the "special advantages" the state gives them to "amass wealth." He warned, in a memorable phrase, that the state "need not permit its own creation to consume it."

Defenders of the Court's decisions striking down campaign finance regulations argue that the Court is genuinely concerned about protecting free speech, and that its goal is not to expand the role of money in politics or to increase the influence of the wealthy and powerful. That is hard to square, however, with its rulings from the same time in cases involving political speech by poor and middle-class speakers. In those cases, it repeatedly turned away people who were trying to speak not by spending money, but in more traditional, less expensive ways.

In 1981, the Court decided a challenge by citizens' associations in Westchester County, New York, to a federal law prohibiting people from leaving unstamped material in private mailboxes used by the Postal Service. The Council of Greenburg Civic Associations said that leaving its circulars in letterboxes was one of the group's main ways of communicating with community members. The Court upheld the law by a 7–2 vote. Rehnquist, writing for the majority, insisted that even though homeowners buy their own mailboxes, once they designate them as a place where U.S. mail is left, no one else has a right to use them. In dissent, Marshall argued that the law was a class-biased restriction on speech. "By traveling door to door to hand-deliver their messages to the homes of community members," he said, association members "employ the method of written expression most accessible to those who are not powerful, established, or well financed."

A few years later, the Court upheld a Los Angeles law that barred candidates from posting campaign signs on utility poles and other public property. The six-justice majority conceded that the ban interfered with candidates' ability to communicate with voters, but it insisted that the posters created "visual clutter" and that the city was within its rights to prevent this "significant substantive evil." In dissent, Brennan argued that the First Amendment did not permit cutting off such a critical method of political communication simply for aesthetic reasons. Posters on public property were a particularly inexpensive way of communicating, he said, "essential to the poorly financed causes of little people."

The contrast between the Court's approach to campaign spending by wealthy individuals and corporations and lower-income people was stark. When the wealthy and powerful wanted to use their money to influence elections, the Court swept aside an elaborate campaign finance regime that had been enacted by Congress and signed by the president, responding to strong popular demand, to help a nation heal after a scandal that went all the way to the White House. When poor and middle-class people challenged bans on their ability to hand out leaflets or post campaign signs, the Court suppressed their speech, out of deference to Postal Service mailbox rules and municipal concerns about clutter. It is hard to avoid the conclusion that the Court had two very different First Amendment standards for political speech, one for the wealthy and powerful and another for the "little people."

THERE WAS A BRIEF PERIOD WHEN THE COURT APPEARED TO BE RELAtively sympathetic to campaign finance laws, and in those years it issued two major rulings upholding regulation on money in politics. In 1990, in *Austin v. Michigan Chamber of Commerce,* it held that Michigan could prevent corporations from spending money to elect candidates. It was a different issue from *Bellotti*—this time corporations wanted to support not ballot referendums but individuals running for office. By a 6–3 vote, the Court said Michigan had the right to keep corporate money out of candidate elections. Marshall, writing for the Court, said Michigan's law was aimed not at ordinary political corruption, but at "the corrosive and distorting effects of immense aggregations of wealth that are accumulated with the help of the corporate form." The Court in *Austin,* speaking through Marshall, sounded a lot like White in his dissent in *First National Bank of Boston v. Bellotti* and J. Skelly Wright in "Money and the Pollution of Politics."

In 2002, Congress enacted the Bipartisan Campaign Reform Act, widely known as McCain-Feingold, a major new law designed to close loopholes that had emerged in existing campaign finance law. Like the 1974 amendments to FECA, which were adopted after Watergate, McCain-Feingold was a response to scandal. It was enacted not long after the controversial 2000 presidential election, which was decided by the Court in *Bush v. Gore,* and the Enron scandal, one of the nation's highest-profile cases of corporate malfeasance.

McCain-Feingold closed a notorious "soft-money" loophole in the existing law that allowed corporations, unions, and wealthy individuals to contribute unlimited amounts of money to political parties, purportedly for party building, getting out the vote, and other activities not related to electing a specific candidate. The soft-money loophole allowed corporations to pour money into elections, and it let individuals do the same, in larger amounts than they were legally allowed to give to candidates.

McCain-Feingold also cracked down on phony issue ads—television commercials that purported to be about an issue but actually were an attack on or argument for a candidate. These advertisements, which jammed the airwaves in the weeks leading up to elections, used language like "Call Senator Smith and tell him to stop destroying our economy," with the goal of getting the audience not to call Senator Smith but to vote against him. Corporations were barred from spending money directly to support or oppose candidates, but by running a phony issue ad, they could spend corporate money on elections and technically not violate the law. McCain-Feingold classified phony issue ads as regular campaign commercials and barred corporations from funding them. A group of plaintiffs led by then–Majority Whip Mitch McConnell challenged key parts of the law.

In 2003, in *McConnell v. Federal Election Commission,* the Court upheld McCain-Feingold. It was a long and fractured decision, with three separate majority opinions, but on the most important points the vote was 5–4, with Sandra Day O'Connor, who was the swing justice at the time, joining the liberal justices to create a majority. The main majority opinion, co-written by O'Connor and Stevens, upheld McCain-Feingold's closing of the soft-money loophole and its ban on phony issue ads.

The conservative dissenters, in an opinion by Kennedy, objected that the ruling "leaves us less free than before." They made it clear that they were eager to start striking down campaign finance regulations again if they could find the votes—and they soon would. The majority for upholding McCain-Feingold was possible only because O'Connor joined it. When she retired, President George W. Bush nominated Samuel Alito, who was strongly supported by conservative activists, to succeed her. Alito was more conservative than O'Connor in general, and he was considerably less supportive of campaign finance regulations. Once he arrived, a new reality set in: there were no longer five votes to uphold laws like McCain-Feingold, and the Court would be more divided than ever along ideological lines.

In 2007, in *Federal Election Commission v. Wisconsin Right to Life,* the Court made its U-turn, reversing a key victory that campaign finance advocates had already won in *McConnell v. Federal Election Commission.* The *Wisconsin Right to Life* case was also about phony issue ads, this time ones run by an anti-abortion group against Wisconsin senator Russ Feingold. The Court, by a 5–4 vote, ruled that Wisconsin Right to Life could run the ads. Roberts, writing for the majority, set out a new test for when an ad would be deemed to be a phony issue ad: only when it is "susceptible of no reasonable interpretation other than as an appeal to vote for or against a specific candidate." The new test all but obliterated McCain-Feingold's effort to rein in these ads. Writing for the four liberal dissenters, Souter said that, "after today, the ban on contributions by corporations" and the "limitation on their corrosive spending when they enter the political arena" were "open to easy circumvention."

The Court's new hardline conservative majority made its big move in 2010 in *Citizens United v. Federal Election Commission,* a case that did not start out big. Citizens United was a small conservative nonprofit organization that produced a ninety-minute documentary attacking Hillary Clinton. *Hillary: The Movie* was something between a traditional documentary and an hour-and-a-half attack ad, featuring commentators like conservative provocateur Ann Coulter and descriptions of Clinton as "ruthless" and "the closest thing we have in America to a European socialist." The group made the film using its own money and funds from for-profit corporations, and it planned to distribute it through video-on-demand. It was not clear if *Hillary: The Movie,* which was far from a typical political advertisement, fell under McCain-Feingold's restrictions. Citizens United sued the Federal Election Commission to establish that it could air *Hillary: The Movie* in the run-up to the 2008 election without violating McCain-Feingold. The lawsuit had the potential to chip away further at McCain-Feingold, but the scope of the challenge appeared to be narrow.

The *Citizens United* lawsuit did not arrive at the Supreme Court by chance. A well-funded network of conservative activists, with strong ties to corporate America, had mobilized against campaign finance regulations. James Bopp, a prominent Republican election lawyer, was one of the leaders. With help from Senator Mitch McConnell, Bopp had established the James Madison Center for Free Speech, which served as a brain trust for campaign finance litigation. Bopp encouraged Citizens United to use *Hillary: The Movie* to further roll back campaign finance regulation and played a large role in crafting the lawsuit in its early stages. Bopp had ambitious goals. He told *The New York Times*, "If we do it right, I think we can pretty well dismantle the entire regulatory regime that is called campaign finance law."

Citizens United v. Federal Election Commission reached the Court for the first time in March 2009. Citizens United hired Ted Olson, one of the nation's preeminent Republican lawyers, who had argued *Bush v. Gore* for Bush, to represent it before the Court. Citizens United became more ambitious once the Court agreed to hear its case, and it no longer wanted merely to chip away at McCain-Feingold. Now it wanted to ask the Court to make major changes in campaign finance law. It would be necessary, however, to proceed cautiously. The big issues Citizens United wanted to raise had not been briefed and argued from the start of the case, and the Court generally did not like being told it should overturn decades of its previous holdings. In his briefs to the Court, Olson made the narrow arguments for his client to prevail, but he also went further. He asked it to reverse *Austin v. Michigan Chamber of Commerce* and hold that corporations like Citizens United had a First Amendment right to spend their money in support of candidates. It was a cursory argument, and few observers thought the Court would take such a radical step.

There were many good reasons for the Court to reject Olson's plea and issue a narrow ruling. One was that the ban on corporate money in candidate elections was so well established. The Tillman Act, which barred corporations from contributing to political candidates, had been one of the great accomplishments of the Progressive Era, adopted to make politics cleaner and more responsive to the people. A few decades later, Congress extended the ban on corporate contributions to corporate spending on campaigns. The Court ratified the ban in *Austin v. Michigan Chamber of Commerce* and again in *McConnell v. Federal Election Commission*. It was a lot of law and history to ask the Court to toss out in such a casual manner.

Another reason for the Court to reject Olson's argument was the doctrine of "constitutional avoidance," which held that courts should look for ways to decide cases, if possible, without interpreting the Constitution. With Citizens United's challenge, it would have been easy for the Court to avoid constitutional issues. It could simply have held that a ninety-minute documentary like *Hillary: The Movie* did not fall under the definitions set out in McCain-Feingold for a political commercial and issued a ruling that did not significantly change the law.

The conservative justices, however, were eager to use *Citizens United* to issue a very broad ruling. Kennedy quickly wrote a draft opinion reversing *Austin* and striking down McCain-Feingold's limits on corporations spending money on candidate elections. Souter, who would have dissented, reportedly made a personal appeal to Roberts to slow the case down. Deciding such a critical issue so hastily, Souter insisted, with virtually no briefing from the parties, would do lasting damage to the Court. The justices had an intense debate, according to accounts from behind the scenes, and ultimately decided not to rush an outcome they all knew was coming.

The Court set *Citizens United* down for a second argument in the fall of 2009, and it asked the parties to submit new briefs addressing whether the ban on corporate spending in elections should be struck down. The Court was still rushing—rather than wait for the term to begin, on the first Monday in October, it scheduled a rare September argument. Elena Kagan, as President Obama's solicitor general, argued for the government. After everything that had occurred, supporters of campaign finance regulations were not optimistic about winning, but they hoped the Court would decide the case on narrow grounds.

That was not what happened. On January 21, 2010, the Court, by a 5–4 vote, issued the sweeping ruling it had been waiting to deliver. It struck down the part of McCain-Feingold that prohibited corporate expenditures on campaigns, reversing *Austin* and *McConnell* in the process. It was a stunningly broad decision that opened the floodgates to unlimited amounts of corporate money in elections. As was increasingly becoming the norm in campaign finance cases, the Court broke down precisely into conservative and liberal camps.

Kennedy wrote the majority opinion, and he was in many ways the ideal person to write it. Kennedy had earned a reputation as a relative moderate, because, as the Court's swing justice, he occasionally broke with his fellow conservatives to give the liberals a majority. In a few areas, including gay rights and the death penalty, the Court had issued important liberal rulings because of his vote. Kennedy was no moderate, however, on business cases. He had strong corporate sympathies that had deep roots.

Kennedy grew up in Sacramento, the son of a lawyer-lobbyist father and a mother who was active in civic affairs. Kennedy, who was raised Catholic and served as an altar boy, attended Stanford, the London School of Economics, and Harvard Law School. He went to work for a leading law firm in San Francisco, but when his father died he returned to Sacramento to take over his father's law and lobbying practice. Kennedy also helped then-governor Ronald Reagan's staff with the drafting of a ballot initiative to limit taxes.

Kennedy was nominated to the San Francisco–based U.S. Court of Appeals for the Ninth Circuit by President Ford in 1975, when he was just thirty-eight. As an appeals court judge, Kennedy had a reputation as a low-key but reliable conservative. One of Kennedy's judicial colleagues described him as having difficulty understanding less fortunate people who faced barriers in life, a product of the exclusive neighborhoods and elite schools in which he spent his formative years. "It's a different life experience," the judge told a reporter. "He just doesn't know any of those people." Kennedy arrived on the Supreme Court as a third choice. When Lewis Powell retired, in 1987, after the failed nominations of Robert Bork and Douglas Ginsburg, President Reagan turned to Kennedy, who he thought would be an uncontroversial nominee. He was right: the Senate confirmed him by a vote of 97–0.

Kennedy's opinion in *Citizens United* elevated corporate speech to a new level—the level of people's speech. What mattered for the First Amendment, Kennedy said, was not the source of the speech, but its content. "Political speech is indispensable to decision-making in a democracy," he said, "and this is no less true because the speech comes from a corporation rather than an individual."

There was a great deal wrong with *Citizens United*. The majority was reckless, almost lawless, in its rush to overturn well-established law. The conservative justices may have been in a hurry to free up corporations to participate in the 2012 presidential election, or they may have wanted to act while they had five votes for their position—since, with the departure of just one justice, that could have changed. Whatever the reason, the majority's haste was hard to miss, and criticism of it came from the Court itself. "Five Justices were unhappy with the limited nature of the case before us, so they changed the case to give themselves an opportunity to change the law," Stevens protested in an unusually sharply written dissent. They "blaze[d] through our precedents, overruling or disavowing" a long line of cases that had come out precisely the opposite way, he said, to get the result they wanted.

The Court's First Amendment analysis was also deeply flawed. It was wrong to say that corporations are equivalent to people as speakers. Corporations lack the attributes that matter most in expressive communication. They have "no consciences, no beliefs, no feelings, no thoughts, no desires," Stevens wrote in dissent. Corporate "personhood" can be a useful legal fiction, Stevens said, but corporations "are not themselves members of 'We the People' by whom and for whom our Constitution was established."

It was also deeply unfair to treat corporations as persons—unfair to actual people, whose voices were now in danger of being drowned out by the far greater resources of corporations. The law gives corporations enormous advantages in accumulating wealth, something White mentioned in his dissent in *First National Bank of Boston v. Bellotti.* They pay lower taxes than people, they are able to raise capital through the sale of stock, and the law allows them to "live" forever. Society gives corporations these advantages in the belief that the general public will benefit from their commercial activity, employment, and wealth creation—not to create super-speakers with the power to change the outcome of elections. With the Court's decision in *Citizens United,* White's warning from decades ago was coming to pass: the nation was permitting "its own creation to consume it."

Few Supreme Court decisions have been more sharply criticized from the moment they appeared than *Citizens United.* President Obama, who once taught constitutional law at the University of Chicago, issued a statement on the day of the ruling calling it "a green light to a new stampede of special interest money." It was, he said, "a major victory for big oil, Wall Street banks, health insurance companies and the other powerful interests that marshal their power every day in Washington to drown out the voices of everyday Americans."

The public shared Obama's reaction. A *Washington Post*–ABC News poll found that eight in ten respondents opposed the *Citizens United* decision, and 65 percent were "strongly" opposed. Unlike the Court, the public was not sharply divided on ideological lines: 85 percent of Democrats, 81 percent of independents, and 76 percent of Republicans disapproved.

Critics were quick to mobilize. MoveOn.org, the grassroots progressive group, organized protests nationwide. Within months, 400,000 people had signed a MoveOn.org petition that called for amending the Constitution to overturn *Citizens United.* The same call went out from twenty states and about eight hundred cities, towns, and other units of government.

Citizens United was, as one scholar observed, "the end of campaign finance law as we knew it." Beyond its damaging holding allowing corporations to spend on candidate elections, it opened the door to a new campaign finance scourge: the rise of the "super PAC." Regular political action committees, or PACs, raise money from individual donors and contribute it to candidates. Campaign finance regulations apply to them: there are limits on the size of the contributions they can accept, and they cannot take money from corporations. There was, however, another kind of PAC, which used its money only for independent expenditures. SpeechNow.org, which was one of these expenditure-only PACs, argued that, because it did not give money to candidates, it should be able to accept contributions of any size, and to take them from corporations. There was strong support for this in *Citizens United,* since, among its various holdings, it had just stated for the first time that the government had *no* anti-corruption interest in regulating expenditures. This made no sense: of course a special interest could corruptly influence an elected official by spending a large amount to get him elected, expecting favors in return. This illogical holding was, however, now the law—and it meant there was no legal basis for reining in super PACs like SpeechNow.org.

Within months, SpeechNow.org persuaded the U.S. Court of Appeals for the D.C. Circuit to hold, based on *Citizens United,* that it could accept contributions of any size. Shortly thereafter, the Federal Election Commission decided, also because of *Citizens United,* that expenditure-only PACs like SpeechNow.org could accept contributions from corporations. With these two rulings, the super PAC was born—a political action committee that could accept contributions of any size, from individuals *or* corporations. With their ability to engage in "nearly limitless fundraising," super PACs quickly became one of the most powerful forces in politics. A Republican campaign finance lawyer declared that the emergence of super PACs was "pretty much the holy grail that people have been looking for."

As destructive as super PACs were, they were made worse by another fast-growing trend in campaign spending: "dark money," or money whose source is hidden from the public. Normally, contributions to PACs and super

PACs must be disclosed. There is, however, a loophole: wealthy individuals and entities can give money to a nonprofit that turns around and gives it to the super PAC. The super PAC need only disclose the nonprofit from which it accepted money, and the nonprofit does not need to disclose where that money came from originally. Dark money makes up an increasingly large share of all election spending. On the fifth anniversary of *Citizens United,* President Obama warned in his State of the Union address that the nation was "drowning in dark money for ads that pull us into the gutter."

The deep unpopularity of *Citizens United* did not slow the Court down. The following year, it struck down an Arizona law enacted by referendum in response to a major political scandal. The law provided public funding for campaigns and gave additional money to candidates running against high-spending opponents. The Court, by the same 5–4 vote as in *Citizens United,* held that Arizona's law violated the speech rights of well-funded candidates because it could make them feel pressure to spend less, so they did not trigger the part of the law that gave more money to their opponents. It did not matter to the Court that the law was funding more speech—and not preventing any. Kagan, in dissent, captured the ruling's perversity. "Except in a world gone topsy-turvy," she said, "additional campaign speech and electoral competition is not a First Amendment injury."

In 2014, the anti-campaign-finance-regulation majority struck again. The Court, by the same ideologically divided 5–4 vote, overturned another part of McCain-Feingold, which limited the total contributions an individual could make in a two-year cycle to candidates, political parties, and PACs. The "aggregate contribution limit" was $123,200 for a two-year election cycle, which Alabama businessman Shaun McCutcheon and the Republican National Committee insisted was too low. Roberts, in the main opinion, said the restrictions did not sufficiently advance the government's interest in fighting corruption to justify its infringement on speech. Breyer got to the heart of the case in a dissent he delivered from the bench. The Court was raising the overall contribution limit to "infinity," he said, and he warned that "if the court in *Citizens United* opened a door, today's decision may well open a floodgate."

THE *BUCKLEY* LINE OF CASES, CAPPED BY *CITIZENS UNITED*, HAS TRANSformed American politics—and government. In the deregulated campaign finance environment the Court created, the wealthiest Americans now play an extraordinarily large role in funding electoral politics. When *Politico* analyzed money flowing to candidates, parties, PACs, and super PACs in the 2014 campaign cycle, it found that the one hundred largest individual donors gave $323 million—almost as much as the amount that came from the 4.75 million Americans who gave $200 or less. In the 2018 midterm elections, a single donor and his wife gave $113 million. Campaign finance has "reached a tipping point where mega donors completely dominate the landscape," according to political consultant Mark McKinnon. Candidates are now, he said, "genuflecting before an audience of 100 wealthy individuals to fuel their campaigns."

As dominant as mega-wealthy individuals have become in funding politics, *Citizens United* opened the system up to a group of influence seekers with significantly more money at their disposal: corporations. In 2019, the ten wealthiest Americans had a net worth ranging from nearly $51 billion to $131 billion, according to *Forbes* magazine. That same year, *Forbes* reported that the ten most valuable American companies had market capitalizations ranging from $343 billion to $961 billion. The impact the largest corporations can have on politics when they choose to spend freely far outstrips the impact the wealthiest individuals can have.

After *Citizens United*, the "stampede of special interest money" that President Obama warned of began almost immediately. The amount of money raised by outside groups not directly affiliated with a campaign or a party has soared. In the first five years after the ruling, corporations, super PACs, labor unions, and other outside groups spent almost $2 billion on federal elections—about two and a half times what they spent in the eighteen years from 1990 to 2008, according to the Brennan Center for Justice. From the 2008 presidential election, just before *Citizens United*, to the 2012 election, just after, outside spending almost tripled. There were similar increases in state and local elections.

Since *Citizens United*, dark money is playing an increasingly important role in elections. Nearly one-third of the almost $2 billion in outside spending since *Citizens United*, or at least $618 million, has been in the form of dark money. In 2018, according to the Center for Responsive Politics, the majority of outside election spending was either from dark money spenders or groups that accepted dark money.

Even if it were possible to trace all of the money that has poured through the floodgates the Court opened, it would still understate the damage of the campaign finance decisions. The money-saturated political landscape the Court created is one in which wealthy individuals and special interests do not need to spend their money to wield influence. Bob Kerrey, the former Democratic senator from Nebraska, has described the powerful impact that special-interest money can have even when it is not spent. Kerrey said that when he was in Congress, if he was considering trying to reduce carbon in the atmosphere to combat global warming, he knew that Charles and David Koch—the archconservative brothers who were each worth billions of dollars—would spend heavily to defeat him for reelection. If he voted to raise the minimum wage, he said, he knew the Chamber of Commerce would support his opponent. It was all so clear that nothing had to be said and no money had to be spent. "They don't have to threaten me," Kerrey said. "I just know they're going to do it."

The new campaign finance regime has created some bizarre rituals that reflect who now holds the power. An infamous example played out in Las Vegas in the spring of 2014, when prospective Republican presidential candidates descended for what the press dubbed the "Sheldon primary." They came to pay homage to casino magnate Sheldon Adelson, who had a net worth of nearly $40 billion. *The Atlantic* reported on the lengths to which the visitors went to ingratiate themselves with Adelson on issues he cared about, in an article headlined "The Sheldon Adelson Suck-up Fest." The candidates came to pledge their fealty to Adelson's favorite causes, including stopping the spread of internet gambling, which competed with his casinos.

The Sheldon primary, for all its eccentricities, reflected a larger reality: the extraordinary lengths to which candidates now go to please wealthy donors. This ingratiation occurs largely out of the sight of ordinary voters, most of whom would be shocked by it. In 2016, *60 Minutes* investigated fundraising by members of Congress after *Citizens United* and found that both political parties expected their members to spend up to thirty hours a week in secretive call centers on Capitol Hill soliciting potential donors, working from a prepared script. Representative David Jolly, a Florida Republican, said his party's leadership told him he was responsible for raising $18,000 a day. Jolly considered the Republican call center to be a "cult-like boiler room" and said the whole process was "beneath the dignity of the office."

In the *60 Minutes* report, which was titled "Are Members of Congress Becoming Telemarketers?," Congress members made it clear that the Court's campaign finance rulings were a major reason for their constant fundraising. Representative Steve Israel, a New York Democrat who was then head of the Democratic Congressional Campaign Committee (DCCC), said "everything changed" after *Citizens United*. Before the ruling, he said, he had to put in an hour every day fundraising, or two at most; after the decision, he had to spend as much as four hours. The schedule the DCCC prepared for freshman members in 2013 recommended that they spend four hours a day making fundraising calls, and just two hours a day doing congressional "committee" and "floor" work. Another member of Congress *60 Minutes* spoke to, Rick Nolan, a Minnesota Democrat, served for six years before *Citizens United* and returned in 2013, after it had been handed down. "It seems like I took a nap," Nolan said, "and I came back and I say, 'Wow, what happened to this place? What's happened to democracy?'"

The intense pressure to make fundraising calls ensures that members of Congress are in constant contact with wealthy Americans, talking with them about their legislative priorities. Big contributors are hardly representative of the American public as a whole. In the 2018 election cycle, the top ten interest groups among contributors to congressional campaigns included real estate, securities/investment, health professionals, lawyers, pharmaceuticals, and oil and gas. Minimum-wage employees and the unemployed were not on the list.

Not surprisingly, in a system where large campaign contributions play such a central role, wealthy people have a disproportionate impact on government policy. In an oft-cited study, Martin Gilens of Princeton University and Benjamin Page of Northwestern University examined a data set on 1,779 policy issues to answer the question "Who really rules?" Their answer was economic elites, including large campaign donors. "In the United States, our findings indicate, the majority does *not* rule—at least not in the causal sense of actually determining policy outcomes," the authors concluded. "When a majority of citizens disagrees with economic elites or with organized interests, they generally lose."

Elites get their way on many important issues through their campaign contributions. A classic example is the "carried interest" loophole, which allows wealthy hedge fund managers and private equity executives to pay a little more than half the tax rate on their compensation that average Americans pay on their salaries. The carried-interest rule makes no sense as a matter of tax policy, but a very wealthy group of Americans wants it very much, and they make large contributions to the elected officials who keep it in place. Even President Trump has said that, as a result of the rule, "the hedge fund guys are getting away with murder."

The carried-interest loophole increases the nation's inequality in two ways. It makes some of the nation's wealthiest people even wealthier, by allowing them to pay less in taxes than they should. No less important, it deprives the government of revenue that could be used to help the poorest Americans. Victor Fleischer, a tax expert at the University of California–Irvine Law School, estimated a few years ago that the carried-interest loophole costs the U.S. Treasury $18 billion a year. There are many ways that money could have been used instead of giving it to hedge fund and private equity executives. The Legal Services Corporation, the badly underfunded federal nonprofit corporation that provides civil legal assistance to low-income Americans who face eviction, the loss of child custody, and other life-altering legal challenges, had a budget of just $410 million in 2018.

Reformers have tried to end the carried-interest loophole, but the resistance has been fierce. During one campaign to abolish it, Stephen Schwarzman, the chairman and CEO of the Blackstone Group, made headlines when he compared the effort to "when Hitler invaded Poland in 1939." The private equity industry has had an impressive record of success in defending its privileged position. One of the biggest battles was in 2007, when Representative Sander Levin, a Michigan Democrat, introduced a bill to close the loophole. In an analysis of its defeat, *The New Yorker* recounted how the private equity industry began with strong support from Republicans and worked to win over Democrats. The industry trade association, the Private Equity Council, and twenty lobbying firms did much of the persuading. The bill died quietly in the Senate Finance Committee.

The campaign against the Levin bill was not decided by compelling policy arguments. It was won by campaign contributions. The industry gave more than $22 million in the 2008 election cycle and nearly three times that amount in 2012. The Center for Responsive Politics, a nonprofit organization that tracks campaign contributions, noted that the industry "didn't emerge as a significant political player or campaign contributor until 2007," the year the Levin bill was defeated.

There are many other government policies that have been driven by special-interest money. The Medicare prescription drug benefit that Congress adopted in 2003 is one of them. Medicare Part D, as it is known, was widely recognized as a giveaway to the pharmaceutical industry, inflating drug company profits while increasing costs for consumers and taxpayers. *Mother Jones* ran an exposé of it under the blunt headline "This Is Why Your Drug Prescriptions Cost So Damn Much."

Part D barred the government from negotiating with pharmaceutical companies for lower drug prices. A study released by Carleton University's School of Public Policy and Administration and Public Citizen compared Part D with programs that were allowed to negotiate. It found that Part D paid an average of 73 percent more than Medicaid and 80 percent more than the Veterans Benefits Administration for brand-name drugs. It calculated that if Part D could obtain the same prices those programs do, it would save as much as $16 billion a year.

This windfall for the pharmaceutical industry has meant higher premiums and co-payments for senior citizens. The cost, however, goes beyond dollars and cents. Studies show that many Part D participants do not fill all of their prescriptions because they cannot afford to, a practice known as cost-related non-adherence (CRNA). One survey found that 16 percent of diabetes patients covered by Part D declined to fill at least one prescription every year for financial reasons.

Members of Congress have tried to lift the ban on negotiating drug prices, but the pharmaceutical industry has successfully defended its special treatment, with the help of large campaign contributions. From 2003 to 2016, drug manufacturers and wholesalers gave $147.5 million in federal contributions to presidential and congressional candidates, party committees, and political advocacy groups. In 2015, the pharmaceutical industry employed a staggering 894 lobbyists to promote its agenda with the 535 members of Congress, and more than 60 percent of these lobbyists were former members of Congress, congressional staff, or government officials.

The single biggest recent example of a government policy that favored big donors over the public good was a windfall not for one industry but for all of them: President Trump's 2017 tax law. The Tax Cuts and Jobs Act of 2017, which was projected to add more than $1 trillion to the deficit, sharply reduced taxes for the wealthy while giving the middle class and the poor far smaller cuts. According to an analysis by the Tax Policy Center, nearly 83 percent of the cuts will go to the wealthiest 1 percent.

Corporations, which were given both lower rates and new tax shelters, were the biggest winners of all. A *Bloomberg* analysis of the law, when it was passed, ran under the headline "Tax Bill Will Deliver a Corporate Earnings Gusher." After it operated for a year, the windfall for corporations was even bigger than many critics had feared. In 2018, sixty profitable Fortune 500 companies paid no taxes at all, including General Motors, IBM, and Netflix. A number of the nation's wealthiest corporations reported negative taxation. IBM earned $500 million in U.S. income and received a federal income tax rebate of $342 million. General Motors had $4.3 billion in income and reported a negative tax rate.

There is no way to calculate all the campaign contributions that went to members of Congress and President Trump to promote the tax bill, because it was a priority for so many wealthy individuals and corporations that gave money in the year it passed. Enormous lobbying resources were also deployed to rewrite the tax law in favor of wealthy individuals and corporations. Of the 11,078 lobbyists registered in Washington the year the bill was passed, about 58 percent were working on tax policy, and in the first nine months of that year, those lobbyists contributed $9.6 million to members of Congress.

Little effort was made to hide the role campaign contributions played in rewriting the tax law to favor the wealthy. Doug Deason, a wealthy Texan, was quoted telling congressional Republicans that the "Dallas piggy bank" would be closed until the tax bill was passed. "Get it done," he said, "and we'll open it back up." Members of Congress spoke bluntly about what donors expected. Representative Chris Collins, Republican of New York, said, "My donors are basically saying, 'Get it done or don't ever call me again.'" Senator Lindsey Graham, Republican of South Carolina, warned his colleagues that if Republicans did not get the tax bill passed, "the financial contributions will stop" and many incumbents would likely lose their seats.

The influence of campaign contributions was particularly noticeable because the 2017 tax law was so unpopular with voters. There was, not surprisingly, little support among the general public for slashing taxes on wealthy individuals and corporations. A CNN poll found that 55 percent of Americans opposed the law and only 33 percent supported it. Fully 66 percent said they believed it would do more to help the wealthy than the middle class. The high levels of opposition to the bill were widely publicized before Congress voted, but they did not slow its momentum.

Wealthy contributors upheld their side of the bargain. After the new tax law was signed, *Politico* proclaimed in a headline, "Big Donors Ready to Reward Republicans for Tax Cuts: The Checkbooks Are Open Again, Just in Time for a Challenging Midterm Election Cycle." Within months, Adelson's company, Las Vegas Sands, reported a $670 million income tax benefit from the new tax law. The month after that, Republican House Speaker Paul Ryan visited Las Vegas and Adelson gave $30 million to a super PAC working to maintain the Republican House majority. The Charles and David Koch brothers or Koch Industries stood to save as much as $1.4 billion a year in taxes as a result of the new law, according to an analysis by Americans for Tax Fairness. The month after President Trump signed the law, a network of groups affiliated with the Koch brothers said that it would spend as much as $400 million to support conservative candidates and causes in the 2018 midterm elections.

In the years since the *Buckley* decision, it is striking how successful wealthy individuals have been in getting their taxes lowered. Americans have made it clear that they want higher taxes on the wealthy in poll after poll. In a 2017 Reuters/Ipsos poll, released while Congress was debating the new tax law, three-quarters of respondents said the rich should pay more. Congress, however, has lowered the highest marginal tax rate from 70 percent in 1976, when *Buckley* was decided, to just 37 percent in 2018. With the role that large campaign contributions and independent expenditures play in politics and government, popular opinion has exerted little impact on tax policy.

ECONOMISTS AND POLITICAL SCIENTISTS SAY THAT IN THE WORLD CREated by *Buckley* and *Citizens United*, there is a "feedback loop" at work between wealth and political power. Rich individuals and corporations are more able than ever to use their money to elect candidates and drive government policies that make them even richer. The wealthier they become, the more favorable policies they can buy. "The result," says Nobel Prize–winning economist Paul Krugman, "is a sort of spiral, a vicious circle of oligarchy."

The government policies the wealthy are demanding and getting are not merely ones that bring them a small incremental advantage: they are major structural changes in how income and wealth are allocated in society. The same *World Inequality Report 2018*, co-produced by Thomas Piketty, that cited "massive educational inequalities" as one of the two primary causes of the United States' "income-inequality trajectory" found that "a tax system that grew less progressive" was the other. Progressive tax systems, which have higher tax rates for the wealthiest taxpayers, are "a proven tool to combat rising income and wealth inequality," the report said. In the last five decades, American taxes have become far less progressive, helping the wealthiest individuals and corporations become wealthier.

Taxes are far from the only policy area in which wealthy individuals and corporations are winning victories that are increasing economic inequality on a large scale. Economic elites have secured labor laws that are tilted toward management and against unions, which has driven down workers' wages. The political influence of the wealthy, particularly large corporations, is the main reason the federal minimum wage has not increased since 2009, which has significantly driven down the inflation-adjusted wages of low-income workers. The influence of economic elites was also a major factor in the elimination of the right to welfare in the mid-1990s, which has greatly diminished the incomes of already poor Americans.

The *Buckley* line of cases has had another important negative effect: it has helped to erode Americans' faith in their democracy. The campaign finance laws the Court has been rapidly dismantling, in rulings sharply divided along ideological lines, are extremely popular with the general public. In a Pew Research Center poll taken in 2018, 77 percent of the respondents said there should be limits on the amount individuals and organizations can spend on political campaigns. Support for limits crossed party lines, with 85 percent of Democrats and Democratic leaners and 71 percent of Republicans and Republican leaners in favor.

The post–*Citizens United* regime has left Americans disillusioned. For decades, public opinion polls have asked people whether they believe the government is run "for the benefit of all the people" or "by a few big interests looking out for themselves." In 1964, 64 percent of respondents said "for the benefit of all," and just 29 percent said "by a few big interests." By 2016, only 7 percent said "for the benefit of all," and 92 percent said "by a few big interests."

This near-unanimous belief that the government is benefiting only special interests is likely part of the explanation for the electorate's current level of anger. The 2016 election, in which a socialist nearly won the Democratic nomination and a right-wing populist was elected president, was widely hailed as the year of the angry voter. A report on "Voter Anger with Government and the 2016 Election," from the University of Maryland School of Public Policy, argued that the "most fundamental source of anger and dissatisfaction" was that the government was "seen as ignoring the people in favor of special interests, campaign donors, and political parties." Fully 91 percent of those surveyed for the report agreed with the statement "Big campaign donors have too much influence," with 23 percent somewhat agreeing and 68 percent strongly agreeing.

It did not have to be this way, and the Supreme Court is the main reason it is. After Watergate, the political system responded remarkably well. Congress passed a strong campaign finance law that imposed strict limits on campaign contributions and expenditures, designed to keep special-interest money out of elections. The president signed it, and the U.S. Court of Appeals for the D.C. Circuit upheld it. Then the Supreme Court, which had four justices nominated by Nixon—who had been forced from office by the scandal that led to the law—dismantled the protections Congress put in place. It has been opening the floodgates wider ever since.

CHAPTER ◆ 5

DEMOCRACY

On December 11, 2000, the Supreme Court held oral arguments, and the eyes of the nation were on Sandra Day O'Connor. The stakes that day could hardly have been higher: the presidency. The election contest between Democrat Al Gore and Republican George W. Bush would be won by whoever received Florida's electoral votes, and the case the Court was deciding would play a large role in determining who that would be.

The margin in Florida was razor-thin, and there were many irregularities in the state's results. Among them were tens of thousands of "undervotes," ballots that had not registered a vote for president, in many cases because of the state's glitchy voting machines. Both sides rushed into court, and state and federal courts began issuing a flurry of rulings. On December 8, with Bush officially leading by just 537 votes, the Florida Supreme Court ordered a statewide manual recount of the undervotes, which might well have changed the outcome of the election. The Supreme Court halted the recount, however, and scheduled arguments in *Bush v. Gore*.

The Court that heard *Bush v. Gore* had five conservative justices and four liberal ones. O'Connor was the swing justice, the most moderate of the conservatives and the one who most often broke ranks with them. If the Court just voted its political preferences, Bush would win 5–4 and he would become president. Many Court watchers, however, thought the Court would not want to resolve one of the most important cases in history by dividing on ideological lines, giving the appearance that it was a partisan body. In other historic rulings, including *Brown v. Board of Education* and *United States v. Nixon,* which ordered Nixon to turn over the White House tapes and ended his presidency, the Court had spoken unanimously. If anyone was going to break ideological ranks or lead the Court to a bipartisan solution, O'Connor seemed to be the justice most likely to do it.

At oral argument, however, O'Connor shocked many people in the gallery. In an exchange with Gore's lawyer over what standard should be used to count undervotes, many of which had the notorious "hanging" chads—caused when the chad in a paper ballot was not completely punched out—O'Connor sounded like the most partisan of the Bush lawyers. Rather than sympathize with voters who had been thwarted by Florida's flawed voting technology, O'Connor blamed them. "Well, why isn't the standard the one that voters are instructed to follow, for goodness' sakes?" she asked testily. "I mean, it couldn't be clearer."

It did not appear from the exchange that O'Connor was going to break ranks with the conservative justices, and she did not. On December 12, the Court ruled for Bush by a 5–4 vote, with O'Connor in the majority. The decision handed Bush Florida's electoral votes, and ultimately the presidency.

The Court that decided *Bush v. Gore* was a direct heir to the Nixon Court that formed in January 1972, when Rehnquist and Powell arrived. There had been considerable turnover in the intervening twenty-nine years, but the Court's ideological composition remained what it was then: a conservative chief justice presiding over a conservative majority. There was another point of continuity with 1972: the chief justice was Rehnquist, who, as one of Nixon's assistant attorneys general, had helped to drive Fortas off the Court and then was plucked from obscurity to be one of the four Nixon justices.

To many observers, *Bush v. Gore* had every appearance of being a political ruling. The five conservative justices voted to stop the ballot counting in Florida, allowing Bush to win. The four liberal justices voted for Gore. Nothing in the justices' analysis of the legal issues led a single one to vote in favor of a candidate who did not share his or her ideology.

Another reason the decision appeared to be political was that its legal reasoning made little sense. The majority opinion, which was unsigned, stopped the recount that the Florida Supreme Court had ordered, holding that it would violate Bush's rights under the Equal Protection Clause. The explanation it gave was that there were not uniform standards from county to county for deciding which ballots counted. Some counties might count a ballot with a dimpled chad while others would not. There was a danger, the majority said, of "arbitrary and disparate treatment" of voters in different parts of the state. That disparate treatment, it said, would violate the Equal Protection Clause.

What the analysis omitted was that the American system of voting has always been rife with disparate treatment, and it is too diffuse, chaotic, and underfunded to expect any kind of uniformity. Voting varied from county to county across the country, not just in Florida. Some jurisdictions used lever machines and others used electronic voting machines. Some areas had long lines to vote on Election Day while others did not. The Court had never said that election mechanics had to be uniform throughout a state, and as a practical matter, it would require herculean efforts and a great deal of money to even approach that standard. The right to uniform election mechanics, it appeared, applied only to presidential recounts in Florida and belonged only to George Bush.

The Court's equal protection holding was also hypocritical. The conservative Court that formed after Nixon took office had ended the Warren Court's "rights revolution," much of which had been based on reading the Equal Protection Clause broadly. When the Burger Court ruled against Linda Williams in *Dandridge v. Williams,* it insisted that a government policy is not unconstitutional merely because it is "not made with mathematical nicety or because in practice it results in some inequality." In the years since, skepticism toward equal protection claims had become an article of faith for the conservative justices. One Harvard law professor wrote after *Bush v. Gore,* with only mild exaggeration, that those justices "almost never find equal-protection violations (except, perhaps, when white people are 'discriminated' against by affirmative action)."

The conservative justices all but admitted their bad faith in *Bush v. Gore*'s most notorious feature: the statement in the majority opinion that the decision was "limited to the present circumstances." It is a fundamental principle of American law that court rulings have precedential value, and that Supreme Court decisions are binding on the lower federal courts. Scalia, one of the five justices in the majority, had written in an opinion only a few years earlier that the Supreme Court "does not sit to announce 'unique' dispositions." The Court's "principal function," he said, was "to establish *precedent*—that is, to set forth principles of law that every court in America must follow." In *Bush v. Gore,* however, the majority announced that its decision would be just the sort of "'unique' disposition" that Scalia had disclaimed. To the decision's critics, its "limited to the present circumstances" language was proof that the Court had, as one commentator put it, "explicitly embraced lack of principle, ad hocery, vulgar partisanship."

The dissenting justices strongly objected to the Court's decision to stop the vote counting and award the presidency to Bush, though they fell into two camps in their legal analysis. Stevens and Ginsburg disagreed with the Court's holding that the lack of a single standard for counting votes violated the Equal Protection Clause. Souter and Breyer agreed with the majority that there was an equal protection violation, but they argued that there was still time to fix it and that the Court should have sent the case back to Florida courts to establish uniform standards.

What all four dissenters agreed on was that the Court was not only wrong on the law, but guilty of an overreach of historic proportions. Stevens ended his dissent by declaring that "although we may never know with complete certainty the identity of the winner of this year's Presidential election, the identity of the loser is perfectly clear. It is the nation's confidence in the judge as an impartial guardian of the rule of law." Ginsburg seemed most indignant of all. While the other dissenters wrote in their opinions that they "respectfully" dissented, as is customary, Ginsburg wrote only "I dissent."

Bush v. Gore was met with vociferous criticism. *The New York Times,* in an editorial, declared that the Court's decision to stop the recount in Florida "comes at considerable cost to the public trust and the tradition of fair elections." Six hundred seventy-three law professors signed a statement condemning the Court for using "its power to act as political partisans, not as judges of a court of law." Many scholars expressed outrage in their own articles and essays. Margaret Jane Radin, a professor at Stanford Law School, declared that *Bush v. Gore* made it difficult for her to remain in the "intellectual heights" of the academic world. "When I was faced with a gross, bald-faced violation of the rule of law," she wrote, "I wanted to protest in the streets."

When the Supreme Court spoke, however, the nation complied. Bush, who lost the popular vote to Gore by more than 500,000 votes, was awarded Florida's electoral votes, and with them he became the first president since Benjamin Harrison, in 1888, to be elected while losing the popular vote. Exactly twenty-four hours after the Court ruled, Bush addressed the nation from a podium in the Texas House of Representatives and pledged to serve the entire nation "whether you voted for me or not." Gore, speaking from his vice presidential office in Washington, declared that, while he differed with the Court's decision, "I offer my concession."

There was one more winner in *Bush v. Gore:* the conservative majority on the Court. If Gore had become president and managed to win reelection, he would certainly have chosen a liberal to replace William Rehnquist when he died, in 2005. There would have been a liberal chief justice with a liberal majority behind him—a new ideological orientation that could have lasted for decades. The five conservative justices who stopped the voting were not only choosing the next president—they were ensuring that the conservative Court that Nixon had established in 1972 lived on into the twenty-first century.

BUSH V. GORE HAD ENORMOUS SIGNIFICANCE FOR AMERICAN HISTORY, for the Supreme Court, and for constitutional law. What was largely lost in the early reaction to the case, however, was what it meant, specifically, for election law. In its rush to stop the Florida recount and put Bush in the White House, the Court had issued a landmark decision on the law governing elections, with a deep ambivalence at its center. In principle, the Court had handed down a bold ruling insisting that election rules had to be highly uniform to meet a very demanding standard of equal protection. Practically, however, it had used that lofty principle to stop validly cast ballots from being counted—and it had told courts never to apply that standard of election fairness again.

The Court's attitude toward voting was once far less ambivalent. Expanding voting rights was a central part of the Warren Court's "rights revolution," starting with legislative districting. In the early 1960s, state legislative districts were not required to be equal in population, and in many cases they were wildly unequal. In Alabama, Jefferson County, with a population of 634,864, had the same number of state senators—one—as Lowndes County, with a population of 15,417. The Warren Court issued a series of landmark rulings, starting with the 1962 case *Baker v. Carr,* that established the principle of "one man, one vote," requiring both state legislative and congressional districts to have roughly equal populations. After these rulings, district lines were redrawn nationwide, making state legislatures and Congress dramatically more democratic. When Warren was asked at the end of his career what he considered the most important case in his time on the Court, he said it was *Baker,* because it "gave to the courts the power to determine whether or not we were to have fair representation in our governmental system."

The Warren Court also strongly supported Congress's power to protect the rights of minority voters. In 1966, it upheld the "preclearance" provision of the Voting Rights Act of 1965, which required certain states and localities to get approval from the Justice Department or a federal court before they could make changes in their voting rules that could make it harder for minorities to vote. In the same year, the Court struck down the poll tax, which had long been used to keep poor and minority voters from casting ballots.

It was hard to know how *Bush v. Gore* fit into this tradition. Even though the Court had stopped votes from being counted and said the decision had no precedential value, its formal holding appeared to help future voting rights claims, since it insisted on a high level of equality in the administration of elections. While the media and most Americans focused on the decision's impact on the presidential election, some legal scholars and voting rights advocates were considering whether *Bush v. Gore* could be used to make elections better-run and fairer. It could be "an advancement in voting rights doctrine," one prominent election law professor wrote in an op-ed piece in *The New York Times* two days after the ruling. "It has asserted a new constitutional requirement: to avoid disparate and unfair treatment of voters."

If the Court had been principled about providing all Americans with the exacting level of equal protection in elections that it insisted on for Bush, *Bush v. Gore* could indeed have been a major "advancement." Elections are administered in notoriously unequal ways that almost always disadvantage poor and minority voters. Studies have shown that blacks and Latinos are forced to wait in longer lines to vote than whites are—nearly twice as long in the 2012 election, according to a Massachusetts Institute of Technology voter survey. Early voting is often administered unevenly, with some areas having many early voting locations while others have few or none. There are also significant differences in the failure rates of various voting methods, with punch card systems generally failing to record votes more often than newer electronic machines. In theory, *Bush v. Gore* should have provided a powerful legal weapon for ending these and other voting disparities. It is difficult to see how it could have, however, when the justices who signed on to its broad equality holding did not actually believe in it, and the Court told other courts not to follow it. *Bush v. Gore* cannot be taken seriously, Richard Hasen, a professor at the University of California–Irvine Law School, has said, "because the Court itself did not take its holding seriously."

History has proven the skeptics right. The Supreme Court for years acted as if *Bush v. Gore* had never existed. No opinion cited the case until 2013, when Thomas "did what wasn't supposed to be done," as one commentator described it. The Court that year struck down an Arizona law that required people to submit proof of citizenship to register to vote, holding that it conflicted with a federal voter registration law. Thomas, in a solo dissent, cited a relatively obscure part of *Bush v. Gore:* its holding that state legislatures have broad authority in choosing their state's electors to the Electoral College. He argued that it meant that the Arizona Legislature should be able to require voters to submit proof of citizenship. So the first time *Bush v. Gore* appeared in a Supreme Court opinion, it was cited as a reason for making it *harder* for people to vote. Lower federal courts have occasionally cited *Bush v. Gore* to argue that election procedures should be fairer and more equal, but it is not an idea that has caught on.

Underneath *Bush v. Gore*'s words about "the equal dignity owed to each voter" was a dark view of elections and democracy. Lani Guinier, a Harvard law professor and former head of the NAACP Legal Defense and Educational Fund's voting rights project, argued in 2002 that *Bush v. Gore*'s real holding did not lie in what it said—all of the language about equality and fairness in voting. It lay, rather, in what it did: stop Florida from counting many ballots cast by eligible voters. Florida had hard-to-use voting technology that prevented many Floridians—particularly the poor, the elderly, and racial minorities—from casting ballots that were counted in the final vote tallies. The Court weighed in on the side of the flawed technology, not the thwarted voters. It believed, according to Guinier, that voters "had to pass a test to have their ballots counted, and the implicit suggestion was that only those who passed this test actually deserve to participate in the democratic process." Its real message, she said, was that democracy is a "domain of governing elites, not robust and engaged citizens."

IN THE YEARS SINCE *BUSH V. GORE*, IN CASES INVOLVING VOTING, THE Court has repeatedly sided with "governing elites" over "robust and engaged citizens." One area where this has notoriously been true is challenges to partisan gerrymandering, the practice of drawing legislative district lines to help one political party win. In addition to tilting elections toward the favored party, partisan gerrymandering takes power away from ordinary voters, because it means that in many cases, elections are all but decided before the voting even begins. Partisan gerrymandering is a new version of the sort of anti-democratic legislative line drawing that the Warren Court struck down in the *Baker v. Carr* line of cases. The post-1969 Court's approach, however, has been very different.

The first major test of partisan gerrymandering after *Bush v. Gore* came in 2004, in *Vieth v. Jubelirer.* Democrats challenged Pennsylvania's highly gerrymandered congressional districts, which had been drawn after the 2000 election, when there was a Republican governor and Republicans controlled the legislature. Under pressure from Karl Rove, President Bush's political adviser, and congressional Republicans, the legislature drew lines designed to create as many districts as possible that would elect Republicans to Congress.

Democrats argued that the plan violated voters' equal protection rights. They showed that the legislature had gone to extraordinary lengths to draw districts that would elect Republicans. Although there were more registered Democrats than Republicans in Pennsylvania, Democrats were likely to win only seven of the nineteen congressional seats, or less than 37 percent.

The Court ruled 5–4, along the same ideological lines as in *Bush v. Gore,* that the Democrats had not made a strong enough case. Scalia, writing for himself, Rehnquist, O'Connor, and Thomas, argued that partisan gerrymandering cases were "nonjusticiable," or not resolvable by the courts, because there was no workable constitutional standard for deciding them. Kennedy, who provided the fifth vote for the majority, wrote a separate opinion saying he believed there could be a case in which the challengers proved that a partisan gerrymander was unconstitutional, and in which the Court identified a workable standard, but this was not that case.

Stevens, in dissent, insisted that the Court had a good basis for striking down Pennsylvania's district lines but that the justices in the majority simply did not want to. The problem was not the lack of a workable standard, he said, but "a failure of judicial will to condemn even the most blatant violations of a state legislature's fundamental duty to govern impartially." Stevens did not invoke *Bush v. Gore,* but he could well have pointed out that the Court had forgotten the commitment it expressed to "the equal weight accorded to each vote and the equal dignity owed to each voter."

Challenges to partisan gerrymandering did not end with *Jubelirer.* The main reason was that Kennedy had held open the possibility that in a future case he might provide the fifth vote to strike down gerrymandered district lines. Another reason the issue stayed alive was that it was a large and growing threat to democracy. As voting data became more voluminous and redistricting software more powerful, legislators were able to draw their lines with greater precision, locking in majorities for their parties more effectively and making voters' wishes ever less relevant—a phenomenon that was being described as "extreme gerrymandering."

The Court returned to partisan gerrymandering in 2018. It accepted a pair of cases that presented the issue squarely and on a bipartisan basis, one a challenge to Republican-drawn legislative lines in Wisconsin, the other a challenge to Democratic-drawn lines in Maryland. Many Court watchers expected Kennedy to follow through on the promise of *Jubelirer* and vote with the liberal justices to strike down partisan gerrymanders. At the oral argument, the focus was on him. When it was over, CNN headlined its story "Anthony Kennedy Doesn't Tip His Hand in Gerrymandering Case." After all the buildup, on June 18, the Court found technical reasons in both cases to let the district lines stand, and partisan gerrymandering law remained the same.

Nine days later, Kennedy announced his retirement. President Trump nominated Brett Kavanaugh, a conservative judge on the U.S. Court of Appeals for the D.C. Circuit, to replace him. Kavanaugh, who had worked for the independent counsel investigating President Bill Clinton and for the Bush campaign in the 2000 Florida recount, was a favorite of movement conservatives. They expected that he would be a solid fifth vote for the Court's conservative bloc, rather than an unreliable, at times wavering one, as Kennedy had been. The confirmation battle over Kavanaugh was one of the most hard-fought in history, with Dr. Christine Blasey Ford, a psychology professor at Palo Alto University, testifying that Kavanaugh had attempted to rape her when they were teenagers, a charge the nominee vigorously denied. Despite the controversy, on October 6, the Senate approved Kavanaugh by a 50–48 vote. His confirmation fulfilled "a long-held dream of conservatives," *The New York Times* reported.

Within six months of Kavanaugh's arrival, the Court heard arguments in another partisan gerrymandering case. *Rucho v. Common Cause* was a challenge to congressional district maps in North Carolina and Maryland. North Carolina was roughly evenly divided between Democrats and Republicans, but the Republican-controlled legislature drew lines that led to Republicans winning about 77 percent of the state's congressional seats. In Maryland, Democrats redrew the lines of a Republican congressional seat, moving hundreds of thousands of voters into or out of the district, until it became a solid Democratic seat.

The arrival of Kavanaugh made all the difference: the conservatives finally had the five votes they needed to hold that partisan gerrymandering was nonjusticiable. Roberts, who wrote the Court's opinion in *Rucho,* declared that the case presented "political questions beyond the reach of the federal courts." The Court finally abandoned Kennedy's search for an appropriate standard to use in partisan gerrymandering challenges. "There are no legal standards discernible in the Constitution for making such judgments," Roberts said, "let alone limited and precise standards that are clear, manageable, and politically neutral."

Kagan, writing for the four liberals, delivered a blistering dissent, which she read from the bench. Kagan castigated the majority for deciding that the legal issues presented by partisan gerrymandering were beyond the Court's reach. "Of all times to abandon the Court's duty to declare the law, this was not the one," she wrote. "The practices challenged in these cases imperil our system of government." The Court had a duty, Kagan said, to defend the "foundations" of American government, and "none is more important than free and fair elections." Kagan said that she dissented with "deep sadness." Once again, the Court had reduced voting to what Guinier called "an existential gesture," in which "ordinary people" were limited to "the act of casting a ballot that may not count."

THE COURT HAS ALSO DEFERRED TO "GOVERNING ELITES" ON ANOTHER issue that is fundamental to the working of American democracy: voter ID laws. In 2008—after *Vieth v. Jubelirer* and before the Wisconsin and Maryland gerrymandering cases—it decided a challenge to Indiana's voter ID law. Indiana's Democratic Party and groups representing elderly, disabled, poor, and minority residents argued that the law, which was one of the strictest in the nation, violated the Equal Protection Clause. Once again, the "robust and engaged citizens" challenging the law could not find a majority on the Court to take their side.

Crawford v. Marion County Election Board came at a pivotal time: the run-up to the 2008 election, which would choose the successor to President George W. Bush. It was no secret that voter ID laws were a part of the Republicans' strategy for keeping their hold on the White House. The Republican voting base—older, whiter, wealthier, and less urban—was more likely to have driver's licenses and other government-issued ID than the Democratic base. One study found that 25 percent of black citizens of voting age lacked current government-issued photo ID, compared with 8 percent of white voting-age citizens. According to the same study, at least 15 percent of voting-age citizens who earned less than $35,000 a year lacked valid government-issued photo ID, more than twice the percentage of those earning more than $35,000.

National Republican strategists, including Karl Rove, had worked to put laws like Indiana's in place. They had help from the American Legislative Exchange Council, a business-supported group that lobbies state legislatures. Indiana's law, which was part of this national effort, was pushed through the Indiana General Assembly in 2005 by the Republican leadership without winning a single Democratic vote.

Advocates for voter ID laws argue that they are needed to prevent voter fraud. When they speak more honestly, however, they often admit that their actual purpose is to suppress voting among Democratic constituencies, particularly black voters. From time to time these statements, generally made behind closed doors, become public. One aide to a Republican state legislator in Wisconsin spoke about attending a Republican caucus meeting on a pending voter ID bill where "GOP Senators were giddy about the ramifications and literally singled out the prospects of suppressing minority and college voters."

The Crawford of *Crawford v. Marion County Election Board* was William Crawford, an Indiana House of Representatives member whose Indianapolis district was one of the poorest in the state. He heard often from his constituents that they did not have the ID they needed to vote. Until the new law was enacted, Indiana voters only had to sign their names at the polls. Afterward, they needed a valid photo ID issued by the federal or Indiana government—more than was required in many other states, which accepted a wider variety of ID, including employee ID, or did not require ID at all. The Indiana Legislature expected most voters to use a driver's license or a state-issued non-driver ID. To get either one, however, a prospective voter had to produce a birth certificate, a passport, or similar documents, which many did not have.

Fees for birth certificates, the document many Indianans would have to use, could be up to $20 or more, which made the law resemble a poll tax.

The challengers also showed that there was no need for the voter ID law. There was no evidence that in-person voter fraud occurred to a significant extent in Indiana or anywhere else in the country. Having people who are not eligible vote in person is an ineffective way to steal an election, far harder to pull off on a mass scale than other tactics, such as absentee ballot fraud. One study released after the Indiana case was decided, by professors at the University of Wisconsin and Stanford University, concluded that the proportion of people reporting voter impersonation in a presidential election was "indistinguishable from" the proportion reporting "abduction by extraterrestrials."

On April 28, 2008, the Court in *Crawford* upheld Indiana's voter ID law, by a 6–3 vote. It divided along ideological lines, with the conservatives in the majority and the liberals in dissent, with one exception. Stevens—a Ford nominee who had become a reliable part of the liberal bloc—gave the conservatives a sixth vote. Writing what amounted to the opinion of the Court, he said the law advanced Indiana's legitimate "interest in protecting the integrity and reliability of the electoral process." On the other side of the balance, he said, the challengers had not shown that the law "imposes 'excessively burdensome requirements' on any class of voters." Stevens left open the possibility that if the Court was presented with a stronger factual record at some point, it could come out the other way.

In dissent, Souter said there was "no reason to doubt" that many Indianans would be discouraged or prevented from voting. Against that harm, he said, the state's interests were minor. There was, he said, simply "no evidence of in-person voter impersonation fraud in" Indiana. The case, Souter maintained, was similar to the 1966 case in which the Court struck down the poll tax. In both circumstances, he said, the laws at issue wrongly made wealth a consideration in eligibility to vote.

It took little time for Stevens to be proven wrong in his belief that the law did not impose "'excessively burdensome requirements' on any class of voters." Just over a week after the ruling, on primary day, twelve nuns in their eighties and nineties, including one who was ninety-eight, were prevented from voting at the polling place at Saint Mary's Convent, in South Bend, because they did not have a federal or state photo ID. None of the nuns had driver's licenses, but some brought outdated passports. "Indiana's Voter ID law applies to everyone," Indiana's secretary of state said when the nuns were turned away. "From all accounts that we've heard, the sisters were aware of the photo ID requirements and chose not to follow them."

Critics of the *Crawford* decision predicted that it would encourage more states to adopt restrictions like Indiana's, and that is, in fact, what happened. Since 2008, voter ID laws have been adopted in Wisconsin, Texas, Pennsylvania, Missouri, Alabama, Mississippi, Arkansas, Iowa, Kansas, Rhode Island, South Carolina, Tennessee, Virginia, Idaho, North Carolina, West Virginia, Oklahoma, Utah, New Hampshire, and North Dakota. Some of the laws are stricter than others, but all make it more difficult to vote.

There is evidence that voter ID laws are doing their job, the one they were really enacted for: suppressing the vote from certain parts of the electorate. After the 2016 election, a study of two large Wisconsin counties estimated that the state voter ID law may have kept nearly 17,000 voters from the polls in those counties alone—in a state Donald Trump won by 22,748 votes. It also found that black registered voters were more than three times as likely as white registered voters to be deterred from voting by the law, and that registered voters earning less than $25,000 a year were almost eight times as likely to be deterred as registered voters making $100,000 or more. The Wisconsin study was part of a growing body of research showing that voter ID laws disproportionately disenfranchise racial minorities and the poor. These studies confirm what Souter said in his *Crawford* dissent: that Indiana's voter ID law "crosses a line" because it "targets the poor and the weak."

In 2016, Stevens, who was then retired, discussed the *Crawford* decision with Kagan on a panel at a judicial conference in Chicago. He said he had learned of many problems with voter ID outside of the record in the case, but he felt he had to limit himself to the facts that the parties had presented to the Court. The result, Stevens said, was "a fairly unfortunate decision." Judge Richard Posner, who had written the opinion for the Chicago-based U.S. Court of Appeals for the Seventh Circuit upholding the law before it got to the Supreme Court, was more direct. Posner, a prominent conservative nominated to the court by President Reagan, said a few years earlier that his court and the Supreme Court had gotten the case wrong. Indiana's voter ID law, Posner said, is "a type of law now widely regarded as a means of voter suppression rather than of fraud prevention."

IN 2013, THE COURT HAD ANOTHER CHANCE TO SIDE WITH "ROBUST AND engaged citizens" who wanted to vote, when it heard a challenge to a key part of the Voting Rights Act of 1965. The act, one of the most important civil rights laws in history, was adopted after Martin Luther King Jr. led a campaign across the South protesting the intimidation, rigged literacy tests, and other tactics being used to prevent blacks from registering and voting. Demonstrators marching from Selma to Montgomery to demand voting rights were violently attacked by Alabama state troopers on the Edmund Pettus Bridge on March 7, 1965, which came to be known as "Bloody Sunday." After the violence appeared on the network news, Congress passed the Voting Rights Act, and President Johnson signed it on August 6, with King and Rosa Parks, the heroine of the Montgomery Bus Boycott, looking on.

The Voting Rights Act allowed individuals to sue when state or local officials interfered with minority voting, but Congress understood how difficult it was to bring a lawsuit. They included a provision, Section 5, that was designed to avoid the need for litigation. It required states and localities to preclear possibly discriminatory changes in rules and procedures with the Justice Department or a federal court before they could take effect. Another provision, Section 4, set out which parts of the country would be subject to the preclearance requirement. It brought most of the South under the act, along with other jurisdictions outside of the South, based on a formula that took into account an area's history of erecting obstacles to voting and its past registration and voting rates.

Congress provided that the Voting Rights Act would expire and have to be reauthorized, to ensure that the burdens it placed on states and localities were not imposed needlessly. It extended the act every time it expired, and presidents of both parties signed the extensions. President Reagan signed an extension in 1982, declaring that "the right to vote is the crown jewel of American liberties, and we will not see its luster diminished."

When Congress reauthorized the Voting Rights Act in 2006, it knew the Court had become more hostile to voting rights. To strengthen the act for the next challenge, it created an extensive record to show why its protections were still needed. It held extensive hearings, which produced a more than fifteen-thousand-page record reviewing the ways in which minorities were still discriminated against in voting. The reauthorization passed the Senate 98–0 and the House 390–33, and George W. Bush signed it into law.

The case the Court heard in 2013, *Shelby County v. Holder*, challenged the Voting Rights Act's preclearance process. Shelby County, Alabama, which brought the case, focused on Section 4, arguing that its formula for determining which jurisdictions should be covered was unconstitutional. If the Court struck down the Section 4 formula, it would effectively end the whole preclearance requirement, because there would be no valid list of which jurisdictions were required to seek preclearance.

In *Shelby County*, the Court, by a 5–4 vote, struck down Section 4's coverage formula. Roberts, writing for the conservative justices, said that when Congress applied preclearance to some states and not others, it violated "the fundamental principle of equal sovereignty" among the states. That put a heavy burden on Congress to justify its decisions about which states to include, he said. Section 4 failed to meet this burden, according to Roberts, because it relied on "40-year-old data" on voting discrimination, from when the Voting Rights Act was first adopted, rather than information on current conditions.

Roberts couched his concerns in the language of equal treatment of the states, but he also made it clear that he did not believe discrimination in voting was still a very serious problem. There were, he noted, no more literacy tests or poll taxes. "Our country has changed," he said. "Congress must ensure that the legislation it passes to remedy that problem speaks to current conditions." He was not impressed or dissuaded by the fact that Congress had compiled a fifteen-thousand-page record of evidence to prove just this point.

Roberts conceded that declaring Section 4's formula unconstitutional was an extreme step. "Striking down an Act of Congress" was "'the gravest and most delicate duty that this Court is called on to perform,'" he said, quoting Justice Oliver Wendell Holmes. His concession, however, understated the enormity of what the Court was doing. It was not merely striking down any act of Congress. The Court was invalidating a law that was a crowning achievement of the civil rights movement, and one that had won overwhelming bipartisan support in Congress and from presidents for decades. The law also regulated a subject, voting in federal elections, that the Constitution specifically and repeatedly assigned to Congress. Article I of the Constitution states that Congress shall regulate the "times, places, and manner" of federal elections, and the Fifteenth Amendment, which bars racial discrimination in voting, says that Congress "shall have power to enforce this article by appropriate legislation." The senators who heard Roberts say at his confirmation hearing that he intended to be an "umpire" on the Court, simply calling "balls and strikes," could not have been expecting a ruling like this.

Making matters worse, the legal principle Roberts invoked to strike down Section 4 was a made-up one. This was not merely the view of the dissenters and the ruling's many liberal critics. Judge Richard Posner of the U.S. Court of Appeals for the Seventh Circuit, the same judge who came to regret his opinion on voter ID, stated flatly after *Shelby* was decided that "there is no doctrine of equal sovereignty." It was, he said, "a principle of constitutional law of which I had never heard—for the excellent reason that . . . there is no such principle." Posner, a Reagan nominee and a prominent conservative, insisted that the whole majority opinion in *Shelby County* "rests on air."

The other part of the Court's reasoning that lacked a basis in reality was its suggestion that preclearance was no longer needed because the nation had changed so much. Ginsburg, in a dissent for the four liberal justices, insisted that a major reason there was less discrimination in voting was precisely because of the preclearance requirement, which prevented it. "Throwing out preclearance when it has worked and is continuing to work to stop discriminatory changes," she wrote, in a memorable line, "is like throwing away your umbrella in a rainstorm because you are not getting wet."

In fact, there was still a great deal of racial discrimination in voting, and Ginsburg provided examples. In Kilmichael, Mississippi, the white mayor and the all-white board of aldermen canceled the 2001 town election when an "unprecedented number" of black candidates announced and it appeared that power in the town would shift from whites to blacks. The Department of Justice ordered Kilmichael to hold an election, and the town elected its first black mayor and a majority-black board of aldermen.

When the Court struck down Section 4's coverage formula, Section 5 was effectively nullified and preclearance ended. Congress could, in theory, enact a new Section 4, with a different formula for choosing covered jurisdictions, but it would be extremely difficult for members of Congress to agree on which parts of the country to include. Even if it did adopt a new formula, as long as it did not cover every jurisdiction in the country, it would be vulnerable to another challenge under the Court's invented doctrine of "equal sovereignty."

Supporters of voting rights were deeply disturbed by *Shelby County*'s brazenness. John Lewis, the Georgia congressman who had been beaten as a young man on the Edmund Pettus Bridge on Bloody Sunday, said that the Court had stuck "a dagger into the heart of the Voting Rights Act." President Obama said he was "deeply disappointed," noting that "for nearly 50 years, the Voting Rights Act—enacted and repeatedly renewed by wide bipartisan majorities in Congress—has helped secure the right to vote for millions of Americans." He promised that his administration would "continue to do everything in its power to ensure a fair and equal voting process."

Shelby County had an immediate impact, as jurisdictions across the country were emboldened to change their election procedures, freed from the requirement to get approval first. Five years after the decision, *The New York Times* noted the ways in which Alabama had made it harder to vote. Within twenty-four hours of the ruling, the state announced that it would start requiring photo ID, reviving a plan that had been blocked by the Voting Rights Act. Alabama then announced that it would close thirty-one driver's license offices, one of the main places where voters obtained ID that could be used to vote. There was a clear racial pattern: eight of the ten counties with the highest percentages of black voters lost offices, compared with just three of the ten counties with the lowest percentages.

At the national level, a Pew Charitable Trusts report found that, five years after *Shelby County*, nearly a thousand polling places had been closed, many of them in black communities in the South. In Indiana, the Republican secretary of state eliminated 170 voting precincts in Lake County, where the state's largest Latino and second-largest black communities were located. Reducing the number of polling places is an effective way of reducing voter turnout—and as a result of the Court's ruling, it is happening a lot more.

In 2018, the Court handed down another ruling on the mechanics of democracy, this one on voter roll purges, and once again it upheld the right of "governing elites" to make it more difficult for ordinary citizens to vote. Voter roll purges have been a sensitive subject since 2000, when Florida conducted an error-filled purge before the presidential election that may have made the difference in George W. Bush's victory. Republican elected officials hired a private firm to remove felons from the rolls and, owing to mistakes in how it was done, as many as twelve thousand voters who were wrongly labeled felons were taken off. In the end, Bush won Florida by just 537 votes. The U.S. Commission on Civil Rights, which investigated what went wrong with the voting in Florida in 2000, estimated that 4,752 black Gore voters were wrongly prevented from voting by the pre-election purge, and it concluded that the purge was "outcome-determinative."

The justification for voter roll purges is that they promote election efficiency and integrity by removing people who have moved, died, or become ineligible. In many purges, however, voters are removed even if they are still alive, still living at their address, and still eligible to vote. They have simply failed to meet bureaucratic eligibility requirements that "governing elites" have put in place—requirements that often disenfranchise "low-interest" voters, who choose not to vote in some elections.

In other cases, voters are removed by mistake. Voter roll purges are often conducted haphazardly, and they frequently end up, as in Florida in 2000, with voters being wrongly disenfranchised. In 2016, the Arkansas secretary of state notified county clerks of more than fifty thousand voters who were convicted felons and directed that they be removed from the rolls. It later turned out that four thousand of the people on the list did not actually have felony convictions, and as many as 60 percent of the others flagged for purging had actually had their voting rights restored.

As with voter ID laws, the strongest supporters of expansive voter roll purges are Republican elected officials and political operatives, who seem convinced that more Democrats than Republicans will be taken off the rolls. There is reason to believe they may be right, and that the purges may be removing more minority and poor voters. A national study by the Brennan Center for Justice found that people were removed from the rolls at much higher rates in counties with a history of voter discrimination. It also reported that between 2016 and 2018, at least seventeen million voters were removed.

The 2018 Supreme Court case was a challenge to Ohio's voter roll purges, which were among the most aggressive in the nation. In Ohio, voters who had not voted in two years—who had missed just one federal election—received mailed notices from the board of elections. If they did not respond and then did not vote in the next four years or have other interactions with the election system, such as signing a nominating petition, they were purged, even if they still met the legal requirements to vote.

Larry Harmon, the lead plaintiff, was a Navy veteran and software engineer living near Akron. When he went to vote in 2015, he was told that his name was no longer on the rolls. Harmon had voted in 2004 and 2008 but not in 2010, 2012, or 2014. Election officials said they sent a notice in 2011 asking him to confirm that he was eligible to vote, but Harmon said he did not recall receiving it.

The Cincinnati-based U.S. Court of Appeals for the Sixth Circuit ruled for Harmon, holding that the purge violated the National Voter Registration Act of 1993 (NVRA), a federal law that imposes conditions on how states register voters for federal elections. The NVRA has rules for purges, including a requirement that they not result in anyone being removed "by reason of the person's failure to vote." The Sixth Circuit said Ohio's purge of Harmon, which was triggered by his not voting in some elections, violated the NVRA's failure-to-vote clause.

On June 11, 2018, in *Husted v. A. Philip Randolph Institute,* the Supreme Court upheld Ohio's purge by a 5–4 vote. Alito, writing for the five conservative justices, said the NVRA's failure-to-vote provision prohibited a state from removing a voter from the rolls *solely* because of his or her failure to vote. It did not apply to the Ohio purge, he said, because failure to vote was only part of the process that led to his being removed.

In his dissent, Breyer agreed with the Sixth Circuit that the purge violated the NVRA's failure-to-vote provision because it was failing to vote that got Harmon removed. He went on, however, to make a larger point about how Ohio's purge undermined American democracy. The purpose of election processes, he said, was "not to test the fortitude and determination of the voter, but to discern the will of the majority." Sotomayor, in a solo dissent, tied Ohio's purge to larger "efforts to prevent minorities from voting and to undermine the efficacy of their votes," which, she said, were "an unfortunate feature of our country's history."

Husted was important in part because of Ohio's traditional role as a swing state with enormous influence in presidential elections. Its implications, however, went beyond any single state. Before the decision, Kristen Clarke, executive director of the Lawyers' Committee for Civil Rights Under Law, said she was "deeply concerned" that if Ohio won, "we will see states taking a copy-cat approach" and working to "gut the voter rolls across the country." In fact, those efforts were already under way. Even before the ruling came down, the Trump Justice Department had written to forty-four states asking questions about what they were doing to keep their voter rolls up to date. A head of the Justice Department Civil Rights Division under President Obama called the letter "virtually unprecedented" and warned that it was "a prelude to voter purging."

Months after *Husted*, purges became an issue in the Georgia governor's race, when it was revealed that the Republican candidate, Secretary of State Brian Kemp, had purged as many as 1.5 million voters between 2012 and 2016, and another 665,000 in 2017. More than 100,000 of the voters purged in 2017 were removed for not voting—the issue in *Husted*. Critics charged that Kemp had conducted the purges to increase his own chances of winning the gubernatorial election. He won the governor's race by about 55,000 votes. In her concession speech, his Democratic challenger, Stacey Abrams, charged that Kemp had used "deliberate and intentional" voter suppression to win.

Voter roll purge rates have been increasing. The seventeen million voters removed from the rolls between 2016 and 2018 represented a sharp increase from 2006 to 2008, when about twelve million voters were purged, according to the Brennan Center for Justice. Partisan organizations have been suing states and localities to conduct more purges. One suit by a conservative group demanded that Noxubee County, Mississippi, a poor, majority-black county, purge its rolls more aggressively. "They went after minority counties who didn't have the financial resources to push back," a Noxubee County election commissioner said.

With the Court's green light in *Husted*, aggressive voter roll purges are likely to become even more common, and more eligible voters will be removed. When the Brennan Center released a follow-up study after *Husted*, in the three states it focused on—Florida, Georgia, and North Carolina—it found "cause for alarm." In her *Husted* dissent, Sotomayor said that "communities that are disproportionately affected by unnecessarily harsh registration laws should not tolerate efforts to marginalize their influence in the political process." It was the right advice, but what was less clear was what those communities could do to stop it.

BUSH V. GORE DID USHER IN A NEW ERA FOR THE LAW OF DEMOCRACY, but it was not one of fairer elections, as its equal protection holding seemed to promise. Instead, the Court all but banished the equality principles of the 2000 ruling from its collective memory and it built further on its true holding: that governing elites should be allowed to make it more difficult for ordinary citizens to vote. It was the exact opposite of the Warren Court's approach to voting rights cases, which had always made voters' rights paramount.

The Court's election law decisions starting with *Bush v. Gore* and its campaign finance rulings starting with *Buckley v. Valeo* are a potent antidemocratic combination. The campaign finance decisions have expanded the rights of wealthy individuals and corporations to use their money to gain influence over government. The election law decisions on partisan gerrymandering, voter ID, the Voting Rights Act, and voter roll purges have diminished the ability of those with less money to use the one thing they have at their disposal to win influence over government: their votes.

The Court's election law rulings since 2000 have made a real difference in whose votes count and who is elected. With partisan gerrymandering, the outcomes of many elections are now virtually foreordained. In North Carolina, after the 2010 census, Republicans drew lines designed to elect Republicans from ten of the state's thirteen congressional districts. That is precisely what happened, even though the state's electorate was almost evenly divided between Democrats and Republicans. When voting does not matter, or hardly matters, the poor and the middle class, who do not have much to offer elected officials except their votes, have little leverage.

The Court's other significant rulings—on strict voter ID laws, the Voting Rights Act, and voter roll purges—have also weakened the influence of lower-income Americans. They have, as a group, helped to make the electorate wealthier and whiter. By shifting the demographics of voters in that way, the Court's rulings have created an electorate that is more likely to favor policies that help the well-off, like lowering the top income tax rate, and less likely to demand ones that help the poor and middle class, like increasing the earned income tax credit for low-income workers.

There is also an unmistakable partisan slant to the Court's major election law rulings since 2000: like *Bush v. Gore*, they have favored Republicans. In the case of partisan gerrymandering, while both parties engage in it, Republicans do it more. The Associated Press analyzed the 2018 election, when Democrats took a majority of the House of Representatives, and concluded that Democratic candidates would have won about sixteen more seats if the Republicans had not had a structural advantage resulting from how district lines were drawn. Not all of that structural advantage was due to partisan gerrymandering, but much of it was.

Strict voter ID laws also have a pro-Republican bias, since racial minorities and poor people—two core constituencies of the Democratic Party—are so much less likely to have acceptable ID. Republican political strategists certainly believe that strict voter ID laws will help their party, and that is why they have worked so hard to get them enacted. Weakening the Voting Rights Act makes it easier for election officials to suppress the votes of blacks and other minorities, which is also likely to help Republican candidates.

Making government more Republican hurts the economic standing of lower-income Americans. The Republican Party promotes a wide array of policies that harm the poor and the middle class, including opposing increases in the minimum wage, fighting labor unions, and resisting more generous social welfare programs. Larry Bartels, a political scientist at Vanderbilt University, studied how different economic classes fared under presidents of each major party. He found that since the late 1940s, the real incomes of middle-class families rose more than twice as fast under Democratic presidents as under Republicans, and the real incomes of working poor families rose ten times as fast under Democratic presidents. "Escalating inequality is *not* simply an inevitable economic trend," Bartels said. A lot of the economic inequality in the United States today, according to Bartels, "is specifically attributable to the policies and priorities of Republican presidents." There is every reason to believe Republican Congresses, governors, and state legislatures have similar effects.

The Court could have chosen a different kind of American democracy. In *Bush v. Gore,* it could have insisted that the primary constitutional value in elections is that all valid votes should be counted. In the cases that followed, it could have decided that partisan gerrymandering and strict voter ID laws violate equal protection, that aggressive voter roll purges violate the National Voter Registration Act, and that the entire Voting Rights Act is constitutional. It could have adhered to the Warren Court's guiding principle that, as Earl Warren himself said, what matters most in election law cases is ensuring that there is "fair representation in our governmental systems." Instead, the Court has taken an approach to election law that defers to the decisions of elites about which voters should be allowed to participate in democracy and whose votes should count. In doing so, it has created an electorate that is less inclined to support policies that help poor and working-class Americans—and a nation that is less likely to get them.

CHAPTER • 6

WORKERS

In November 2006, the Supreme Court heard oral arguments in Lilly Ledbetter's sex discrimination lawsuit against Goodyear Tire & Rubber. The Court had just experienced major changes: Rehnquist was replaced by Roberts in the fall of 2005, and in early 2006, O'Connor's seat was filled by Alito. The Court shifted to the right as a result, in a number of areas—and workers' rights was one of them. Alito, who was generally more conservative than O'Connor, had particularly strong views about employment law, and his arrival set the stage for a new era of anti-worker rulings—starting with the Court's decision in Ledbetter's case.

Ledbetter was one of the remarkable figures whose personal stories are often overlooked when they give their names and their legal claims to Supreme Court cases. She grew up dirt-poor in Possum Trot, Alabama, where she started picking cotton before she entered first grade. Ledbetter spent her early years without indoor plumbing. When her mother made it clear that she could not attend college, even though she was near the top of her class in high school and Jacksonville State University was just down the road, she married her high school sweetheart. After a few false starts to her career, Ledbetter came across an article in *BusinessWeek* about Goodyear Tire & Rubber, which mentioned that women were becoming part of its management team. Ledbetter, who was concerned about being able to afford to send her children to college while she was saving for her own retirement, decided to apply to Goodyear's Gadsden, Alabama, plant.

She soon discovered that the plant was loud and foul-smelling—her first time there, she said, she "felt like I'd stuck my head in a barrel of hot roofing tar." It was also, Ledbetter quickly realized, a very tough place for women. Over the years, men groped her, threatened her, and tampered with her car's brake cable. Men who were supposed to report to her said to her things like "I take orders from a bitch at home, and I'm not taking orders from a bitch at work." When the going got rough, she brought a knife to work, and eventually she bought a gun.

Ledbetter kept her cool through a lot of abuse, but toward the end of her career she encountered something that filled her with rage. Someone left an anonymous, handwritten note in her office mailbox with her salary written out by hand alongside the salaries of three male managers who had started the same year she did. Ledbetter never knew what other managers made, since Goodyear regarded salary information as confidential. In fact, when she started at Goodyear, a secretary had told her that if she wanted to succeed, she should do two things: contribute to the United Way every year and never discuss her paycheck. "The way she said it," Ledbetter recalled, "made me feel like I'd disappear into the night if I didn't do exactly what she said."

Now, however, Ledbetter found herself reeling as she read the anonymous note confirming her suspicion that she was not being paid as much as the male managers. When Ledbetter retired, after nineteen years, she was the only woman among sixteen area managers, and she had the lowest salary of all of them, including ones with less seniority. The male managers made between $4,286 and $5,236 a month, while she was paid just $3,727. "To see the real pay disparity there on paper and to see how cheap I was compared to my male coworkers made me realize that I must have been just a joke to Goodyear's human resources department," she later said. "It was clear that Goodyear didn't play fair, never had, and never would as far as I was concerned."

Ledbetter decided to fight. She filed a complaint with the Equal Employment Opportunity Commission (EEOC), charging that she had been underpaid on account of her sex, in violation of Title VII of the Civil Rights Act of 1964. The act said that victims of discrimination had to file a complaint within 180 days of an unlawful employment practice. Ledbetter showed that within 180 days of when she filed her complaint, her pay was less than that of men doing the same work. She presented evidence that her low pay was due to sex discrimination, not inadequacies in her performance. Ledbetter also introduced evidence of discrimination beyond unequal pay, including testifying that a manager told her that the "plant did not need women, that [women] didn't help it, [and] caused problems." When the case went to trial, a jury awarded her more than $3.5 million, though the trial judge reduced the award.

On May 29, 2007, in *Ledbetter v. Goodyear Tire & Rubber Co.*, the Court ruled against Ledbetter 5–4, dividing along the usual ideological lines. It held that she had filed her discrimination claim too late. Alito, writing for the Court, said that the 180-day window for filing began the first time Ledbetter was paid less than her male counterparts, which had been many years earlier. It did not matter, he said, that she had filed within 180 days of receiving a paycheck that was less than those of the male managers.

Ginsburg, the former women's rights litigator, dissented, and she felt so strongly that she took the unusual step of reading her dissent from the bench. The case, Ginsburg said, was not as complicated as the majority made it out to be. Ledbetter had presented all the necessary evidence to win under Title VII: she was in one of the law's protected classes, namely, women; she did substantially similar work to the men at her work site; she was paid less; and the disparity was due to discrimination. She also complained within 180 days of receiving paychecks from Goodyear that reflected its discrimination against her.

Ginsburg rejected Alito's contention that Ledbetter needed to file her complaint within 180 days of her first discriminatory paycheck. It was at odds with Congress's clear desire for Title VII to provide "robust protection" against discrimination, she said, and it ignored the "realities of the workplace." Workers know immediately if they are fired or not hired or demoted, Ginsburg observed, but not if they are being underpaid, because they generally have no way to learn what their colleagues earn. Ledbetter had no way to know until her anonymous note appeared.

Ginsburg ended her dissent by encouraging Congress to amend Title VII to undo the Court's decision. Since *Ledbetter* was based on an interpretation of a law Congress had written, it was free to rewrite the law to allow claims like Ledbetter's. Congress had already done that, she noted, to reverse other unduly narrow readings of Title VII. "Once again," she wrote, "the ball is in Congress' court."

The reaction to *Ledbetter* was overwhelmingly negative, which was not surprising. The case had an appealing plaintiff with a sympathetic story. She had worked hard and performed well and was underpaid by the Alabama factory bosses because she was a woman—and the Court had sided with the discriminators. Unlike many court decisions, this one was easy for non-lawyers to understand, and the injustice was obvious. As Ledbetter concisely described the unfairness of the ruling, "Goodyear was exonerated for its wrongdoing, simply because" it "had been doing me wrong long enough to make it legal." Hillary Clinton, who was beginning to campaign for president, said Ledbetter's story made her think about "all the women I know around the country, who are doing the very best they can, often with very little support or recognition."

Although the issue in *Ledbetter* seemed like a small technicality—it *was* a small technicality—it mattered a great deal, because timeliness is often a critical issue in employment discrimination lawsuits. Marcia Greenberger, a co-president of the National Women's Law Center, called *Ledbetter* "a very important setback" in the fight "to eliminate discriminatory pay." Judges would go on to invoke Alito's opinion in hundreds of cases under Title VII, the Age Discrimination in Employment Act, and other laws, and in many of them it would prove fatal to workers' claims.

Congress took up Ginsburg's invitation. Supporters of equal pay drafted a bill that made it clear that every new paycheck resulting from a discriminatory pay decision violates Title VII and resets the deadline for filing a complaint. The Lilly Ledbetter Fair Pay Act was the first law that President Obama signed, nine days after being sworn in. With Ledbetter looking on, he said he was signing it in honor of not only her, but his own grandmother, "who worked in a bank all her life, and even after she hit that glass ceiling, kept getting up again."

THE *LEDBETTER* RULING WAS ESPECIALLY DISAPPOINTING TO AMERICANS who remembered an earlier era when the Court was on the side of victims of employment discrimination. In the early 1960s, the civil rights movement's protests and sit-ins throughout the South created pressure for a sweeping civil rights law. President Kennedy pushed Congress to act, and after his assassination, President Johnson continued to twist arms. In July 1964, Congress responded with the Civil Rights Act of 1964, which barred discrimination in a wide array of areas, including public accommodations, voting, and employment, which was covered by Title VII of the act. It was not clear, however, how strong the new law's employment protections would be. Congress had used vague language in some critical parts, and it would be up to the courts to interpret them.

The Court's first major decision about what Title VII meant for racial discrimination in the workplace came in 1971. The NAACP Legal Defense Fund brought a lawsuit on behalf of thirteen black employees of a power plant in rural North Carolina that had an entrenched racial hierarchy, with blacks in the lowliest and worst-paid jobs. The workplace had Jim Crow–style racial segregation, down to separate drinking fountains and bathrooms for whites and blacks. The day the Civil Rights Act of 1964 took effect, making racial discrimination in the workplace illegal, Duke Power adopted two new employment tests—a high school graduation requirement and a standardized intelligence test—for the better entry-level jobs. Although they were formally race-neutral, they strongly favored whites in hiring and promotions.

The NAACP Legal Defense Fund filed the lawsuit during the Warren Court, when there was a strong liberal majority, but it arrived at the Court after Burger and Blackmun had replaced Warren and Fortas. When the case was argued, in December 1970, the Burger Court had already decided *Dandridge v. Williams,* with its sharp rebuke to the poverty law movement. Many legal experts expected that the newly emerging conservative majority would use *Griggs v. Duke Power Co.* to push back against the rising tide of civil rights.

The *Griggs* case raised the question of what should count as employment discrimination. The Civil Rights Act of 1964 did not contain a precise definition, and there were many views, in Congress and throughout the nation. Intentionally treating people worse in hiring, promotion, and other aspects of work because of race, sex, or other protected characteristics was clearly discrimination, but the civil rights lawyers who brought *Griggs* thought the scope should be wider. They argued that even if an employer did not directly discriminate, if it adopted selection criteria that disadvantaged a protected group, and the criteria were not related to the job, it should be held to be a violation of Title VII. These lawyers wanted the Court to hold that tests like the ones Duke Power adopted, which had the practical effect of excluding racial minorities, could be regarded as illegal discrimination.

The Court ruled for the *Griggs* plaintiffs unanimously, declaring that Title VII barred "not only overt discrimination, but also practices that are fair in form, but discriminatory in operation." Duke Power had decided it was going to ignore the civil rights movement and the laws Congress had passed in response to it and use purportedly nonracial tests to continue its traditional southern racial hierarchy. The ruling was a clear message from the Court that Jim Crow was over.

The Court in *Griggs* adopted a "disparate impact" test for discrimination. Under disparate impact, the question was not whether Duke Power had acted intentionally to disadvantage black employees. If the criteria the company adopted—the diploma requirement and the intelligence tests—had an unequal impact on black workers and job applicants, the employer had to show that there was a "business necessity" for them. "If an employment practice which operates to exclude Negroes cannot be shown to be related to job performance, the practice is prohibited," Burger wrote.

Griggs made disparate impact the new test of employment discrimination. By shifting the focus from intention to discriminate to having policies with the effect of discriminating, the disparate impact test made it considerably easier for workers to win discrimination lawsuits. It also forced employers to give serious consideration to whether their policies were harming racial minorities in ways that could lead to being sued. *Griggs* was quickly recognized as one of the Court's most important civil rights rulings, not far below *Brown v. Board of Education* in impact.

The decision set off "the *Griggs* revolution," which changed the racial composition of workplaces nationwide. It encouraged racial minorities to challenge a wide array of hiring qualifications and employee practices. After *Griggs*, employers began to self-police, removing hiring and promotion criteria that were not clearly work-related and undertaking voluntary measures to make their workforces more diverse. *The New York Times* called *Griggs* "a powerful engine of demographic change in the workplace."

There was opposition to *Griggs* from the day it was decided. Many critics argued that it made discrimination lawsuits too easy to bring, and that it could lead employers to abandon selection criteria that were legitimately job-related. They also warned that employers would adopt racial quotas so they did not have to worry about being sued. Even as the Court became more conservative, however, it stood by *Griggs* for years.

In 1986, in the final months of the Burger era, the Court handed down another important employment discrimination ruling in favor of workers. In *Meritor Savings Bank v. Vinson*, the Court considered the case of a young bank employee who said she had been coerced by her supervisor into having sex repeatedly over several years, which she said she went along with out of fear of losing her job. She also said that the supervisor groped her, exposed himself to her, and raped her. The Court ruled unanimously that sexual harassment by a supervisor could violate Title VII. If sexual harassment is "sufficiently severe or pervasive" to create "a hostile or abusive work environment," it said, the employer could be held liable. With its holding, the Court gave women a significant new tool to use in combating on-the-job harassment, and helped to launch the field of sexual harassment law.

In 1989, the Rehnquist Court changed direction on employment law in a dramatic way: it abandoned the *Griggs* test. The case in which it did involved two salmon canneries in Alaska that had racial hierarchies much like the ones at Duke Power. There were two job categories: skilled "noncannery" jobs and unskilled "cannery" jobs. The worst jobs were filled almost entirely by Alaska Natives and Filipinos, while the better jobs were held mainly by whites. Nonwhite employees sued, charging that the segregated workplaces violated Title VII. They pointed to practices that they said reinforced the plants' racial divisions, including different hiring tracks for the two kinds of jobs and a policy of not promoting from within.

On June 5, 1989, in *Wards Cove Packing Co. v. Atonio,* the Court ruled, 5–4, that the plaintiffs had not proved their case. While the facts were not so different from those in *Griggs,* the Court had changed. In addition to considerable turnover among the justices since 1970, it now had a different outlook toward employment discrimination. It no longer saw racial disparities in a workforce as evidence that an employer was resisting the civil rights movement, which was by now far in the past.

White wrote the majority opinion for himself and the conservative justices: Rehnquist, O'Connor, Scalia, and Kennedy. White's opinion changed *Griggs*'s rule that, once employees had shown that a policy had a disparate racial impact, the employer had to show that there was a "business necessity" for it. Now, the Court said, employees had to prove both that the practices they were challenging had a disparate racial impact and that they were not necessary for the job. It was difficult—and, given the expert testimony required, costly—for workers to prove that a challenged practice was not necessary for the job.

The dissenting justices accused the majority of turning away from years of employment discrimination law. Blackman said that Alaska's salmon industry resembled a "plantation economy," with the kind of racial separation the Court had decried in *Griggs*. The Court's new test, he said, "essentially immunize[d] these practices from attack" by a disparate-impact claim. "One wonders," he concluded, "whether the majority still believes that race discrimination—or more accurately, race discrimination against nonwhites—is a problem in our society, or even remembers that it ever was."

Wards Cove was one of several rulings, all decided the same month, that made it harder for employees to sue for discrimination. In another case, the Court narrowed a different civil rights law, Section 1981 of the Civil Rights Act of 1866, holding that it applied only to discrimination in hiring, not discrimination on the job. In a third case, brought by white firefighters in Birmingham, Alabama, the Court made it easier for white workers to reopen affirmative action settlements.

Taken together, these decisions marked a new era for employment discrimination law. In a news story, *The New York Times* said the rulings showed that Reagan, who had left office five months earlier, had "finally succeeded in a goal that had appeared to elude him for much of his eight years in the White House: to shift the Supreme Court's direction on civil rights." The paper noted that the *Wards Cove* majority was composed of three justices Reagan had appointed—O'Connor, Scalia, and Kennedy—and a chief justice he had elevated, Rehnquist, joined by White, who had drifted far to the right on civil rights since his days in the Kennedy Justice Department.

Civil rights supporters called on Congress to enact legislation reversing *Wards Cove* and the other rulings, and it did. On November 21, 1991, President George H. W. Bush signed the Civil Rights Act of 1991. The law, among other things, restored the *Griggs* test for disparate impact. It was an indication of how far the Court had shifted on employment discrimination that the act passed the House of Representatives 381–38, with most Republicans voting in favor, and the Senate 93–5. The Court, which had once been in the vanguard on civil rights, was now substantially more hostile to employment discrimination claims than were Congress and a Republican president.

The 1991 law was a rebuke to the Court, one that may have slowed its turn against workers suing for discrimination. In the years that followed, as one commentator noted, the "Court moved cautiously and plaintiffs fared much better." The cease-fire was not permanent, however, and eventually a new wave of rulings came—helped along by Alito taking O'Connor's seat in 2006. One of the most prominent of these new rulings was *Ledbetter*, in 2007, which was followed, once again, by a rebuke from Congress, in the form of the Lilly Ledbetter Fair Pay Act of 2009.

The Court, however, continued on its anti-worker path, with a trio of cases putting up obstacles to employment discrimination lawsuits. In June 2009, less than six months after President Obama signed the Ledbetter Act, it handed down a ruling making it more difficult for older Americans to sue for age discrimination. The plaintiff in the case, Jack Gross, had grown up in farm country, in one of Iowa's poorest counties. He developed chronic ulcerated colitis at age five and spent his childhood in chronic pain. Gross worked throughout high school, doing farm chores, delivering newspapers, and moonlighting as a janitor. He married his high school sweetheart after his first year in college.

When Gross graduated, he had two young children to support. He became an adjuster for Farm Bureau Life Insurance (FBL) and eventually rose to claims administration vice president. He was given demanding assignments, at which he excelled, as reflected in his annual reviews, which were in the top 3 percent of the company for thirteen consecutive years. In 2003, Gross, who was fifty-four, was replaced by a younger woman he had supervised who did not have the skills he had. He was one of a dozen employees demoted on the same day, all workers over the age of fifty. "It just jumped off the page," he said later. "Everybody that they're naming here is my age or older. Nobody under 50 was getting demoted. The only promotions were people who were basically a generation younger than us." Gross learned that the demotions had occurred when his employer merged with another company, and the merged company, it appeared, was intent on removing employees over the age of fifty. "They claimed that this was not discrimination," Gross said, "but simply a reorganization."

Gross sued under the Age Discrimination in Employment Act of 1967 (ADEA). A jury ruled that he had been a victim of age discrimination and it awarded him $46,945 in lost compensation. The trial judge found that the jury had ample evidence to support its verdict. The St. Louis–based U.S. Court of Appeals for the Eighth Circuit overturned the jury verdict, and Gross took the case to the Supreme Court.

The Court ruled, by a 5–4 vote along ideological lines, that Gross had not proven his case. The majority, in an opinion by Thomas, said that age discrimination victims had to show that age was not only *one* of the factors in what was done to them, but the *crucial* factor. It was a surprising decision, because the Court had previously held that workers suing for discrimination under Title VII for race and sex discrimination only had to prove that the discrimination was *one* of the factors—and the language of the ADEA and Title VII was the same. One barred negative employment actions "because of" age, the other "because of" race or sex.

The liberal dissenters, in an opinion by Stevens, insisted that the "most natural" way to read "because of age" was to mean that age was *a* factor in the decision. They strongly objected to the majority interpreting the ADEA's "because of" language in a more anti-worker way than Title VII's "because of" language. The Court had engaged in "an unabashed display of judicial lawmaking," Stevens said, to get the result it wanted.

Gross agreed. "I feel like my case has been hijacked by the high court for the sole purpose of rewriting both the letter and spirit of the ADEA," he said.

After his defeat, Gross tried to persuade Congress to overrule the Court, as it had with the Civil Rights Act of 1991 and the Lilly Ledbetter Fair Pay Act. Iowa's senators introduced a bill to reverse *Gross* in 2012, and Gross testified in favor of changing the law. He tried to give the Senate Judiciary Committee a sense of the toll that age discrimination was having on people he knew. "Many of my friends are also farm or small town 'kids' who now feel like they are the forgotten minority," Gross said. "Many of them have been forcibly retired or laid off." Some of his friends, he said, "have been aggressively looking for work for months, only to find doors closed when they reveal the year they graduated." He had other friends, he said, who "accepted janitor jobs in spite of successful careers and college educations." Gross said his friends "all know that age discrimination is very real and pervasive."

Gross told the Senate that he knew he had been "set aside" in the labor market. "What you do here, how you change the law may or may not help me," he said, "but I know for sure you are in the position to help those who come after me." Since *Gross v. FBL Financial Services, Inc.*, hundreds of plaintiffs had abandoned their lawsuits because they would have difficulty succeeding under the new standard. "Personally, that's one of the things that I resent most," Gross said. "That my name is being associated with so much injustice and unfairness." Congress has still not enacted a law to reverse the *Gross* decision.

In 2011, the Court delivered another major setback to workers alleging discrimination, this time by limiting their ability to bring large class action lawsuits. The plaintiffs sued Wal-Mart for sex discrimination on behalf of a class of 1.5 million current or former female employees. The plaintiffs had a good reason for suing as a large class: it would have been difficult for individual plaintiffs or even a small class to take on the enormous work and expense of bringing a lawsuit charging systemic discrimination against a corporation of Wal-Mart's size. They could also see that Wal-Mart's treatment of all of them was similar in many important ways.

The six lead plaintiffs told of being frustrated in their attempts to rise into management and to be treated with dignity. Betty Dukes, a greeter at a Wal-Mart near San Francisco, started out earning $5.50 an hour and, despite years of wanting to move into management, could not. Kimberly Miller worked for about eight years at an Ocala, Florida, Sam's Club, which was owned by Wal-Mart. Although she received strong evaluations and recommendations, she could not get promoted into management, either. Christine Kwapnoski had a similar experience at a Wal-Mart in Missouri. "I observed co-workers, mostly male, suddenly being moved into positions as soon as the positions were opened and before I had an opportunity to express interest," she said. Kwapnoski transferred to a Sam's Club in Concord, California, but still could not rise into management. "When I was working as the freezer/cooler associate, I was passed over four times for the promotion to team lead, an hourly supervisor position," she said. Every time, a man got the position. Kwapnoski was finally promoted two weeks after the discrimination suit was filed, but her pay decreased because she was no longer eligible for overtime.

The Court, by the usual 5–4 vote, held that the case could not proceed as a class action. Scalia's majority opinion said that in order to be part of the same class, all the women had to show not only that they had been discriminated against by Wal-Mart but that they had suffered the "same injury." The Court made it clear that it would interpret that standard narrowly, limiting it to cases in which employees had the "same supervisor" or some other close similarity in their experiences.

Ginsburg, writing for the liberal dissenters, said the Court's ruling rejecting the class was too sweeping. There was clear evidence that "gender bias suffused Wal-Mart's company culture," she said. There was statistical evidence, like the fact that women were 70 percent of Wal-Mart's hourly employees but only 33 percent of its managers. There was also anecdotal evidence, including the fact that senior managers often referred to female associates as "little Janie Q's." The dissenters would have allowed the plaintiffs to try to use a different part of the class action rules to support their very large class.

Two years later, the Court handed down yet another anti-worker decision, this time making it more difficult to sue for on-the-job harassment. The plaintiff in the case, Maetta Vance, was a black woman who said she had been racially harassed while working at Ball State University, in Muncie, Indiana. Vance, a catering assistant, was the only black employee in the catering department, and she said she was tormented by a white female catering specialist who had authority to direct her work. The catering specialist allegedly slapped Vance, who reported it at the time. Vance said the woman subjected her to a stream of racial harassment and used the words "Buckwheat" and "Sambo." Vance also said that the woman at one point asked her, in a southern accent, "Are you scared?" and stood by laughing while her husband and daughter used racial slurs against Vance and physically threatened her. Vance also complained about another colleague who boasted of her family in the Ku Klux Klan.

Vance sued Ball State University under Title VII, charging that she had been subjected to unlawful racial harassment and that the university was legally responsible. Under the Court's Title VII rulings, it was far easier for workers to prevail in a harassment lawsuit against their employer if they could show that the harasser was a supervisor and not a co-worker. In her lawsuit, Vance asserted that the catering specialist was a supervisor, since she had the authority to oversee Vance's work on a daily basis, including regularly giving her assignments.

The Court ruled against Vance, by a 5–4 vote. Alito wrote for the five conservative justices again, as he had in Lilly Ledbetter's case. He insisted that the catering specialist did not qualify as a "supervisor" under Title VII. Alito adopted a narrow interpretation of which managers were supervisors, counting only ones who could make major decisions about a worker's job, such as firing or demoting them. Controlling a subordinate's daily schedule and assignments, he said, was not enough.

Ginsburg, writing for the liberal dissenters, said that the Court had relieved employers of responsibility for the bad acts of many of their supervisors. She insisted that the majority's rigid interpretation of who was a supervisor did not reflect the reality of the nation's workplaces. Ginsburg saw the ruling as part of a larger trend. The Court was proceeding, she said, "on an immoderate and unrestrained course" of weakening Title VII. It was a striking thing to say about a Court that had once used Title VII, one of the great capstones of the civil rights movement, to lead the nation in the opposite direction: toward greater fairness for all workers.

WHILE THE COURT HAS MADE IT HARDER FOR AMERICAN WORKERS TO fight for fair treatment through employment discrimination lawsuits, it has also undermined their ability to act collectively to protect their rights through labor unions. Unions have a long and often contentious history in the United States. They emerged in the nineteenth century in response to the nation's increasing industrialization. In its early years, the labor movement faced concerted, often violent opposition, including incidents like the Ludlow Massacre in Colorado in 1914, in which more than twenty striking coal miners and their family members died. Much of this early suppression of unions and violence against union organizers was done in coordination with local law enforcement and with the active support of the government.

The status of organized labor changed considerably during the Great Depression, when, for the first time, the nation threw its support behind unions. In 1935, Congress adopted the National Labor Relations Act (NLRA), which recognized the right to organize and engage in collective bargaining, and it created the National Labor Relations Board to protect those rights. The NLRA, which is often called the Magna Carta of American labor, proceeded from an assumption that unions were good not only for workers but for the nation as a whole. A new model of the workplace emerged, in which management and labor were expected to negotiate in good faith and arrive at contracts that met the needs of both the company and its workers. In the protective environment created by the NLRA, union membership grew rapidly.

After World War II, as the political climate turned more conservative, corporate America persuaded Congress to enact the Taft-Hartley Act of 1947, which tilted the law more toward management in a variety of ways, including banning certain kinds of strikes and picketing. With the legal climate worsening and the nation's economy evolving, union membership declined, and it has continued to decline ever since. In 1949, nearly 35 percent of private-sector workers belonged to a union, while today only a little more than 6 percent do. The United States has fallen well below other industrial democracies, including Germany, Sweden, Canada, and France, in the percentage of its workforce that is unionized. As one commenter said of the international numbers, "lackluster union presence is largely an American phenomenon."

Many forces have driven down union membership, including ones that have little to do with the law. The labor market has changed in recent decades, with employment declining in sectors that have traditionally had high rates of unionization, such as manufacturing, and rising in ones with lower unionization rates, such as health care.

Anti-union government policies have also played a large role. Some of the main ones were adopted long ago, such as Taft-Hartley, which, in addition to its limits on union activities, authorized states to enact "right to work" laws, which prohibit unions from negotiating contracts that require workers to join a union or pay union fees to hold a job. Other anti-union policies are more recent. A major turning point came in 1981, when President Reagan fired eleven thousand striking members of the Professional Air Traffic Controllers Organization. The firings killed off PATCO, and Reagan's hardline response has been credited with drastically reducing the number of strikes in both the public and private sectors.

The Court has also played a significant role. Just a few years after the adoption of the NLRA, in 1938, it delivered a tough blow to unions that severely limited their power to protect workers. In a case involving the Mackay Radio & Telegraph Company, the Court held that when workers go on strike, employers are free to fill their positions with permanent replacements. The "Mackay doctrine" greatly diminished the effectiveness of strikes by making workers afraid to participate in them. The Mackay decision was a "judicial de-radicalization" of the NLRA, critics say, and elevated "entrenched property rights" over "workers' rights."

The Court that adopted the Mackay doctrine seems to have been driven by a pro-business, free-market ideology, not by a fair reading of the NLRA. It was a Court that had just struck down several major New Deal programs and that had been pushing back against the federal social safety net Roosevelt was working to create. Congress had put language in the NLRA that expressly prohibited employers from discharging or otherwise discriminating against workers who engaged in concerted activities—and filling a worker's job permanently for striking, leaving them unemployed, would seem to be just that.

By inventing the Mackay doctrine, the Court neutralized the threat of strikes, which should have been one of the most powerful tools of organized labor. To call a strike after the Mackay ruling, unions had to try to persuade their members to put their jobs at risk, something the NLRA specifically said should not happen. The Mackay doctrine has, according to New York University law professor Cynthia Estlund, "rendered the strike useless and virtually suicidal for many employees, and has become employers' Exhibit Number One in union organizing campaigns."

After decades of rulings hostile to organized labor, the Warren Court began to shift the law back toward unions, promoting, as the *Industrial Relations Law Journal* said, "strong unionism and vigorous support of the principle of collective bargaining." In one of the most important decisions of the era, involving a union drive at a factory in Holyoke, Massachusetts, the Court held that an employer could not threaten its workers with losing their jobs if they joined the union. Almost as powerful as its rulings on the law was the message the Warren Court sent about the value of organized labor. In a case pitting a union against a Wisconsin manufacturing plant, Brennan said that the nation's labor policy was built on the conviction that "by pooling their economic strength and acting through a labor organization freely chosen by the majority," workers "have the most effective means of bargaining for improvements in wages, hours, and working conditions."

With the end of the Warren era, the Court reverted to its historic hostility to unions. One of the modern Court's most damaging rulings came in 1992, in a case about union organizers who wanted access to a workplace to speak to employees. Lechmere, a retail store located in a shopping plaza, threatened to arrest the organizers for trespassing if they placed union literature on employees' cars in the shopping mall's parking lot. The union said that because the workers scattered after their shifts, without leafleting in the parking lot it would be unable to reach 80 percent of the workers who would be voting in the union recognition election. The Court held, in an opinion by Clarence Thomas, that Lechmere could keep the union out of the parking lot.

It was not surprising that one of the leading anti-union decisions of recent decades would be written by Thomas, who had joined the Court just months earlier but was already acquiring a reputation as the most conservative justice. When President Bush nominated Thomas to replace Thurgood Marshall, the confirmation battle was an incendiary one. Anita Hill, who had worked for Thomas when he was the head of the EEOC, accused him of sexual harassment. Thomas denied the charge and called his treatment "a high-tech lynching for uppity blacks who in any way deign to think for themselves." He was confirmed by the Senate on a 52–48 vote, the closest margin for a nominee to the Court in more than a century.

Thomas had grown up in extreme poverty in Pin Point, Georgia, during the era of Jim Crow racial segregation. Unlike Marshall, whose exposure to racism and poverty made him a champion of the disadvantaged, Thomas had little sympathy for society's downtrodden. When he was head of the EEOC, Thomas shifted the agency away from large lawsuits and toward small ones with individual victims. One critic accused him of transforming the EEOC "into a claims adjustment bureau." Thomas served briefly on the U.S. Court of Appeals for the D.C. Circuit before President George H. W. Bush nominated him to the Court.

Thomas was strikingly unsympathetic to victims of discrimination and adversity. His harsh attitude extended to his own sister, Emma Mae Martin, a single mother who had been deserted by her husband. She worked two minimum-wage jobs to support her family while her aunt cared for her children, and when the aunt suffered a stroke, Martin quit work and went on welfare so she could care for her aunt. In speaking to a group of conservatives, Thomas said of his sister, who later went back to work as a cook in the local hospital, "she gets mad when the mailman is late with her welfare check."

Some of Thomas's confidants have argued that his views became even more conservative as a result of the ordeal liberals put him through at his confirmation hearings. "I'm gonna live long enough; I'm gonna stay on the Court long enough; and I'm gonna write the decisions that will get them," one of them said. "I don't think that's his conscious thinking, but that's his way of getting revenge." The confidant added that Thomas was "very angry" and that "it shouldn't affect his thinking on the Court, but it does." If Thomas's jurisprudence was a reaction to the liberals who supported Anita Hill and opposed his confirmation, he would have had particular reason to hold a grudge against labor unions in cases like *Lechmere, Inc. v NLRB*. Organized labor came out strongly against Thomas, with the AFL-CIO calling his nomination "disgraceful" and part of an attempt to "make the Court the preserve of the far right wing."

In a wide range of cases, Thomas has voted against the weak—including racial minorities, the poor, and prisoners—often in ways that provoke outrage from liberals. A month after the *Lechmere* decision, Thomas wrote a particularly mean-spirited dissent in a case in which a Louisiana prison inmate sued after being beaten by prison guards while he was shackled, leaving him with bruises, facial swelling, loosened teeth, and a cracked dental plate. In an editorial, *The New York Times* called Thomas's dissent, which argued that the prisoner had no constitutional claim, "alarming" and declared Thomas to be the "youngest, cruelest justice."

The *Lechmere* case gave Thomas an opportunity to side with a large corporation against a scrappy group of union organizers who hoped to improve conditions in retailing, a particularly low-wage industry. In his majority opinion, Thomas said that unions had a right to access an employer's premises only when they could show they had no other reasonable means of communicating their organizing message to the employees. If they could not reach the workers in person, he said, they could always try mailings and phone calls.

Many labor law experts insisted that Thomas's opinion misread the NLRA, ignoring Congress's intent that the act be read broadly to promote the right of unions to organize. They also said that, as a practical matter, the decision was a major setback for the labor movement. A critic writing in *The American Prospect* said that by cutting off access to unorganized workers so thoroughly, the Court had made it "almost impossible for organized labor to expand into new areas or even to retain its strongholds."

The Congress that enacted the NLRA and President Roosevelt, who signed it, wanted to create a legal climate in which labor unions would thrive. The Court, with the brief exception of the Warren years, has not interpreted it that way. In 2015, Julius Getman, an emeritus professor of labor law at the University of Texas, wrote a scholarly article looking back at the Court's rulings under the NLRA going back to the 1930s. Getman argued that, by adopting the Mackay doctrine and issuing rulings like *Lechmere,* the Court had imposed its own anti-union values on the act. It had gone so far in an anti-union direction, he said, that some supporters of unions even believed it would be better to repeal the NLRA entirely and start over. Getman urged reform rather than repeal, and put forth practical solutions, including trying to persuade Congress to adopt a law overturning the Mackay doctrine. He was, however, more weary than optimistic. "There is a great need for change," he concluded, "but little hope in the present climate that sensible voices will prevail."

THE COURT RECENTLY TOOK ITS ANTI-UNION RULINGS TO A NEW LEVEL. It used a new interpretation of the First Amendment to deliver a serious blow to public-sector unions, the unions that represent government workers. The decision was an extreme example of conservative judicial activism: the Court twisted a constitutional provision, and reversed years of settled precedents, to overturn decisions of the elected branches of government. In doing so, it seriously imperiled the finances of the largest and fastest-growing part of the labor movement.

The story of the Court and public-sector unions goes back to 1977, when the Burger Court decided *Abood v. Detroit Board of Education*. D. Louis Abood, a Detroit schoolteacher, and some colleagues challenged a Michigan law that allowed unions and local governments to agree to an "agency shop" contract. In an agency shop, all employees have to either join the union or pay an "agency fee" in lieu of dues to cover the costs of their representation. Abood and the other teachers who sued said the union was using their fees for political, economic, and religious purposes they did not agree with. For the government to force them to subsidize those activities, they said, violated their First Amendment rights.

The Court understood why Abood was objecting, but it also saw that there was a need for agency fees, which are also called "fair share fees." Unions negotiate wages, benefits, and health and safety rules for all workers in a bargaining unit, whether they are members of the union or not. If workers could receive the benefits of union representation without having to pay dues or agency fees, many would save their money by getting benefits without paying for them. If enough workers decided not to pay, it could bankrupt the union.

The *Abood* Court, in a unanimous ruling, struck a compromise. It acknowledged that teachers had a right not to pay for political activities they did not agree with. At the same time, it recognized that if workers did not have to pay a fee of any kind, they could become "free riders" who refused "to contribute to the union while obtaining benefits of union representation." Addressing both concerns, the Court held that non-union members could be required to pay an agency fee to the union, but the fee could represent only the cost of collective bargaining and other core union activities. After *Abood*, unions calculated agency fees as the Court directed and sent nonmembers notices of how much to pay. Since *Abood* was a unanimous decision, the question of union fees seemed to be settled.

Anti-union activists, however, did not give up on their hope of ending public-sector agency fees entirely. One reason for their interest was that public-sector unions were growing and becoming a larger part of the overall labor movement. In 1969, nearly 84 percent of union members worked for private employers, while only about 16 percent worked for the government. By 2017, public-sector unions had surpassed private-sector unions, representing more than 51 percent of the nation's unionized workforce.

In 2011, states with Republican governors and legislatures began a push to scale back the rights of unions. Wisconsin enacted a law backed by newly elected governor Scott Walker that sharply limited the ability of unions representing government workers to engage in collective bargaining. In early 2012, Indiana adopted a "right to work" law, the first state to do so in a decade. In a news story headlined "Strained States Turning to Laws to Curb Labor Unions," the head of the American Federation of State, County and Municipal Employees was quoted as saying he believed that the state-level attacks on public-sector unions were "payback" from Republicans for the unions' support of Democrats in the 2010 elections. "Now there's a bull's-eye on our back," he said.

While Republican elected officials were declaring war on public-sector unions, Alito, who had written the opinions rejecting the claims of Lilly Ledbetter and Maetta Vance, launched a similar war at the Court. In a 2012 case about how agency fees should be calculated, he dropped a strong hint that the Court might be willing to overturn the careful compromise it had worked out decades earlier in *Abood* and perhaps hold that imposing any agency fee at all violated the First Amendment. With the arrival of Roberts and Alito, in 2005 and 2006, the conservative majority was more pro-business than it had been in decades. All five of the conservative justices signed Alito's opinion suggesting that public-sector union dues were back in play.

The Court's statement was an invitation to the same forces that were fighting labor unions in state legislatures around the country to bring the battle to the Court—and many were waiting for the chance. Since the 1980s, a large, well-funded conservative legal movement had been forming to promote corporate America's interests, just as Powell had called for in the Powell Memorandum. Some organizations in the movement had a focus on unions, including the National Right to Work Legal Defense Foundation, the Center for Individual Rights, and the Liberty Justice Center. They received substantial funding from billionaires like the Koch brothers, either directly or through intermediaries, and right-wing foundations. The Economic Policy Institute, which investigated the financing of anti-union legal groups, concluded that "challenging fair share fees in the courts appears to be part of a broader billionaire-financed agenda to weaken unions and shift power away from ordinary workers."

Two years later, the Court decided a case brought to it by one of these groups, the National Right to Work Legal Defense Foundation. In another opinion by Alito, writing for the five conservatives, the Court struck down agency fees that home health care workers in Illinois were being required to pay. It was another narrow ruling, but Alito again attacked *Abood* and strongly hinted that the Court might rule in a future case that all agency fees for public-sector unions violated the First Amendment. It appeared that Alito did not yet have the five votes he needed for such a bold ruling but that he intended to keep trying.

After two opinions threatening to wipe out agency fees for public-sector unions, it was clear that Alito was on a crusade. If the Court was waging an ideological war on unions, Alito—or, as one opinion journal called him, "the Court's leading union-hater, Justice Samuel A. Alito, Jr."—was the justice to do it. Alito was not as well known as Scalia and Thomas, the two most outspoken conservative justices, but he was no less of an ideological warrior. When President Bush was considering nominees in 2005, Alito was deeply popular with conservative activists. In his years on the Court, he had not disappointed them. On the most important issues to movement conservatives, including abortion and civil rights, Alito was distinctly to the right of O'Connor, whose seat he had filled. In a few years, an essay in *The Yale Law Journal* would pronounce Alito "the Court's most consistent conservative."

It did not take long for anti-union activists to bring the Court yet another case about public-sector union agency fees. In this one, the Center for Individual Rights represented a group of California teachers and other school employees challenging a state law that required them to pay agency fees. Many Court watchers thought this would be the case in which Alito finally assembled the five votes he needed to strike down agency fees. After it was argued, however, Scalia died, and when it was decided, in early 2016, the Court split, 4–4. Public-sector agency fees had survived yet again, but just barely.

On March 16, 2016, President Obama nominated Merrick Garland to fill Scalia's seat. If the Senate had confirmed Garland, there would have been a liberal majority on the Court for the first time since the rise of the Nixon Court, in 1972. A liberal majority would, among other things, almost certainly foil Alito's campaign to end mandatory agency fees for public-sector unions.

One of the reasons Obama settled on Garland was that he seemed highly confirmable. Garland was chief judge of the U.S. Court of Appeals for the D.C. Circuit, a court whose judges were often elevated to the Supreme Court. He was a liberal, but there were aspects of his career that would appeal to conservative and moderates, including his experience coordinating the Justice Department's response to the 1995 Oklahoma City bombing.

Conservative activists and their wealthy backers, however, were intent on blocking Garland's nomination to preserve the conservative majority. The Judicial Crisis Network, a secretive conservative legal organization, launched a well-funded television, radio, and digital advertising campaign focusing on states with senators who might be undecided. Much of the money spent to block Garland came from sources that could not be identified.

Senate majority leader Mitch McConnell went into full obstruction mode, declaring that there would be no hearings, no vote—in fact, no action at all—on Garland's nomination. McConnell insisted that it was a "long-standing tradition" not to fill Supreme Court vacancies in election years, but there was little basis for his claim. In the past century, there had been four nominations during presidential elections, and the Senate confirmed three of the nominees. The exception was Fortas's nomination for chief justice, but the Senate gave Fortas full consideration until President Johnson withdrew his name. PolitiFact, the Pulitzer Prize–winning fact-checking site, rated McConnell's statement that he was merely acting in accordance with tradition "false." In 2019, McConnell made it clear that he did not even believe in the "tradition" himself when he told a conservative audience that if a vacancy opened in 2020, the Senate would confirm President Trump's nominee.

Refusing to consider Garland was another instance of the Republicans playing hardball over control of the Court, in the tradition of Nixon nearly fifty years earlier. Driving Fortas off the Court had been a critical step in creating a conservative majority. Refusing to confirm Garland was now crucial in keeping it. When Trump defeated Hillary Clinton in November, with Scalia's seat still open, it was clear the conservative lock on the Court would continue.

Within two weeks of taking office, Trump nominated Neil Gorsuch, a judge on the Denver-based U.S. Court of Appeals for the Tenth Circuit. Gorsuch, a veteran of the George W. Bush Justice Department, was the son of Anne Gorsuch Burford, President Reagan's Environmental Protection Agency administrator, who did battle with environmentalists and resigned after Congress cited her for contempt for refusing to turn over documents. The Senate confirmed Gorsuch in April 2017, by a vote of 54–45. It would be Gorsuch, not Garland, who would break the Court's 4–4 deadlock on public-sector union agency fees.

There was every reason to believe that Gorsuch would share Alito's views on the subject. He was one of the most conservative federal appeals court judges on employment issues, among others. His best-known opinion, which had been a point of controversy at his confirmation hearings, was a harsh rejection of workers' rights. It concerned a truck driver whose brakes had frozen. The driver, Alphonse Maddin, stayed in the truck for hours in subzero temperatures waiting for a repair truck. When he grew numb, despite a supervisor telling him to remain, Maddin unhitched his truck from its trailer and drove to a service station. He was fired, and he sued under a law protecting drivers from being fired for refusing to operate unsafe vehicles. The majority ruled that Maddin was entitled to back pay, but Gorsuch dissented, insisting that he *had* operated the vehicle and therefore was not protected by the law. Maddin said that Gorsuch had adopted the company's dubious defense to try to get the world "to forget that a man was about to freeze to death."

After Gorsuch's arrival, the Court did not wait long to take yet another public-sector union agency fee case. In this one, the National Right to Work Legal Defense Foundation represented Mark Janus, a child support specialist in the Illinois Department of Healthcare and Family Services. Janus had chosen not to join the American Federation of State, County and Municipal Employees, and he did not want to pay its $44.58-a-month agency fee.

In 2018, the Court decided *Janus v. American Federation of State, County and Municipal Employees.* With Gorsuch's vote, Alito was finally able to reverse *Abood* and hold that mandatory agency fees for public-sector unions violate the First Amendment. Even requiring fees for a union's nonpolitical work, such as collective bargaining, he said, "violates the free speech rights of nonmembers by compelling them to subsidize private speech on matters of substantial public concern."

The main dissent was written by Kagan, who had a family connection to the labor movement. Kagan had grown up on Manhattan's liberal Upper West Side. Her father was a tenants' lawyer and community activist, and her mother taught for two decades at Hunter College Elementary School. One of her brothers, after graduating from Yale, took a job as a subway yard mechanic and became a leader in the Transport Workers Union Local 100. After attending Oxford and Harvard Law School, Kagan became the first woman dean of Harvard Law School. She also held important government positions, including as a domestic policy adviser to President Clinton and as the first female solicitor general, under President Obama. Kagan was a liberal with a strong pragmatic streak, who had an exceptional legal mind and a much-admired writing style.

Kagan took the unusual step of reading a summary of her *Janus* dissent from the bench. She framed the case as being about not only public-sector unions, but also the right of "the American people, acting through their state and local officials," to make "important choices about workplace governance." In a particularly sharp turn of phrase, Kagan called the justices in the majority "black-robed rulers overriding citizens' choices." They were "weaponizing the First Amendment," she said, "to intervene in economic and regulatory policy." The First Amendment, she insisted, "was meant for better things."

The *Janus* decision had an immediate impact on the more than twenty states that allowed unions to impose agency fees—the ones without "right to work" laws. In these states, 4.8 million workers were instantly given the right to not pay at all for the union representation they received. They were suddenly able to become "free riders," as the Court had put it in *Abood*. It was widely predicted that when workers were not required to pay dues or agency fees, many would opt out, leaving public-sector unions smaller, poorer, and less able to advocate for their members.

The unions themselves had reached similar conclusions. The American Federation of State, County and Municipal Employees surveyed 600,000 members and found that 35 percent would pay the fee no matter what, 15 percent would likely not pay dues, and the remaining 50 percent were on the fence. Even before *Janus* was decided, government unions began cutting their budgets in anticipation of losing members. The National Education Association, the largest teachers' union, estimated just before the decision came down that it could lose as many as 307,000 members over two years. When

Janus was decided, *The New York Times* declared that most public-sector unions in the affected states "are going to get smaller and poorer."

Anti-union groups announced plans to aggressively use *Janus* to drive down union membership. The State Policy Network, a nationwide alliance of conservative think tanks, prepared "State Workplace Freedom Toolkits" to help its affiliates exploit *Janus* to "deliver a mortal blow" to public-sector unions. The Freedom Foundation, another anti-union organization, declared in a fundraising letter that it intended to use *Janus* to destroy public-sector unions by driving "the proverbial stake through their hearts."

Early reports on public union membership showed relatively modest declines. The National Education Association said it lost 72,325 members and fee payers from August 2017 to August 2018, or just over 2 percent of its membership. The declines could grow over time, however, as more members learn about their right to stop paying dues or fees and as new employees decide not to join in the first place. Unions would do well to brace for worse. After Michigan adopted a right-to-work law—which had the same effect as *Janus*, allowing workers to stop paying union dues or fees—the Michigan Education Association lost about 28 percent of its members in less than six years.

In addition to weakening organized labor, *Janus* will almost certainly have another effect: helping the Republican Party. Public-sector unions are one of the main sources of support for Democratic candidates. In the 2016 election cycle, the top ten donors to Democratic and liberal causes included the Service Employees International Union, the American Federation of Teachers, and the National Education Association—all public-sector unions. Public-sector unions also register their members to vote and turn them out on Election Day, most often for Democratic candidates. There is statistical evidence that weakening unions in general helps Republicans. One study of the effect of right-to-work laws found that they reduce the Democratic vote share for president, Congress, governor, and state legislators by about 3.5 percent.

Janus fit neatly into a partisan pattern going back to *Bush v. Gore*. The conservative justices stopped the vote counting in Florida; struck down campaign finance restrictions, including the prohibition on corporate spending on elections; upheld strict voter ID laws and aggressive voter roll purges; invalidated a key part of the Voting Rights Act; rejected challenges to partisan gerrymandering; and, now, voted to defund public-sector unions. All of these rulings greatly helped the electoral chances of Republican candidates. The conservative movement had long made defunding unions a priority. Grover Norquist, the founder of Americans for Tax Reform, said that if laws reining in the power of public-sector unions "are enacted in a dozen more states, the modern Democratic Party will cease to be a competitive power in American politics." Whether or not the conservative justices were thinking about the political implications of *Janus,* the president who appointed the justice who cast the deciding vote certainly was. In a tweet the morning the case was decided, President Trump exulted, "Big loss for the coffers of the Democrats!"

THERE IS ONE MORE SET OF COURT RULINGS THAT, ALTHOUGH NOT DIrectly related to employment, has done substantial harm to workers: the campaign finance decisions, starting with *Buckley v. Valeo.* By striking down restrictions on spending in elections, the Court dramatically shifted the balance of power toward wealthy individuals and corporations. Those increasingly empowered individuals and corporations have used their influence to persuade elected officials to adopt anti-worker laws and policies.

In the years since *Buckley,* corporations have eclipsed organized labor in political spending, reflecting the decline of organized labor and the growth of American business. In 1978, labor PACs gave more to congressional candidates than corporate PACs did. By the 2017–18 cycle, corporate PACs were giving nearly seven times as much. In that same cycle, OpenSecrets.org looked at the breakdown in overall donations in federal elections and found that ones supportive of business interests outspent ones aligned with labor interests by about 16 to 1.

Contributions by wealthy individuals who run corporations have soared, and now vastly outstrip labor union spending. In the 2018 election cycle, Sheldon Adelson and his wife contributed more than $123 million to federal candidates, and Michael Bloomberg gave more than $95 million. Richard Uihlein, a far-right business supplies magnate, contributed nearly $40 million. The highest-contributing union gave just over $42 million. Although these individuals have a number of policy priorities, opposition to unions is often high on their list. The Ed Uihlein Family Foundation, which Richard Uihlein controls, has been a major funder of the Liberty Justice Center, and *The Guardian* has called Adelson "one of the country's most high-profile and powerful opponents of labor unions."

Corporate contributions and spending also flow heavily at the state level. In 2018, candidates for governor, state legislature, and other state offices raised $2.2 billion, nearly as much as Senate and House candidates raised, and much of it came from corporate interests. A Center for Public Integrity report on the 2018 election cycle found that corporate donors gave large amounts to governors who were almost certain to win their elections. "Why Are Corporations Pouring Millions into Shoo-in Governor Races?," the report's title asked. The center answered its own question: it was "likely an effort to court power," the report said. "Donations can open the door to face time with state executives, which especially benefits regulated businesses . . . And the safer the seat, the safer the bet."

One of the main anti-worker policies that corporate interests have been buying in recent years is state right-to-work laws, the laws that prevent both public- and private-sector unions from signing contracts requiring workers to pay union dues or fair-share fees. The corporate-funded American Legislative Exchange Council (ALEC), which has a strong presence in state legislatures across the country, has been a major force in promoting pro-business laws at the state level, including right-to-work legislation. The large amount of corporate money flowing to state legislators helps to give ALEC a receptive audience.

The drive for right-to-work laws has scored a series of recent successes. After a long period in which few of these laws were enacted, there was suddenly a flurry of them: Michigan and Indiana in 2012, Wisconsin in 2015, West Virginia in 2016, and Kentucky and Missouri in 2017. These anti-union laws are popular with corporations and their lobbyists, but less so with the public. In 2018, Missouri voters overturned the right-to-work law enacted by its legislature by a roughly 2–1 margin.

When states adopt right-to-work laws, rates of union membership go down. One study found that the decline was generally about 5 to 10 percent, but the falloffs can be greater. In Wisconsin, which adopted a right-to-work law and other anti-union legislation, private-sector union membership fell from nearly 16 percent in 2009 to just 8.1 percent in 2016. These declines hurt workers, because non-union workers receive lower wages and benefits than union workers.

Another way corporate campaign contributions have hurt workers is by helping to keep the federal minimum wage low. When Congress established the minimum wage in 1938, it left it to future Congresses to periodically raise the wage so it kept up with inflation. That has not happened consistently. Congress has not increased the minimum wage since 2009, when it rose to $7.25. The United States has what *The Washington Post* has called "one of the stingiest minimum wage policies of any wealthy nation." In France, the minimum wage is 60.5 percent of the median wage, and in the United Kingdom it is 49 percent. In the United States, it is below 35 percent.

One of the main reasons the minimum wage is so low is that large corporations have lobbied Congress not to increase it. Before a key 2014 vote on a bill to raise the minimum wage to $10.10 in three years, twenty trade associations representing restaurants, hotels, and other industries wrote a letter urging Congress to reject it. The groups behind the letter had given more than $5.5 million in contributions to members of Congress in the previous two years and spent more than $91 million on lobbying in the previous year.

The working poor who relied on the minimum wage could not match these corporate campaign contributions or high-priced lobbyists. They did, however, have strong popular support on their side. In a Gallup poll shortly before the vote, 76 percent of Americans said they supported raising the minimum wage from $7.25 to $9; just 22 percent opposed the increase.

Low-income workers also had respected allies advocating for them. President Obama had called for the minimum wage to be raised to $9 in his 2013 State of the Union address. The U.S. Conference of Catholic Bishops wrote to Congress in support of an increase, noting that "a full-year, full-time worker making the minimum wage does not make enough money to raise a child free from poverty." Newspapers across the country, from *The New York Times* to *The Salt Lake Tribune,* urged Congress to vote for the increase. In the end, the minimum-wage bill failed in the Senate, where it fell short of the sixty votes needed to overcome a threatened filibuster.

After the Senate vote, Obama criticized the Republicans for letting down "28 million hard-working Americans." The Senate majority leader, Harry Reid, accused Republicans of "fighting for the billionaires." No one thought to blame the Court, even though it was its decades of campaign finance rulings that made the billionaires' wishes count for so much and public opinion count for so little.

There are many other government policies that have been harmful to workers that can be traced to the influence of pro-corporate campaign donors. In a wide array of areas, workers are being harmed by corporate malfeasance that Congress, legislators, and regulators should address through stronger laws and stronger enforcement. Their unwillingness to do so almost certainly results in large part from the influence of large donors.

One of these areas is wage theft. Many employers, including large companies, force their employees to work off the clock, deny them overtime pay, or otherwise cheat them out of money they have earned. The amounts involved are sizable. A study entitled "Grand Theft Paycheck," released in 2018, identified more than four thousand legal cases since 2000 in which large corporations paid a penalty for wage theft and calculated that they led to more than

$9.2 billion in verdicts and settlements. The study's lead author said that its findings made it clear that "wage theft goes far beyond sweatshops, fast-food outlets, and retailers" and was "built into the business model of a substantial portion of corporate America." The report called for stronger laws at the federal and state levels and stricter enforcement—both of which corporate interests have strongly resisted using campaign contributions as leverage.

The government has also failed to provide adequate regulation of workplace safety. In 2017, nearly 5,200 workers were killed on the job, and more than 2.85 million more suffered injuries that required medical care or time off from work. Occupational Safety and Health Administration (OSHA) enforcement is so starved for resources that it would take OSHA 150 years to visit every workplace it is responsible for just once. The National Employment Law Project warned in 2018 that OSHA enforcement was being cut back further, "putting workers' lives at risk."

One of the main reasons for this failure to protect workers on the job is corporate campaign contributions. The Center for Public Integrity, in a report entitled "The Campaign to Weaken Worker Protections," found that the nation's unnecessarily high levels of work-related illnesses, injuries, and deaths are in large part the result of decades of corporate efforts to weaken OSHA and fend off efforts to improve it. Those efforts have prevailed, the report said, in large part because of corporate money flowing to the elected officials responsible for guiding OSHA. Those funds have created, one of the report's experts said, "a culture in the regulatory process of extreme deference to industry."

THE COURT'S ANTI-WORKER RULINGS HAVE ALL CONTRIBUTED TO THE nation's growing economic inequality. It is certainly true of the employment discrimination decisions, which have taken a direct hit on the finances of millions of workers. For every Jack Gross, Maetta Vance, and Betty Dukes who lost before the Court, there are millions more whose chance to be compensated for discrimination was foreclosed before they even got to court.

Taken as a whole, these decisions represent a significant transfer of money from poor and middle-class workers to the companies that employ them.

Each employment discrimination ruling has inflicted a particular kind of damage. In the case of *Gross*, the Court made it extremely difficult for a class of workers to sue just as discrimination against them was soaring. The case was decided in the depths of the Great Recession, when there were widespread layoffs targeting older workers. Even as the economy has recovered, there is extensive evidence from journalistic investigations, lawsuits, and other sources that employers engage in age discrimination on a massive scale. ProPublica took a close look at one such employer in a 2018 exposé headlined "Cutting 'Old Heads' at IBM." It reported that IBM had fired as many as twenty thousand older workers over five years, using selection criteria that were slanted against older workers even when they were rated as high performers. In some cases, ProPublica found, the money IBM saved from pushing these workers out was used to hire younger and cheaper replacements.

The Court in *Gross* left older workers who were pushed out at IBM and other companies with almost no chance of prevailing if they sued. In 2012, NPR surveyed the state of age discrimination litigation and concluded that "wins are elusive," and it reported that "employment law experts say that has a lot to do with one particular case." A lawyer with the AARP Foundation said, nearly four years after the ruling, that "plaintiffs' attorneys have told us that they will not take age cases anymore because of the Gross decision."

This collapse of age discrimination law hurts victims in a variety of ways. It means that workers like Jack Gross who were demoted or lost their jobs will not be compensated for the salary and benefits they were denied. In many cases, the victims will also end up with sizable uncompensated lawyers' fees and litigation expenses. They also are often left unemployed, and forced to enter the job market at a time when it is particularly hostile to them.

Older job seekers take significantly longer to find a job than younger ones. When they do get a new position, they often take a substantial pay cut, like the friends Gross testified about to the Senate who went from being

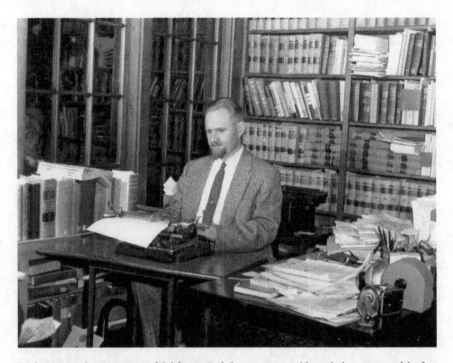

Jacobus tenBroek, a University of California–Berkeley constitutional law scholar, was one of the first advocates for the legal rights of the poor, arguing in a 1955 paper that laws making new arrivals in a state wait to apply for welfare benefits violated their "right of free movement."

Earl Warren, who became chief justice in 1953, presided over the Warren Court's "rights revolution," which expanded the legal rights of the poor, racial minorities, criminal defendants, and other disadvantaged groups.

1

DIVISION OF CORRECTIONS

CORRESPONDENCE REGULATIONS

MAIL WILL NOT BE DELIVERED WHICH DOES NOT CONFORM WITH THESE RULES

No. 1 -- Only 2 letters each week, not to exceed 2 sheets letter-size 8 1/2 x 11" and written *on one side only*, and if ruled paper, do not write between lines. *Your complete name* must be signed at the close of your letter. *Clippings, stamps, letters* from other people, *stationery* or *cash must not be enclosed* in your letters.

No. 2 -- All *letters* must be addressed in the *complete prison name* of the inmate. *Cell number*, where applicable, and *prison number* must be placed in lower left corner of envelope, with your complete name and address in the upper left corner.

No. 3 -- *Do not send any packages without a Package Permit.* Unauthorized *packages* will be destroyed.

No. 4 -- *Letters* must be written in English only.

No. 5 -- *Books, magazines, pamphlets,* and *newspapers* of reputable character will be delivered *only if* mailed direct from the publisher.

No. 6 -- *Money* must be sent in the form of *Postal Money Orders* only, in the inmate's complete prison name and prison number.

INSTITUTION ______________ CELL NUMBER ______________

NAME ______________ NUMBER ______________

In The Supreme Court of The United States
Washington D.C.

clarence Earl Gideon
Petitioner
vs.
H.G. Cuchray, Jr, as
Director, Divisions
of corrections state
of Florida

Petition for a writ
of Certiorari Directed
to The Supreme Court
state of Florida.

No. 890 Misc.
OCT. TERM 1961
U. S. Supreme Court

To: The Honorable Earl Warren, Chief
Justice of the United States

Comes now the petitioner, Clarence Earl Gideon, a citizen of The United states of America, in proper person, and appearing as his own counsel. Who petitions this Honorable Court for a Writ of Certiorari directed to The Supreme Court of The State of Florida, To review the order and Judgement of the court below denying The petitioner a writ of Habeus Corpus.

Petitioner submits That The Supreme Court of The United States has The authority and jurisdiction to review The final Judgement of The Supreme Court of The State of Florida The highest court of The State Under sec. 344(B) Title 28 U.S.C.A. and Because The "Due process clause" of The

Clarence Gideon, who was convicted of a poolroom burglary in Panama City, Florida, hand-wrote a petition to the Supreme Court that led to *Gideon v. Wainwright*, the Supreme Court decision creating a right to counsel for poor criminal defendants.

On August 6, 1965, with Martin Luther King Jr. and other civil rights leaders present, President Lyndon Johnson signed the Voting Rights Act, requiring many states and localities to get approval before adopting rules that could make it harder for minorities to vote—until the Supreme Court invalidated that part of the law in 2013.

Thurgood Marshall, who had served as director-counsel of the NAACP Legal Defense and Educational Fund and argued *Brown v. Board of Education* before his appointment as a justice, was one of the Court's most passionate defenders of the rights of poor and powerless Americans.

Abe Fortas, a pillar of the Warren Court's liberal majority, was pressured into resigning in 1969 as part of President Richard Nixon's plan for creating a conservative majority on the Court.

When Chief Justice Warren retired in 1969, President Nixon replaced him with Warren Burger, a conservative appeals court judge who was eager to reverse the legacy of the Warren Court.

William Rehnquist, who came to Washington to be an archconservative lawyer in the Nixon Justice Department, ended up as an archconservative chief justice who regularly sided with the wealthy and powerful over the poor and weak.

Lewis Powell was presented to the nation as a moderate southerner with a strong commitment to public education, but he cast the deciding votes in landmark cases in 1973 and 1974 that rejected poor children's claims to equal educational opportunity.

The Burger Court in 1976, the year it decided *Buckley v. Valeo*, which established the principle that money equals speech—the first of a long series of decisions striking down limits on campaign spending by wealthy individuals and corporations.

The Supreme Court on a White House visit to Jimmy Carter, the only president in the last fifty years who did not have an opportunity to appoint a Supreme Court justice—which helped conservatives keep their hold on the Court.

President Ronald Reagan appointed Sandra Day O'Connor, the first woman justice, who was more centrist than most of the conservative justices but still voted to stop the Florida recount in *Bush v. Gore* and to deny an impoverished nine-year-old girl the right to a free bus ride to school.

Anthony Kennedy, another Reagan nominee, had a reputation for moderation, but he consistently sided with the wealthy and powerful in decisions like *Citizens United v. Federal Election Commission*, which held that corporations have a First Amendment right to spend money on elections.

President Reagan on a 1981 visit to the Court, which he would make significantly more pro-business by appointing justices who favored corporations on a wide range of issues.

In 1993, President Bill Clinton nominated Ruth Bader Ginsburg, putting one of the nation's leading women's rights advocates on the Court.

President George W. Bush nominated John Roberts to be the seventeenth chief justice in 2005, continuing a conservative lock on the position that had begun with President Nixon's nomination of Warren Burger in 1969.

In 2005, George W. Bush nominated Samuel Alito, a favorite of conservative activists, who would lead the Court to create a First Amendment right of government workers not to pay union fees, striking a major blow against organized labor.

After the Supreme Court overturned Lilly Ledbetter's damage award against Goodyear Tire & Rubber for discrimination in pay, President Barack Obama signed the Lilly Ledbetter Fair Pay Act of 2009, reversing the decision.

When Brett Kavanaugh was confirmed in 2018, despite charges that he had committed a sexual assault in high school, some legal experts predicted it would be the start of an even more conservative Court that would make "epochal" changes in the law.

professionals to being janitors. One study found that older workers who lose their jobs end up taking new ones that pay more than 13 percent less. A substantial number of older workers who lose jobs never find another one. In addition to the immediate loss of income, late-career unemployment can greatly undermine workers' retirement plans, both because they stop making regular contributions to their retirement funds when they are close to retirement and because they draw on those funds to live on while they are looking for work.

The *Vance* case is also having a large impact, making it harder for victims of racial and sexual harassment to sue. On-the-job harassment is widespread in the workplace, as the Me Too movement has made clear. As a result of *Vance*, however, it is more difficult to sue employers when it occurs. After the ruling, the National Women's Law Center identified forty-three sexual harassment cases that were dismissed as a result, including the case of a seventeen-year-old Safeway employee who was fondled and kissed by a manager who controlled her work schedule but did not have the power to hire or fire her. Now, many of these cases are not being brought at all, because they are so difficult to win unless the harasser is a very high-level manager.

Discussions of on-the-job harassment often focus on the emotional toll, but the economic impact can also be considerable. One study of sexual harassment released in 2018 by the Stanford Center on Poverty and Inequality reported that 4 to 7 percent of working women are victims of sexual harassment each year. It found that 80 percent of women subjected to severe sexual harassment changed jobs within two years, 6.5 times the rate of women who were not harassed. Many took jobs that paid less and worked fewer hours. The study found that "sexually harassed women report significantly greater financial stress two years after the harassment than those who are not harassed." Other forms of harassment have similar negative economic effects on victims.

The damage *Wal-Mart v. Dukes* has done to workers has been particularly far-reaching. Dismissing the case was a setback for 1.5 million women like

Christine Kwapnoski who said they were subjected to sex discrimination in their careers at Wal-Mart but will likely never be compensated. It also set a high bar for many millions more who had yet to file their own discrimination suits. There is already evidence showing that fewer class actions are being filed since the decision, that the cases are smaller, and that settlements are more modest.

The financial impact from all of the Court's employment discrimination rulings go beyond lost wages and benefits. Victims of discrimination also frequently experience medical consequences that translate into economic harm. There is a growing body of scientific literature connecting discrimination with physical and mental health problems, including stress, depression, anxiety, substance abuse, and cardiovascular disease. These physical and mental injuries can significantly increase medical expenses for discrimination victims. They can also interfere with victims' ability to obtain and retain new employment. These secondary economic harms can be particularly acute for victims of age discrimination. Workers fired late in their careers have high rates of major depression, anxiety, and other forms of mental illness.

The greatest harm of the Court's employment discrimination decisions, however, may be prospective: they send a message to employers that if they discriminate against their employees, they are unlikely to be held liable or required to pay damages. After the *Gross* case, companies have less reason to worry about firing their oldest workers. After *Vance,* they have less incentive to root out harassers on their staff. After *Dukes,* employers can worry less about broadly discriminatory policies that affect large numbers of workers. As a result of these new incentives, workers in groups that are often discriminated against, including older workers, women, and racial minorities, are more likely to be economically harmed.

The Court's rulings against labor unions have also increased economic inequality, by driving down workers' wages and benefits. There is extensive evidence that unions raise the salaries of their members. One study found that they produce a "wage premium" of 20 percent or more for the workers they represent. Barry Hirsch, a Georgia State University economist who has researched the union wage gap, said that "one cannot avoid the conclusion" that the higher salaries and benefits unionized workers receive help to explain "the fierce management opposition to union organizing."

Unions have an even greater effect on benefits. Union members have more access to health care than do workers who are not in a union, and it is more affordable. Unionized workers are significantly more likely than non-unionized workers to have health care benefits and employer-provided pension plans. When benefits are taken into account, the compensation gap between unionized and non-unionized workers rises to about 28 percent.

Experts who have examined the increasing economic inequality in the United States say that one of the main driving forces has been the decline in union membership. A study by Bruce Western of Harvard and Jake Rosenfeld of the University of Washington, looked at the period from 1973 to 2007, when private-sector union membership declined from 34 to 8 percent for men and 16 to 6 percent for women. In these years, inequality in hourly wages increased by more than 40 percent. The study found that as much as one-third of the growth in inequality was due to reduced levels of union membership. As unions lost members and influence, the authors said, workers were increasingly left to fend for themselves against "unbridled market logic."

The Court's campaign finance rulings have also hurt workers and increased economic inequality. The right-to-work laws that states have adopted, largely because of corporate campaign contributions and lobbying, have demonstrably hurt workers' finances. In right-to-work states, unionization rates are lower than in other states, and wages are lower. The Economic Policy Institute found that states with right-to-work laws have wages that are 3.1 percent lower than those in non-right-to-work states, all other things being equal.

The failure to raise the federal minimum wage since 2009, which has largely been due to the influence of corporate campaign contributors, has also exacerbated economic inequality. Since the minimum wage reached its peak in inflation-adjusted dollars in 1968, it has lost about one-third of its value. In twenty-nine states and the District of Columbia, there are minimum wages that are above the federal minimum wage, but in the remaining states, the lowest-wage workers have fallen far behind.

There is, not surprisingly, evidence that the failure to raise the federal minimum wage has increased poverty. If the minimum wage had kept pace with inflation since 1968, it would be about $12—and, according to one calculation, there would be about 6.6 million fewer Americans living in poverty. There is another, grimmer consequence of the failure of the nation's broken political system to generate increases in the minimum wage. Studies have found a strong connection between poverty and premature death. Not increasing the minimum wage at the rate of inflation has almost certainly led to many thousands, if not millions, of Americans dying early. A University of North Carolina study from 2019 identified a more specific consequence of not raising minimum wages. It found that a $1 increase in a state's minimum wage was associated with a 1.9 percent decrease in suicide rates.

There are other policies driving income inequality that have been adopted in large part because of pro-corporate campaign contributions. The government's inadequate response to wage theft has had a major impact on the incomes of low-wage workers. The Economic Policy Institute produced a study that looked at only one form of wage theft, minimum wage violations, in just the ten most populous states. It found that 2.4 million workers lost $8 billion a year from these violations—an average of $3,300 per worker. The report noted that this form of wage theft affected workers who could least afford to lose earnings and drove many families below the poverty line.

The failure of OSHA to adequately protect American workers has also taken a significant toll on poor and working-class Americans, and again corporate campaign contributions have been a driving factor. The more than five thousand workers killed and nearly three million injured each year represent individuals and families that are devastated in many ways, including economically. In many cases, any compensation these workers or their families receive is greatly limited by workers' compensation laws. A study that examined the impact of workplace injuries found that the financial effects were often "severe," because of uncompensated medical expenses and reduced income. "Many respondents reported depleted savings, borrowing money, taking out retirement funds, and declaring bankruptcy in efforts to cope," the study reported.

Taken together, the Court's decisions involving the rights of workers, including its campaign finance decisions, have had a devastating impact on the economic standing of low- and middle-income Americans. They have denied workers damage awards when they are treated unfairly and encouraged employers to discriminate more in the future. They have deprived workers of the wage and benefit premiums that come with union membership. They are a major reason that the poorest workers have not seen an increase in the minimum wage in a decade and have little recourse when their wages are stolen, and they are a significant factor in the nation's high rates of death and injury on the job. As long as the Court continues to favor employers and campaign contributors so extremely, the economic standing of workers, and particularly low-income workers, will likely continue to decline.

CHAPTER ♦ 7

CORPORATIONS

In June 2008, the Supreme Court decided a case arising out of the *Exxon Valdez* oil spill, which had occurred nearly two decades earlier. The *Exxon Valdez* oil tanker ran aground in March 1989 after going off course in Alaska's Prince William Sound. The resulting oil spill was catastrophic: more than one thousand miles of coastline polluted, hundreds of thousands of animals killed, and serious economic damage to about one-third of Alaska's commercial fishermen.

Exxon was sued for negligence, and much of the lawsuit's focus was the role that the *Exxon Valdez* captain's alcohol consumption played in the disaster. Joseph Hazelwood, a serious alcoholic, had completed a twenty-eight-day treatment program while he worked for Exxon. Hazelwood reportedly continued drinking heavily in an array of settings, including bars, restaurants, hotels, and airports. There was testimony that Hazelwood had drunk at least five double vodkas in waterfront bars before the incident and evidence suggesting that his blood alcohol level at the time of the spill was three times the legal limit for driving in most states. It was not clear why, given Hazelwood's record, Exxon would entrust him with captaining an oil tanker.

After a monthlong trial, on June 14, 1994, a federal jury found that Exxon was reckless for putting a captain with a known history of alcohol abuse in command of the *Exxon Valdez.* It also found that Hazelwood was negligent for drinking heavily on the afternoon before the accident. The jury awarded compensatory damages to more than ten thousand fishermen and over twenty thousand other Alaskans affected by the spill, which ultimately came to $507.5 million.

A few months later, the jury awarded $5 billion in punitive damages against Exxon. Financial analysts said that Exxon, which had revenue of $111.2 billion in 1993, would not be greatly harmed by the award, and Exxon stock rose after the verdict came in. Exxon chairman Lee R. Raymond took a harder line. He called the award "excessive by any legal or practical measure" and declared that Exxon would "use every legal means available to overturn this unjust verdict." On appeal, Exxon got the award cut in half, to $2.5 billion. Even after that, Exxon took its case to the Supreme Court, arguing that $2.5 billion in punitive damages was excessive and violated its rights under the Due Process Clause.

To anyone not following the Court's punitive damages decisions, Exxon's claim must have seemed like an odd one. Punitive damages have a venerable history. The law has imposed higher awards when defendants engaged in particularly bad behavior as far back as the Code of Hammurabi, in ancient Babylon. In American law, punitive damages, which trace back to English legal traditions, were uncontroversial by the middle of the nineteenth century. In an 1851 dispute between the owners of adjacent mill dams in Great Barrington, Massachusetts, the Court said that it was already well established that "a jury may give what are called exemplary or vindictive damages depending upon the peculiar circumstances of each case."

Punitive damages punish egregious conduct, such as intentional or reckless behavior that exposes others to considerable risk of harm. They also allow a jury to "send a message" to a defendant, especially a large or powerful one that might not be deterred by merely having to pay for the actual damage it caused.

There was no formula for assessing punitive damages—it was left to jurors to figure out after weighing all the relevant circumstances. In exceptional cases, trial or appellate judges could reduce an award they considered excessive.

It would also not have been obvious to the casual observer why the Due Process Clause of the Fourteenth Amendment should be relevant to Exxon's punitive damages challenge. Its text, which says that "no state" shall "deprive any person of life, liberty, or property, without due process of law," did not appear to have anything to do with the size of punitive damages imposed on large corporations. Nor did the history of the Fourteenth Amendment, which was adopted after the Civil War to help lift freed slaves up to equality, suggest it was meant to protect a corporation that had injured thousands of people from a large punitive damages award.

This discussion of the Due Process Clause and punitive damages was occurring against the backdrop of a decades-long campaign by corporate America to rein in litigation against businesses. Starting in the 1970s, insurance companies and other large companies had promoted a "tort reform" movement, which was coordinated in large part by the U.S. Chamber of Commerce. The business community was concerned about the cost to its bottom lines from lawsuits over "torts"—negligent or intentional actions that cause harm, which could be over anything from a defective product to fraud. Tort reform advocates insisted that there was a litigation crisis, with out-of-control jury verdicts that were unfair to corporations, medical professionals, and other defendants. They wanted Congress and state legislatures to adopt punitive damages caps and other restrictions that would make it harder to hold defendants liable for large amounts of money.

The movement worked to win over popular opinion with an expensive propaganda campaign. Industry-funded think tanks and advocacy organizations like the American Tort Reform Association churned out reports, position papers, and model legislation. The reformers played up the threat posed by "frivolous lawsuits," including a highly distorted story about a purportedly greedy plaintiff who had made off with a $2.9 million jury verdict because she spilled a too-hot cup of McDonald's coffee on herself. Tort reformers put up billboards declaring: SPILL HOT COFFEE, WIN MILLIONS: PLAY LAWSUIT LOTTO.

Consumer groups, plaintiffs' lawyers, and many legal scholars resisted the move to cap punitive damages, arguing that it was an effort by big business to avoid responsibility for its actions—and that it would remove an important deterrent that kept corporations from harming more people. These opponents refuted many of the tort reform movement's specific claims, including its account of the hot-coffee case. The truth was that the elderly woman involved had been served coffee so unusually hot that, when it spilled on her, she required a series of skin grafts and was partially disabled for almost two years.

The tort reform movement had limited legislative success. While Republicans and the business community pushed hard to get laws passed, Democrats, consumer advocates, and trial lawyers worked just as hard to oppose them. Only a small minority of state legislatures adopted punitive damages caps. Tort reformers also made little progress in Congress, scoring only modest victories in a few specific areas.

The one bright spot for the movement was the judiciary. Presidents Reagan, George H. W. Bush, and George W. Bush all supported tort reform, and they nominated justices who shared their concern about protecting corporations from litigation. Starting in the 1990s, the Court began to adopt the kinds of aggressive caps on punitive damages that Congress and most state legislatures were unwilling to impose. It was a case of what one legal commentator called "do-it-yourself tort reform."

The Court's war on punitive damages began in 1996, in *BMW of North America, Inc., v. Gore,* a case about a defective BMW automobile. Dr. Ira Gore Jr. had bought a new black BMW sports car from an authorized dealer in Birmingham, Alabama. Gore later found out that the car had been repainted, which BMW had not told him. His car's top, hood, trunk, and quarter panels had all been given a new coat of paint before it was sold to him as new, apparently because the car had been exposed to acid rain in transport from Germany. BMW had a policy, it turned out, that if a new car was damaged and the cost of repair was less than 3 percent of the retail price, it would sell the car as new without telling the dealer.

Gore sued for damages, and at trial his expert witness testified that his new car, for which he paid $40,750.88, was worth about 10 percent less than an undamaged one. The jury awarded Gore $4,000 in actual damages. It also found that BMW's policy constituted "gross, oppressive or malicious" fraud and awarded him another $4 million in punitive damages. On appeal, the Alabama Supreme Court held that the jury had erred in its calculations and lowered the punitive damages award to $2 million. BMW thought the award was still too high and took the case to the Supreme Court.

The Court ruled 5–4, in a vote that did not break down neatly on ideological lines, that the $2 million punitive damages award was excessive and violated the Due Process Clause. Stevens, writing for the majority, said that "elementary notions of fairness" dictated that corporations and individuals should have fair notice of the severity of punishment they may be subjected to. To offer that kind of guidance, he said that punitive damages should be analyzed for excessiveness according to a set of "guideposts," including how bad a defendant's conduct was and what the ratio was between actual and punitive damages. BMW's conduct was not sufficiently "reprehensible," Stevens said, to warrant $2 million in punitive damages. He also objected that the punitive damages were disproportionate to the actual damages of $4,000. "The ratio is a breathtaking 500 to 1," Stevens said. The Court ruled that the award was "grossly excessive" and "transcends the constitutional limit."

The Court continued to refine its doctrine of excessive punitive damages. In 2003, it rescued another corporate bad actor from a jury's damage award. Curtis Campbell, a Utah man, had been sued for his part in a serious car accident. The injured parties offered to settle for $50,000, which was the limit of his insurance policy with State Farm. State Farm rejected the settlement offer and insisted on going to trial, but it promised Campbell he would not be personally liable for any award over $50,000 if they lost the case, and that he did not need his own lawyer. They did lose the case, and Campbell was held liable for $185,849. Despite its promise, State Farm refused to cover the extra $135,849 and Campbell had to hire his own lawyer to appeal. Campbell ended up suing State Farm for bad faith, fraud, and intentional infliction of emotional distress.

Campbell's lawyers later turned up evidence that State Farm had forced him to go to trial as part of a corporate strategy to increase its profits by limiting payouts, which it called its "Performance, Planning and Review" program. Former employees testified that they were told to target the "weakest of the herd," State Farm's most vulnerable customers, including the elderly, the poor, and others considered "least knowledgeable about their rights and thus most vulnerable to trickery or deceit." Campbell fit the profile: he had Parkinson's disease and had suffered a stroke. A jury found State Farm liable, and Campbell was awarded $1 million in actual damages and $145 million in punitive damages, amounts later approved by the Utah Supreme Court. State Farm took the case to the Supreme Court.

On April 7, 2003, the Court reversed the Utah Supreme Court by a 6–3 vote and held that the punitive damages were excessive. In *State Farm Mutual Automobile Insurance Co. v. Campbell*, which again did not break down on ideological lines, the Court said more about the limits that due process placed on punitive damages. Kennedy, writing for the majority, conceded that State Farm's conduct "merits no praise," but he insisted that the punitive damages were unconstitutionally large. The Court was more precise than in the BMW case, declaring that "few awards exceeding a single-digit ratio between punitive and compensatory damages . . . will satisfy due process." When it said "single-digit ratio," the Court meant that punitive damages should not be more than about nine times the size of the compensatory damages. In this case, where the compensatory damages were $1 million, the Court suggested the punitive damages award against State Farm should have been closer to $9 million, or even $1 million, than $145 million.

In dissent, Ginsburg said the Court was changing the law on punitive damages very quickly—in favor of corporate defendants. Until the BMW case, in 1996, it had never held a state-court punitive damages award to be unconstitutionally excessive. Now the Court was imposing what looked like a mathematical cap. The "flexible guides" of the BMW case were, she said, starting to "resemble marching orders." Ginsburg also disputed the majority's suggestion that State Farm's conduct was not all that reprehensible. A jury might well want to send a message, she pointed out, about State Farm's Performance, Planning and Review program, which seemed expressly designed to provide bad service, to the point of creating serious financial problems, for the "weakest of the herd." It might also, she said, have wanted to punish conduct it regarded as "egregious and malicious."

In 2007, the Court came to the rescue of another corporation that had been hit with a large punitive damages award, this time the world's largest tobacco company. An Oregon jury had ordered Philip Morris to pay the widow of Jesse Williams, who had died of lung cancer, $821,000 in compensatory damages and $79.5 million in punitive damages. The Oregon Supreme Court upheld the punitive damages, even though the ratio to the compensatory damages was almost 100 to 1. It found that Philip Morris's conduct was "extraordinarily reprehensible," since it "knew that smoking caused serious and sometimes fatal disease, but it nevertheless spread false or misleading information" for nearly half a century.

The Supreme Court in *Philip Morris USA v. Williams*, by a 5–4 vote, again with liberal and conservative justices on both sides, overturned the Oregon Supreme Court's decision. Breyer, writing for the majority, said the award had been made in a way that suggested the jury might have been punishing Philip Morris for harm to smokers who were "strangers to the litigation"—not part of the lawsuit. He worried that Philip Morris was being punished for an indeterminate number of victims, whose precise injuries were not known, which would "add a near standardless dimension to the punitive damages equation."

Ginsburg again dissented, emphasizing that the jury had been responding to the "reprehensibility" of Philip Morris's conduct. It was not punishing the tobacco giant for harm to smokers who were strangers to the litigation, she said. It was properly considering "the harm that Philip Morris was prepared to inflict on the smoking public at large."

The Court's decision was widely criticized by the media, legal scholars, and the general public. Many people who did not follow the intricacies of punitive damages law saw the Court protecting a large tobacco company that had marketed cigarettes in misleading ways long after their lethality had been scientifically settled. In an editorial headlined "Shielding the Powerful," *The New York Times* lamented that the Court had stretched "due process in a way that will make it easier for companies that act reprehensibly to sidestep serious punishments." A case note in the *Harvard Law Review* objected that the Court had turned the Fourteenth Amendment, which was intended to help the least powerful, "into a boon for railroads, monopolies, utility companies, bankers, and other large commercial interests."

THESE CASES—INVOLVING A CAR BMW KNEW WAS DEFECTIVE, A STATE Farm policy that hurt some of its most vulnerable customers, and the death of a cigarette smoker—provided the backdrop for Exxon's challenge to its own punitive damages award. Exxon's case had an unusual wrinkle: because of where the injuries had occurred, the Court considered it under maritime law, rather than relying on the Due Process Clause. Maritime law is a separate field of law, with its own precedents handed down over centuries. Although the Court took into account its past rulings under the Due Process Clause, it did a new analysis, which looked at what punitive damages awards were considered reasonable by judges and juries in maritime cases, and tried to come out in the middle of that range.

The Court decided, by a 5–3 vote, that the $2.5 billion punitive damages award against Exxon Shipping Company was excessive. The $2.5 billion was actually well within the "single-digit" ratio of punitive damages to compensatory damages the Court had called for in its State Farm decision. The compensatory damages were $507.5 million, so the ratio was about 5:1. Souter concluded, however, that in maritime cases like this one, a "fair upper limit" for the ratio of punitive damages to compensatory damages was 1 to 1. Therefore, he said, the punitive damages against Exxon should be reduced to $507.5 million.

Once again, Ginsburg protested in dissent. She objected to the 1:1 ratio as "the Court's lawmaking" and insisted that if there was going to be a limit on the ratio of punitive damages to compensatory damages it should come from Congress. She also worried that the 1:1 ratio the Court was creating for maritime law would one day be imported into due process law and a new rule would emerge prescribing that punitive damages could never be more than compensatory damages.

The punitive damages decisions are one of the few controversial legal issues involving corporations where the Court has not broken down predictably along ideological lines. In these cases, ideology worked in an erratic way. Some of the conservatives took their expected pro-business positions, and some of the liberals sided against the corporation. Other liberal justices, however, were inclined to impose a limit on punitive damages because they were drawn to the idea of using the Due Process Clause to make punishment more predictable and fair. Some conservative justices disliked the idea of reading broad rights into vaguely worded constitutional provisions. One thing, however, went according to ideological script: Ginsburg, who was among the most committed liberals, reacted with sustained outrage as the Court's new, pro-corporate punitive damages doctrine emerged.

The punitive damages decisions are disturbing on several levels. One problem with them is that the Court was clearly not particularly concerned that it was taking away an important function of punishment: deterring future bad conduct. BMW, State Farm, and Philip Morris had all intentionally engaged in seriously harmful actions, and Exxon Shipping had been extraordinarily negligent. They were also all corporate behemoths, with annual revenue and market capitalizations that far exceeded the punitive damages that were imposed on them. State Farm was the nation's largest insurance company and in 2003 it was number 21 on the Fortune 500, with annual revenue of just under $50 billion. The jury's punitive damages award of $145 million was just 0.29 percent of what it brought in that year, an amount that might easily be ignored. The $9 million maximum award the Court approved, representing 0.018 percent, certainly *would* be ignored. The Court's decisions made it far more likely that when juries wanted to send a message to corporations to stop engaging in bad conduct that hurt the little people, those messages would not be heard.

Another troubling aspect of the punitive damages decisions is that the Court took the perverse position that corporations deserved special protection in the justice system. One of the reasons it gave for reducing the award against State Farm was that juries have "wide discretion in choosing amounts" of punitive damages, "and the presentation of evidence of a defendant's net worth creates the potential that juries will use their verdicts to express biases against big businesses." The Court did not explain why juries, which are entrusted not to use their verdicts to express biases against defendants' race, religion, sex, and other attributes, should not be trusted to treat big business fairly.

The pro-corporate bias of these decisions is unmistakable. In its punitive damages rulings, the Court flipped the principle of *Carolene Products*' footnote 4 on its head. Footnote 4 said that "discrete and insular minorities" who faced discrimination and lacked influence in the political system deserved special protection under the Equal Protection Clause. The modern Court has decided that wealthy corporations, which exert outsized influence in the political system, deserve special protection against jurors' possible "biases against big businesses." It was a sad conclusion to the Warren Court debate about whether the poor should be recognized as a suspect class under the Equal Protection Clause. Poor people never were, but in punitive damages cases, at least, the Court has extended special protection to wealthy corporations under the Due Process Clause.

A final disturbing aspect of the punitive damages cases is the difference in how the Court viewed the constitutional issues in punishing corporations and punishing people. A month before it decided the State Farm case, the Court had rejected an Eighth Amendment challenge to California's "three strikes and you're out" law. The challenge was brought by an Army veteran and father of three who stole nine children's videotapes from Kmart and, because of the "three strikes" law, was sentenced to two consecutive terms of twenty-five years to life. The Court ruled that there was no unconstitutional disproportionality in sentencing a human being to spend fifty years to life in prison for a $153.54 theft. A month later, it declared that it violated the Constitution to impose more than $9 million in punitive damages on a corporation with $50 billion in annual revenue that had badly abused a physically disabled customer.

THE CAMPAIGN AGAINST PUNITIVE DAMAGES WAS PART OF A LARGER agenda: the Court, which in the Warren era had looked for ways to use the law to improve conditions for the nation's poor, was now championing corporations. This transformation was due, more than anything else, to a dramatic change in the Court's membership. The Warren Court was led by a chief justice who made increasing racial, economic, and political equality a personal mission and who cared deeply about the poor. The liberal majority behind him included justices like Thurgood Marshall, the legal architect of the civil rights movement. The Court that decided the Exxon Shipping case was led by John Roberts, a former corporate lawyer and son of a steel plant manager, who strongly favored business interests. His conservative majority included Clarence Thomas, who had moved the EEOC in a pro-employer direction and attacked his own struggling sister for accepting welfare.

Legal experts who followed the Court were increasingly calling out its pro-business transformation. A few months before the decision in the Exxon Shipping case, *The New York Times* published an article under the headline "Supreme Court Inc." In it, George Washington University law professor

Jeffrey Rosen discussed the Court's embrace of a "pro-business jurisprudence" that valued free markets. That same year, Erwin Chemerinsky, who is now the dean of the University of California–Berkeley Law School, declared that in its first three years, from 2005 to 2008, the Roberts Court had shown itself to be "the most-pro-business Court of any since the mid-1930s."

This widely held view that the Court had veered sharply in the direction of the rights of corporations was backed up by statistical data. A scholar who analyzed the Court's rulings in business cases going back to the 1960s found a steady progression in how often it ruled in favor of business: 28 percent for the Warren Court, 48 percent for the Burger Court, 54 percent for the Rehnquist Court, and 64 percent for the Roberts Court. The study, which was published in the *Santa Clara Law Review* in 2009, noted that, while the justices nominated by Republican presidents were the driving force, a contributing factor was that recent Democratic nominees were more pro-business than the Democratic nominees of the Warren era.

The evidence showed that the Court's conservative justices were not just pro-business—they were extraordinarily so by historical standards. A study released in 2013 calculated that all five members of the conservative majority at that time—Roberts, Scalia, Thomas, Kennedy, and Alito—were among the top ten most pro-business justices to serve on the Court since 1946. Strikingly, the study—by Lee Epstein, of the University of Southern California Law School; William Landes, of the University of Chicago Law School; and Judge Richard Posner, of the U.S. Court of Appeals for the Seventh Circuit—found that Alito was the single most pro-business justice of the thirty-five who had served since 1946, and Roberts came in second. Agreeing with the *Santa Clara* study, the authors found that the Court's extreme shift in corporate cases was due in significant part to the fact that the conservative justices were "extremely" conservative, while the liberal justices were only "moderately" liberal.

Just as the Warren Court systematically looked for ways in which the poor were unfairly disadvantaged—in the criminal justice system, in voting, and in welfare benefits—the Rehnquist and Roberts Courts appeared to be looking for ways to protect corporations from oppression. In many cases, the Court seemed to be following corporate America's own list of ways it felt aggrieved by the law and providing it with the relief it was not getting from the political branches.

Another long-standing goal of corporate America was reining in the use of class action lawsuits. Class actions made it possible for large numbers of employees or consumers to band together and file a single lawsuit. In many cases, poor and middle-class people who would not have been able to sue on their own because of the cost of hiring a lawyer were able to do so as part of a class. Large class actions often produced sizable damage awards, which had a noticeable effect on a company's bottom line. When Public Citizen examined more than five hundred cases litigated by the U.S. Chamber of Commerce, it found that the biggest legal issue area it was involved in was "court access," which included trying to rein in class actions. It was such a priority that Chamber of Commerce president Thomas Donohue once said, "We spend half our time trying to reduce the number of suits by class-action lawyers."

Class action lawsuits have a long history as a populist legal tool. The concept traces back to medieval England, and versions of it existed in the earliest American law. Class actions became more important in the industrial age, when corporations began to engage in conduct that harmed large groups of people in the same way. A single mass-produced product could create a class of victims with similar injuries, who could most efficiently bring their claims together. Class actions entered a new, modern era in 1966, when it was widely recognized that they could play an important role in challenging racial segregation in the South. The drafters of the federal class action rule, Rule 23 of the Federal Rules of Civil Procedure, liberalized it to make it easier for victims of racial discrimination and other injured individuals to proceed as a class.

In the 1960s, legal scholars and advocates for disadvantaged groups believed class actions would be a revolutionary tool for ordinary Americans to achieve justice. Benjamin Kaplan, Harvard Law School's Royall Professor of Law, who played a key role in drafting the newly expanded class action rule, emphasized its populist possibilities. The changes would, he said, advance the class action's "historic mission of taking care of the smaller guy."

In the golden age after the 1966 liberalization of Rule 23, class action lawsuits were used by civil rights lawyers to desegregate public schools, restaurants, and transit systems and to improve conditions in prisons and mental hospitals. The leading poverty law cases of the 1960s and '70s were class actions. *King v. Smith* was brought on behalf of families receiving AFDC benefits in Alabama. *Rodriguez v. San Antonio Independent School District* was brought on behalf of students in poor school districts throughout the state of Texas.

Class action lawsuits have proved invaluable to consumers, employees, shareholders, and other "smaller guys" suing large corporations. They allow many individuals to share a lawyer, who is often paid from money won in the lawsuit, and to put on a single case. Class actions also allow courts to impose sweeping remedy orders vindicating the rights of many people at once. Another major advantage is their ability to aggregate a large number of small claims. Corporations often cheat many customers or employees out of small amounts of money. It is not worth it for a customer to sue over a $10 overcharge, but through a class action, a lawyer can sue on behalf of a million customers who were each cheated out of $10 by the same company.

Class action lawsuits have held corporations accountable for a wide range of malfeasance, with damage awards that have run into the billions of dollars. A class action by Vietnam veterans and their families against manufacturers of the Agent Orange herbicide, for death and disabilities among veterans and birth defects in their children, led to the creation of a $180 million victim compensation fund. Investors in WorldCom, the telecommunications giant, brought class actions against banks and an accounting firm after the company collapsed in 2002, charging that they had helped WorldCom inflate revenue and hide expenses, or should have discovered what the company was doing. They reached $6.1 billion in settlements.

Class actions have not been a perfect tool, and at times they have faced criticism not only from the corporations and others they target, but from more neutral observers. A common complaint is that class action lawyers often do better financially than members of the victim class. While that certainly happens, the criticism has been overstated. In a scholarly article entitled "Do Class Action Lawyers Make Too Little?" Vanderbilt University law professor Brian Fitzpatrick calculated that in the three hundred or so class actions settled in federal court annually in the years he examined, there was about $16 billion in settlements, and the lawyers were awarded about $2.5 billion in fees. That amounted to roughly 15 percent of the amount won, which was, Fitzpatrick noted, considerably less than what lawyers generally earn when they take a case on a contingency basis. Fitzpatrick concluded that in class actions whose main purpose is deterring bad corporate behavior, from the vantage point of maximizing social welfare, class action lawyers were actually underpaid.

As class actions proliferated and large awards became more common, corporations pushed back, arguing that class actions were part of the "litigation explosion" that was terrorizing businesses, enriching greedy lawyers and undeserving plaintiffs, and ultimately hurting consumers. Tort reform advocates, many of whom were paid by business interests, insisted that class actions were unfair to corporations—even ones that had harmed people on a mass scale.

The corporate campaign against class actions began to score some significant victories. In 1998, a change to the Federal Rules of Civil Procedure allowed defendants to appeal immediately when a class was certified by a court, instead of having to go to trial first, which reduced pressure on corporations to settle when a class action was filed. In 2005, Congress enacted the Class Action Fairness Act, a law heavily promoted by big business, which made it easier to move class actions from state court to federal court, where the rules and judges were generally more sympathetic to defendants. Ed Markey, who was then a Massachusetts congressman, called the law a "payback to the tobacco industry, to the asbestos industry, to the oil industry, to the chemical industry at the expense of ordinary families."

For decades, the Court largely remained on the sidelines of the war that corporate America was waging on class actions. In recent years, however, the pro-business Roberts Court has handed corporations a pair of major victories in their drive to rein in class actions. In 2011, it issued its ruling in Betty Dukes's class action lawsuit against Wal-Mart, which said that women suing Wal-Mart could not proceed as a class unless they could show that they had all suffered the "same injury." The flip side to the case's being an enormous setback for employees suing for discrimination is that it made it far easier for companies being sued to insulate themselves from legal liability. The ruling "tipped the balance in favor of powerful employers over everyday workers," Suzette Malveaux, a Catholic University of America law professor, wrote in an analysis of the case, titled "How Goliath Won." Erwin Chemerinsky, dean of the University of California–Berkeley Law School, and Catherine Fisk, a professor of law there, examined the Wal-Mart decision and concluded that it was "premised on a frank hostility to class actions and an expressed desire to protect big business."

The Court's ruling in the Wal-Mart case has "reshaped the American legal landscape" in favor of corporate defendants, a study by ProPublica found. In its first two years, federal and state courts cited it more than twelve hundred times, and it led to jury verdicts being reversed, plaintiff classes decertified, and settlements undone. Its new standards have helped defense contractors, media conglomerates, and other large corporate defendants fend off lawsuits filed by their employees.

In 2013, the Court protected corporations from consumer class actions the same way it had protected them from employee class actions in the Wal-Mart case. A group of cable customers in New Jersey, Pennsylvania, and

Delaware, led by a consumer named Caroline Behrend, sued Comcast for $875 million for overcharging them. They said that Comcast had violated antitrust law by using a strategy of establishing local monopolies, which it secured by swapping territories with competitors. Behrend and several other named plaintiffs were seeking to represent a class of more than two million current and former Comcast subscribers.

The Court refused to recognize the class of customers suing Comcast. The vote was 5–4, as it had been in the Wal-Mart case, with the justices again divided on ideological lines. Scalia, writing for the conservatives—himself, Roberts, Kennedy, Thomas, and Alito—said the two million people in the class had been injured in different ways depending on what state and county they lived in and the "permutations" in the cable services offered. The liberal dissenters insisted that there was "well nigh universal" recognition that class actions should not be rejected because members of the class were entitled to different damages—or, at least, there had been up until then.

The Wal-Mart and Comcast decisions were two more examples of the Court providing corporate America with "do-it-yourself tort reform." The rulings reduced the chances that big business would be held accountable for harm to their employees and customers, particularly in the largest cases, which corporations worried about most. With these decisions, the Court significantly eroded the class action, and its ability to serve as a revolutionary tool for the "smaller guy" to obtain justice.

The Court's campaign against class actions has shown no sign of slowing down. The old rhapsodic scholarship about the extraordinary possibilities of class action lawsuits has been replaced in recent years with articles with titles like "The Failing Faith in Class Actions," "The Decline of Class Actions," and "A Bleak Future for Class Actions?" In "The End of Class Actions?" a law professor declared that his assessment was "a pessimistic one," and he warned that it was hard for him "to conclude that a world without class actions will be anything other than a world with greater corporate wrongdoing."

THE COURT HAS ALSO BEEN TILTING THE LAW IN FAVOR OF CORPORATIONS in the arcane but critically important area of "forced arbitration," the requirement that businesses are increasingly building into their contracts with consumers, employees, and smaller businesses to waive the right to sue in court. These forced arbitration clauses ensure that disputes will be resolved not by neutral judges and jurors, but through a system that is heavily stacked in favor of corporations. Advocates for workers and consumers have been sounding the alarm against forced arbitration. In its report on forced arbitration, the Employee Rights Advocacy Institute for Law & Policy used the subtitle "How America's Wealthiest, Most Powerful Companies Use Fine Print to Subvert Employee Rights." The Court has been a strong supporter of forced arbitration clauses, generally, in recent years, by a 5–4 vote.

Arbitration once had positive associations. In 1976, in what has been called the "big bang" moment for alternative dispute resolution, Harvard Law School professor Frank Sander gave a speech to a distinguished legal conference on "Varieties of Dispute Processing," which argued that arbitration, mediation, and other alternative mechanisms could resolve certain kinds of disputes more efficiently and fairly than litigation. Before long, a movement was born.

Sander was a passionate and persuasive advocate for the cause, who presented alternative dispute resolution in idealistic terms. Sander had escaped Germany after Kristallnacht and made his way to the Netherlands and England without his family. He reunited with them in the Boston area and gained admission to Harvard College. After attending Harvard Law School and clerking for Frankfurter when *Brown v. Board of Education* was before the Court, Sander returned to Harvard Law School and became a pioneer in the field of family law. After a sabbatical in Sweden, he returned to Harvard with ideas about reforming the American legal system. In his 1976 speech, which he delivered to the Pound Conference, a special conference of judges and lawyers called by Warren Burger, Sander made a high-minded argument for abandoning the "one-size-fits-all" justice system and replacing it with a more modern one that matched disputes with the most effective way of resolving them.

In the years after Sander's speech, an alternative dispute resolution movement took hold. Reformers argued that arbitration, mediation, and other alternative mechanisms would allow litigants to avoid the formality, complexity, high costs, and delay of traditional litigation. Much of the arbitration early on was done under the supervision of courts, and the costs associated with it were often minimal.

Before long, however, corporations began to transform how alternative dispute resolution worked. They saw arbitration as a more advantageous way for them to resolve disputes than going to court, and they began writing mandatory arbitration agreements into their contracts with customers and employees, often buried in small print. Since the corporations were drafting the agreements, they could include terms that benefited them.

There were many ways these agreements became slanted in favor of the corporations that drew them up. In some cases, arbitration agreements specified that employees or customers had to file complaints in as little as thirty days. The employee or customer could also be required to travel long distances for the arbitration, at their own expense. Arbitration agreements often contained class action waivers so that employees and consumers who had been cheated could not band together in a single arbitration, represented by the same lawyer. Employees and consumers also often had to pay significant fees, and it was not always clear in advance how much it would cost. Corporations had enormous freedom in setting the terms, because, unlike litigation, which runs according to established laws and procedures, arbitration can take any form that the drafter of an arbitration agreement wants. As one arbitration firm said in a Q&A on its website, "What rules of evidence apply? The short answer is none."

For corporations, the biggest advantage of arbitration was who made the final decision. When disputes go to arbitration, they are not resolved by judges or juries, whose independence is protected. Federal judges have life tenure, and state court judges are rarely removed from office. Juries resolve a single case and do not face any negative consequences for the decisions they reach. Arbitrators, by contrast, generally have no job security. In most cases, they are hired for specific arbitrations, and they always need to worry about where their next case will come from. This creates a strong incentive to rule in favor of corporations, who generally select either the arbitrators or the companies that employ them.

Arbitrators who take on corporate matters can easily find themselves blackballed if they rule for an employee or consumer. Harvard law professor Elizabeth Bartholet experienced this firsthand when she was recruited by a prominent arbitration firm. In fourteen months, she arbitrated, and issued decisions in, nineteen cases involving a single credit card company, ruling for the company eighteen times. In the nineteenth, she ruled for the cardholder and awarded about $48,000 in damages. Bartholet said the arbitration firm removed her from seven pending cases she was scheduled to preside over. She resigned, and publicly decried the company's "apparent systematic bias in favor of the financial services industry."

Many arbitrators keep their jobs by not ruling against powerful interests. In an article headlined "Is Justice Served?" the *Los Angeles Times* quoted a Los Angeles attorney, Mitchell Shapiro, whose partner gave him a heads-up before he went into arbitration on a franchise matter. "You're not going to lose," the partner told him. Their law firm gave the arbitrator so much business, the partner said, that "he has never decided against us." The prediction proved correct: the arbitrator ruled for Shapiro's client.

Ruling exclusively, or almost always, in favor of corporations can be a lucrative career. While federal district court judges make just over $200,000, and state court judges can make far less, some arbitrators charge as much as $10,000 a day and make over $1 million a year. A California appellate justice told the *Los Angeles Times* that "private judging," an oft-used expression, "is an oxymoron," because arbitrators "are businessmen. They are in this for money."

Arbitrators understand the incentive structure well. When they arbitrate disputes between corporations and customers or employees, they do not often rule against the corporation. Public Citizen examined more than nineteen thousand cases involving arbitrators who worked for a company that is often hired by the credit card industry to resolve disputes with customers. It reported, under the bullet point "Stunning Results that Disfavor Consumers," that 94 percent of the decisions sided with business.

In addition to arbitrator bias, the arbitration process has other attributes that work in favor of corporations. The proceedings are usually secret, and generally there is no transcript or written explanation of the reasoning behind the arbitrator's ruling. As a result, companies that hire arbitrators often know how they have ruled in previous cases, while consumers do not. The secrecy also makes it difficult for media and public interest organizations to monitor arbitration proceedings for systematic bias or misconduct. Public Citizen concluded in its report that forced arbitration was "a deliberate strategy to substitute a secret, pro-business kangaroo court for an open trial on the merits."

As with campaign finance, the Court was not divided along ideological lines about arbitration in its early days. In the years after Sander's "big bang" speech on the virtues of alternative dispute resolution, many liberals supported mandatory arbitration as a more flexible, speedy, and cost-effective way of resolving legal conflicts. That included liberal justices. In 1983, Brennan wrote the Court's opinion in a decision that required a North Carolina hospital to arbitrate a dispute with a contractor, saying that doubts about the scope of issues for arbitration "should be resolved in favor of arbitration."

In time, however, the Court began to view arbitration cases more ideologically, with the conservative justices generally in favor and the liberal ones opposed. The division emerged as it became clear how corporations were using arbitration. The cases arriving at the Court showed that arbitration, which had arrived on the scene with so much idealism behind it, was becoming a means for corporations to deny the less powerful and less sophisticated people they had harmed a day in court.

A major turning point came in 1991, when the Court decided a case that posed a critical question: whether employees could be forced to arbitrate legal disputes, including discrimination cases, with their employers. Robert Gilmer, a financial services manager, had sued the company that fired him under the Age Discrimination in Employment Act. When he registered with the New York Stock Exchange, he had signed a form saying that any legal actions he had over his employment had to be resolved through arbitration. Gilmer wanted to bring his age discrimination suit in federal court, where he would have a far greater chance of prevailing, but his former employer insisted he had to go into arbitration.

The Court ruled against Gilmer by a 7–2 vote, holding that he could not bring his discrimination claim in federal court. White, writing for the majority, relied heavily on the Federal Arbitration Act, a federal law enacted in 1924, which he said created a strong national policy in favor of arbitration. Stevens, in a dissent joined by Marshall, argued that the Federal Arbitration Act made clear in its own text that it did not apply to employment contracts. He also insisted that it was wrong to force someone into arbitration when he was suing under a federal law that Congress had enacted to protect Americans from discrimination, something only the courts could be relied on to do effectively.

The dissenters were right in their reading of the Federal Arbitration Act. The act was adopted in 1924 at the urging of New York merchants to give them a fast and efficient way of resolving their disputes with each other. Congress passed the law to help those merchants, not to change employment relationships across the country. In fact, as Stevens pointed out, the arbitration act expressly said that it was not intended to apply to any workers "engaged in foreign or interstate commerce." The Federal Arbitration Act "was about agreements between two sophisticated business people," Imre Szalai, a law professor at Loyola University New Orleans, has said. "Unfortunately, the Supreme Court . . . has grossly misinterpreted the statute. It was never intended to apply to workers."

With its 1991 ruling, the Court sent a clear message to corporations nationwide: if they wanted to take their disputes with the workers they fired, or discriminated against, or cheated out of wages, out of the court system, they could do so by putting a forced arbitration agreement in their employment contract. It was a generous offer the corporations were quick to take the Court up on. In the future, many more workers would find themselves in Gilmer's position, of desperately wanting their claim against their employer to be heard by a judge or jury, and being forced to take it to an arbitrator.

In 2000, the Court's conservative majority made it clear that it would enforce arbitration agreements against consumers just as unrelentingly as it had against workers. The case before it was brought by Larketta Randolph, who had purchased a mobile home in Opelika, Alabama, with financing from Green Tree Financial Corporation. Randolph sued Green Tree, charging that it had violated federal truth-in-lending laws. The contract she signed with Green Tree contained a forced arbitration clause. Green Tree insisted that their dispute had to go to arbitration. Randolph had a specific and very reasonable objection: the arbitration clause in her contract did not specify how much she would have to pay in fees for the arbitration, and she did not think she could afford it. She did not believe that to vindicate her rights under a federal consumer law she should be forced into a private arbitration process that could drive her into bankruptcy.

The Court ruled for Green Tree by a 5–4 vote. Rehnquist, writing for the conservative justices, made the perverse argument that Randolph had no grounds for objecting to the cost of arbitration, since she had no idea how much the fees would be. That was, of course, precisely Randolph's point—that it was the not knowing that was unfair to her. The Court did not seem to care that for a person of modest means like Randolph, being told that she had no right to know the cost of arbitration in advance made it very likely she would simply not bring her claim at all.

Ginsburg, writing for the four liberal justices, said she would have given Randolph a chance to be told the cost of arbitration in advance. It was notable that the Court divided 5–4 along ideological lines, something it would increasingly do in forced arbitration cases. It was around this time, as one commentator observed, that "the Court's liberal wing woke up to the potential of arbitration to simply preclude the prosecution of claims by consumers and workers."

With the Court strongly on their side, corporations had enormous power to use forced arbitration clauses that protected them from being sued in court and to force people into arbitration when they did not want to go. They also had great freedom to write terms that stacked the arbitration process heavily in their favor. There was, however, one aspect of forced arbitration that still eluded them: they wanted the courts to make it clear that they had the right to include a provision in their mandatory arbitration clauses prohibiting employees and customers from bringing class actions in arbitration. Corporations knew that when employees and customers were forced to go into arbitration alone, they were deprived of the many advantages that came with proceeding as a class—and often, they did not bother to bring their claims at all. In recent years, both of these groups—consumers and employees—have asked the Court to hold that the class action waivers in their arbitration agreements were not enforceable, for different reasons. The Court, however, has come down strongly on the side of enforcing class action waivers, in a series of ideologically charged rulings.

In 2011, the Court considered a case involving consumers locked into a forced arbitration agreement with their cell phone provider. Vincent and Liza Concepcion had signed a cell phone service contract with AT&T that offered free phones. The Concepcions sued after they were told that they had to pay $30.22 in sales tax for their "free" phones, based on the retail value of their phones. The Concepcions filed a class action lawsuit against AT&T, alleging that charging tax on free phones was fraud.

AT&T said the contract the Concepcions signed required them to resolve any complaints in arbitration and did not allow them to enter arbitration as part of a class action. If AT&T got its way, the Concepcions would, as a practical matter, have no recourse. If people are cheated out of $30.22, they are not likely to file a non-class-action lawsuit or to go into arbitration as individuals. It would not be worth the time and expense.

The federal district court that heard the case said that the Concepcions had a right to go into arbitration as part of a class action. It relied on California state law, which held that class action waivers are legally "unconscionable," or so one-sided and unfair that they are not enforceable. The San Francisco–based U.S. Court of Appeals for the Ninth Circuit agreed and held that the Concepcions could proceed as a class in arbitration.

The Supreme Court, by a 5–4 vote, ruled that the Concepcions had to proceed in individual arbitration. Scalia, writing for the majority, said that the Federal Arbitration Act gave anyone drawing up a contract the right to include a class action waiver. Under the doctrine of "preemption," when there is a conflict between federal and state law, the federal law generally takes precedence, because of the Constitution's Supremacy Clause. As a result, Scalia said, California's law was not valid—and AT&T could force the Concepcions into individual arbitration.

In his dissent, Breyer, writing for the four liberals, emphasized that the Federal Arbitration Act expressly says that arbitration agreements should not be enforced in ways that are inconsistent with state laws. Congress had made it clear that it wanted states to have "an important role" in deciding how arbitration would work, Breyer said, and it wanted to respect state rules like California's ban on class action waivers. Breyer also underscored the real-world impact of the Court's decision: if companies like AT&T were allowed to put bans on class actions in their forced arbitration agreements, they would be free to cheat their consumers out of small amounts of money with impunity. "What rational lawyer would have signed on to represent the Concepcions in litigation for the possibility of fees stemming from a $30.22 claim?" Breyer asked.

The AT&T case might have been a dispute over forced arbitration in consumer contracts, but it was really yet another ruling against class action lawsuits—and, in some ways, the most damaging one of all. It gave corporations an easy way to protect themselves against being sued in class actions by their customers. They simply had to bury two provisions somewhere in the fine print of their sales contracts: a forced arbitration clause and a class action waiver. There was virtually no chance customers would notice them, and even less that they would raise any objections. The Court's ruling, one class action expert said, "basically lets companies escape class actions, so long as they do so by means of arbitration agreements."

Two years later, the Court enforced a class action waiver even though it meant that the party being forced into individual arbitration would effectively have no chance to protect its rights. Italian Colors Restaurant, in Oakland, California, sued American Express, claiming that the credit card giant was using its monopoly power to force it to pay higher fees than other cards charged. American Express said Italian Colors had to go into individual arbitration, based on the contract it had signed. The restaurant said it would not be able to bring its claim if it had to proceed on its own. To prove its case about monopoly power, it would need to hire an antitrust expert who would cost hundreds of thousands of dollars or more, while the maximum damage award it could receive would be less than $39,000.

The Court ruled for American Express by a 5–3 vote, in another opinion by Scalia for the five conservative justices. For the majority, the case was simple: the contract Italian Colors Restaurant had signed with American Express, and its bar on class actions, was binding. The Federal Arbitration Act, Scalia said, required arbitration clauses to be enforced "rigorously."

Kagan, in dissent, said the majority was wrong to force Italian Colors into individual arbitration. The Court had a doctrine, she noted, called the "effective vindication" rule, which said that arbitration agreements were not binding if they forced parties into arbitration under circumstances that would not allow them a fair chance to enforce congressionally created rights.

The rule clearly applied to Italian Colors Restaurant, which was asserting its rights under federal antitrust law, she said. Taking away its ability to bring its claim as a class action effectively meant denying it an opportunity to protect its federal right not to be injured by a monopoly. Kagan provided what she said was a "nutshell version" of the majority's opinion: "Too darn bad."

In 2018, the Court imposed individual forced arbitration on a group that corporations were particularly eager to extend it to: employees. The case was a lawsuit by Jacob Lewis, a technical writer, against Epic Systems, the health care software company he worked for, charging that it had failed to pay him and other technical writers for overtime hours. Lewis filed his case as a class action lawsuit, but Epic Systems said that an arbitration agreement he had consented to required him to go into individual arbitration. There was, however, a strong argument that employees could not be denied the right to bring class actions with fellow employees. As Lewis pointed out, Section 7 of the National Labor Relations Act guarantees workers the right to work together to protect their interests.

The Court, in an opinion by Gorsuch, again said that the Federal Arbitration Act required arbitration agreements to be enforced as written. This time, the conservatives were more emphatic than ever about using the act as a battering ram against any attempts to rein in mandatory arbitration. Gorsuch said that it protected "pretty absolutely" the enforceability of class action waivers in arbitration agreements. That included, he said, a class waiver in a contract with workers, despite the protections of Section 7.

In a dissent that she read from the bench, Ginsburg underscored that the conservative justices were ignoring decades of well-established labor law in reaching their decision. When Congress enacted the NLRA, she said, during the Great Depression, it had become clear to the nation that the only way for "vulnerable workers" to protect their rights was to band together and work for their interests collectively. To ensure their ability to do so, Congress included Section 7, which guaranteed workers the right to engage in "concerted activities . . . for mutual aid or protection." Jacob Lewis's class action was the sort of concerted action the 1935 Congress was intent on protecting. The Court's conservatives, however, would not allow even the Magna Carta of American labor to stop its mandatory arbitration juggernaut.

The *Epic Systems Corp. v. Lewis* decision was a major victory for corporations and an enormous setback for workers. If corporations put the right provisions in their employment contracts—a mandatory arbitration clause and a class action waiver—they would now be protected against class actions from their employees in court or in arbitration. Lawyers for employees immediately began looking for ways around the ruling, but it would almost certainly bring to a standstill the vast majority of class actions by employees of corporations that had drafted their employment contracts well. That would leave many employees forced to enter a hostile, and often costly, arbitration system on their own—or simply not bother to bring their claims at all.

THERE ARE MANY OTHER AREAS IN WHICH THE COURT HAS ACTIVELY pushed the law in favor of corporations, to the detriment of consumers, employees, and other victims of their harmful acts. The Court has often sided with corporations that are accused of violating environmental protection laws. One of these rulings came in 2009 in a challenge to Coeur Alaska, a mining company that pumped "slurry discharge," a toxic form of wastewater, into an Alaska lake, even though Environmental Protection Agency rules prohibited it. The Court held that the Clean Water Act permitted Coeur Alaska to do the pumping with just a permit from the U.S. Army Corps of Engineers, and that it did not need one from the EPA, as environmental groups insisted it did. The permit that Coeur Alaska received from the Army Corps of Engineers allowed it to dump 4.5 million tons of waste, even though it would wipe out all life in the lake.

Ginsburg, writing for herself, Stevens, and Souter, said the Court had allowed mines to improperly classify their discharge to evade the EPA's pollution standards. The holding, she said, was "antithetical to the text, structure, and purpose of the Clean Water Act." Earthjustice, an environmental group, warned that the Court's misreading of environmental laws would have wide-ranging implications. "If a mining company can turn Lower Slate Lake in Alaska into a lifeless waste dump," it said, "other polluters with solids in their wastewater can potentially do the same to any body in America."

The Court has also moved antitrust law in corporations' direction, giving wealthy monopolists more room to stifle competition and extract unfair profits. One important area in which the Court has favored corporate monopolies is the essential facilities doctrine, which could have helped to rein in large technology companies, including broadband internet companies and platforms like Facebook and Google. The doctrine was designed to prevent companies from abusing their monopoly over a service or product that its competitors need. The Court recognized the essential facilities doctrine in a 1912 decision that ordered a railroad consortium organized by robber baron Jay Gould, which controlled the only railroad bridges over the Mississippi River in St. Louis, to allow competing railroads to use them at a reasonable cost. In a 2004 decision involving the prices phone companies charge competitors to use their phone lines, the Court gutted the doctrine.

Diane Wood, a judge on the Chicago-based U.S. Court of Appeals for the Seventh Circuit, suggested in a 2019 speech that the Court had made a mistake by eviscerating the essential facilities doctrine—and at just the wrong time. Wood, who taught antitrust law at the University of Chicago Law School before President Clinton nominated her to the bench, and who was a leading contender for a Supreme Court nomination under President Obama, noted that as a result of the 2004 ruling, the main legal doctrine for taking on so-called bottleneck monopolies had been badly weakened just when the digital revolution might make it more necessary than ever.

Many technology activists share Wood's concerns. The Electronic Frontier Foundation, which promotes civil liberties in the digital world, has called on the Federal Trade Commission to "revitalize" the essential facilities doctrine. The doctrine is, the group said, one of the most obvious ways of challenging the threat of monopolistic behavior and censorship posed by the dominant technology platforms. The timing is "ideal for a fresh look at the doctrine," the EFF said, with the "harmful effects of Internet platform dominance" becoming increasingly obvious. It is unlikely, however, that even if the FTC wanted to breathe new life into the essential facilities doctrine, the current Court, with its skeptical approach to antitrust, would allow it to be revived.

THE COURT'S PRO-CORPORATE RULINGS HAVE INCREASED ECONOMIC inequality in many ways, large, small, and incalculable. Each of the Court's business decisions is a financial transfer—from the Alaska fishermen to Exxon Shipping, from Curtis Campbell to State Farm, from Betty Dukes to Wal-Mart, from Jacob Lewis and his colleagues to Epic Systems, and from other corporate victims to corporations everywhere. The dollar amounts are enormous.

In the punitive damages decisions, the economics are straightforward: the Court's rulings have saved corporations many billions of dollars that otherwise would have gone to people they had injured or cheated. In the single year 2001, just before the *State Farm* decision, more than $162 billion in punitive damages were awarded at trial or affirmed on appeal. Punitive damages were also growing rapidly. In 1992, there were no punitive damages awards over $100 million, but by 2001 there were sixteen. Corporations were worried about this fast-growing expense, as their enthusiasm for the tort reform movement showed. After the Court established its single-digit-ratio formula, corporations could worry a lot less.

Much of the hundreds of billions of dollars corporations were saving came directly from ordinary Americans, who would have been awarded the punitive damages. The loss to society, however, goes beyond the money damages that will not be awarded or distributed. The Court's decisions also encourage more corporate wrongdoing in the future.

Lawsuits that are filed when corporations engage in misconduct operate as what New York University law professor Arthur Miller has called a "satellite regulatory system." Working alongside the government's regulatory system, these lawsuits pressure corporations not to harm people. This satellite system is necessary because the real regulatory system does not always work properly. Administrative agencies are invariably short of resources. They are also often "captured" by the industries they are supposed to regulate, giving their loyalty to the corporations they are meant to watch over rather than to the public. The problem of regulatory capture has been particularly severe in recent years as President Trump has appointed corporate executives and lobbyists to watchdog positions, including a onetime coal lobbyist chosen to run the EPA and an acting director of the Consumer Financial Protection Bureau who once called his own bureau a "sick, sad" joke.

The result of the Court's weakening of the satellite regulatory system will be more of the conduct that punitive damages once discouraged. Companies will sell more products with hidden defects, like the BMW that Ira Gore bought. Insurance companies will cheat their customers more often, as State Farm did Campbell, and energy companies will take fewer precautions against massive oil spills. Corporations will save money, while customers and employees and innocent bystanders will face a higher likelihood of being hurt. The injured parties will still be able to sue for the actual damages they suffer, but as a practical matter, people like Gore will in many cases not go to the trouble of suing for actual damages of $4,000 and very small punitive damages.

The Court's class action decisions have created another windfall for corporations that have infringed on the rights of consumers and employees. As predicted, many class actions have been thrown out under the new rules. A year after the Concepcions lost their case against AT&T, Public Citizen found that at least seventy-six class action lawsuits had been stopped from going forward, including ones the presiding judges said should have proceeded. After three years, the group released a report that described some of the class action lawsuits that were blocked. One was a suit by car detailers who said that CarMax had refused to pay them the overtime wages they earned. Public Citizen said that "potentially hundreds of CarMax employees" had been "left without any recourse because their only option is to pursue their claims individually in a private arbitration."

The result of this decline in class actions is that corporations are paying out far less in damages and settlements to groups of people they have harmed. In 2018, class action settlements fell to $1.32 billion, from $2.72 billion in 2017, according to the *Workplace Class Action Blog*—a more than 50 percent decline. The author of the report attributed much of the plunge to the *Dukes* case's higher barriers to certifying a class and the individual arbitration rule upheld in *Epic Systems*.

The Court's forced arbitration rulings are also having the effect many experts predicted. Corporations are increasingly insulating themselves from consumer lawsuits by placing mandatory arbitration clauses in their sales contracts. Of the Fortune 100, eighty-one have used arbitration agreements in connection with consumer transactions, according to a study published in 2019 in the *UC Davis Law Review*. There were more than 826 million consumer arbitration agreements in force in 2018, in a nation with fewer than 330 million people, the study found. "The ability to access the courthouse is disappearing for American consumers because of the proliferation of arbitration agreements among the majority of America's leading companies," the study concluded.

Corporations have also been including forced arbitration clauses in more of their employment contracts. The number of employers using forced arbitration clauses was already growing rapidly before the *Epic Systems* ruling. In 1992, only 2 percent of non-unionized employers used mandatory arbitration clauses, but by 2018, 54 percent did. After *Epic Systems*, the growth is almost certain to speed up, since forced arbitration clauses are more valuable to employers when they also contain a class action waiver.

Now that the Court has given corporations a green light to include class action waivers in their forced arbitration agreements, those, too, are proliferating. The UC Davis study found that of the eighty-one Fortune 100 companies with forced arbitration clauses in their customer contracts, seventy-eight included class action waivers. In 2019, JPMorgan Chase, the nation's largest bank, announced that its credit card customers would be required to go into private arbitration in any dispute with the bank, even if the original agreement they signed did not contain an arbitration clause, unless they filed for a waiver. The new policy, which affected about forty-seven million accounts, specified that customers would not have the right to proceed in arbitration as part of a class.

Corporations have also been emboldened, in the wake of *Epic Systems*, to put class action waivers in more of their employment contracts. After the ruling, management-side labor lawyers rushed to advise their corporate clients to add the waivers with an enthusiasm that at times bordered on the unseemly. "You Had Me at 'Class Action Waiver,'" the global law firm Baker McKenzie declared in its *Employer Report* blog. "For employers looking to take advantage of the benefits of individual arbitration," the firm said, the key was "show me the class action waiver!"

These massive changes have largely occurred under the radar. Deepak Gupta, a lawyer with Public Citizen who represented the Concepcions against AT&T, said the general public is missing the enormous harm the Court has been doing to consumers, because "issues like class-action rules and preemption and arbitration" can make "most people fall asleep." Although these cases are overshadowed by the Court's major civil rights rulings, he says, "they actually have, I think, a much bigger impact on our everyday lives as consumers and workers."

It is impossible to put a dollar figure on the enormous societal transformation from a system in which consumer and employee injuries were compensated to one in which they very likely will not be. Millions of Americans will eventually find out, if they have not noticed it already, that when an employer fires them or fails to pay them overtime, a bank imposes exorbitant fees, or a manufactured product injures them, they will not have their day in court. Their only remedy will lie in an arbitration system set up to deny their claims.

Just as there is no way to put a price tag on the Court's steady erosion of Americans' right of access to the courts, there is no way to calculate the cost of its many other aggressively pro-corporate rulings. It is impossible to know how much consumers will ultimately pay in monopolistic costs of all kinds, because the Court eviscerated the essential facilities rule just before the rise of dominant technology platforms in online retailing, internet search, and social media. A full accounting would have to include the damage done by having a small number of technology companies dominating whole areas of public life, and using their dominant position, in many cases, to exploit low-wage workers, drive journalistic organizations out of business, and exert extraordinary influence over the nation's elections and government.

The cost of the Court's decision to allow a mining company to turn Alaska's Lower Slate Lake into a "lifeless waste dump," and other environment-destroying rulings like it, likewise cannot be gauged. In the aggregate, however, the damage these decisions will cause in cancer, heart disease, lung disease, and global climate change is sizable. In 2017, Britain's Lancet Commission on Pollution and Health tried to quantify the cost of pollution in a single year worldwide, and it estimated that in 2015 it caused economic damage of $4.6 trillion and killed nine million people. The Court's anti-environmental rulings are responsible for a modest but definite part of this global economic reckoning.

The Court's business rulings are not only unfair to the individual litigants who lose their cases but to whole economic classes. They have caused a massive transfer of wealth to corporations, corporate executives, and shareholders. That wealth is coming from ordinary Americans who interact with corporations not as owners or managers but as consumers, employees, and innocent bystanders. In its decisions involving corporations, the Court has made especially clear something that is true across virtually every area of the law: that it is a Court for the 1 percent, not the 99 percent.

CHAPTER ♦ 8

CRIMINAL JUSTICE

In February 2013, the Supreme Court heard a case about the police interrogation of a criminal suspect in custody. Alonzo King was an unremarkable criminal defendant, charged with menacing people with a shotgun. The jurisdiction in which he was arrested was just as mundane: Wicomico County, a sleepy part of southern Maryland that is home to Perdue Farms' headquarters. What made King's case of interest to the Court was that when he was arrested, the police took a DNA sample from the inside of his cheeks with a swab. They acted pursuant to the Maryland DNA Collection Act, which authorized the police to take DNA samples from criminal suspects. The state uploaded King's DNA to the Combined DNA Index System, a federal database, and it matched a suspect in a six-year-old rape case. King was tried for the rape and convicted.

In appealing his conviction, King argued that the seizure of his DNA violated his Fourth Amendment rights. It is well established that the state can compel a criminal suspect to help its investigation in certain ways, including by giving fingerprints. Forcing a suspect to provide a DNA sample, however, is more intrusive than taking fingerprints, and it raised more profound privacy issues. DNA can reveal not only people's identity but their entire genetic profile. The Court of Appeals of Maryland ruled for King, holding that the seizure of his DNA and the portion of the Maryland DNA law that authorized it violated the Fourth Amendment.

When *Maryland v. King* arrived at the Supreme Court, there was no doubt about its significance. While DNA samples were being collected in states across the country, geneticists were unlocking new secrets from DNA at a rapid pace. It was clear that the rules the Court established for the government's use of the DNA it collected would be of enormous significance as genetic science progressed. At oral argument, Alito called *King* "perhaps the most important criminal procedure case that this Court has heard in decades," and legal commentators were quick to agree.

Experts lined up to explain the scientific issues and to underscore the dangers that lurked in the case. Civil libertarians, scientists, and defense lawyers warned that the way the government was collecting and using DNA—including the Combined DNA Index System (CODIS), which Congress established in 1994—posed an unprecedented threat to privacy. A DNA database gave the government a storehouse of critical information about what physical and mental illnesses a person might have or might develop, their race and ethnicity, who their family members were, and other deeply personal matters.

Law enforcement understood the value of DNA and was constantly looking to expand its use. CODIS began as a small software pilot project serving just fourteen state and local laboratories, but by the time of the *King* case it had expanded to all fifty states and contained more than eleven million DNA profiles. The Electronic Privacy Information Center and twenty-six technical experts and legal scholars explained in a friend-of-the-court brief that CODIS was growing "dramatically and unpredictably" without the necessary legal safeguards and posed a serious threat to "genetic privacy rights."

The American Civil Liberties Union, in another friend-of-the-court brief, emphasized how wide the scope of DNA collection had become. The federal government and thirty-one states had DNA collection laws, and many jurisdictions took DNA from people who had been arrested for crimes far less serious than the gun offense King was charged with. In at least thirteen states, DNA samples were taken at every felony arrest, including relatively minor ones. In California, these included stealing $250 worth of crops from a field or unlawfully subleasing a car. Federal law allowed DNA to be seized from people arrested for misdemeanors, which could include illegal parking or walking a pet with a leash longer than six feet.

Some groups were, predictably, more likely than others to have their genetic privacy invaded by forcible DNA collection. The Howard University School of Law Human and Civil Rights Clinic, in a friend-of-the-court brief, pointed out that the impact of intrusive law enforcement techniques of this kind falls disproportionately on minority populations. Even though the law was racially neutral, the civil rights clinic advised, "history and practice dictate" that it would "be used to harass and infringe upon the rights of people of color."

Despite the serious warnings from experts, the Court, by a 5–4 vote, reversed the Maryland court and upheld King's conviction. The Court broke down on ideological lines, with one switch. Breyer, one of the liberal justices, voted with four of the conservatives—Roberts, Kennedy, Thomas, and Alito—to uphold the conviction. Scalia dissented, along with the remaining three liberals—Ginsburg, Kagan, and Sotomayor.

Kennedy, writing for the Court, said the Fourth Amendment required balancing privacy rights against "law enforcement–related concerns." In his view, the government had legitimate government interests in collecting DNA from a person who had been arrested—most of all, the ability to properly identify him. Kennedy said the privacy interests were "minimal," since the subject was already in police custody, not in his home or on the street, and the search itself was just a "gentle rub" of a swab. He also emphasized that the matching that occurred in CODIS was done with parts of the subject's DNA that do not reveal genetic traits.

Scalia, who wrote the dissent, argued that, although the Court framed the case as being about the ability to identify a suspect, it was actually about much more. The government used the DNA samples to search DNA databases and try to connect a known suspect—in this case King—with unsolved crimes. In Fourth Amendment terminology, that kind of search is one without "individualized suspicion"—the government would be trying to connect King to crimes it had no specific reason to suspect he was involved with. The government is prohibited from searching people without individualized suspicion to convict them of crimes "without exception," Scalia said, and that prohibition "lies at the very heart of the 4th Amendment."

The majority was trying to disguise "the vast (and scary) scope of its holding," Scalia said, by saying that DNA would be taken by the police only from people suspected of "serious offenses." That was, Scalia insisted, "a limitation it cannot deliver." This sort of DNA testing would be done more widely now that the Court had approved it, he said—possibly, one day, even on people applying for driver's licenses or boarding planes. Scalia suggested that the nation could be on its way to becoming a "genetic panopticon," invoking English philosopher Jeremy Bentham's nightmare vision—from the Greek *pan,* for "all," and *optikon,* for "sight"—of a world in which every aspect of a person could be observed.

Law enforcement and its allies welcomed the ruling, but critics of excessive government power on both the left and right worried about where the Court was taking the country. Norman Reimer, the executive director of the National Association of Criminal Defense Lawyers, called the decision a "dangerous precedent" that could "pave the way for an extraordinary degradation of the Fourth Amendment, with far reaching consequences for Americans' individual liberty and privacy rights." Senator Ted Cruz, the conservative Texas Republican, tweeted, "Unfortunate MD v. King #SCOTUS ruling expands govt power, invades liberty & undermines our constitutional rights."

In an earlier era, the Court had taken a very different approach to the rights of criminal suspects. In the "rights revolution" of the 1960s, the

Warren Court significantly expanded the rights of people accused of crimes. It saw criminal suspects, who faced the immense power of police and prosecutors, as a vulnerable group in need of protection.

When the Warren Court began, defendants in state court, where almost 99 percent of criminal prosecutions occurred, had few constitutional rights. States were required to meet a basic standard of "fundamental fairness" under the Fourteenth Amendment, but beyond that, state police and prosecutors had considerable freedom to do what they wanted. If the police obtained forced confessions or seized evidence through unreasonable searches, there was no federal requirement that state courts exclude them from being introduced at trial, and about half of the states allowed prosecutors to use this sort of tainted evidence, which would be barred in federal court.

In 1961, the Court began to change the rules. The case that launched the Court's new direction, *Mapp v. Ohio,* began in Cleveland in May 1957, when the police arrived at Dollree Mapp's home to question a man about a bombing. Mapp was a strong-willed Mississippi native who married one top-ranked boxer and was later engaged to another, the light heavyweight champion Archie Moore. Mapp, who had called her lawyer, refused to let the police in without a warrant, but they broke the glass on a back door and let themselves in. When she demanded to see a search warrant, one of the officers waved a piece of paper he claimed was a warrant. Mapp grabbed the paper and stuffed it in her blouse, and the officer reached in and grabbed it back. When she continued to resist, the police handcuffed her and searched her home. The police did not find the man they were looking for, but they found a trunk in the cellar with sexually explicit pamphlets, pictures, and a "little pencil doodle." Mapp said the material belonged to a boarder who no longer lived there, but she was convicted on obscenity charges and sentenced to one to seven years in prison. The state never produced the paper the officer had waved or any evidence that there was a valid search warrant.

If Mapp had been tried in federal court, the seized evidence could not have been used against her. In 1914, the Court had adopted the "exclusionary rule" for criminal trials in federal court, which barred the use of evidence taken in violation of the Fourth Amendment. The rule kept police honest by removing any incentive to obtain evidence illegally, and it protected the integrity of the justice system by preventing prosecutors from benefiting from such evidence. At the time of Mapp's arrest, however, the Court had not extended the exclusionary rule to state court trials, and Ohio did not have its own exclusionary rule.

On June 19, 1961, in *Mapp v. Ohio*, the Court overturned Mapp's conviction, by a 6–3 vote. The Court said that the sexually explicit materials had been seized from Mapp's home in violation of the Fourth Amendment, since there was no warrant and she did not consent. It then laid down a bold new constitutional rule: the federal exclusionary rule that had developed under the Fourteenth Amendment now applied to the states. The decision instantly expanded defendants' rights nationwide—specifically, it meant that the roughly half of states that did not exclude illegally seized evidence at trial now were required to. The importance of the new rule was obvious immediately. *The New York Times*, in a front-page story, called it "the most significant limitation ever imposed on state criminal procedure by the Supreme Court in a single decision."

There were many reasons for the Warren Court's new interest in expanding the rights of people accused of crimes. In part, it reflected the Court's new membership. The Court had changed with the arrival of Warren as chief justice in 1953, and it would change even more throughout the 1960s. President Kennedy's two nominations in 1962, Goldberg and White, pushed the Court to the left, and Johnson's nomination of Thurgood Marshall in 1967 did so even more. The result was a Court that was increasingly concerned about civil liberties, police misconduct, and all of the other issues embedded in criminal justice.

The Court's championing of defendants' rights was also a reflection of the times. With the rise of the civil rights movement, the nation was learning how much injustice was built into the fabric of American society. As civil rights protesters and Freedom Riders clashed with police, sheriffs, and state troopers across the segregated South, the public's faith in law enforcement began to fray. There was a growing awareness that the criminal justice system was, in many cases, an extension of an oppressive system. "If you examine the criminal law decisions of the Warren Court," Morton Horwitz, a Harvard law professor and legal historian, said, "you can grasp the extent to which race is the central, often unacknowledged, factor."

Not least, there was the reality of how law enforcement behaved at the time. Big-city police departments and small-town sheriffs knew their actions would rarely be second-guessed, and they acted accordingly. The police grabbed people off the street and questioned them, with little or no basis. When officers arrested suspects or interrogated them at the station house, they broke rules, and occasionally bones. As a New York City deputy police commissioner said about obtaining a search warrant in the era before the *Mapp* ruling, "Evidence obtained without a warrant—illegally if you will—was admissible in state courts. So the feeling was: Why bother?" The Warren Court was bringing law to one of the most lawless parts of society: law enforcement.

In 1966, the Court issued a second landmark criminal law decision, *Miranda v. Arizona,* which limited the state's ability to pressure criminal suspects for information. It held that statements made by suspects in police custody could not be used against them at trial unless they had been advised beforehand of their right to remain silent and to be represented by counsel—the famous Miranda warning. *Miranda* expanded suspects' Fifth Amendment rights against self-incrimination the same way that *Mapp* had expanded suspects' Fourth Amendment rights against unreasonable searches.

The ruling was one that Warren himself had been eager to hand down. He had told his law clerks to keep an eye out for a case that raised the issue of the right to counsel for suspects who were in police custody. The case the Court selected arose when Ernesto Miranda was arrested by the Phoenix police, who were investigating the kidnapping and rape of a local woman.

After Miranda was questioned for two hours without being told he had the right to have a lawyer present, the police extracted a signed confession that was used to convict him.

Miranda was even more revolutionary than *Mapp.* Warren's opinion had an undeniable legislative quality, setting out in detail the warning every police department in the country had to deliver to criminal suspects. The Court's rules were so precise that police began carrying cards with the Miranda warning written out: "You have the right to remain silent. Anything you say can and will be used against you in a court of law. You have the right to an attorney. If you cannot afford an attorney, one will be provided for you."

Mapp and *Miranda* were only two of more than six hundred criminal law decisions in the Warren era. There was no question that these rulings had a momentous collective impact on the nation, though there was debate over whether they were a change for the better. To liberals, they represented nothing less than a "criminal justice revolution" that made society significantly fairer. Law enforcement was less enthusiastic. "I guess now," the executive director of the International Association of Chiefs of Police complained after *Miranda,* "we'll have to supply all squad cars with attorneys."

Nixon's nomination of Burger to be chief justice marked the end of the criminal justice revolution. In reporting on the appointment, *The New York Times* noted that Burger's "outspoken opposition to the present trend among judges to broaden the rights of suspects" was consistent with the "specifications" for justices that Nixon had set during his presidential campaign. With Nixon's quick nomination of Blackmun, Powell, and Rehnquist in the next two and a half years, Burger soon had a majority in place to take criminal law in the direction the president wanted.

The Burger Court wasted no time in unraveling Warren-era criminal justice decisions, starting with *Miranda*. In a 1971 case, Burger, writing for a five-justice majority, held that a criminal defendant's confession taken without a *Miranda* warning *could* be used at trial, if it was being used to "impeach," or contradict, his own testimony. It was less than two years into the

Burger Court and already there was a new rule: illegally taken confessions *usually* could not be used at trial.

The Court also created exceptions for what kinds of police custody required a *Miranda* warning. In 1977, it held that *Miranda* did not apply when the police called a suspect in and questioned him at police headquarters if they did not arrest him or physically prevent him from leaving. Marshall, in dissent, protested that "the coercive elements" in the case were "so pervasive" that the Fifth Amendment required a *Miranda* warning.

There was more scaling back to come. In 1984, the Court created a "public safety" exception to *Miranda*. The case involved the arrest of a man who had been seen with a gun but did not have it on him when the police arrived. The police questioned him and he told them where the gun was. In an opinion by Rehnquist, the Court said that his statement was admissible in court, even though he had been handcuffed when he was questioned and he had not been given a *Miranda* warning. The holding that the police could question someone without a *Miranda* warning when the public's safety was at issue was an exception that had the potential to grow very large.

With every passing year, there was less of *Miranda* left. Even when it became far more conservative, however, the Court was unwilling to go so far as to overturn the actual decision, which had become deeply entrenched in American law and culture. In 2000, Rehnquist, who was no great fan of the original ruling, wrote an opinion for a 7–2 majority reaffirming the 1966 decision. "A majority of the Court is unwilling to overrule *Miranda*," one legal scholar observed, "however, a majority is also unwilling to take *Miranda* seriously."

The post-Warren Court also hollowed out *Mapp* and its insistence that evidence that was taken without a warrant or consent could not be used at trial. As with *Miranda*, it created increasingly large exceptions that allowed prosecutors to use improperly seized evidence. In 1973, the Court endorsed a warrantless police search of a car when one passenger gave consent, even though he did not know he had the right to refuse consent. In dissent, Brennan wrote, "It wholly escapes me how our citizens can meaningfully be said to have waived something as precious as a constitutional guarantee without ever being aware of its existence."

Conservatives had long wanted a "good faith" exception to the exclusionary rule that would apply when the police did not know they were seizing evidence illegally. In 1984, the Court created it. The Court ruled, by a 6–3 vote, that if the police had an invalid warrant but they reasonably, in good faith, believed it was valid, the evidence they found in a search could be used at trial. White, writing for the majority, said that more emphasis had to be placed on the "substantial social costs" of the exclusionary rule, including the fact that it could result in some guilty defendants going free.

The idealism of the Warren Court's *Mapp* decision was by now long gone. Brennan, in dissent, objected that the Court was endorsing the use of "illegally obtained evidence" to prosecute defendants "whose rights have been violated—a result that had previously been thought to be foreclosed." He argued that the Court was ignoring the substantial costs to society of accepting illegal searches. "It now appears," Brennan said, "that the Court's victory over the Fourth Amendment is complete."

During the "war on drugs" of the 1990s, the Court endorsed another kind of controversial warrantless search, known as "working the buses." The issue came to the Court in a case in which officers in Broward County, Florida, boarded an interstate bus and interrogated passengers, looking for drug traffickers. They questioned Terrance Bostick, a young black man who was traveling through to Atlanta. The officers awakened Bostick and asked for permission to search his bag, even though they did not have an "articulable suspicion," the legal term for a specific reason to believe he might be breaking the law. Bostick consented, and the police found cocaine in his bag. He was found guilty of drug possession, but the Florida Supreme Court reversed his conviction, holding that the police had not properly gotten consent to the search, since a person on a bus would not have felt free to leave.

The Court reversed the Florida Supreme Court, by a 6–3 vote. O'Connor, writing for the majority, said the question was not whether Bostick felt free to leave the bus, but whether a reasonable passenger would feel free to say no to the search. The Court sent the case back to the Florida courts to answer that question. Marshall, in dissent, agreed with the Florida Supreme Court that Bostick's consent was not freely given. He also noted that "suspicionless, dragnet-style" searches, a common tactic in the nation's war on drugs, were dangerously eroding the right to privacy. He warned that "random knocks on the doors of our citizens' homes seeking 'consent' to search for drugs cannot be far away."

Marshall went on to make another point: that this sort of police activity is more likely to be aimed at racial minorities than at whites. He cited another case in which an officer involved in searching for drugs admitted that one factor police considered in deciding who might be a drug courier was whether the person was black. Searches of the kind the Broward County officers had engaged in were not, Marshall insisted, "completely random."

There was another area in which the Court increased the search powers of police, which became a bigger issue over time: stop-and-frisk. The stop-and-frisk story is different from the others, because it was the Warren Court that first approved of stop-and-frisks, in a 1968 decision that was one of its few major rulings against the rights of criminal suspects. In that initial case, *Terry v. Ohio*, a plainclothes police officer stopped and patted down three men he suspected were casing a store to rob it. The Court held that an officer could stop and frisk someone on the street for weapons if he had reasonable suspicion that they were "armed and dangerous." *Terry* expanded law enforcement's authority to conduct searches, allowing them even when the police did not have "probable cause" for believing the subject had committed a crime. *Terry* was, however, still a narrow ruling, since the Court required an officer to have a reasonable basis for believing he was in a dangerous situation.

The post-Warren Court extended the stop-and-frisk doctrine well beyond the limited circumstances of that 1968 case in a variety of ways. In 2000, it approved a stop-and-frisk when a suspect fled from police in a high-crime area, even though the police had no data suggesting that fleeing in those circumstances made a person likely to be a criminal. The ruling greatly increased the ability of police to stop and frisk people for behaving "suspiciously."

The expansion of stop-and-frisk was important because of the scale of the invasions of privacy involved. Working the buses was a specialized tactic, but stop-and-frisks were in widespread use across the country. In New York City alone, in just the year 2011, 685,000 people were subjected to stop-and-frisk before the program was stopped. In about 83 percent of the cases, the subject was black or Hispanic, although those groups were just over half the city's population. Few law enforcement tactics in recent years have been met with more anger, protests, or charges of racism.

THERE WAS A THIRD CASE, ALONG WITH *MAPP V. OHIO* AND *MIRANDA V. Arizona,* that formed the Warren Court's criminal law "big three." In *Gideon v. Wainwright,* the Court recognized a Sixth Amendment right to counsel for poor defendants. While *Mapp* was about what happened when the police showed up at the door to conduct a search, and *Miranda* offered protection when the police began asking questions, *Gideon* concerned what happened to criminal defendants from interrogation through trial. *Gideon* was the boldest of all in what it promised: a whole system of legal defense for poor criminal defendants in every part of the country. It is a promise the nation has still not managed to live up to.

Clarence Earl Gideon was convicted of breaking into a Panama City, Florida, poolroom. While he was behind bars, he sent an appeal to the Supreme Court, written in pencil on lined prison paper, challenging his conviction, saying that his request for a court-appointed lawyer at trial had been wrongly denied. The Court accepted Gideon's case, and on March 18, 1963, stating that the Sixth Amendment guaranteed poor defendants the right to counsel, it unanimously overturned his conviction.

Black, writing for the Court, noted that governments spend vast sums to prosecute people accused of crimes, and defendants who have money hire the best lawyers they can. That the government and wealthy defendants did this, he said, were "the strongest indications of the widespread belief that lawyers in criminal courts are necessities, not luxuries." The right to counsel "may not be deemed fundamental and essential to fair trials in some countries," Black said, "but it is in ours." The same day, in *Douglas v. California*, the Court ruled that the Fourteenth Amendment Equal Protection Clause guaranteed poor people convicted of a crime appointed counsel to represent them on their first appeal.

Gideon captured the popular imagination in a way the Warren Court's other criminal justice rulings had not. It was not viewed as a court-imposed special privilege for criminals, as the exclusionary rule and the Miranda warning were by many. It was, rather, seen as a reaffirmation of a hallmark of the American system of justice: the adversarial trial, at which the truth is presumed to emerge when both sides have a fair opportunity to make their case. The nation rallied around the decision. "If an obscure convict named Clarence Earl Gideon had not sat down in his prison cell with a pencil and paper to write a letter to the Supreme Court the vast machinery of American law would have gone on functioning undisturbed," Attorney General Robert F. Kennedy declared. "But Gideon *did* write that letter and the whole course of American legal history has been changed." Anthony Lewis, a *New York Times* journalist, told the story of the case in the bestselling book *Gideon's Trumpet*, which was turned into a movie, with Henry Fonda as Clarence Gideon and John Houseman as Earl Warren.

When the Warren Court ended, it did not take long for the Burger Court to begin eroding the right to counsel. It said that the right that *Gideon* recognized applied only to "critical stages," and it began holding that some important parts of the government's efforts to convict a suspect were not critical. In 1972, when all four of the Nixon nominees were in place, the Court ruled, 5–4, that a police lineup used to identify a suspect who had not yet been charged with a crime was not a critical stage and poor defendants were not entitled to have lawyers appointed for them. The ruling was clearly at odds with the logic of Black's opinion in *Gideon:* most wealthy defendants who were told that they had to appear in a police lineup would have a lawyer present for it.

The Burger Court also limited the right to counsel on appeal. On the day it decided *Gideon,* the Court said that poor defendants had the right to an appointed lawyer on their first appeal. In 1974, it held that there was no right to appointed counsel for any further appeals. Rehnquist, writing for the majority, said that poor defendants had an "adequate opportunity" to present their claims even if they were forced to navigate the higher levels of the appellate court system on their own. In dissent, Douglas, writing for himself, Brennan, and Marshall—the remnants of the Warren Court liberal majority—insisted that the "same concepts of fairness and equality" that required counsel for the first appeal should require it for later ones.

The most serious way the Burger Court eroded *Gideon,* however, was by adopting an undemanding standard for what constitutes acceptable legal representation for poor defendants. The Warren Court said that poor people had a right to appointed counsel under the Sixth Amendment, but it did not say how high the quality of that representation had to be. The Court considered that question in 1984 in *Strickland v. Washington.* David Leroy Washington was convicted of three murders in Dade County, Florida. The State of Florida appointed a defense attorney to represent Washington, who pleaded guilty. The judge sentenced Washington to death for each of the three murder counts. In a post-conviction challenge to his death sentences, Washington, represented by a new lawyer, objected to the representation he had received at trial.

Washington's new lawyer made a strong case that his first lawyer had failed to investigate his background properly and had not presented mitigating evidence that might have persuaded the judge not to impose the death penalty. The lawyer submitted new evidence, including affidavits from fourteen friends, relatives, and acquaintances saying they would have testified on his behalf, as well as psychiatric evidence that could have helped his case. The trial lawyer testified at Washington's post-conviction hearing that he had felt "hopelessness" and doubted his client could avoid the death penalty. He also testified that he had made little attempt to develop evidence of Washington's psychological problems.

On May 14, 1984, the Court held, by a 8–1 vote, that Washington's legal representation had been good enough. O'Connor, writing for the Court, insisted that the first lawyer's decision not to seek more character or psychological evidence was a reasonable one. Even if it had not been, she said, Washington could not show that he was prejudiced by it, because there was no reasonable probability that the omitted evidence would have changed the sentencing judge's mind.

The Court's test made it extremely difficult for poor defendants to successfully challenge the quality of their representation. To win a retrial, they had to show both that their lawyer's performance was "deficient" and that if it had not been, there was a "reasonable probability" the case would have come out differently. The second prong of the test was particularly daunting, and Marshall, in dissent, questioned the logic behind it. He insisted that there was no way to know whether a defendant would have prevailed with a better lawyer, because "seemingly impregnable cases can sometimes be dismantled by good defense counsel."

If there was any doubt that the Court had set a low bar for what constituted effective assistance of counsel, the trial and appellate courts that applied *Strickland v. Washington* made it clear. In case after case, they rejected claims by poor defendants that their lawyers had not done an adequate job—even when the quality of the representation was shockingly poor. One extreme area involved lawyers who had slept through their client's trial. A whole jurisprudence developed on how much sleeping, during what parts of a trial, was acceptable. In one case in Michigan, Joseph Muniz, who was convicted of assault with intent to commit murder, challenged his conviction because a juror saw his lawyer sleeping during his cross-examination. The prosecutor asked Muniz a series of questions that led to the admission of additional evidence against him, allegedly while his counsel was asleep. In 2011, the Cincinnati-based U.S. Court of Appeals for the Sixth Circuit rejected Muniz's claim of ineffective assistance of counsel. The court said Muniz failed to meet the *Strickland* test, because he had not shown that his lawyer's sleeping affected the outcome of his case. It led one exasperated legal commentator to ask, "If an attorney sleeping through examination of his client by the government is not enough to trigger relief, what is?"

Drunk lawyers could also meet the *Strickland* standard. In 2014, Robert Wayne Holsey was executed by the State of Georgia for murder. Holsey, who had limited mental capacity, was represented by a court-appointed lawyer who admitted to drinking as much as a quart of vodka a day during the trial, while he was also preparing to be criminally prosecuted for stealing client funds. The lawyer himself said that he "probably shouldn't have been allowed to represent anybody" at the time. Although the lawyer failed to submit evidence that might have persuaded the jury not to vote for the death penalty, the Atlanta-based U.S. Court of Appeals for the Eleventh Circuit and the Supreme Court upheld Holsey's death sentence.

Lawyers could also use drugs and still meet the standard for effective assistance of counsel. In 1990, New Yorker Edwin Badia challenged his murder conviction, which came after a trial at which his defense lawyer used heroin and cocaine. The lawyer was later convicted of conspiracy to distribute narcotics. The New York State appellate court that heard Badia's appeal conceded that his lawyer's conduct was "reprehensible," but it upheld his conviction.

While the Warren Court promised poor defendants a lawyer, the Burger Court said that lawyer barely had to be competent. *Strickland* gave states a green light to operate indigent defense systems that were underfunded and structurally incapable of providing adequate representation. In a landmark 2004 report, *Gideon's Broken Promise*, the American Bar Association, the organization that represents the nation's legal establishment, used words like "alarming" and "national crisis" to describe the state of legal representation for poor defendants. The ABA found that funding for indigent defense was so inadequate that it was difficult to recruit capable lawyers or get their best efforts. Many jurisdictions had extremely low caps on the amount a court-appointed lawyer could charge for representing a poor person, even in serious and complicated cases.

Recent studies of indigent defense programs in specific states identified profound inadequacies. A 2018 report on Mississippi found that poor defendants charged with felonies were not given lawyers between arrest and arraignment, a period during which they could be in jail for as much as a year. The state's cap of $1,000 in fees per case meant that when defendants got a lawyer, they were often pressured to plead guilty so the lawyer did not need to investigate, do legal research, or participate in a trial. If a case did go to trial, it could be financially ruinous for the lawyer. In one capital case that was vigorously defended at trial by two experienced death penalty lawyers, the attorneys earned about $2 an hour. "The court reporter," the judge noted, "was paid far more than defense counsel."

Not surprisingly, the quality of the lawyers who represent indigent defendants in states that rely on appointed counsel is in many cases extremely low. The 2018 Mississippi report noted that since there were no standards for establishing that a lawyer was competent for a specific assignment, a new law school graduate who had just passed the bar could be assigned to represent a defendant facing life in prison. In Kentucky, fully one-quarter of the prisoners recently on death row had lawyers at trial who were later disbarred or resigned to avoid disbarment. As one critic said, the *Strickland* standard, in the real world, requires the state to provide little more than "a warm body with a law degree."

In jurisdictions that use public defenders rather than appointed private lawyers, the caseloads often make it almost impossible to provide clients with adequate representation. The National Advisory Commission on Criminal Justice Standards and Goals recommended that defense lawyers handle no more than 150 felonies a year, or 400 misdemeanors. The American Bar Association report found that in parts of New York State, caseloads were as high as 1,600 per lawyer per year. "Public defenders are the pack mules of the system," Ed Monahan, the head of Kentucky's public defender's office, said shortly before retiring. "Pack mules can carry a lot, but you put one more box on an overburdened mule, and it won't be able to function."

The same American Bar Association report found that poor defendants rarely have their cases investigated in a serious way, either because the funds are not available or their overworked lawyers do not request them. As a result, poor defendants almost invariably go to trial at a significant disadvantage, with the prosecutors having access to extensive evidence collected for them by law enforcement and the defense often having little more than the defendant's own testimony. The report cited a survey of felony case files from contract defenders in four Alabama judicial circuits that found that the lawyers had filed no motions for funds for investigators or experts in 99.4 percent of the cases.

THE NATION'S FOUNDERS BELIEVED SO DEEPLY IN JURY TRIALS THAT THEY put "the right to a speedy and public trial, by an impartial jury," in the Sixth Amendment. The guarantee rings hollow, however, because of the way in which the Court has interpreted the right to appointed counsel. When a poor defendant cannot count on having a lawyer who will investigate his case and prepare the best defense, or when an assigned lawyer may be incompetent or drunk, it makes sense to accept a plea bargain, whether the defendant is guilty or not.

Today, few criminal defendants actually exercise their right to a jury trial. Before the 1960s, between one-fourth and one-third of state felony charges were resolved with a trial. Now, about one-twentieth are. The current ratio works well for the state courts and prosecutors' offices, which lack the resources to bring a significant percentage of the criminal cases they handle through to trial. It does not, however, serve the core purpose of the justice system: to separate the innocent from the guilty and to ensure that all defendants have a fair chance to contest the charges against them.

When poor defendants enter plea-bargaining negotiations, the quality of legal representation they receive is even lower than it is for trials. The American Bar Association reported that defendants facing years in prison often met their lawyers for the first time at a hearing where they had to decide on the spot whether to sign away their freedom. In one Louisiana parish, according to an ABA source, in 83 percent of cases there was nothing to suggest that the public defender had ever met with his client out of court. The ABA cited a source in Alabama who said that lawyers who defend poor defendants there on a contract basis "basically do nothing but process defendants to a guilty plea in as expeditious a manner as possible." The report had a name for this kind of representation: "meet 'em and plead 'em lawyers."

While the Court has helped push poor defendants to plea bargain by setting such low standards for the quality of legal representation they are entitled to, it has also given prosecutors extraordinary power in the plea-bargaining process. In a 1978 case, the Court strongly endorsed aggressive plea bargaining by prosecutors, even when it included threats to retaliate harshly against defendants who refused to accept a deal. The case, *Bordenkircher v. Hayes,* was brought by Paul Hayes, a Kentucky man who was indicted for passing an $88.30 forged check, which was punishable by two to ten years in prison. The prosecutor offered Hayes five years if he pleaded guilty and said that if Hayes turned it down, he would be charged under the state's Habitual Criminal Act and, because of his prior offenses, would face a mandatory life sentence. Hayes rejected the deal, was convicted, and received a life sentence. He argued that the prosecutor's bullying approach, threatening him with a more serious charge and life in prison if he did not accept the plea bargain, violated due process. The Cincinnati-based U.S. Court of Appeals for the Sixth Circuit agreed, stating that the Due Process Clause "protected defendants from the vindictive exercise of a prosecutor's discretion."

The Court reversed the appeals court and upheld Hayes's life sentence.

Stewart, writing for a five-justice majority, conceded that threatening tougher punishment "clearly may have a 'discouraging effect on the defendant's assertion of his trial rights,'" but he insisted that the Constitution did not prohibit that sort of high-stakes coercion. He went on to praise plea bargains as "important components of this country's criminal justice system" that, if properly done, "can benefit all concerned."

The Court could have taken a different approach. It could have recognized that in a constitutional system founded on the right to trial by jury, prosecutors should not be allowed to blackmail defendants into waiving that right. It could have held that due process requires a system in which defendants accept plea bargains because they are actually guilty, not because they are afraid to insist on their innocence. Instead, the Court in *Bordenkircher* allowed prosecutors to bring extreme charges, "no matter how unjust," as long as they could make the facts fit, argued John Pfaff, a Fordham law professor who studies mass incarceration, in his book *Locked In.* That is "a tremendous amount of power for one official to have," Pfaff said, "made all the more powerful by the fact that prosecutors generally wield it out of public view."

Plea bargaining may be an efficient way of moving defendants through overburdened criminal courts, but it is not a system designed to separate the guilty from the innocent. The more prosecutors are allowed to threaten a defendant with added charges and harsher punishment for turning down their offer—to impose a "trial penalty," in plea-bargaining terminology—the more likely it is that innocent defendants will waive their right to a trial and enter a plea. In his *Bordenkircher* dissent, Blackmun described the decision defendants are forced to make as "a devastating gamble."

There is no doubt that, owing to the deficiencies in legal representation given to poor criminal defendants, innocent people are going to prison. A *60 Minutes* exposé of Louisiana's indigent defense system painted a bleak picture of the human cost of these failures. In the report, public defenders described the unrelenting pressure created by their excessive caseloads. New Orleans chief public defender Derwyn Bunton, whose office announced in

2016 that it would no longer accept the most serious felony cases, compared his city's justice system to the famous *I Love Lucy* episode in which Lucy tries to keep up with the chocolates that are moving across a factory conveyor belt. Defendants move through the system so quickly, he said, that there is no time to figure out whether they are actually guilty.

The *60 Minutes* report included an interview with Donald Gamble, a New Orleans resident who was jailed for sixteen months awaiting trial on armed robbery charges before a lawyer accidentally discovered that he was innocent. It was not Gamble's lawyer who figured it out, but a Tulane University law professor who was looking into inadequacies in the legal representation provided by the public defender's office. While reviewing Gamble's case as part of her research, the professor noticed that he did not match the perpetrator caught on surveillance video. She reported what she had discovered, and within days the charges against Gamble were dropped. Gamble told *60 Minutes* that if he had not been freed by the professor's chance involvement in his case, he likely would have accepted a plea deal, despite his innocence. He could have been sentenced to five years in prison, but he would have avoided the possibility of being convicted at trial and sent away for life. As it was, Gamble lost not only sixteen months of his life, but several teeth, which were knocked out in one of several jailhouse beatings he endured before he was freed.

The problem *60 Minutes* found in New Orleans is a national one. Defendants all across the country plead guilty every year to crimes they did not commit. The Innocence Project, which uses DNA to exonerate wrongly convicted people, recently reported that more than 11 percent of the 365 people they have shown to have been wrongly convicted pleaded guilty to crimes they did not commit. The National Registry of Exonerations, which is maintained by Michigan and Northwestern Law Schools, recently reported similar results: of the more than 2,400 exonerations on its list, 12 percent involved false confessions.

Judge Jed Rakoff, of the U.S. District Court for the Southern District of

New York, who regularly presides over criminal cases, has argued that a sizable number of defendants are likely pleading guilty to crimes they did not commit. In an article entitled "Why Innocent People Plead Guilty," he observed that a typical criminal defendant, with limited financial resources and a troubled past, understands that even if he is innocent, he may not have much chance of mounting a successful defense. "If his lawyer can obtain a plea bargain that will reduce his likely time in prison," Rakoff said, "he may find it 'rational' to take the plea."

IF A DEFENDANT IS FOUND GUILTY, SENTENCING FOLLOWS, AND THAT IS another area in which the Court has turned the law against defendants. In the 1980s and '90s, a "get tough on crime" movement led to tougher sentencing laws being adopted at the federal and state levels. The Court could have reined in the excesses of the movement by applying the kinds of constitutional standards it used to limit punitive damages awards against corporations. Instead, it became a willing participant in the nation's mass incarceration crisis.

California became a leader in the tougher-sentencing movement in 1994, when it adopted a "three strikes and you're out" law, partly in response to the highly publicized kidnapping and murder of twelve-year-old Polly Klaas. The new law required a sentence of twenty-five years to life for offenders convicted of a felony who had previously committed two serious or violent felonies. California was not the first state to adopt a repeat-offender law, but its three-strikes law became a trendsetter. Other states followed, and eventually more than half had three-strikes laws. There were also mandatory minimum sentences in all fifty states and laws in forty-nine states allowing for life without parole for certain crimes. The federal government had its own strict sentencing provisions. In 1984, 1986, and 1994, Congress enacted laws ending federal parole, establishing mandatory minimum sentences, and adopting three-strikes at the federal level.

Although three-strikes statutes and other tough sentencing laws were promoted as a way to get the most hardened criminals off the streets, they were often used on people who did not fit that profile. About eight years into the new sentencing regime in California, there were more than three hundred inmates in the state's prisons who were serving sentences of twenty-five years to life for a third strike of petty theft. In 2002, one of those inmates, Leandro Andrade, brought a constitutional challenge to the law.

Andrade, a father of three and an Army veteran, was arrested at a Kmart in Southern California for shoplifting five children's videotapes, including *Casper* and *Snow White,* worth $84.70. Two weeks later, at another Kmart, he shoplifted four more, including *Cinderella* and *Free Willy 2,* worth $68.84. Andrade's shoplifting would normally have been petty theft, punishable by a fine or a short jail sentence. Under California law, however, misdemeanor petty theft becomes a felony if the offender had a prior property offense conviction, which Andrade did. As a result, his shoplifting incidents were converted to two felonies. Andrade was convicted under the three-strikes law, and even though he had never committed a violent crime, he was given two sentences of twenty-five years to life. Andrade was thirty-seven when he was convicted, and he would not be eligible for parole until he was eighty-seven.

For critics of harsh and inflexible sentencing laws, Andrade's sentence provided a nearly ideal test case. It presented the Court with a sympathetic, nonviolent plaintiff who, because of two minor shoplifting incidents, would spend the rest of his life, or close to it, behind bars. Andrade challenged his sentence as a violation of the Eighth Amendment, which prohibits "cruel and unusual punishments." The San Francisco–based U.S. Court of Appeals for the Ninth Circuit ruled for Andrade, holding that his sentence violated the Eighth Amendment because it was "grossly disproportionate to his crimes."

On March 5, 2003, the Court reversed the Ninth Circuit and upheld Andrade's sentence, by a 5–4 vote, along ideological lines. O'Connor, writing for the majority, conceded that the Court had previously acknowledged that a sentence could be so disproportionate to the crime that it violated the Eighth Amendment, but she said that it applied only to "the extraordinary case."

Andrade's sentence, she said, did not rise to that level. Her opinion, which focused on the proper interpretation of the Court's precedents from the 1980s and '90s, did little to explain what she thought would be a constitutionally disproportionate sentence, if sentencing a thirty-seven-year-old man to prison at least until he was eighty-seven for stealing $153.54 in videotapes did not meet the bar. Souter, writing for the four liberal justices, said in dissent that "if Andrade's sentence is not grossly disproportionate, the principle has no meaning."

Neither the majority nor the dissent mentioned the Court's decisions involving punitive damages against corporations, but they added a whole new level of outrage to the ruling. At the time of its decision in Leandro Andrade's case, the Court had already overturned the $2 million punitive damages award against BMW for fraudulently selling damaged but repaired cars as new, saying that the award was "grossly excessive" and "transcends the constitutional limit." Just one month after affirming Andrade's sentence, the Court would overturn the $145 million punitive damages award against State Farm for egregiously deceiving and mistreating a customer. In that case, it would say that a punitive damage award any larger than $9 million would likely be unconstitutional.

The Court had two very different ideas about proportionality of punishment: one for corporations under the Fourteenth Amendment Due Process Clause and another for people under the Eighth Amendment. The Due Process Clause, it said, did not allow a jury to punish one of the world's wealthiest companies with a punitive damages award of $145 million, which was equal to 0.29 percent of its annual revenue—barely enough to get the attention of the company's leadership. The Eighth Amendment did, however, allow California to put a thirty-seven-year-old Army veteran and father who engaged in minor shoplifting behind bars until he was at least eighty-seven.

THE POST-1969 COURT'S CRIMINAL JUSTICE RULINGS, WHICH HAVE DIminished the rights of suspects, defendants, and people convicted of crimes, are not merely individual tragedies for people like Donald Gamble and Leandro Andrade. They have also created systematic injustice, whose impact is felt broadly across society. These rulings are all drivers of the nation's extraordinarily high levels of incarceration. The United States' inmate population of nearly 2.3 million is the world's largest. The United States' incarceration rate, 698 per 100,000, is the world's highest—about five times the rate of the United Kingdom. The United States has about 4.3 percent of the world's population but about 22 percent of its prisoners.

It was not always so. Mass incarceration in the United States started in the early 1970s, the era in which the Nixon Court began. The incarceration rate was about 100 per 100,000 for much of the twentieth century, but prison populations began to soar starting around 1972. After decades of increases, the incarceration rate topped out in 2008 at 760 per 100,000. There are many reasons the prison population expanded during these years, but changes in sentencing laws and policy were a major driver. The incarceration rate has dipped recently, but it remains extremely high by historical and international standards.

Many experts argue that there are significantly more inmates behind bars than need to be there to keep crime rates low. In its report "How Many Americans Are Unnecessarily Incarcerated?" the Brennan Center for Justice contended that about 39 percent of the United States prison population, or about 576,000 people, were incarcerated for little public safety reason. The report argued that if many inmates were given shorter sentences or alternatives to prison, such as drug treatment, both the inmates and society would be better off. Another leading criminology expert has said that many inmates over age forty could be safely released, because criminals generally "age out" of crime.

The post-1969 Court's criminal law decisions have increased the probability of a suspect becoming an inmate at every stage of the criminal justice process. The rulings eroding *Mapp* have made it more likely that a suspect will be searched and that incriminating evidence will be seized. The loopholes the Court has created in *Miranda* have increased the chances that a suspect will say something incriminating to a police officer or be identified in a police lineup. The Court has also made it more likely that people, particularly poor people and racial minorities, will be stopped and frisked on the street, which can lead to the police finding evidence leading to a prosecution. The Court's rulings have made it more likely that evidence seized in any of these ways will be used at trial. The decision on DNA swabbing added a high-tech advantage to law enforcement's arsenal in connecting people to crimes in which they were not even suspects.

The extraordinarily low standard the Court set for effective assistance of counsel has made it more likely that defendants who are innocent will be convicted or will accept a plea bargain rather than risk going to trial. The Court's endorsement of coercive plea-bargaining tactics by prosecutors has provided another incentive for innocent defendants to plead guilty and for defendants who are offered a bad deal in plea bargaining to nevertheless accept it. As Judge Rakoff noted, under these circumstances even innocent defendants may "find it 'rational' to take the plea."

Tough sentencing laws contribute to the nation's high incarceration rates in at least two ways. Most obviously, they lead to large numbers of inmates being kept behind bars who otherwise would not be there, and who in many cases may not need to be there. Sentencing decisions rarely make headlines, particularly when the issue is a defendant being given more prison time than the crime warrants. Occasionally, however, a news story will show the distortive impact that sentencing laws can have. In 2017, Iowa grandmother Susan Rice, who became addicted to methamphetamine, was sentenced for conspiracy to distribute drugs because she drove a dealer around. Under a mandatory sentencing law, she had to receive between five and forty years in prison. The federal judge who sentenced her objected publicly, saying she deserved a year to eighteen months, but he was forced to give her at least five years. "I think it's a miscarriage of justice," he said.

The other way tough sentencing laws drive up the prison population is by giving prosecutors an intimidating weapon to use in plea bargaining. These laws allow prosecutors to demand heavy sentences from defendants who accept a guilty plea. They also create pressure on innocent defendants to accept a plea bargain. Judge John L. Kane Jr., a senior judge on the federal district court in Denver, has spoken out about how often prosecutors use tough sentencing laws to extract guilty pleas from defendants who might otherwise try to assert their innocence. "How many times is a mandatory sentence used as a chip in order to coerce a plea?" asked Judge Kane. "They don't keep records." He noted, however, that "we hardly ever have trials anymore."

There is another trend in the criminal justice system that has driven the nation's incarceration rate up: the increased use of cash bail. About one-quarter of the incarcerated population, or roughly 460,000 people, who are behind bars on an average day are pretrial detainees who have not been convicted of a crime, according to a report by the Brookings Institution. Some of them are not released before trial because a judge has determined that they pose too great a danger to the public or too great a flight risk. Many more, however, are being held because cash bail was set and they were too poor to pay it.

The use of cash bail has been soaring. In 1990, only a little more than half of defendants, 53 percent, were required to post bail to be free pending trial. By 2009, 72 percent of defendants were. Many are accused of property or public order offenses. More than two-thirds of defendants with nonviolent felony charges had bail of $5,000 or higher, according to Brookings. A New York City study found that only 7 percent of criminal defendants met bail set at $5,000. The cash bail system is one of the clearest examples of class bias in the justice system: the people who remain behind bars after bail has been set are not the most dangerous, or the most likely to flee the jurisdiction, but the ones who do not have the money to buy their freedom.

The Court could significantly reform the cash bail system, but it has chosen not to. The Eighth Amendment expressly prohibits "excessive bail," but the Court has not interpreted it in ways that help people trapped behind bars before trial because they cannot afford bail. In 2019, the Court refused to consider the case of Maurice Walker, who was charged with walking while intoxicated and held in a Georgia jail for six days because he could not post bail. The crime he was accused of did not carry jail time, so he served more time for being unable to meet bail than he would have if he had been immediately convicted.

Reformers have identified the cash bail system as one of the main sources of unfairness in the justice system. The American Bar Association has argued that jailing defendants "solely because they cannot afford to purchase their freedom," without considering their ability to pay, violates the Fourteenth Amendment Equal Protection and Due Process Clauses. The American Civil Liberties Union launched a nationwide campaign to end wealth-based incarceration in 2017, declaring, "We can't end mass incarceration without ending money bail." Celebrities have weighed in, including Shawn Carter, better known as Jay Z, who wrote an opinion piece for *Time* headlined "For Father's Day, I'm Taking On the Exploitative Bail Industry."

EVERY PHASE OF THE CRIMINAL JUSTICE SYSTEM—FROM INVESTIGATION of crimes to plea bargaining to trials to sentencing—is infected by racial discrimination, which adds another level of systematic bias and further drives mass incarceration. The Court rarely discusses these racial inequities, and when it does, it is often in a mention in a dissent, such as Marshall's discussion in the Florida "working the buses" case, of how it was not "completely random" whom the police questioned.

There is, however, considerable evidence that the racial discrimination is real and pervasive. In the wake of protests over police conduct in Ferguson, Missouri, and other cities, *The New York Times* examined tens of thousands of traffic stops in Greensboro, North Carolina. North Carolina is the state that collects the most detailed data on traffic stops, and Greensboro is a racially diverse city. The *Times* found that police "used their discretion to search black drivers or their cars more than twice as often as white motorists—even though they found drugs and weapons significantly more often when the driver was white." *The Times* determined that similar disparities existed throughout North Carolina. It also reported that the police were more likely to stop black drivers for no apparent reason and that they were more likely to use physical force with black drivers, even if they did not encounter resistance.

When the San Francisco District Attorney's Office investigated police practices, it came up with similar results. It found, based on the work of a task force of retired federal and state judges, that there were significant racial disparities in traffic stops, searches, and arrests in San Francisco, particularly between black and white drivers. Black people accounted for less than 15 percent of all stops in San Francisco in 2015 but more than 42 percent of the non-consent searches following stops. This focus on blacks was not justified by the results of those searches. Blacks and Hispanics had the lowest "hit rates"—the rate at which searches found contraband. Whites searched without consent were about twice as likely as blacks searched without consent to be carrying contraband.

There is also a growing body of evidence showing racial disparities in sentencing. In 2017, the U.S. Sentencing Commission found that the average federal sentence for black men was 19.1 percent longer than for white men for the same crime, even when criminal history and other factors were held constant. Paul Butler, a professor at Georgetown Law School and a former federal prosecutor, said the study showed that "race infects" each "stage of the process" in the criminal justice system. In 2016, the *Sarasota Herald-Tribune* investigated sentencing in Florida, using two state databases with tens of millions of records. It found that when blacks and whites committed the same crime and scored the same number of points—reflecting the severity of the crime, the offender's prior record, and other factors—blacks received longer sentences in 60 percent of felony cases.

The Court had a chance to do something about the epidemic of racial bias in the criminal justice system in 1987, in a lawsuit brought by the NAACP

Legal Defense Fund. The case was a challenge to Georgia's death penalty by Warren McCleskey, a black death-row inmate convicted of killing a white police officer. McCleskey argued that Georgia had applied the death penalty in a discriminatory way, in violation of the Equal Protection Clause.

The NAACP Legal Defense Fund submitted a study of the role of race in the death penalty, based on an analysis of more than two thousand Georgia murder cases. The study found that blacks were 1.1 times as likely to receive the death penalty as other defendants. It found a much larger disparity, however, based on the race of the victim. Killers of whites were 4.3 times as likely to be sentenced to death as killers of blacks. McCleskey was in the most disadvantaged group, as a black defendant with a white victim. He argued that Georgia's death penalty violated the Equal Protection Clause.

The Court in *McCleskey v. Kemp* rejected McCleskey's claim by a 5–4 vote, along ideological lines. Powell, writing for the Court, rejected the idea that the criminal justice system could be challenged through evidence of racial disparities. Mere statistical evidence about how race affected capital punishment was not enough, Powell said. For McCleskey to have his sentence reversed on the grounds of racial discrimination, he would have to present specific evidence of racial discrimination in his own case. Powell also mentioned something that revealed the Court's deeper concern. "If we accepted McCleskey's claim," he said, "we could soon be faced with similar claims as to other" kinds of criminal sentences—and there might be claims that there were disparities toward other minority groups, or toward women.

Brennan, in dissent, said the majority had missed the essential point. When McCleskey submitted strong statistical evidence about race in capital cases in Georgia, he *was* presenting important evidence about his own case. If McCleskey "asked his lawyer whether a jury was likely to sentence him to die," Brennan said, a "candid reply" would have begun with the lawyer saying that "few of the details of the crime or of McCleskey's past criminal conduct were more important than the fact that his victim was white."

In his dissent, Brennan also addressed the majority's concern that if

McCleskey won, there would be challenges to other kinds of criminal sentences and ones brought by other minority groups. The majority was expressing "a fear of too much justice," Brennan argued. "Surely," he said, the majority believed that "if striking evidence indicated that other minority groups, or women, or even persons with blond hair, were disproportionately sentenced to death," that "would be repugnant to deeply rooted conceptions of fairness." But Brennan was giving the Court too much credit. The majority had made clear that it did not believe that at all.

Many civil rights advocates have come to regard *McCleskey* as one of the Court's worst rulings. On its twenty-fifth anniversary, one legal scholar declared that it had become "firmly entrenched as a resident in the exclusive but not so desirable neighborhood of Notorious Cases." Anthony Amsterdam, a professor at New York University Law School, called it "the Dred Scott decision of our time"—invoking the Court's 1857 decision holding that an enslaved man had no right to sue for his freedom—and one "for which our children's children will reproach our generation and abhor the legal legacy we leave them."

Critics of mass incarceration have identified *McCleskey v. Kemp* as an important contributing factor. If the Court had ruled for McCleskey, it could have been transformational. Powell acknowledged as much when he wrote for the Court that "McCleskey's claim, taken to its logical conclusion, throws into serious question the principles that underlie our entire criminal justice system." The decision could have pushed Congress, state legislatures, and the lower courts to root out racial bias throughout the justice system, including in sentencing. The result would not only have been a fairer system, but likely one with a lower overall rate of incarceration as the extra prison time being imposed on nonwhites was removed.

Instead, the Court has ensured that the criminal justice system need not confront these issues. Michelle Alexander, the professor and author of *The New Jim Crow: Mass Incarceration in the Age of Colorblindness,* said that the Court had "immunized the criminal justice system from judicial scrutiny for racial bias." She noted that since *McCleskey* there have been few racial discrimination challenges to "sentencing schemes, patterns, or results." The reason, she said, is simple: "the exercise is plainly futile."

The Court's harsh approach to most suspects and defendants is even more striking when contrasted with its treatment of white-collar defendants. In criminal cases involving wealthy and powerful defendants or ones who do not fit the "traditional" model of what a criminal is, the Court has frequently second-guessed prosecutors, given defendants the benefit of the doubt, and found ways of reading criminal laws narrowly to overturn convictions. In recent decades, the Warren Court's fierce protection of defendants' rights and its skepticism about prosecutors and police have lived on in one area: cases involving white-collar criminals.

There are many criminal cases in which the Court has demonstrated this sympathy. In 1983, it considered the case of Raymond Dirks, an officer of a firm that provided investment analysis of insurance company stocks to institutional investors. Dirks received insider information that an insurance company had fraudulently overstated its assets. He told investors what he had learned, and some sold their stock in the company as a result. The Securities and Exchange Commission charged Dirks with violating the Securities Act of 1933 by providing insider information. The commission said that when people are tipped off with insider information, "regardless of their motivation," they must disclose the information publicly or refrain from trading. Instead Dirks gave the information to investors who traded on it. The Securities and Exchange Commission found Dirks guilty and censured him.

The Court reversed Dirks's censure by a 6–3 vote, with all five conservative justices in the majority. Powell, writing for himself, Burger, O'Connor, White, Rehnquist, and Stevens, said that Dirks was not liable because he had not personally profited from the insider information—even though he gave it to clients of his who did. In dissent, Blackmun, writing for himself, Brennan, and Marshall, said that Dirk had clearly violated the Securities Act. The majority had simply invented a new rule, he said, that to be convicted of insider trading a person must have acted "from a motive of personal gain." The majority then used this "innovation" in the law, Blackmun said, to acquit Dirks even though he had clearly violated the law.

The Court decided another white-collar criminal case in 1991, the same year it decided the "working the buses" case of Terrance Bostick, the young black man in Florida. John Cheek was an American Airlines pilot who was part of a "tax protest" movement, and had come to believe that wages were not income for purposes of the tax law. Cheek did not file tax returns for six straight years, except for one year when he filed a frivolous one. He said at trial that, based on his own research and the teachings of the tax protest movement, he did not believe he had to pay taxes. Cheek was found guilty by the jury that heard his case. He challenged his conviction, arguing that the tax law said that violations had to be "willful," and the judge had not properly instructed the jury on how his principled opposition to paying taxes should be treated.

The Court reversed Cheek's conviction, by a 6–2 vote. White, writing for the majority, said the jury should have been told that if Cheek truly believed he did not have to pay taxes, no matter how irrational his belief, he could not be convicted, since the law contained a requirement that the evasion be "willful." White said Cheek could possibly be convicted on retrial, but the jury would have to determine specifically that his belief was not sincere.

The ruling was taking a highly indulgent view of tax avoidance. In dissent, Blackmun insisted that it was not a complex case, since it was about "the income tax law in its most elementary and basic aspect: Is a wage earner a taxpayer and are wages income?" It defied belief, he said, that, more than seventy years after the introduction of the federal income tax, a taxpayer "of competent mentality" could think his wages were not taxable. The decision, Blackmun said, invited taxpayers to "cling to frivolous views of the law" to avoid paying taxes.

Cheek did not win in the end. He was retried, and when the jury was directly instructed to consider whether he actually believed that he did not have to pay taxes, it convicted him again. The Court's ruling was extraordinary, however, in its willingness to let Cheek make a defense based on nonbelief in the law. It was particularly notable that the law-and-order conservatives—including Rehnquist, Scalia, O'Connor, and Kennedy—were in the majority, arguing that Cheek's years of intentional tax avoidance were not necessarily criminal. The dissenters, Blackmun and Marshall, who wanted to uphold the conviction, were two of the Court's most liberal members.

There were more rulings like these, including one in which the Court reversed the conviction of a high-rolling gambler convicted of financial improprieties at a Nevada casino, also because it was not convinced that his actions were "willful." It was clear to many observers what the Court was doing. In 2015, after it had reversed another white-collar criminal conviction, *The New York Times* ran an analysis by a criminal law professor describing the pattern. The article, headlined "Narrowing the Definition of White-Collar Crimes," said the Court had been using "mental gymnastics" to reverse convictions of white-collar criminals. The Court's overall message, the professor said, was that the government should be careful about how aggressively it pursued cases that "carry heavy punishments to defendants who pose little threat to the public's physical safety."

The Court's decisions illustrated what J. Kelly Strader, a professor at Southwestern Law School, called the "white collar paradox." The conservative justices, who usually voted to uphold criminal convictions, frequently made an exception for white-collar criminal defendants. The liberals, on the other hand, were more likely to do the reverse—to vote in favor of ordinary criminal defendants and against white-collar defendants—or to vote in favor of all defendants. As a result of this unusual voting pattern, on a Court with five conservative justices, it was far easier for white-collar criminal defendants to win five votes to overturn their convictions than it was for other defendants. The Court had become, as Strader observed, "anti-defendant . . . except in white collar cases."

The idea that the Court was engaged in a "white collar paradox" was supported by statistical evidence. In an article called "The Judicial Politics of White Collar Crime," Strader analyzed the justices' votes over a twenty-four-year period and produced hard numbers illustrating the phenomenon. For some justices, the evidence was particularly stark. Scalia voted for defendants in fewer than 7 percent of non-white-collar criminal cases and nearly 82 percent of white-collar cases. Rehnquist voted for the defendant in just over 8 percent of non-white-collar criminal cases and almost 62 percent of white-collar ones.

There are a variety of possible explanations for this white-collar paradox. Some moral psychologists argue that conservatives are more accepting of hierarchy than liberals are and more respectful toward those with more wealth, power, and social standing. They may, as a result, be more forgiving in their judgments of white-collar criminals and harsher toward other kinds of criminals. The conservative justices' votes in white-collar cases likely also reflect their sympathy for defendants who resemble them. One study of sentencing in white-collar criminal cases, based on interviews with fifty-one federal judges, found that a substantial factor was the judges' tendency to sympathize with defendants of their own social class. One judge told the investigators that it was difficult to avoid being biased when "people like you are standing in front of you." The Court is a long way from the height of the Warren Court, when the five most liberal justices had all grown up in or close to poverty. For years now, the only justices who grew up in poverty have been Sotomayor and Thomas—and Thomas has been outspoken about putting the difficulties of the poor, including his own sister, behind him.

The Court's criminal justice rulings, by driving mass incarceration, have promoted economic inequality. Imprisonment has a highly disproportionate impact on poor individuals, families, and communities. Prisons and jails are filled with people who were poor before they were locked up. The median annual income of incarcerated men aged twenty-seven to forty-two before their incarceration was just $19,650 in 2014, while for non-incarcerated men the median was $41,250. This statistic supports the view, as one commentator noted, "that mass incarceration in the United States is primarily a system of locking up lower class men."

Prisons and jails are filled not only with people who were poor at the time of their arrest but also with people who grew up in poverty and near poverty. One study of the economics of imprisonment found a simple correlation: "the poorer your parents are, the more likely you are to be incarcerated." In a sample of prisoners around the age of thirty, it reported that the bottom 5 percent of families produced about 15 percent of inmates, and the bottom 20 percent produced nearly half.

Mass incarceration also disproportionately affects people of color. In 2017, blacks were 12 percent of the U.S. adult population but 33 percent of the prison population. Hispanics were 16 percent of the adult population and 23 percent of inmates. Whites, by contrast, were 64 percent of adults but just 30 percent of prisoners. The impact of these racial disparities is felt across whole communities. While 6 percent of white men had family members in prison, according to one recent study, 44 percent of black women did.

In addition to reflecting the nation's economic inequality, mass incarceration is a major contributor to it. While behind bars, inmates earn little or no money, and when they are released their wages and likelihood of full employment are significantly harmed. A Pew Charitable Trusts study of the finances of forty-five-year-old males found that the ones who were never incarcerated had an average annual wage of $39,100, while the men who had a prison record had an average wage of $23,500, or 40 percent less. Much of that gap is due, the study says, to the stigma of incarceration and other prison-related factors.

Families suffer economically from a family member's incarceration. About 54 percent of inmates are parents of minor children, and their 2.7 million children represent 3.6 percent of the nation's children. Many of these children grow up in poverty or near poverty as a result of a parent's being behind bars. When a father is imprisoned, the family's income is 22 percent lower on average than it was the year before he left for prison, a substantial decline from an already low level.

The impact of a parent's imprisonment is not just financial. Children with incarcerated parents do worse in school than other children. They are more likely to misbehave, to have learning disabilities, and to drop out of school. About 23 percent of children with fathers who have been incarcerated are suspended or expelled, as compared with 4 percent of other children. The result is a form of intergenerational punishment. The Pew Charitable Trusts study concluded that incarceration makes the "prospect for upward mobility" among the children of inmates "significantly dimmer."

The Court's criminal law decisions are inextricably connected with economic inequality, driving many poor and working-class people further down economically—and, not infrequently, failing to punish higher-income individuals who commit white-collar crimes. There are also indications, however, that something larger is going on: that the Court is turning the criminal justice system into an increasingly efficient means of social control for the growing ranks of Americans who are at the bottom of the economic hierarchy. It might sound alarmist to say that the Court is creating the legal tools for operating a prison state, with a particular focus on people of color and the poor, but a member of the Court, herself a former prosecutor, has warned of just that.

The case was *Utah v. Strieff*, which appeared to be a dispute over a routine drug arrest. It began when the police received a tip about possible drug activity in a South Salt Lake City house. After a man walked out of the house, a narcotics detective followed him to a parking lot and asked him for identification. The detective checked the man's name, Edward Strieff, against police records and found that he had an outstanding arrest warrant for a traffic violation. The detective arrested Strieff, searched him, and found methamphetamine.

Strieff moved to exclude the drug evidence from his trial. He argued that the police had no legal basis for stopping and questioning him and that the drugs they found as a result of the illegal stop should not be used against him. It was a straightforward argument based on two well-established Fourth Amendment doctrines: that to stop someone on the street the police must have a reasonable suspicion of criminal activity and that, if they seize evidence in an illegal search, that "fruit of the poisonous tree," as a long-ago court colorfully expressed it, cannot be used at trial. Prosecutors used the drug evidence against Strieff at trial, and he was convicted. When he appealed, however, the Utah Supreme Court ruled that the evidence should not have been used, and it overturned the conviction.

On June 20, 2016, the Court reversed Utah's highest court by a 5–3 vote and reinstated Strieff's conviction. Thomas, writing for the majority, conceded that the stop had been illegal because the police did not have a reasonable suspicion that Strieff had done anything wrong. Thomas said, however, that the "fruit of the poisonous tree" doctrine did not apply, because when the detective checked his record and found an outstanding arrest warrant, it "attenuated the connection between the unlawful stop and the evidence seized from Strieff."

The *Strieff* decision significantly changed the rules that apply to police stops on the street. The Court gave the police a reason to stop people who have not done anything wrong, or even anything that would reasonably raise suspicions of wrongdoing. As long as the police discovered an open warrant on the person they stopped, any evidence they found could be used against them. This was no small loophole: open warrants are common, especially among populations that have high levels of interaction with the police. Federal and state databases contain more than 7.8 million outstanding warrants, the great majority for minor offenses, and there are many more at the local level. In New York City, there were 1.4 million outstanding arrest warrants in 2016 for "quality of life" offenses, such as being in a park after closing time. In Ferguson, Missouri, according to a Department of Justice study in 2015, out of a population of twenty-one thousand, sixteen thousand people had outstanding warrants. In many cases, warrants are never served, so people who have an outstanding warrant do not even know it.

In dissent, Kagan argued that the ruling "practically invites" the police to stop people with no legal basis. Under the old rules, a police officer who wanted to stop someone improperly would likely decide it was not worth it, since any evidence uncovered could not be used at trial. That was "precisely the deterrence the exclusionary rule is meant to achieve," Kagan said. The Court was now saying, however, that "so long as the target is one of the many millions of people in this country with an outstanding arrest warrant, anything the officer finds in a search is fair game for use in a criminal prosecution." As a result, Kagan said, "the officer's incentive to violate the Constitution . . . increases."

Sotomayor, in her own dissent, went further, delivering a personal warning to the American people. In highly unusual form, she addressed the reader directly: "The Court today holds that the discovery of a warrant for an unpaid parking ticket will forgive a police officer's violation of your Fourth Amendment rights," Sotomayor wrote. "Do not be soothed," she continued, "by the opinion's technical language: This case allows the police to stop you on the street, demand your identification, and check it for outstanding traffic warrants—even if you are doing nothing wrong." As a result, anything the officer finds "by searching you" can be used in a criminal prosecution, a form of "misconduct," Sotomayor said, that the Fourth Amendment should not allow.

Drawing on her own "professional experiences," Sotomayor, who had been a Manhattan assistant district attorney before becoming a judge, underscored what she saw as the "severe consequences" of unlawful police stops. She warned that the police officer can "handcuff you and take you to jail for doing nothing more than speeding" or "jaywalking." At jail, the officer can "fingerprint you, swab DNA from the inside of your mouth, and force you to 'shower with a delousing agent' while you 'lift [your] tongue, hold out [your] arms, turn around, and lift [your] genitals.'"

Sotomayor said it was "no secret that people of color are disproportionate victims of this type of scrutiny," but she underscored that the decision diminished the rights of all Americans. "This case tells everyone, white and black, guilty and innocent," she said, that his or her "body is subject to invasion." Sotomayor warned that the "countless people who are routinely targeted by police" were "the canaries in the coal mine whose deaths, civil and literal, warn us that no one can breathe in this atmosphere." The system the Court was establishing, she said, "implies that you are . . . the subject of a carceral"—or prison—"state, just waiting to be catalogued."

When Sotomayor mentioned the police's ability to "swab DNA from the inside of your mouth," she was referring to the *Maryland v. King* decision. The juxtaposition of *Utah v. Strieff* and *Maryland v. King* was sobering. In these cases, in a period of three years, two justices had sounded alarms that the Court was moving the nation toward two distinct totalitarian nightmares. Scalia, writing for himself and three of the liberal justices, suggested that the United States was in danger of becoming a panopticon, and Sotomayor cautioned that it was sliding toward becoming a prison state. What they agreed on was that the government was assuming—and the Court was allowing—greater control than ever over people's bodies, and more power than ever to investigate, categorize, and incarcerate them.

These dual totalitarian visions are a logical extension of where the Court has taken the nation in the past fifty years. Economic inequality has risen at a furious pace, the middle class has contracted, and the status of the poor has become ever more precarious. This economic transformation makes firmer methods of social control, including more oppressive forms of policing, likely—if not inevitable. As the sociologists explain, "the more economically stratified a society becomes the more it becomes necessary for the dominant groups . . . to enforce through coercion the norms of conduct which guarantee their supremacy."

The more autocratic nation the Court seems intent on creating is not the one the founders intended America to be. The police conduct that the Court countenanced in *Utah v. Strieff* "implies that you are not a citizen of a democracy," Sotomayor warned in her dissent. A police force that can stop people on the street for no reason, search them, and check them against government databases sounds more totalitarian than democratic. A government that can force people who have not been convicted of any crime to turn over their DNA sounds more like a brave new world than a free nation. Scalia made that point caustically in his *Maryland v. King* dissent. "I doubt that the proud men who wrote the charter of our liberties," he said, "would have been so eager to open their mouths for royal inspection."

Conclusion

Brett Kavanaugh was sworn in as a Supreme Court justice on October 6, 2018, just hours after the Senate confirmed him by a tense 50–48 vote. Kavanaugh's nomination was nearly derailed when Christine Blasey Ford accused him of sexually assaulting her in high school. His defenders cast doubt on Ford's story and insisted that Kavanaugh, a judge on the U.S. Court of Appeals for the D.C. Circuit, was being smeared. On the day of the vote, 164 demonstrators were arrested, including 14 who tried to disrupt the roll call. Minority Leader Chuck Schumer called Kavanaugh's nomination "one of the saddest moments in the history of the Senate." Majority Leader Mitch McConnell insisted that the "mob" that had turned out to protest had only made his supporters more resolute.

Much of the anger over the nomination was about the possibility that someone who had sexually assaulted a woman and then lied to the Senate about it was joining the nation's highest court—and in opinion polls, more Americans said they believed Ford than Kavanaugh. The opposition was also fueled, however, by a widespread belief that if Kavanaugh was confirmed, it would mean a new era for the Court. He would be replacing Anthony Kennedy, who had been the swing justice for more than a decade. Kennedy was unmistakably conservative—he had written the opinion in *Citizens United* and had joined enthusiastically in many of the Court's most extreme 5–4 rulings—but he was moderate on some issues. With Kavanaugh in place, it appeared that there would finally be a five-justice majority made up of solid conservatives. Many Court watchers believed his arrival could be the start of an "'epochal' shift," as *The Wall Street Journal* put it.

For anyone who had been following the Court's past fifty years of rulings on issues of economic class, it was strange to think that the experts were saying an epochal shift was coming. What had the past half century been if not a steady process of shifting the Court away from its onetime commitment to the middle class and the poor, in favor of the wealthy and powerful? Since 1969, the year that everything began to change, the Court had obliterated the idea that poor people might have a special right to be protected under the Equal Protection Clause—even though they fit the criteria the Court had laid out for "discrete and insular minorities," groups whose history of oppression and powerlessness entitled them to special consideration. The Court had stopped looking out for the interests of people on welfare, declaring in a landmark 1970 decision that the "intractable economic, social, and even philosophical problems presented by public welfare assistance programs are not the business of this Court."

The Court had not merely stopped its efforts to lift the boots of oppression off the necks of the poor; it had also gotten in some kicks of its own. One of the most notable of these came in the midst of the Affordable Care Act's surprise victory in the Court, when Roberts cast an unexpected vote to uphold most of Obamacare. At the same time as he did, he invoked an obscure constitutional doctrine, in a way that it had never been used before, to take health care away from millions of poor people who had been given it by Congress and the president.

The Court had entrenched inequality and racial segregation in the nation's schools. It decided that the Equal Protection Clause, which was enacted after the Civil War to ensure that all Americans would be treated equally by the government, did not guarantee all of the nation's children an equally funded public education. Nor did it mean that children had a right to a racially integrated education, as long as the whites in a metropolitan area could get themselves to the other side of a school district line. It also did not mean that a little girl from an impoverished rural family who lived sixteen miles from her public school had the right to a bus ride to get there.

It was not just the poor that the Court had turned on over the past fifty years. The middle class, which was also struggling, fared little better. The Court wiped out the claims of millions of workers who were subjected to discrimination on the basis of race, sex, and age, by twisting employment law in favor of employers. The Court had also become hostile to labor unions, interpreting the New Deal law that was intended to promote unionization of the workforce in ways that weakened the right of workers to organize and act collectively. In a particularly audacious move, it had interpreted the First Amendment to strike down mandatory "fair share" fees for public-sector unions, dealing a major blow to the labor movement.

While the Court denied the poor and the middle class rights to which they were entitled, it invented new ones for wealthy individuals and corporations. It decided that spending money in an election was speech and used that novel principle as a bulldozer to sweep away one campaign finance regulation after another. The Court was not deterred by the crisis that special-interest money was creating for democracy, or by the broad support for campaign finance regulation from Congress, presidents, and the people. It went on to issue a radical ruling that corporations have a First Amendment right to spend unlimited amounts of money from their treasuries to win elections, a decision 80 percent of Americans opposed and 65 percent opposed strongly. With these rulings, the Court ensured that the wealthiest and most powerful people and institutions in society would have an almost insurmountable level of control over government.

The Court showered many more legal gifts on corporations. The same Court that abandoned welfare recipients to their lives of poverty—"the problems of government," it said with a shrug, "are practical ones and may justify, if they do not require, rough accommodations"—took on as a mission clearing away some of the biggest problems of wealthy corporations. Punitive damages, which had been used to discourage outrageous actions since ancient times, suddenly became suspect, and the Court rushed to rescue major global corporations from damage awards they would barely notice having paid. The Court came to the defense of corporations that used mandatory arbitration clauses to deny consumers they had cheated and workers whose wages they had stolen their day in court.

The Court also eroded the voice that poor and middle-class people had over government—what little was left after it threw open the floodgates of special-interest money. The same Court that would not allow Congress to limit political spending gave its endorsement to voter ID laws that were designed to suppress the votes of poor people and racial minorities, voting roll purges that disenfranchised eligible voters, and partisan gerrymanders that were intended to make the voters as irrelevant to the election process as possible. While the Court gave its blessing to all of these, it removed the heart of the Voting Rights Act—one of the crowning achievements of the civil rights movement, which had been repeatedly reauthorized by large bipartisan majorities in Congress and signed into law by presidents of both parties—by invoking a purported constitutional doctrine that it all but made up.

While the Court was driving the poor and the middle class further down and lifting up wealthy individuals and corporations, it was also changing the criminal law in a way that two justices—one liberal, one conservative—warned had more than a whiff of tyranny. The Court gave its blessing to the police stopping and searching people without any reason to suspect they had done anything wrong, and to seizing the DNA of people who had not been convicted of a crime. As the gap between the wealthiest and poorest Americans was growing to record levels—in significant part because of its own rulings—the Court was helping to usher in what one of its own members warned could be a prison state.

Given that the Court's past half century was made up of all of this, it raised an obvious question about the talk of an impending epochal change. For fifty years, the conservative majority had waged an unrelenting war on the poor and the middle class and enthusiastically championed wealthy individuals and corporations—and changed the law dramatically to suit its vision of society. After all of this, what could a conservative "epochal shift" mean?

The answer, of course, lay partly in important hot-button social issues. Hardcore conservatives hoped that a purer conservative majority would finally deliver an array of victories that had long eluded them. Anti-abortion activists thought the Court might at last overturn *Roe v. Wade* and end the constitutional right to abortion. Opponents of affirmative action expected that there might at last be five votes to hold that all selection criteria that take race into account are unconstitutional. Critics of the Court's decisions recognizing a right to same-sex marriage believed the new majority might declare those rulings a mistake.

The truth was, all of these things were possible. For decades, *Roe v. Wade* had survived because one of the conservative justices—Sandra Day O'Connor or Anthony Kennedy—defected to the liberals and voted to uphold it. Now that O'Connor was gone and the Court had shifted rightward, it was not certain how long the abortion-rights era would continue.

Affirmative action was also vulnerable. Roberts had laid down a marker in 2007 when he declared that the "way to stop discrimination on the basis of race is to stop discriminating on the basis of race." He had only four votes for his position, however, with Kennedy writing a separate opinion that was more supportive of race-based remedies. In a big case about affirmative action in university admissions in 2016, Kennedy had voted with the liberals to uphold the use of race, but the mathematics might well be different now.

The future of a constitutional right to same-sex marriage was also unclear. Kennedy had broken with the conservative bloc and voted with the liberals on same-sex marriage. It was possible that with Kennedy gone, the new conservative majority might do away with the right to marriage or hollow it out so that it meant little.

If the Court reversed course in any of these areas, it could have a devastating personal impact on millions of Americans—young women forced into back-alley abortions, racial minorities turned away from leading universities and desirable jobs, gay people denied an equal right to marry. It could also have significant economic effects. Millions of Americans would be made poorer, whether because of the cost of raising a child they did not want or the diminished income from being denied educational and employment opportunities, or the added expenses associated with living as an unmarried couple.

Any of these reversals would advance a long-standing conservative goal: rolling back the progress the nation made in the 1960s—or, in the case of gay rights, that started in the 1960s. Ending the right to abortion, holding that the Constitution does not protect same-sex marriage, or ending affirmative action could all amount to an epochal shift—all the more so if the Court did two or three of them. The epochal shift that some conservative activists have in mind, though, is focused on reversing the gains of an even earlier era: the 1930s.

For many conservatives, the real battleground has always been the New Deal and the way in which it vastly expanded the federal government's role in the life of the nation. Until President Franklin Roosevelt took office, in 1933, there were virtually no government social welfare programs and nearly no regulatory state: the poor had to look to their families or private charities when they needed help, and the economy operated almost entirely by the principles of laissez-faire capitalism. It was Roosevelt's New Deal that produced Social Security, federal welfare programs, the federal minimum wage, and a federal right to unionize—and that established agencies to supervise things like the sale of stock and relations between labor and management.

There is a part of the conservative movement that believes the federal government did not have the authority to do any of this. That was true in the 1930s, when the New Deal safety net was being established, and for several years the Supreme Court agreed. It struck down major New Deal legislation, including laws adopted to revive the industrial economy and rescue impoverished farmers. The Court backed down only in 1937, after Roosevelt announced his Court-packing plan, which would have allowed him to appoint additional justices so he could create a pro–New Deal majority on the Court. In the "switch in time that saved nine," the Court changed course and began upholding New Deal laws.

The goal of these conservatives is returning to a pre-1937 view of the Constitution, before the Court gave in and accepted the New Deal. This has been a drumbeat on the right for some time. At the start of the George W. Bush administration, another time when conservatives were feeling energized, the Federalist Society—the legal group that would later help President Trump choose his Court nominees—sponsored a conference on "Rolling Back the New Deal." It included a presentation by a prominent law professor on "The Mistakes of 1937."

More recently, a leading political magazine dubbed these anti–New Deal activists "the Rehabilitationists," for their goal of bringing back an antiquated understanding of the Constitution. A member of the movement, writing in *National Review* in 2012, insisted that the powers of the federal government were limited to a few areas, like declaring war and building post offices, and did not include Social Security, health care, or other social welfare programs. "Don't be cowed," he said, "by shrieking from the Left."

A main article of faith among these constitutional conservatives is that the Court has interpreted the Commerce Clause, which provides the basis for upholding much of the federal social safety net, too broadly. Before 1937, the Court regularly struck down legislation, including laws designed to end child labor, for exceeding Congress's power under the Commerce Clause. If the Court returned to a pre-1937 interpretation of the Commerce Clause, it could conceivably strike down major social welfare and labor laws, including the National Labor Relations Act, which protects the right to form unions, and the Fair Labor Standards Act, which established the federal minimum wage and the federal right to overtime pay.

It is hard to imagine that the Court would ever do anything so radical—and certainly the pressure on it not to strike down laws that are so broadly popular with the American people would be considerable. There was, however, a period in the 1930s when the Court did precisely that. It has also had more recent episodes of Commerce Clause radicalism. In 1995 and 2000, the Rehnquist Court struck down the Gun-Free Schools Act and parts of the Violence Against Women Act, both popular laws, on the grounds that they exceeded the power of Congress under the Commerce Clause.

There have been significant hints from the current Court that it might be interested in changing its approach to the Commerce Clause. Most notably, when Roberts provided the fifth vote to uphold the Affordable Care Act, he refused to say that Congress had the power under the Commerce Clause to impose the individual mandate and instead upheld it under Congress's taxing power. In his opinion, he emphasized that "the commerce clause is not a general license to regulate an individual from cradle to grave."

There are ways to read Roberts's words about the Commerce Clause as not enormously significant, and the specific facts of the case were unusual. Hardline conservatives, however, were enormously excited by the possibilities. "We finally won a three-decades-long battle over the commerce clause," John Eastman, a conservative law professor at Chapman University, said of Roberts's opinion. Even Akhil Amar, a liberal Yale law professor, said the decision "reinvigorates a stricter understanding of all the powers of government." When Barack Obama, as a senator, voted against Roberts's confirmation, he specifically said that he did not trust Roberts on questions like "whether the Commerce Clause empowers Congress to speak on those issues of broad national concern that may be only tangentially related to what is easily defined as interstate commerce."

There are other legal hooks, beyond a more restrictive reading of the Commerce Clause, that the Court could use to strip away the legal edifice of the New Deal. By making changes in the arcane area of administrative law, the Court could begin to drastically scale back the power of federal agencies, which since the 1930s have become an important force for keeping abusive business practices in check. In the area of workers' rights, the erosion has already begun. In *Janus v. American Federation of State, County and Municipal Employees,* the Court significantly wounded public-sector unions with a ruling under the First Amendment. In *Epic Systems v. Lewis,* it struck a major blow against the right of workers to act collectively under the NLRA by invoking the Federal Arbitration Act. At the oral argument in *Epic Systems,* Breyer made clear precisely what the Court was up to: the case, he said, was aimed at "the entire heart of the New Deal." These rumblings of opposition to federal power, the social safety net, and workers' rights could just be the start of a truly epochal change in the law—and the nation.

THE SUPREME COURT IS MORE THAN A LEGAL TRIBUNAL, RULING ON disputes between parties—it is also an architect. The Court's interpretations of the Constitution and other laws become blueprints for the nation, helping to determine what form it will take and how it will continue to rise. For the past half century, the Court has been drawing up plans for a more economically unequal nation, and that is the America that is now being built.

The Court's rulings have helped to produce historic gaps between the most well-off and the least. Wealth inequality is once again where it stood at in 1929, just before the Great Depression began. The top 1 percent of Americans control about 40 percent of the nation's wealth. Much of the rest of the country is only scraping by. A survey by an employment website in 2017 found that 78 percent of Americans said they were living paycheck to paycheck.

The inequality trajectory the nation is on is not sustainable, something societal leaders have begun to speak out about. President Obama has called income inequality "the defining challenge of our time," and Warren Buffett has said that wealth inequality "has widened and will continue to widen unless something is done about it." In 2019, Ray Dalio, the founder of one of the world's largest hedge funds, declared that increasing economic inequality poses an "existential threat" to America. He warned that inequities of this kind—the kind that saw his own personal net worth soar to more than $18 billion—lead to "increasing conflict," "populism of the left and populism of the right," and, often, "revolutions of one sort or another." Dalio called on the nation's leaders to start treating wealth and income inequality as the national emergency it is.

In October 2020, Amy Coney Barrett took the seat of the late Ruth Bader Ginsburg, which brought the conservative majority to six justices and exacerbated fears about where the Court would lead the nation. As the right wing expanded its size and power, it was hard to remember that there was a time when the Court was moving in the opposite direction. Under only slightly different historical circumstances, the Warren Court could have continued on its path, as Warren and President Johnson hoped it would when they met in June 1968. It could have designated the poor as a suspect class and used that special level of protection to ensure that the nation's welfare programs did a better job of providing for the Americans who needed them. It could have ensured equal school funding for all children, and it could have required states to provide integrated education regardless of school district lines. It could have upheld limits on campaign spending and struck down barriers to voting. It could have sided with workers more than corporations, and defendants more than prosecutors.

That different set of blueprints would have built a different society. For the past five decades, all families could have been lifted above the poverty line. All children could have attended schools that were adequately funded and racially integrated. There could have been elections that were decided by the most persuasive arguments to the electorate, not by special-interest money, and a government that put the public's interest ahead of the billionaires'. There could have been workplaces with less discrimination and more unions, and prisons with fewer inmates.

The Court, in other words, could have helped to create a society with more equality, inclusion, and opportunity for all. As Edward Sparer, the leader of the poverty law movement, said so many years ago, it "could have led to a different America."

ACKNOWLEDGMENTS

There are books that take authors on new journeys and ones authors have lived with their whole lives. This book falls squarely in the second category. I grew up in the afterglow of the Warren Court, and I went to law school and became a public interest lawyer in large part because of its idealistic vision of the law. I left the law and became a journalist, to a significant extent, because the Court so drastically reversed direction after the Warren era ended.

I first formed many of the ideas in this book at Harvard College, where I was fortunate to study constitutional law with the legendary Archibald Cox, and at Harvard Law School, where I learned from many professors whose own views of what the law could be were shaped by the Warren Court, among them Gerald Frug, Lance Liebman, Laurence Tribe, Stephen Breyer, David Shapiro, Lloyd Weinreb, Susan Estrich, Charles Nesson, Daniel Meltzer, and Martha Minow.

As a lawyer for the Southern Poverty Law Center in Montgomery, Alabama, and the American Civil Liberties Union in New York, Alabama, and Connecticut, I saw firsthand what the law can do for those who need it the most. I worked alongside extraordinary people, including the ACLU's Alabama team, which was working to establish the right to an adequate education in the state's poorest school systems, after the Supreme Court let them down so profoundly in *Rodriguez v. San Antonio Independent School District*. There are no truer heirs to Earl Warren's legacy than Olivia Turner, Bobby Segall, and Martha Morgan.

As a journalist at *The New York Times* and *Time*, I had the chance to write extensively about the Court and legal issues and to have my thoughts refined by impressive minds. At *The New York Times*, my appreciation to Dorothy Samuels, Gail Collins, Frank Rich, Carolyn Curiel, Brent Staples, Eduardo Porter, Teresa Tritch, Philip Taubman, Ethan Bronner, Adam Moss, Terry Tang, David Shipley, Francis X. Clines, Robert Semple, Carol Giacomo, Lawrence Downes, Philip Boffey, Verlyn Klinkenborg, and Eleanor Randolph.

At *Time*, I had the great pleasure of working with Walter Isaacson, Jim Kelly, Joelle Attinger, Priscilla Painton, John Stacks, Rick Hornik, Rick Stengel, Bill Saporito, Dan Goodgame, Josh Quittner, Jan Simpson, Richard Zoglin, Jim Gaines, Aisha Labi, Karl Taro Greenfeld, Daniel Eisenberg, Barbara Maddux, Vicki Rainert, Eric Roston, Michael Krantz, Tammy Drummond, Stacy Perman, Nadya Labi, Joel Stein, and Josh Tyrangiel.

In writing this book, I benefitted enormously from insightful journalism and legal scholarship. I would like to acknowledge, in particular, the work of Dahlia Lithwick, Jeffrey Toobin, Adam Winkler, Linda Greenhouse, Emily Bazelon, Adam Liptak, Charles Lane, Jeffrey Rosen, Joan Biskupic, Richard Hasen, Jacobus tenBroek, Edward Sparer, Charles Reich, Frank Michelman, Laurence Tribe, Lani Guinier, Laura Kalman, Peter Edelman, Erwin Chemerinsky, Charles Fried, Mark Tushnet, Ganesh Sitaraman, Bruce Allen Murphy, Peter Rubin, Donald Black, Suzanna Sherry, Margaret Jane Radin, Richard Posner, Eric Posner, Lee Epstein, William Landes, Cynthia Estlund, Julius Getman, Myron Orfield, Brian Fitzpatrick, Suzette Malveaux, Catherine Fisk, Elizabeth Bartholet, Imre Szalai, Michele Gilman, Arthur Miller, Morton Horwitz, John Pfaff, Paul Butler, Michelle Alexander, Kelly Strader, J. Mitchell Pickerill, Martha Davis, Felicia Kornbluh, Elizabeth Bussiere, Adam Lioz, Ezra Rosser, Henry Freedman, Clare Pastore, Melanie Abbott, and Julie Nice.

I drew on conversations with many of those impressive thinkers, as well as interviews and conversations with several of the justices—including my administrative law professor, Stephen Breyer—and a good number of Supreme Court law clerks. My special thanks to Walter Slocombe, for his recollections of Abe Fortas, and Ira Feinberg, who was with Thurgood Marshall at a critical time.

There is no better publishing house than Penguin Press, and it is my incredible good fortune that I have been able to work with the extraordinary Ann Godoff on this, our third book together. Ann's brilliance spans the whole publishing process, from helping the author refine a book's central ideas until they are just right, to strengthening arguments and improving sentences, to choosing the perfect cover and subtitle. My deep gratitude to her for doing all of these things for my book, and to Casey Denis, Colleen Boyle, Bruce Giffords, and the whole team at Penguin Press for their own invaluable work.

I was enormously lucky that I found my very wise and adept agent, Kris Dahl at ICM, for my first book, and that she has stuck with me through this one. My thanks, also, to the incomparable Josie Freedman of ICM's west coast office, which arranged a movie deal for my last book, *Imbeciles: The Supreme Court, American Eugenics, and the Sterilization of Carrie Buck*. I am honored that the endlessly talented Dakota Johnson is bringing Carrie Buck's story to the big screen.

Columbia Law School's public interest program chose *Imbeciles* as the one book it recommended all incoming students read in the fall of 2019. My thanks to Ibrahim Diallo, Hannah Rosner, and Madeleine Kurtz, and to Jamal Greene, Rose Cuison-Villazor, and Elisabeth Benjamin for joining me at Columbia for a panel on the book.

My great appreciation also to Michael Waldman and Jeanine Chirlin and the entire staff of the Brennan Center for Justice at NYU Law School; Juliet Lapidos of *The Atlantic*; Lisa Lucas of the National Book Foundation; Amy Goodman of *Democracy Now!*; Marcy Euler and the Tucson Festival of Books; and Jane Kulow and the Virginia Festival of the Book for their support.

I had the honor of serving as a Pulitzer Prize juror for feature writing in 2018 and commentary in 2017, and I learned an enormous amount from fellow jurors Keith Campbell, Audrey Cooper, Rachel Morris, Eli Sanders, Paige Williams, Madeleine Blais, Jay Stowe, Manuela Hoelterhoff, and Danielle Henderson.

Friends were a great source of insights and support—and, often, food—at every stage. I'd like to thank Eileen Hershenov first, because she asked so many times to be listed first. Elizabeth Taylor has long been my partner in all things literary, and Paul Engelmayer, who has taught me so much about the law, generously read and commented on an early draft of this book. Also, with affection and gratitude: Elisabeth Benjamin, Caroline Arnold, Amy Chua, Loren Eng, Amy Gutman, Patti Galluzzi, Tina Smith, Maria Laurino, Elizabeth Glazer, Amy Schwartz, Carol Owens, David Propp, Lavea Brachman, Laura Haight, P. J. Posner, Michael Dubno, Dan Pool, Noah Benjamin-Pollak, Kathy Bishop, Kirk Swinehart, Claudia Dowling, Ed Barnes, and Hope Hamashige.

I am fortunate to go on an annual fishing trip, organized by the estimable Judge Engelmayer, that has for years produced far more witty banter, camaraderie, and intellectual musings than fish. For this, I'd like to thank Paul Engelmayer, Jim Rosenthal, Antony Blinken, Peter Mandelstam, Michael Abramowitz, Eric Washburn, Peter Vigeland, and Jacob Schlesinger.

I am grateful also to my family: Stuart Cohen, Noam Cohen, Aviva Michaelov, Harlan Cohen, and Kika and Nuli Cohen, who informed me not long ago that I am not only their uncle but their friend.

And finally, in writing this book I thought often of three people who left us too soon, and who never lost their outrage at what those at the top of society do to those at the bottom: my great friends Elaine Rivera and Chuck Young, both immensely talented journalists, and my remarkable mother, Judge Beverly Sher Cohen, whose kitchen walls were decorated not with images of food or drink, but rather with a poster bearing the injunction from Deuteronomy 16:20: "Justice, justice shalt thou pursue."

NOTES

Introduction

xiii **Vance said a different woman:** *Vance v. Ball State University,* 570 U.S. 421 (2013).

xiv **She also warned that the Court's decision:** *Vance,* 570 U.S. 421.

xiv **A jury ruled:** *Gross v. FBL Financial Services, Inc.,* 557 U.S. 167 (2009); *Workplace Fairness: Has the Supreme Court Misinterpreted Laws Designed to Protect American Workers? Hearing Before the Senate Committee on the Judiciary,* 111th Cong. (2009) (statement of Jack Gross), judiciary.senate.gov/download/testimony-of-grosspdf.

xiv **The dissenting liberal justices:** *Gross,* 557 U.S. 167.

xiv **Ledbetter sued for sex discrimination:** *Ledbetter v. Goodyear Tire & Rubber Co.,* 550 U.S. 618 (2007); Lilly Ledbetter with Lanier Scott Isom, *Grace and Grit: My Fight for Equal Pay and Fairness at Goodyear and Beyond* (New York: Three Rivers Press, 2012), 15.

xiv **The ruling against Ledbetter:** *Ledbetter,* 550 U.S. 618; Sheryl Gay Stolberg, "Obama Signs Equal-Pay Legislation," *New York Times,* January 29, 2009.

xv **"That is money," he said:** *Workplace Fairness* (statement of Jack Gross), judiciary .senate.gov/download/testimony-of-grosspdf.

xv **It occurred to her that:** Ledbetter, *Grace and Grit,* 265–66, 273.

xvi **When the South rose up:** *Brown v. Board of Education,* 347 U.S. 483 (1954).

xvi **It expanded the rights:** *Miranda v. Arizona,* 384 U.S. 436 (1966); *Shapiro v. Thompson,* 394 U.S. 618 (1969); *Engel v. Vitale,* 370 U.S. 421 (1962); Erwin Chemerinsky, *The Case Against the Supreme Court* (New York: Penguin, 2014), 155.

xvi **By 1968, Richard Nixon:** Edgar McManus and Tara Helfman, *Liberty and Union: A Constitutional History of the United States* (New York: Routledge, 2014), 488;

Michael Tackett, "The Justice Who Changed a Way of Life," *Chicago Tribune*, September 24, 2006; Ed Cray, *Chief Justice: A Biography of Earl Warren* (New York: Simon & Schuster, 1997), 497.

xvii **Warren, however, had a plan:** Laura Kalman, *The Long Reach of the Sixties: LBJ, Nixon, and the Making of the Contemporary Supreme Court* (New York: Oxford University Press, 2017); Bob Woodward and Scott Armstrong, *The Brethren: Inside the Supreme Court* (New York: Simon & Schuster, 1979); Lucas A. Powe Jr., *The Warren Court and American Politics* (Cambridge, Mass.: Belknap Press, 2000), 465; John A. Jenkins, *The Partisan: The Life of William Rehnquist* (New York: PublicAffairs, 2012), 89; Fred Graham, "Johnson Appoints Fortas to Head Supreme Court; Thornberry to Be Justice," *New York Times*, June 27, 1968; G. Edward White, *Earl Warren: A Public Life* (New York: Oxford University Press, 1982), 142, 307.

xvii **Many of these initiatives:** Cray, *Chief Justice*, 496.

xviii **In his first three years in office:** *San Antonio Independent School District v. Rodriguez*, 411 U.S. 1 (1973).

xviii **The role of one man:** Fred P. Graham, "Profile of the 'Nixon Court' Now Discernible," *New York Times*, May 24, 1972; John Ehrlichman, *Witness to Power: The Nixon Years* (New York: Simon & Schuster, 1982), 134; Woodward and Armstrong, *The Brethren*, 189; Jenkins, *The Partisan*, 103–4; Lesley Oelsner, "Harlan Dies at 72; On Court 16 Years," *New York Times*, December 30, 1971.

xviii **Since January 1972:** Nate Silver, "Supreme Court May Be the Most Conservative in Modern History," FiveThirtyEight, March 29, 2012.

xviii **since 1969, Republicans:** White House, "Presidents," available at whitehouse.gov/about-the-white-house/presidents/.

xix **An analysis conducted in 2014:** Maureen Dowd, "The Supreme Court; Conservative Black Judge, Clarence Thomas, Is Named to Marshall's Court Seat," *New York Times*, July 2, 1991; David Stout, "Ceremony Follows Senate Vote Confirming Nomination, 78–22," *New York Times*, September 30, 2005; Richard Berke, "The Supreme Court; The Overview; Clinton Names Ruth Ginsburg, Advocate for Women, to Court," *New York Times*, June 15, 1993; David Leonhardt, "The Supreme Court Blunder That Liberals Tend to Make," *New York Times*, June 2, 2014; Michael Isikoff, "The Truth Behind the Pillars," *Newsweek*, December 24, 2000; Stephanie Mencimer, "What the Cult of Ruth Bader Ginsburg Got Wrong," *Mother Jones*, November 24, 2018; Michael Shear, "Supreme Court Justice Anthony Kennedy Will Retire," *New York Times*, June 27, 2018.

xix **Fortas's forced resignation:** Ron Elving, "What Happened with Merrick Garland in 2016 and Why It Matters Now," NPR.org, June 29, 2018.

xix **As President Trump said:** Donald Trump (@realDonaldTrump), "THE SECOND AMENDMENT WILL NEVER BE REPEALED!," Twitter, March 28, 2018, 5:52 a.m., twitter.com/realdonaldtrump/status/978932860307505153; Eileen Sullivan, "Trump Says Second Amendment 'Will Never Be Repealed,'" *New York Times*, March 28, 2018.

xx **In a 1940 case:** *Chambers v. Florida*, 309 U.S. 227, 241 (1940); Alden Whitman, "Earl Warren, 83, Who Led High Court in Time of Vast Social Change, Is Dead," *New York Times*, July 10, 1974.

xx **Hollywood has yet to make:** *Brown*, 347 U.S. 483; *Gideon v. Wainwright*, 372 U.S. 335 (1963); *Shelby County v. Holder*, 570 U.S. 529 (2013); IMDb, s.v. "Separate but Equal," imdb.com/title/tt0102879/; IMDb, s.v. "Gideon's Trumpet," imdb.com/title/tt0080789/.

xx **In the years after the war:** *Dred Scott v. Sandford*, 60 U.S. 393 (1856); *Plessy v. Ferguson*, 163 U.S. 537 (1896).

xxi **During World War II:** *Lochner v. New York*, 198 U.S. 45 (1905); *Hammer v. Dagenhart*, 247 U.S. 251 (1918); *Adair v. United States*, 208 U.S. 161 (1908); *A.L.A. Schechter Poultry Corp. v. United States*, 295 U.S. 495 (1935); *United States v. Butler*, 297 U.S. 1 (1936); Bernard Schwartz, *A History of the Supreme Court* (New York: Oxford University Press, 1993), 232–34; *Korematsu v. United States*, 323 U.S. 214 (1944).

xxi **The justices have also:** *Roe v. Wade*, 410 U.S. 113 (1973); *Lawrence v. Texas*, 539 U.S. 558 (2003); *Obergefell v. Hodges*, 135 S. Ct. 2584 (2015); *Bowers v. Hardwick*, 478 U.S. 186 (1986); *Crawford v. Marion County Election Board*, 553 U.S. 181 (2008).

xxii **The current Court:** Nolan McCaskill, "Trump Releases Updated Short List of Potential Supreme Court Nominees," *Politico*, November 11, 2017; Seth McLaughlin, "Kavanaugh a 'Man of Integrity,' Pence Tells Values Voter Summit," *Washington Times*, September 22, 2018.

xxii **"These decisions are not the work":** Lee Epstein and Tonja Jacobi, "Super Medians," *Stanford Law Review* 61, no. 1 (April 2010): 37, 69–72; Silver, "Supreme Court May Be the Most Conservative in Modern History;" Michael Graetz and Linda Greenhouse, *The Burger Court and the Rise of the Judicial Right* (New York: Simon & Schuster, 2016), 4–5; Charles Fried, "Not Conservative," *Harvard Law Review Blog*, July 3, 2018.

xxii **Poor people had always been seen:** William Quigley, "Reluctant Charity: Poor Laws in the Original Thirteen States," 31 *University of Richmond Law Review* 111 (1997); *Edwards v. California*, 314 U.S. 160 (1941); Fried, "Not Conservative."

xxiii **Four years later, it greatly increased:** David Zarefsky, *President Johnson's War on Poverty: Rhetoric and History* (Tuscaloosa: University of Alabama Press, 2005), xvii–xix; *Harper v. Virginia Board of Elections*, 383 U.S. 663 (1966); *Goldberg v. Kelly*, 397 U.S. 254 (1970).

xxiii **In its opinion, the Court:** *Sniadach v. Family Finance Corp.*, 395 U.S. 337 (1969).

xxiv **In a number of rulings:** *United States v. Carolene Products Co.*, 304 U.S. 144 (1938); Bertall L. Ross II and Su Li, "Measuring Political Power: Suspect Class Determinations and the Poor," *California Law Review* 104 (2016): 323, 325.

xxiv **It also decided that the poor:** *Dandridge v. Williams*, 397 U.S. 471 (1970); Ross and Li, "Measuring Political Power," 323, 325.

xxiv **If Nixon had not:** *Rodriguez*, 411 U.S. 1; *Milliken v. Bradley*, 418 U.S. 717 (1974); Lee Epstein, William Landes, and Richard Posner, "How Business Fares in the Supreme Court," *Minnesota Law Review* 97 (2013): 1431, 1451.

xxiv **That decision is likely:** *Janus v. AFSCME,* 138 S. Ct. 2448 (2018).

xxv **It upheld strict voter ID laws:** *Shelby County v. Holder,* 570 U.S. 529 (2013); *Crawford v. Marion County Election Board,* 553 U.S. 181 (2008); *Husted v. A. Philip Randolph Institute,* 138 S. Ct. 1833 (2018); Nina Totenberg, "Supreme Court Upholds Controversial Ohio Voter-Purge Law," *All Things Considered,* NPR, June 11, 2018.

xxv **These decisions have contributed:** Stephen Smith, "The Rehnquist Court and Criminal Procedure," *University of Colorado Law Review* 73, no. 4 (2002): 1337; John Gramlich, "America's Incarceration Rate Is at a Two-Decade Low," Pew Research Center Fact Tank, May 2, 2018, pewresearch.org/fact-tank/2018/05/02/americas-incarceration-rate-is-at-a-two-decade-low/; *Utah v. Strieff,* 136 S. Ct. 2056 (2016).

xxv **As a result of these rulings:** Spencer Overton, "The Donor Class: Campaign Finance, Democracy, and Participation," *University of Pennsylvania Law Review* 153, no. 1 (2004): 73.

xxv **It gave corporations:** Brian Fitzpatrick, "The End of Class Actions?," *Arizona Law Review* 57, no. 162 (2015); Jeffrey Fisher, "The Exxon Valdez Case and Regularizing Punishment," *Alaska Law Review* 26, no. 1 (2009).

xxvi **A *New York Times* analysis:** Epstein, Landes, and Posner, "How Business Fares in the Supreme Court," 1431, 1449, 1471; Jeffrey Rosen, "Supreme Court Inc.," *New York Times,* March 16, 2008.

xxvi **The richest 0.1 percent:** Drew DeSilver, "U.S. Income Inequality on Rise for Decades, Is Now Highest Since 1928," Pew Research Center Fact Tank, December 5, 2013; "Nine Charts About Wealth Inequality in America (Updated)," Urban Institute, apps.urban.org/features/wealth-inequality-charts/; Max Ehrenfreund, "Bernie Sanders Is Right: The Top 0.1 Percent Have as Much as the Bottom 90 Percent," *Washington Post,* November 19, 2015; Chad Stone et al., "A Guide to Statistics on Historical Trends in Income Inequality," Center on Budget and Policy Priorities, December 11, 2018; Facundo Alvaredo et al., *World Inequality Report 2018,* World Inequality Lab, 78, wir2018.wid.world/files/download/wir2018-full-report-english.pdf.

xxvi **To "reverse these trends":** Joseph Stiglitz, *The Price of Inequality: How Today's Divided Society Endangers Our Future* (New York: Norton, 2013), 7.

xxvii **The Supreme Court is rarely included:** Emily Horton, "The Legacy of the 2001 and 2003 'Bush' Tax Cuts," Center on Budget and Policy Priorities, October 23, 2017; Dylan Scott and Alvin Chang, "The Republican Tax Bill Will Exacerbate Income Inequality in America," *Vox,* December 4, 2017; Arloc Sherman, "After 1996 Welfare Law, a Weaker Safety Net and More Children in Deep Poverty," Center on Budget and Policy Priorities, August 9, 2016; Dylan Matthews, "'If the Goal Was to Get Rid of Poverty, We Failed': The Legacy of the 1996 Welfare Reform," *Vox,* June 20, 2016.

xxvii **The Court's campaign finance decisions:** Alvaredo et al., *World Inequality Report 2018,* 8–20, 78.

xxviii **Public health experts connect:** Anna Bahney, "40% of Americans Can't Cover a $400 Emergency Expense," CNN, May 22, 2018; "Deaths of Despair: The Opioid Epidemic Is Just Part of the Problem," *Science Daily,* September 27, 2018; Lenny Bernstein, "U.S. Life Expectancy Declines Again, a Dismal Trend Not Seen Since World War I," *Washington Post,* November 29, 2018; Meilan Solly, "United States Drops 21 Spots in Global Life Expectancy Rankings," *Smithsonian,* October 19, 2018.

xxviii **That translates into more than:** "Understand Food Insecurity," Hunger and Health: Feeding America, hungerandhealth.feedingamerica.org/understand-food-insecurity/; Maia Szalavitz, "Income Inequality's Most Disturbing Side Effect: Homicide," *Scientific American,* November 1, 2018; "24 Million Americans—Poverty in the United States: 1969," U.S. Department of Commerce, December 26, 1970; "What Is the Current Poverty Rate in the United States," Center for Poverty Research, University of California at Davis, updated October 15, 2018.

xxviii **"Once those are gone":** Ganesh Sitaraman, "Divided We Fall," *New Republic,* April 10, 2017; "The Other Moore's Law," *Economist,* February 14, 2009.

xxix **"Economic growth that is spread":** Richard V. Reeves and Katherine Guyot, "Fewer Americans Are Making More Than Their Parents Did—Especially If They Grew Up in the Middle Class," Brookings Institution, July 25, 2018; Raj Chetty et al., "The Fading American Dream: Trends in Absolute Income Mobility Since 1940" (working paper, National Bureau of Economic Research, Cambridge, Mass., 2016).

Chapter One: Protecting the Poor

1 **The problem, Stancil said:** *Smith v. King,* 277 F. Supp. 31 (M.D. Ala. 1967); *King v. Smith,* 392 U.S. 309, 309–16 (1968); Felicia Kornbluh, *The Battle for Welfare Rights: Politics and Poverty in Modern America* (Philadelphia: University of Pennsylvania Press, 2007), 67; Henry Freedman, "Sylvester Smith, Unlikely Heroine: *King v. Smith* (1968)," in *The Poverty Law Canon: Exploring the Major Cases,* ed. Marie Failinger and Ezra Rosser (Ann Arbor: University of Michigan Press, 2016), 52, 56; Martha F. Davis, *Brutal Need: Lawyers and the Welfare Rights Movement, 1960–1973* (New Haven, Conn.: Yale University Press, 1993), 60; Walter Goodman, "The Case of Mrs. Sylvester Smith," *New York Times,* August 25, 1968; Martin Garbus, *Ready for the Defense* (New York: Avon Books, 1971), 147–48.

2 **Alabama's top welfare official:** *Smith,* 277 F. Supp. 31; *King,* 392 U.S. at 309–16; Kornbluh, *Battle for Welfare Rights,* 67; Freedman, "Sylvester Smith," 52–54, 56; Davis, *Brutal Need,* 60; Goodman, "Case of Mrs. Sylvester Smith"; Garbus, *Ready for the Defense,* 147–48.

2 **"Ain't much he can do":** Freedman, "Sylvester Smith," 51–52; Davis, *Brutal Need,* 60, 68; Garbus, *Ready for the Defense,* 148–49.

2 **"If God had intended for me":** *King*, 392 U.S. at 309–16; Kornbluh, *Battle for Welfare Rights*, 67; Freedman, "Sylvester Smith," 56; Davis, *Brutal Need*, 61; Goodman, "Case of Mrs. Sylvester Smith"; Garbus, *Ready for the Defense*, 149.

2 **Nationwide, the numbers were far larger:** Goodman, "Case of Mrs. Sylvester Smith"; Mark A. Graber, "The Clintonification of American Law: Abortion, Welfare, and Liberal Constitutional Theory," *Ohio State Law Journal* 58, no. 3 (1997): 787–88.

3 **Smith also lost the minimal support:** Freedman, "Sylvester Smith," 56; Goodman, "Case of Mrs. Sylvester Smith."

3 **The rule put the welfare mother:** Freedman, "Sylvester Smith," 51.

3 **Governor George Wallace had stood:** Freedman, "Sylvester Smith," 155.

4 **The statute required states:** Freedman, "Sylvester Smith," 54–55, 61–62; Garbus, *Ready for the Defense*, 155, 184–85; *Smith*, 277 F. Supp. 31.

4 **Marshall, the first black justice:** *King*, 392 U.S. 309; Freedman, "Sylvester Smith," 54–55, 62–63; Davis, *Brutal Need*, 68.

4 **Alabama's rule was invalid:** Freedman, "Sylvester Smith," 64; *King*, 392 U.S. 309.

5 **"All responsible government agencies":** Freedman, "Sylvester Smith," 54–55, 63, 65; *King*, 392 U.S. 309; Andrew Nolan, *The Doctrine of Constitutional Avoidance: A Legal Overview*, Congressional Research Service, CRS Report No. R43706, September 2, 2014; Graber, "Clintonification of American Law," 787–88.

5 **"The *King* decision is a salutary one":** C. Frank Goldsmith Jr., "Social Welfare—The 'Man in the House' Returns to Stay," *North Carolina Law Review* 47 (1968): 228, 234–35; Garbus, *Ready for the Defense*, 203–8.

5 **In 1938, in the obscure commercial case:** *United States v. Carolene Products*, 304 U.S. 144, 152n4 (1938).

5 **If a law imposed a special burden:** *Carolene Products*, 304 U.S. at 152n4; Henry Rose, "The Poor as a Suspect Class Under the Equal Protection Clause: An Open Constitutional Question," *Nova Law Review* 34 (2010): 407, 408–9; James Curry, Richard Riley, and Richard Battistoni, *Constitutional Government: The American Experience* (Eagen, Minn.: West Publishing, 2003), 282.

6 **One factor it said:** *Carolene Products*, 304 U.S. at 152n4.

6 **Throughout American history:** Rose, "The Poor as a Suspect Class," 419–21; Kenji Yoshino, "The New Equal Protection," *Harvard Law Review* 124, no. 3 (2011): 747, 756; Erin Blakemore, "Poorhouses Were Designed to Punish People for their Poverty," History.com, January 30, 2018, history.com/news/in-the-19th-century-the-last-place-you-wanted-to-go-was-the-poorhouse.

7 **Later in his presidency:** David Kennedy, *Freedom from Fear: The American People in Depression and War, 1929–1945* (New York: Oxford University Press, 1999), 469–70.

7 **Edwards was convicted of violating:** *Edwards v. California*, 314 U.S. 160, 184–85 (1941); Clare Pastore, "When Paupers Became People: *Edwards v. California* (1941)," in *The Poverty Law Canon: Exploring the Major Cases*, ed. Marie Failinger and Ezra Rosser (Ann Arbor: University of Michigan Press, 2016), 13–15, 18; Rose, "The Poor as a Suspect Class," 407, 410–11.

8 **"Poverty and immorality":** *Edwards,* 314 U.S. at 172–73, 177; Pastore, "When Paupers Became People," 13–15, 18; Rose, "The Poor as a Suspect Class," 410–11.

8 **Jackson, however, had only his own vote:** *Edwards,* 314 U.S. at 172–73, 177, 184–85.

9 **As it happened, though:** Jim Newton, *Justice for All: Earl Warren and the Nation He Made* (New York: Riverhead, 2006), 308; Carlton F. W. Larson, "What If Chief Justice Fred Vinson Had Not Died of a Heart Attack in 1953?: Implications for *Brown* and Beyond," *Indiana Law Review* 45, no. 1 (2011): 131, 142; Richard Kluger, *Simple Justice: The History of* Brown v. Board of Education *and Black America's Struggle for Equality* (New York: Vintage, 2005), 593–94, 618.

9 **Eisenhower promised to nominate Warren:** Newton, *Justice for All,* 248–56.

9 **It was one of the great miscalculations:** White, *Earl Warren,* 148–49, 152; Alden Whitman, "Earl Warren, 83, Who Led High Court in Time of Vast Social Change, Is Dead," *New York Times,* July 10, 1974; Kluger, *Simple Justice,* 666; Bernard Schwartz, "Chief Justice Earl Warren: Super Chief in Action," *Tulsa Law Journal* 33 (1977): 477.

10 **Warren's hero was Hiram Johnson:** White, *Earl Warren,* 11–12, 21; Newton, *Justice for All,* 15–16.

10 **He warned that, with the government:** Whitman, "Earl Warren, 83"; Kluger, *Simple Justice,* 663–65; White, *Earl Warren,* 49, 73–75; Newton, *Justice for All,* 35–40, 69–71.

10 **At a 1943 governors' conference:** Whitman, "Earl Warren, 83"; Kluger, *Simple Justice,* 663–65; White, *Earl Warren,* 49, 73–75, 153; Newton, *Justice for All,* 158–59, 184–86.

11 **Potter Stewart, a moderate conservative:** *Brown,* 347 U.S. 483; Kermit Hall, "The Warren Court: Yesterday, Today, and Tomorrow," *Indiana Law Review* 28, no. 2 (1995): 309; Kluger, *Simple Justice,* 598; Bernard Schwartz, *The Warren Court: A Retrospective* (New York: Oxford University Press, 1996), 297.

12 **So Black's strong words:** *Griffin v. Illinois,* 351 U.S. 12, 17–19 (1956).

12 **TenBroek argued that these durational residency requirements:** Kornbluh, *Battle for Welfare Rights,* 30; Jacobus tenBroek, *The Constitution and the Right of Free Movement* (New York: National Travelers Aid Association, 1955); Stacie Dubnow, "Fifty Years After tenBroek: The Right to Live in the World Today and Tomorrow," *Braille Monitor,* February 2019, nfb.org/sites/www.nfb.org/files/publications/bm/bm19/bm1902/bm190203.htm.

12 **TenBroek suggested that poverty:** Kornbluh, *Battle for Welfare Rights,* 30; Davis, *Brutal Need,* 20–21; Michael Grossberg and Christopher Tomlins, eds., *The Cambridge History of Law in America,* vol. 3 (Cambridge, England: Cambridge University Press, 2008), 367; Jacobus tenBroek, "California's Dual System of Family Law: Its Origin, Development and Present Status," *Stanford Law Review* 16, no. 2 (1964): 257; Jacobus tenBroek, "California's Dual System of Family Law: Its Origin, Development and Present Status: Part II," *Stanford Law Review* 16, no. 4 (1964): 900; Jacobus tenBroek, "California's Dual System of Family Law: Its Origin, Development and Present Status: Part III," *Stanford Law Review* 17, no. 4 (1965): 614; Lucas A. Powe Jr.,

The Warren Court and American Politics (Cambridge, Mass.: Belknap Press, 2000), 449–50.

13 **President Kennedy embraced Harrington's call to arms:** David Zarefsky, *President Johnson's War on Poverty: Rhetoric and History* (Tuscaloosa: University of Alabama Press, 2005), xvii–xix; Maurice Isserman, "Michael Harrington: Warrior on Poverty," *New York Times,* June 19, 2009.

13 **For the first time since he became chief justice:** Russell W. Galloway, *Justice for All?: The Rich and Poor in Supreme Court History, 1790–1990* (Durham, N.C.: Carolina Academic Press, 1991), 138; Powe, *The Warren Court,* 210–11.

13 **All five understood from personal experience:** Seth Stern and Stephen Wermiel, *Justice Brennan: Liberal Champion* (Boston: Houghton Mifflin, 2010), 4–6, 8–9, 16–23; Powe, *The Warren Court,* 211; Laura Kalman, *The Long Reach of the Sixties: LBJ, Nixon, and the Making of the Contemporary Supreme Court* (New York: Oxford University Press, 2017), 47; Howard Ball, *Howard L. Black: Cold Steel Warrior* (New York: Oxford University Press, 1996), 40.

14 **In ruling for Gideon:** *Gideon v. Wainwright,* 372 U.S. 335 (1963); Michael Mushlin, "Gideon v. Wainwright Revisited: What Does the Right to Counsel Guarantee Today," *Pace Law Review* 10 (1990): 327, 329–30; Anthony Lewis, "Supreme Court Extends Ruling on Free Counsel," *New York Times,* March 19, 1963.

14 **Sounding like tenBroek:** *Douglas v. California,* 372 U.S. 353, 355 (1963); *Gideon v. Wainwright,* 372 U.S. 335, 344 (1963); Jerold Israel, "Gideon v. Wainwright: The 'Art' of Overruling," in *The Supreme Court and the Judicial Function,* ed. Philip Kurland (Chicago: University of Chicago Press, 1975), 73–74, 74n7.

15 **The march's leaders later unveiled:** Martin Luther King Jr., "I Have a Dream" speech (August 28, 1963, Washington, D.C.), National Archives, archives.gov/files/press/exhibits/dream-speech.pdf; William Forbath, "Constitutional Welfare Rights: A History, Critique and Reconstruction," *Fordham Law Review* 69 (2001): 1821, 1842, 1850–51; A. Philip Randolph and Bayard Rustin, "How the Civil-Rights Movement Aimed to End Poverty," 1967, reprinted in *Atlantic* (King Issue), April 2018, theatlantic.com/magazine/archive/2018/02/a-freedom-budget-for-all-americans-annotated/557024/.

15 **Congress began passing laws establishing:** Lyndon Johnson, Annual Message to Congress on the State of the Union (January 8, 1964, Washington, D.C.), Lyndon Baines Johnson Presidential Library, lbjlibrary.net/collections/selected-speeches/november-1963-1964/01-08-1964.html.

15 **Welfare recipients, he insisted:** Charles Reich, "The New Property," *Yale Law Journal* 73 (1964): 733, 783, 786.

15 **In 1963, after law school:** David Margolick, "Edward Sparer, 55; Legal Advocate for the Poor," *New York Times,* June 25, 1983; Davis, *Brutal Need,* 22–23, 26–27, 30; Gary Smith, "Remembering Edward Sparer: An Enduring Vision for Legal Services," *Clearinghouse Review* 39, no. 5–6 (2005): 329, 330; Sylvia A. Law, "Edward V. Sparer," *University of Pennsylvania Law Review* 132, no. 3 (1984): 425.

16 **Sparer's list included the right to privacy:** Davis, *Brutal Need*, 34–36; Edward Sparer, "The Role of the Welfare Client's Lawyer," *UCLA Law Review* 12 (1965): 361, 366–67; Grossberg and Tomlins, *Cambridge History*, 368.

16 **The mission of this new class:** Elizabeth Bussiere, *(Dis)Entitling the Poor: The Warren Court, Welfare Rights, and the American Political Tradition* (University Park: Penn State University Press, 1997), 95; R. Shep Melnick, *Between the Lines: Interpreting Welfare Rights* (Washington, D.C.: Brookings Institution Press, 1994), 65; Kornbluh, *Battle for Welfare Rights*, 69–73; Bryant Garth, *Neighborhood Law Firms for the Poor: A Comparative Study of Recent Developments in Legal Aid and in the Legal Profession* (Rockville, Md.: Sijthoff & Noordhoff, 1980), 24.

16 **In holding that New York State:** Freedman, "Sylvester Smith," 55; *Anderson v. Burson*, 300 F. Supp. 401 (N.D. Ga. 1968); Israel Shenker, "Guarantee of 'Right to Live' Is Urged," *New York Times*, September 28, 1969; *Rothstein v. Wyman*, 303 F. Supp. 339, 346 (S.D.N.Y 1969).

17 **"We won the vast majority":** Ezra Rosser, introduction to *The Poverty Law Canon: Exploring the Major Cases*, ed. Marie Failinger and Ezra Rosser (Ann Arbor: University of Michigan Press, 2016), 3; Patricia Wald, "Ten Admonitions for Legal Services Advocates Contemplating Federal Litigation," *Clearinghouse Review*, May 1993, 11–12.

17 **Fortas's views on the law:** Kalman, *Long Reach of the Sixties*, 60–67.

17 **"Lines drawn on the basis":** *Harper v. Virginia Board of Elections*, 383 U.S. 663, 668 (1966); Bussiere, *(Dis)Entitling the Poor*, 89.

18 **In Connecticut, welfare recipients:** Forbath, "Constitutional Welfare Rights," 1850–54; Kornbluh, *Battle for Welfare Rights*, 14–16, 48–50; Grossberg and Tomlins, *Cambridge History*, 367.

18 **Under the leadership of George Wiley:** Davis, *Brutal Need*, 43–45.

19 **King described the Poor People's Campaign:** Sylvie Laurent, *King and the Other America: The Poor People's Campaign and the Quest for Economic Equality* (Oakland: University of California Press, 2019), 12, 103–4; *Martin Luther King, Jr. Encyclopedia* (King Institute, Stanford University), kinginstitute.stanford.edu/encyclopedia/poor-peoples-campaign.

19 **The other four justices were somewhere between:** Wil Haygood, *Showdown: Thurgood Marshall and the Supreme Court Nomination That Changed America* (New York: Knopf, 2015), 15; Bussiere, *(Dis)Entitling the Poor*, 101.

19 **When Marshall took his seat:** Fred P. Graham, "President Sees Marshall Take Supreme Court Seat," *New York Times*, October 3, 1967; C. Frank Goldsmith Jr., "Social Welfare—The 'Man in the House' Returns to Stay," *North Carolina Law Review* 47 (1968): 235

20 **Johnson did not ask:** Kalman, *Long Reach of the Sixties*, 125; Newton, *Justice for All*, 506–7.

20 **"As a Southerner":** Laura Kalman, *Abe Fortas: A Biography* (New Haven, Conn.: Yale University Press, 1992), 10, 12; Bruce Allen Murphy, *Fortas: The Rise and Ruin*

of a Supreme Court Justice (New York: William Morrow, 1988), 4; Abe Fortas, "March to Decency," *New York Times*, July 18, 1972.

20 **Fortas accepted a teaching position:** Kalman, *Abe Fortas*, 10, 17, 25, 67.

21 **Douglas would later say:** Kalman, *Abe Fortas*, 136, 182–83, 200–202; Martin Tolchin, "How Johnson Won Election He'd Lost," *New York Times*, February 11, 1990.

21 **Fortas continued to advise Johnson:** Kalman, *Abe Fortas*, 217, 240–41; Murphy, *Fortas*, 234.

21 **One of his law clerks recalled:** Kalman, *Abe Fortas*, 250; *Tinker v. Des Moines School District*, 393 U.S. 503 (1969).

22 **Thornberry, a self-made son:** John C. Jeffries, *Justice Lewis F. Powell, Jr.* (New York: Charles Scribner's Sons, 1994), 223; Fred Graham, "Johnson Appoints Fortas to Head Supreme Court; Thornberry to Be Justice," *New York Times*, June 27, 1968; Kalman, *Long Reach of the Sixties*, 129–30, 140–179; Robert McG. Thomas Jr., "Homer Thornberry, Appeals Judge, Dies at 86," *New York Times*, December 13, 1995.

22 **He overestimated how many Democratic votes:** Kalman, *Long Reach of the Sixties*, 126–29; Bob Woodward and Scott Armstrong, *The Brethren: Inside the Supreme Court* (New York: Simon & Schuster, 1979); Powe, *The Warren Court*, 465; John A. Jenkins, *The Partisan: The Life of William Rehnquist* (New York: PublicAffairs, 2012), 89; Graham, "Johnson Appoints Fortas"; White, *Earl Warren*, 142, 307; Newton, *Justice for All*, 492.

22 **The cronyism charge:** Kalman, *Long Reach of the Sixties*, 126–29; Pat Buchanan, "Q&A with Pat Buchanan," C-SPAN, July 24, 2014, c-span.org/video/?320563-1/qa-pat-buchanan; Patrick J. Buchanan, *The Greatest Comeback: How Richard Nixon Rose from Defeat to Create the New Majority* (New York: Crown Forum, 2014); Jeffries, *Justice Lewis F. Powell, Jr.*, 223; Christine Compston, *Earl Warren: Justice for All* (New York: Oxford University Press, 2001), 140.

23 **Patrick Buchanan, a top aide:** Murphy, *Fortas*, 444; Kalman, *Long Reach of the Sixties*, 156–57; Buchanan, "Q&A with Pat Buchanan"; Buchanan, *The Greatest Comeback*, 275.

23 **James Eastland of Mississippi:** Kalman, *Long Reach of the Sixties*, 145; Kyle Longley, *LBJ's 1968: Power, Politics, and the Presidency in America's Year of Upheaval* (Cambridge, England: Cambridge University Press, 2018), 183.

23 **That struck many senators:** Murphy, *Fortas*, 380–90.

24 **Other justices taught classes:** Jeffries, *Justice Lewis F. Powell, Jr.*, 223; Kalman, *Long Reach of the Sixties*, 66–67.

24 **He "wanted the Fortas nomination":** Kalman, *Long Reach of the Sixties*, 126–29, 160–61, 162–64, 173–76; Linda Greenhouse, "Ex-Justice Abe Fortas Dies at 71; Shaped Historical Rulings on Rights," *New York Times*, April 7, 1982; Laura Kalman, "Abe Fortas: Symbol of the Warren Court?," in *The Warren Court in Political and Judicial Perspective*, ed. Mark Tushnet (Charlottesville: University of Virginia Press, 1993), 155–68; Newton, *Justice for All*, 492; Jeffries, *Justice Lewis F. Powell, Jr.*, 223; Calvin

Woodward, "Fact Check: Republicans Thwarted Supreme Court Picks Too," *Chicago Tribune,* April 2, 2017; Charles Babington, "Filibuster Precedent? Democrats Point to '68 and Fortas," *Washington Post,* March 18, 2005; "Filibuster and Cloture," U.S. Senate, senate.gov/artandhistory/history/common/briefing/Filibuster_Cloture.htm.

24 **He would later call:** Kalman, *Long Reach of the Sixties,* 175–76; Longley, *LBJ's 1968.*

25 **"As I sat listening to him":** John Ehrlichman, *Witness to Power: The Nixon Years* (New York: Simon & Schuster, 1982), 115; David Stout, "John D. Ehrlichman, Nixon Aide Jailed for Watergate, Dies at 73," *New York Times,* February 16, 1999; John Dean, *The Rehnquist Choice: The Untold Story of the Nixon Appointment That Redefined the Supreme Court* (New York: Free Press, 2002), 5.

25 **The Justice Department began:** Kalman, *Long Reach of the Sixties,* 188–89; Dean, *The Rehnquist Choice,* 1–2, 5–9.

25 **There was no rule:** Woodward and Armstrong, *The Brethren,* 14–17; Powe, *The Burger Court,* 478; Jenkins, *The Partisan,* 91–92, 164; Kalman, *Long Reach of the Sixties,* 188–89; Kalman, *Abe Fortas,* 324–25, 360–62; Dean, *Rehnquist Choice,* 1–2, 5–9; Fred Graham, "Judiciary Group Bars U.S. Judges from Taking Fees," *New York Times,* June 11, 1969; Frank, "Conflict of Interest," 744, 754; Walter Slocombe (former law clerk to Abe Fortas), interview with the author, October 5, 2018; Abe Fortas to Earl Warren, May 14, 1969, reprinted in Robert Shogan, *A Question of Judgment: The Fortas Case and the Struggle for the Supreme Court* (Indianapolis: Bobbs-Merrill, 1972), 279–82.

26 **nor had Fortas violated:** Woodward and Armstrong, *The Brethren,* 14–17; Powe, *The Burger Court,* 478; Jenkins, *The Partisan,* 91–92, 164; Kalman, *Long Reach of the Sixties,* 188–89; Kalman, *Abe Fortas,* 324–25, 360–62; Dean, *Rehnquist Choice,* 1–2, 5–9; Graham, "Judiciary Group Bars U.S. Judges from Taking Fees"; Frank, Conflict of Interest," 744, 754; Slocombe, interview, October 5, 2018; Murphy, *Fortas,* 208–9; 552; Fortas to Warren, May 14, 1969, in Shogan, *A Question of Judgment,* 279–82.

26 **Mitchell plotted against Fortas:** Woodward and Armstrong, *The Brethren,* 14–17; Powe, *The Burger Court,* 478; Jenkins, *The Partisan,* 91–92, 164; Kalman, *Long Reach of the Sixties,* 188–89; Dean, *Rehnquist Choice,* 5, 8–9; Murphy, *Fortas,* 549–51.

26 **The confirmation, however:** Murphy, *Fortas,* 555–56.

26 **Rehnquist prepared a memorandum:** Woodward and Armstrong, *The Brethren,* 14–17; Powe, *The Burger Court,* 478; Jenkins, *The Partisan,* 91–92, 164; Kalman, *Long Reach of the Sixties,* 188–89; Dean, *Rehnquist Choice,* 6–7; Murphy, *Fortas,* 555; Fred P. Graham, "Inquiry on Fortas Described in Book," *New York Times,* April 17, 1972.

27 **Mitchell's pursuit of Agger:** Woodward and Armstrong, *The Brethren,* 14–17; Jeffries, *Justice Lewis F. Powell, Jr.,* 224; Jenkins, *The Partisan,* 93; Kalman, *Abe Fortas,* 366; Dean, *Rehnquist Choice,* 10.

27 **Some of his old Republican enemies:** Murphy, *Fortas,* 556–60.

27 **He would not want to end his tenure:** Woodward and Armstrong, *The Brethren,* 14–17; Jeffries, *Justice Lewis F. Powell, Jr.,* 224; Jenkins, *The Partisan,* 93; Kalman, *Abe*

Fortas, 366–67; Dean, *Rehnquist Choice*, 9; Murphy, *Fortas*, 563; Ed Cray, *Chief Justice: A Biography of Earl Warren* (New York: Simon & Schuster, 1997), 509–10.

28 **Mitchell and Warren met:** Woodward and Armstrong, *The Brethren*, 15–17; Jeffries, *Justice Lewis F. Powell, Jr.*, 224; Jenkins, *The Partisan*, 93; Kalman, *Abe Fortas*, 366–68; Kalman, *Long Reach of the Sixties*, 185, 192–93; Dean, *Rehnquist Choice*, 5, 9.

28 **According to Dean:** Dean, *Rehnquist Choice*, 9; Ehrlichman, *Witness to Power*, 116; Murphy, *Fortas*, 566–68; Shogan, *A Question of Judgment*.

28 **After the unpleasantness:** Woodward and Armstrong, *The Brethren*, 15–17; Jeffries, *Justice Lewis F. Powell, Jr.*, 224; Jenkins, *The Partisan*, 93; Lesley Oelsner, "Mitchell, Haldeman, Ehrlichman Are Sentenced to 2½ to 8 Years, Mardian to 10 Months to 3 Years," *New York Times*, February 22, 1975; Kalman, *Long Reach of the Sixties*, 193–95; "Slander by Indirection" (editorial), *New York Times*, May 14, 1969; Dean, *Rehnquist Choice*, 9; Slocombe, interview, October 5, 2018.

28 **In an editorial:** Woodward and Armstrong, *The Brethren*, 15–17; Jeffries, *Justice Lewis F. Powell, Jr.*, 224; Murphy, *Fortas*, 570; Kalman, *Abe Fortas*, 366–68; Kalman, *Long Reach of the Sixties*, 183, 192–93; "Slander by Indirection" (editorial), *New York Times*; Dean, *Rehnquist Choice*, 5, 9; Fred Graham, "Mitchell Confirms That He Gave Warren 'Certain Information' About Fortas," *New York Times*, May 13, 1969.

29 **The following day, May 14:** Murphy, *Fortas*, 570–73.

29 **"He had persuaded Abe Fortas to resign":** Kalman, *Abe Fortas*, 375–76; Ehrlichman, *Witness to Power*, 116; Slocombe, interview, October 5, 2018; Cray, *Chief Justice*, 510; Murphy, *Fortas*, 570.

29 **"Mitchell's bluff had succeeded":** Woodward and Armstrong, *The Brethren*, 15–17; Jeffries, *Justice Lewis F. Powell, Jr.*, 224; Jenkins, *The Partisan*, 93; Dean, *Rehnquist Choice*, 10–11.

29 **He concluded that:** Murphy, *Fortas*, 592–93.

30 **In the old English model:** *Shapiro v. Thompson*, 394 U.S. 618 (1969); Elisa Minoff, "Legal Services Attorneys and Migrant Advocates Join Forces: *Shapiro v. Thompson* (1969)," in *The Poverty Law Canon: Exploring the Major Cases*, ed. Marie Failinger and Ezra Rosser (Ann Arbor: University of Michigan Press, 2016), 73, 82, 84.

31 **If the Court took either route:** Henry Rose, "The Poor as a Suspect Class Under the Equal Protection Clause: An Open Constitutional Question," *Nova Law Review* 34 (2010): 407, 408–9; Israel Shenker, "Guarantee of 'Right to Live' Is Urged," *New York Times*, September 28, 1969.

31 **If the Court accepted either of these arguments:** *Edwards v. California*, 314 U.S. 160 (1941); Bussiere, *(Dis)Entitling the Poor*, 103–6.

31 **The Court struck down:** *Shapiro v. Thompson*, 394 U.S. 618.

32 **His parents had been born:** Stern and Wermiel, *Justice Brennan*, 4–8.

32 **He quickly became a pillar:** Stern and Wermiel, *Justice Brennan*, 4–6, 8–9, 16–23, 418.

32 **holding that Connecticut's durational residency:** *Shapiro*, 394 U.S. 618; Bussiere, "Failure of Constitutional Welfare Rights," 116.

33 **On that point they were right:** Bussiere, *(Dis)Entitling the Poor,* 102–3.

33 **The result was a decision:** Bussiere, *(Dis)Entitling the Poor,* 103.

33 **Philip Kurland, a University of Chicago law professor:** *Shapiro,* 394 U.S. at 627; Minoff, "Legal Services Attorneys," 84; Bussiere, *(Dis)Entitling the Poor,* 103–4, 120; Bussiere, "Failure of Constitutional Welfare Rights," 105, 115, 117, 121; Philip Kurland, "The Judicial Road to Social Welfare," *Social Service Review* 48, no. 4 (1974): 480, 490.

33 **During the New Deal:** *A.L.A. Schechter Poultry Corp. v. United States,* 295 U.S. 495 (1935); *United States v. Butler,* 297 U.S. 1 (1936); *National Labor Relations Board v. Mackay Radio & Telegraph,* 304 U.S. 333 (1938).

34 **The Court ruled:** *Sniadach v. Family Finance Corp.,* 395 U.S. 337 (1969).

34 **He also expressed concern:** *Sniadach,* 395 U.S. at 341–42.

35 **As he stepped down:** Whitman, "Earl Warren, 83."

35 **When asked what had been:** Schwartz, "Chief Justice Earl Warren," 477–78; Whitman, "Earl Warren, 83"; White, *Earl Warren,* 148–49, 152; 4; Kluger, *Simple Justice,* 666.

35 **Burger "wanted a seat":** Robert B. Semple Jr., "Warren E. Burger Named Chief Justice by Nixon; Now on Appeals Bench," *New York Times,* May 22, 1969; Ehrlichman, *Witness to Power,* 114.

35 **When Eisenhower won:** Michael Graetz and Linda Greenhouse, *The Burger Court and the Rise of the Judicial Right* (New York: Simon & Schuster, 2016), 347–48; Linda Greenhouse, "Warren E. Burger Is Dead at 87; Was Chief Justice for 17 Years," *New York Times,* June 26, 1995; *Peters v. Hobby,* 349 U.S. 331 (1955); Woodward and Armstrong, *The Brethren,* 30; *The Supreme Court Justices: A Biographical Dictionary,* ed. Melvin I. Urofsky (Oxford, England: Taylor & Francis, 1994), s.v. "Warren Earl Burger," 69.

36 **"If I were to stand still":** Kalman, *Long Reach of the Sixties,* 187.

36 **During the visit, Burger urged:** Woodward and Armstrong, *The Brethren,* 6–7; Kalman, *Long Reach of the Sixties,* 187; Greenhouse, "Warren E. Burger Is Dead"; Ehrlichman, *Witness to Power,* 114.

36 **"RN can only straighten":** Jeff Shesol, "Opening the Door to a Conservative Court," *New York Times,* June 22, 2016; Woodward and Armstrong, *The Brethren,* 14, 20, 22; "Senate Confirms Burger by 74 to 3," *New York Times,* June 10, 1969; Semple, "Warren E. Burger Named Chief Justice."

37 **Other progressive legal scholars:** Shenker, "Guarantee of 'Right to Live'"; Grossberg and Tomlins, *Cambridge History,* 369; Davis, *Brutal Need,* 37–38.

37 **That guarantee could include:** Frank I. Michelman, "Foreword: On Protecting the Poor Through the Fourteenth Amendment," *Harvard Law Review* 83, no. 1 (1969): 13; Samuel Warren and Louis Brandeis, "The Right to Privacy," *Harvard Law Review* 4 (1890): 193; Frank Michelman, interview with the author, September 11, 2017.

37 **Herbert Wechsler, an eminent constitutional law professor:** Michelman, "On Protecting the Poor," 35; Warren and Brandeis, "Right to Privacy," 193; Michelman, interview, September 11, 2017.

38 **Mobilization for Youth's Legal Unit:** Melanie Abbott, "Dignity and Passion: *Goldberg v. Kelly* (1970)," in *The Poverty Law Canon: Exploring the Major Cases*, ed. Marie Failinger and Ezra Rosser (Ann Arbor: University of Michigan Press, 2016), 94.

38 **When the caseworker learned:** Abbott, "Dignity and Passion," 94; Stern and Wermiel, *Justice Brennan*, 339–40.

38 **The city, for its part:** Michelman, "On Protecting the Poor"; Charles Reich, "The New Property," 733.

39 **The Court found it in:** Stern and Wermiel, *Justice Brennan*, 338–39.

39 **Brennan said the Due Process Clause:** *Goldberg v. Kelly*, 397 U.S. 254, 264 (1970).

39 **With a single ruling:** Mark Stern, "Social Policy: History (1950–1980), *Encyclopedia of Social Work* (2019), available at https://www.oxfordbibliographies.com/view/document/obo-9780195389678/obo-9780195389678-0223.xml.

40 **It was now viewing poverty:** *Goldberg*, 397 U.S. at 265; Rosser, introduction to *Poverty Law Canon*, 4.

40 **The decision was a declaration:** *Goldberg*, 397 U.S. at 265; Rosser, introduction to *Poverty Law Canon*, 4.

40 **The fifth vote Brennan won:** *Goldberg*, 397 U.S. at 265.

40 **In the midst of one of the greatest victories:** *Goldberg*, 397 U.S. at 279; *Wheeler v. Montgomery*, 397 U.S. 280, 282 (1970) (Burger, C.J., dissenting) (dissent also applied to the related case of *Goldberg v. Kelly*); Wheeler, 397 U.S. at 282 (Stewart, J., dissenting) (dissent also applied to the related case of *Goldberg v. Kelly*); David Rosenbloom, Rosemary O'Leary, and Joshua Chanin, *Public Administration and Law*, 3rd ed. (Boca Raton, Fla.: CRC Press, 2010), 140; Woodward and Armstrong, *The Brethren*, 70; Galloway, *Justice for All?*, 144.

Chapter Two: Turning Against the Poor

41 **It was, instead:** Elizabeth Bussiere, "The Failure of Constitutional Welfare Rights," *Political Science Quarterly* 109, no. 1 (1994): 123; *Dandridge v. Williams*, 397 U.S. 471 (1970).

41 **The cap meant that small families:** Julie Nice, "A Sweeping Refusal of Equal Protection: *Dandridge v. Williams* (1970)," in *The Poverty Law Canon: Exploring the Major Cases*, ed. Marie Failinger and Ezra Rosser (Ann Arbor: University of Michigan Press, 2016), 135–36; *Williams v. Dandridge*, 297 F. Supp. 450, 450–55 (D. Md. 1968); Martha F. Davis, *Brutal Need: Lawyers and the Welfare Rights Movement, 1960–1973* (New Haven, Conn.: Yale University Press, 1993), 119; *Dandridge*, 397 U.S. 471.

42 **Nationally, the average AFDC benefits:** Mollie Orshansky, "Counting the Poor: Another Look at the Poverty Profile," *Social Security Bulletin* 10 (January 1965): 3; *Williams*, 297 F. Supp. 450; James Jennings, *Understanding the Nature of Poverty in Urban America* (Westport, Conn.: Greenwood Publishing Group, 1994), 75.

42 **When Maryland adopted its maximum grant rule:** C. Thomas Dienes, "To Feed the Hungry: Judicial Retrenchment in Welfare Adjudication," *California Law Review* 58

(1970): 555, 556–58; Nice, "A Sweeping Refusal," 135–6; *Collins v. State Board of Social Welfare,* 81 N.W.2d 4, 135–36 (Iowa 1957); Robert Cover, "Federal Judicial Review of State Welfare Practices," *Columbia Law Review* 67 (1967): 84, 87–88; W. Michael Mayock, "Redefining Federal Largess Through State Maximum Grant Regulations: Dandridge v. Williams," *Loyola of Los Angeles Law Review* 4 (1971): 182, 184–85.

42 **The maximum grant cap:** *Dandridge,* 397 U.S. 471; Davis, *Brutal Need,* 130–131; Mayock, "Redefining Federal Largess," 186.

43 **The poverty law movement, however:** Elizabeth Bussiere, *(Dis)Entitling the Poor: The Warren Court, Welfare Rights, and the American Political Tradition* (University Park: Penn State Press, 2010), 101, 107; Davis, *Brutal Need,* 120; Nice, "A Sweeping Refusal," 135.

43 **Even if the Court did not recognize a right to subsistence:** Bussiere, *(Dis)Entitling the Poor,* 108–9; Nice, "A Sweeping Refusal," 142–45.

44 **That would have been similar:** Bussiere, *(Dis)Entitling the Poor,* 108–9; Nice, "A Sweeping Refusal" 145.

44 **On this new Burger Court:** *Dandridge,* 397 U.S. at 483–86.

44 **He practiced at white-shoe law firms:** John MacKenzie, "Potter Stewart Is Dead at 70, Was on High Court 23 Years," *New York Times,* December 8, 1985; Ernest Kolowrat, *Hotchkiss: A Chronicle of an American School* (New York: New Amsterdam Books, 1998) 33; Joel Jacobsen, "Remembered Justice: The Background, Early Career and Judicial Appointments of Justice Potter Stewart," *Akron Law Review* 35 (2002): 227, 230–35.

44 **Therefore, he said:** *Dandridge,* 397 U.S. at 484–86.

45 **"The problems of government":** *Dandridge,* 397 U.S. at 485.

45 **As Stewart saw it:** *Dandridge,* 397 U.S. at 476–77.

45 **Using language that signaled:** *Dandridge,* 397 U.S. at 487.

45 **Marshall said that Maryland had not:** *Dandridge,* 397 U.S. at 490–508 (Douglas, J., dissenting); *Dandridge,* 397 U.S. at 508–30 (Marshall, J., dissenting); John C. Jeffries, *Justice Lewis F. Powell, Jr.* (New York: Scribner's Sons, 1994), 259.

46 **"The Constitution may impose":** Bussiere, "Failure of Constitutional Welfare Rights," 126; *Dandridge,* 397 U.S. at 487.

46 **As a result of the decision:** Mayock, "Redefining Federal Largess," 205.

47 **If the Court had been willing:** Julie Nice, "No Scrutiny Whatsoever: Deconstitutionalization of Poverty Law, Dual Rules of Law & Dialogic Default," *Fordham Urban Law Journal* 35 (2008): 629; Peter Edelman, "Dandridge v. Williams Redux: A Look Back from the Twenty-First Century," *Drake Law Review* 60 (2012): 981; *James v. Valtierra,* 402 U.S. 137, 145 (1971) (Marshall, J., dissenting); Nice, "A Sweeping Refusal," 149.

48 **Nixon was looking:** Laura Kalman, *The Long Reach of the Sixties: LBJ, Nixon, and the Making of the Contemporary Supreme Court* (New York: Oxford University Press, 2017), 211, 214–15, 231, 237; Bob Woodward and Scott Armstrong, *The Brethren: Inside the Supreme Court* (New York: Simon & Schuster, 1979), 63; Gary Mormino,

"Nixon's Southern Court Strategy," *Tampa Bay Times*, March 11, 2016; Jeffries, *Justice Lewis F. Powell, Jr.*, 225–26; John Ehrlichman, *Witness to Power: The Nixon Years* (New York: Simon & Schuster, 1982), 118.

48 **Rehnquist, the assistant attorney general:** Kalman, *Long Reach of the Sixties*, 211, 214–15, 231, 237; Woodward and Armstrong, *The Brethren*, 63; Mormino, "Nixon's Southern Court Strategy"; Jeffries, *Justice Lewis F. Powell, Jr.*, 225–26.

48 **Thinking the confirmation vote:** Kalman, *Long Reach of the Sixties*, 214–15, 231, 226, 237; Woodward and Armstrong, *The Brethren*, 63; Mormino, "Nixon's Southern Court Strategy"; Jeffries, *Justice Lewis F. Powell, Jr.*, 225–26.

49 **"They are entitled":** Kalman, *Long Reach of the Sixties*, 214–15, 228, 231, 237; Woodward and Armstrong, *The Brethren*, 63; Mormino, "Nixon's Southern Court Strategy"; Rick Perlstein, "The Southern Strategist," *New York Times Magazine*, December 30, 2007; "Carswell Disavows '48 Speech Backing White Supremacy," *New York Times*, January 22, 1970.

49 **He was being forced:** Mormino, "Nixon's Southern Court Strategy"; Richard Reeve, *Nixon: Alone in the White House* (New York: Simon & Schuster, 2002), 186; John A. Jenkins, *The Partisan: The Life of William Rehnquist* (New York: PublicAffairs, 2012), 101; Ehrlichman, *Witness to Power*, 128–29; Jonathan Aitken, *Nixon: A Life* (New York: Simon & Schuster, 2015), 465.

49 **Top Justice Department lawyers:** Woodward and Armstrong, *The Brethren*, 100–103; Linda Greenhouse, *Becoming Justice Blackmun: Harry Blackmun's Supreme Court Journey* (New York: Times Books, 2005), 47.

49 **The replacement of Fortas with Blackmun:** Warren Weaver Jr., "Blackmun Approved 94–0; Nixon Hails Vote by Senate," *New York Times*, May 13, 1970; Fred Graham, "Blackmun Is Sworn In as 98th Justice," *New York Times*, June 30, 1970; Woodward and Armstrong, *The Brethren*, 62–3, 100–103, 144; Kalman, *Long Reach of the Sixties*, 247–48; Greenhouse, *Becoming Justice Blackmun*, 62–63.

50 **Rarick inserted purportedly incriminating documents:** John Dean, *The Rehnquist Choice: The Untold Story of the Nixon Appointment That Redefined the Supreme Court* (New York: Free Press, 2002), 24; Seth Stern and Stephen Wermiel, *Justice Brennan: Liberal Champion* (Boston: Houghton Mifflin, 2010), 319; Michael Newton, *White Robes and Burning Crosses: A History of the Ku Klux Klan from 1866* (Jefferson, N.C.: McFarland & Co., 2014), 162.

50 **There was little left:** Stern and Wermiel, *Justice Brennan*, 319–23.

50 **Douglas, who was a committed environmentalist:** *Sierra Club v. Morton*, 405 U.S. 727 (1972); *United States v. O'Brien*, 391 U.S. 367 (1968); Woodward and Armstrong, *The Brethren*, 14; Stern and Wermiel, *Justice Brennan*, 319.

51 **FBI director J. Edgar Hoover:** Woodward and Armstrong, *The Brethren*, 14; "F.B.I. Kept Close Watch on Douglas," *New York Times*, July 22, 1984; Joshua Kastenberg, "Safeguarding Judicial Integrity During the Trump Presidency: Richard Nixon's Attempt to Impeach Justice William O. Douglas and the Use of National Security as

a Case Study," *Campbell Law Review* 40 (2018): 1, 132–33; Ehrlichman, *Witness to Power,* 116, 122; Dean, *Rehnquist Choice,* 24–25.

51 **Ford held up an issue:** Woodward and Armstrong, *The Brethren,* 87; Gerald R. Ford, "House Floor Speech: Impeach Justice Douglas, April 15, 1970," Box D29, Gerald R. Ford Congressional Papers, Gerald R. Ford Presidential Library, fordlibrarymuseum .gov/library/document/0054/4526271.pdf; Kenneth Davis, "The History of American Impeachment," Smithsonian.com, June 12, 2017; Kastenberg, "Safeguarding Judicial Integrity," 136–37; Ehrlichman, *Witness to Power,* 122; Dean, *Rehnquist Choice,* 27.

51 **Ford was unable:** Kastenberg, "Safeguarding Judicial Integrity," 167; Ehrlichman, *Witness to Power,* 130; Dean, *Rehnquist Choice,* 26.

51 **Nixon took comfort:** Ehrlichman, *Witness to Power,* 130–33

52 **Marshall told a Navy officer:** Stuart Taylor Jr., "Marshall Puts Reagan at 'Bottom' Among Presidents on Civil Rights," *New York Times,* September 9, 1987.

52 **the lawyer she spoke to:** Michele Estrin Gilman, "Privacy as a Luxury Not for the Poor: *Wyman v. James* (1971)," in *The Poverty Law Canon: Exploring the Major Cases,* ed. Marie Failinger and Ezra Rosser (Ann Arbor: University of Michigan Press, 2016), 153, 156

53 **The plaintiffs cooperated:** Gilman, "Privacy as a Luxury," 155–56; Edward Sparer, "The Role of the Welfare Client's Lawyer," *UCLA Law Review* 12 (1965): 366–67.

53 **A three-judge federal district court:** Gilman, "Privacy as a Luxury," 157–58; *Wyman v. James,* 400 U.S. 309 (1971); Marcia Coyle, *The Roberts Court: The Struggle for the Constitution* (New York: Simon & Schuster, 2013), 15.

53 **Blackmun, in his majority opinion:** *Wyman,* 400 U.S. at 317–18; Jordan Budd, "A Fourth Amendment for the Poor Alone: Subconstitutional Status and the Myth of the Inviolate Home," *Indiana Law Journal* 85 (2010): 355, 368–69; Greenhouse, *Becoming Justice Blackmun,* 63.

54 **Now, with the steadily forming conservative majority:** *Wyman,* 400 U.S. at 347.

54 **The provision, Article 34:** *James,* 402 U.S. 137; Liam Dillon, "A Dark Side to the California Dream: How the State Constitution Makes Affordable Housing Hard to Build," *Los Angeles Times,* February 3, 2019.

54 **Poor people eligible for public housing sued:** Dillon, "Dark Side to the California Dream"; Thomas Mizo, "Constitutional Law—Equal Protection—Mandatory Referendum on Low-Income Housing—James v. Valtierra," *Boston College Law Review* 13 (1972): 603–4.

55 **By the same logic:** Mizo, "Constitutional Law—Equal Protection."

55 **Requiring voter approval:** *James,* 402 U.S. 137.

55 **All of those opinions:** *James,* 402 U.S. 137.

55 **Matthew Lassiter, a University of Michigan:** Dillon, "Dark Side to the California Dream."

56 **John Dean said Black:** Woodward and Armstrong, *The Brethren,* 189; Jenkins, *The Partisan,* 103; Ehrlichman, *Witness to Power,* 133; Dean, *Rehnquist Choice,* 33; "Justice Black Dies at 85; Served on Court 34 Years," *New York Times,* September 25, 1971.

56 **The news that Harlan had:** Ehrlichman, *Witness to Power*, 134; Woodward and Armstrong, *The Brethren*, 189; Jenkins, *The Partisan*, 103–4; Lesley Oelsner, "Harlan Dies at 72; On Court 16 Years," *New York Times*, December 30, 1971.

57 **Still, his outright support:** Joyce Baugh, *The Detroit School Busing Case:* Milliken v. Bradley *and the Controversy over Desegregation* (Lawrence: University of Kansas Press, 2011), 17; Dean, *Rehnquist Choice*, 66; Paul Vitello, "Richard H. Poff, Who Withdrew Court Bid, Dies at 87," *New York Times*, July 1, 2011; Mark Tushnet, *A Court Divided: The Rehnquist Court and the Future of Constitutional Law* (New York: Norton, 2006), 27; "The Southern Manifesto of 1956," History, Art & Archives, United States House of Representatives, history.house.gov/Historical-Highlights/1951-2000/The-Southern-Manifesto-of-1956/.

57 **Powell, a former president:** John Darnton, "Lewis Franklin Powell Jr.," *New York Times*, October 22, 1971; Dean, *Rehnquist Choice*, 263–64.

57 **The paper presented:** Darnton, "Lewis Franklin Powell Jr."

57 **Whether that was true:** Jeffries, *Justice Lewis F. Powell, Jr.*, 139–40, 233–34; Kalman, *Long Reach of the Sixties*, 249, 292; B. Drummond Ayres Jr., "Court Ruling Is a Bitter Irony for Richmond Blacks," *New York Times*, January 25, 1989.

58 **When he resigned as chairman:** Jeffries, *Justice Lewis F. Powell, Jr.*, 7, 140–43.

58 **Representative John Conyers Jr.:** Jeffries, *Justice Lewis F. Powell, Jr.*, 140–43; Fred Graham, "Senate Confirms Powell by 89 to 1 for Black's Seat," *New York Times*, December 7, 1971; James Naughton, "Harlan Retires; Nixon Hints Poff Is a Court Choice," *New York Times*, September 24, 1971; "Rehnquist Confirmed by Senate, 68–26," *New York Times*, December 11, 1971; Robert Semple, "Justice Black, 85, Quits High Court, Citing His Health," *New York Times*, September 18, 1971; Kalman, *Long Reach of the Sixties*, 249, 292.

58 **In a show of allegiance:** Walter Sullivan, "Cigarettes Peril Health, U.S. Report Concludes," *New York Times*, January 12, 1964; Robert Bedingfield, "Philip Morris Chief Questions Finding of Smoking Study," *New York Times*, April 15, 1964; Jeffries, *Justice Lewis F. Powell, Jr.*, 188–89.

58 **The one vote against him:** Jeffries, *Justice Lewis F. Powell, Jr.*, 240; Graham, "Senate Confirms Powell"; Jenkins, *The Partisan*, 134, 238–40.

59 **Barry Goldwater, the Arizona senator:** Tushnet, *A Court Divided*, 13; Jenkins, *The Partisan*, 124; Ehrlichman, *Witness to Power*, 136–37; Dean, *Rehnquist Choice*, 129, 265.

59 **He went on to Stanford Law School:** Tushnet, *A Court Divided*, 14, 22–23; *Encyclopedia Britannica*, s.v. "William Rehnquist," britannica.com/biography/William-Rehnquist; Linda Greenhouse, "William H. Rehnquist, Chief Justice of Supreme Court, Is Dead at 80," *New York Times*, September 4, 2005. Jenkins, *The Partisan*, 1, 3; George Lardner Jr. and Saundra Saperstein, "A Chief Justice-Designate with Big Ambitions," *Washington Post*, July 6, 1986.

60 **In addition to his contributions:** Tushnet, *A Court Divided*, 14, 22–23; "William Rehnquist," *Encyclopaedia Britannica;* Greenhouse, "William H. Rehnquist"; Jenkins, *The Partisan*, 1, 60, 69–70.

60 **John Dean, Nixon's White House counsel:** Fred Graham, "Rehnquist Role in Election Confirmed," *New York Times,* November 13, 1971; Dean, *Rehnquist Choice,* 272–73.

60 **In *Simple Justice*:** Graham, "Rehnquist Role in Election Confirmed"; Leon Friedman, "Rehnquist: He Was a Very Elusive Target," *New York Times,* December 12, 1971; Darnton, "Lewis Franklin Powell Jr."; Kalman, *Long Reach of the Sixties,* 303; Woodward and Armstrong, *The Brethren,* 196; Adam Liptak, "New Look at an Old Memo Casts More Doubt on Rehnquist," *New York Times,* March 19, 2012; Brad Snyder and John Barrett, "Rehnquist's Missing Letter: A Former Law Clerk's 1955 Thoughts on Justice Jackson and Brown," *Boston College Law Review* 53 (2012): 631; Jenkins, *The Partisan,* 38–39, 135; Richard Kluger, *Simple Justice: The History of* Brown v. Board of Education *and Black America's Struggle for Equality* (New York: Vintage, 2005), 609–15; Dean, *Rehnquist Choice,* 284–5.

61 **"Just be as mean":** "Nixon's Final Advice to Rehnquist," The Presidency: Educational Resources, University of Virginia Miller Center, millercenter.org/the-presidency/educational-resources/nixon-s-final-advice-to-rehnquist; Darnton, "Lewis Franklin Powell Jr."; Kalman, *Long Reach of the Sixties,* 303; Woodward and Armstrong, *The Brethren,* 196; Tushnet, *A Court Divided,* 31; Jenkins, *The Partisan,* 135–36; Stanley Kutler, "Why Nixon Matters," Reuters, August 7, 2014; Dean, *Rehnquist Choice,* 284–5.

61 **"The next Court":** Naughton, "Harlan Retires"; Fred Graham, "Stewart Tells of Barring His Elevation," *New York Times,* May 28, 1968; Fred Graham, "Profile of the 'Nixon Court' Now Discernible," *New York Times,* May 24, 1972.

61 **When it was clear:** Ann Burkhart, "The Constitutional Underpinnings of Homelessness," *Houston Law Review* 40 (2003), 211, 212n6.

61 **When they failed to persuade:** *Lindsey v. Normet,* 405 U.S. 56, 58–59 (1972); Lisa Alexander, "Occupying the Constitutional Right to Housing," *Nebraska Law Review* 94 (2015): 245, 258.

62 **"We do not denigrate":** *Lindsey,* 405 U.S. at 74; Steven Quaintance McKenzie, "Fast Food Justice: The Denial of Tenants' Due Process Rights in Chicago's Eviction Courts," *Public Interest Law Reporter* 9 (2004): 1, 3–4.

62 **Instead, the Court made it clear:** *Lindsey,* 405 U.S. at 74; *Lindsey,* 405 U.S. at 90 (Douglas, J., dissenting).

62 **He sued, arguing that:** *United States v. Kras,* 409 U.S. 434 (1973); Henry Rose, "Denying the Poor Access to Court: *United States v. Kras* (1973)," in *The Poverty Law Canon: Exploring the Major Cases,* ed. Marie Failinger and Ezra Rosser (Ann Arbor: University of Michigan Press, 2016), 188–90.

63 **The Court had also held:** *Griffin v. Illinois,* 351 U.S. 12 (1956); *Douglas v. California,* 372 U.S. 353 (1963); *Harper v. Virginia Board of Elections,* 383 U.S. 663 (1966); *Boddie v. Connecticut,* 401 U.S. 371 (1971).

63 **The weekly payments:** *Kras,* 409 U.S. at 444–48.

63 **"I cannot agree":** *Kras,* 409 U.S. at 458 (Douglas, J., dissenting); *Kras,* 409 U.S. at 460; William Douglas, *Go East Young Man* (New York: Random House, 1974), 172.

63 **When the court refused:** *Ortwein v. Schwab*, 410 U.S. 656 (1973); *Kras*, 409 U.S. at 445; Stephen Loffredo and Don Friedman, "Gideon Meets Goldberg: The Case for a Qualified Right to Counsel in Welfare Hearings," *Touro Law Review* 25 (2009): 274, 296.

64 **Applying the lenient rational-basis:** *Ortwein*, 410 U.S. 656.

64 **The Court's decision:** *Ortwein*, 410 U.S. 656.

64 **When President Kennedy nominated White:** Michael Bailey, "Measuring Court Preferences, 1950–2011: Agendas, Polarity and Heterogeneity" (Georgetown University, August 2012), available at semanticscholar.org; Woodward and Armstrong, *The Brethren*, 74–75; *Miranda v. Arizona*, 384 U.S. 436 (1966); *Bowers v. Hardwick*, 478 U.S. 186 (1986); Lyle Denniston, "The Mystery of Justice Byron White," *Constitution Daily*, May 3, 2012; Jeffries, *Justice Lewis F. Powell, Jr.*, 263; Linda Greenhouse, "Byron R. White, Longtime Justice and a Football Legend, Dies at 84," *New York Times*, April 16, 2002.

64 **White was an often unpredictable:** Bailey, "Measuring Court Preferences"; Woodward and Armstrong, *The Brethren*, 74–75; *Miranda*, 384 U.S. 436; *Bowers*, 478 U.S. 186; Denniston, "Mystery of Justice Byron White"; Jeffries, *Justice Lewis F. Powell, Jr.*, 263; Greenhouse, "Byron R. White."

65 **When the elderly Douglas:** Russell W. Galloway, *Justice for All?: The Rich and Poor in Supreme Court History, 1790–1990* (Durham, N.C.: Carolina Academic Press, 1991), 158–59; Woodward and Armstrong, *The Brethren*, 474.

65 **Comparing noncitizens to racial minorities:** *Graham v. Department of Public Welfare*, 403 U.S. 365 (1971).

66 **A few years later:** *Reed v. Reed*, 404 U.S. 71 (1971); *Frontiero v. Richardson*, 411 U.S. 677 (1973); Woodward and Armstrong, *The Brethren*, 306; *Craig v. Boren*, 429 U.S. 190 (1976).

66 **For poor people and poverty lawyers:** Joseph Stiglitz, *The Price of Inequality: How Today's Divided Society Endangers Our Future* (New York: Norton, 2013), 18–19; Thomas Simon, "Suspect Class Democracy: A Social Theory," *Miami Law Review* 45, no. 1 (1990): 107, 141; Marcy Strauss, "Reevaluating Suspect Classifications," *Seattle Law Review* 35 (2011): 135, 140–41; Henry Rose, "The Poor as a Suspect Class Under the Equal Protection Clause: An Open Constitutional Question," *Nova Law Review* 34 (2010): 407, 420; Frank I. Michelman, "Foreword: On Protecting the Poor Through the Fourteenth Amendment," *Harvard Law Review* 83, no. 1 (1969): 21; Bertall L. Ross II and Su Li, "Measuring Political Power: Suspect Class Determinations and the Poor," *California Law Review* 104 (2016): 323, 344; Nice, "No Scrutiny Whatsoever," 629–36.

68 **When New York City:** Felicia Kornbluh, *The Battle for Welfare Rights: Politics and Poverty in Modern America* (Philadelphia: University of Pennsylvania Press, 2007), 183.

68 **It was less a rallying cry:** Kornbluh, *Battle for Welfare Rights*, 183; Susan Sheehan, *A Welfare Mother* (New York: Houghton Mifflin Harcourt, 1976).

68 **Eldridge sued for the right:** John Capowksi, "Reflecting and Foreshadowing: *Mathews v. Eldridge* (1976)," in *The Poverty Law Canon: Exploring the Major Cases*, ed. Marie Failinger and Ezra Rosser (Ann Arbor: University of Michigan Press, 2016), 219, 221.

68 **Still, Powell insisted:** *Mathews v. Eldridge,* 424 U.S. 319, 342–43 (1976).

69 **The record showed:** *Mathews,* 424 U.S. at 349–50 (Brennan, J., dissenting).

69 **Patricia Wald, the onetime neighborhood legal services lawyer:** Patricia Wald, "Ten Admonitions for Legal Services Advocates Contemplating Federal Litigation," *Clearinghouse Review,* May 1993, 11–12.

70 **If he was making:** Linda Greenhouse, "Warren E. Burger Is Dead at 87; Was Chief Justice for 17 Years," *New York Times,* June 26, 1995.

70 **Her nomination was historic:** Sheryl Gay Stolberg and Charlie Savage, "Stevens's Retirement Is Political Test for Obama," *New York Times,* April 9, 2010; "Texts on Retirement of Justice Douglas," *New York Times,* November 13, 1975; Richard W. Stevenson, "O'Connor to Retire, Touching Off Battle over Court," *New York Times,* July 2, 2005.

70 **A few years earlier:** Tushnet, *A Court Divided,* 32; Robert McFadden, "Comments by Meese on Hunger Produce a Storm of Controversy," *New York Times,* December 10, 1983; Jenkins, *The Partisan,* 210–13.

71 **Reagan officials appreciated:** Tushnet, *A Court Divided,* 32; Linda Greenhouse, "Senate, 65 to 33, Votes to Confirm Rehnquist as 16th Chief Justice," *New York Times,* September 18, 1986; Stuart Taylor Jr., "Rehnquist and Scalia Take Their Places on Court," *New York Times,* September 27, 1986; Jenkins, *The Partisan,* 210–13; Stuart Taylor Jr., "Rehnquist's Court: Tuning Out the White House," *New York Times,* September 11, 1988; Bernard Weinraub, "Burger Retiring, Rehnquist Named Chief; Scalia, Appeals Judge, Chosen for Court," *New York Times,* June 18, 1986.

71 **When Kennedy asked:** Tushnet, *A Court Divided,* 32; Greenhouse, "Senate, 65 to 33"; Jenkins, *The Partisan,* 40–41, 216–19; Ronald Ostrow and Robert Jackson, "Rehnquist Denies That He Harassed Minority Voters," *Los Angeles Times,* July 31, 1986; Stuart Taylor, "4 Rebut Testimony of Rehnquist on Challenging of Voters in 60's," *New York Times,* August 2, 1986.

71 **confirmed him by a 65–33 vote:** Tushnet, *A Court Divided,* 32; Greenhouse, "Senate, 65 to 33"; Jenkins, *The Partisan,* 40–41, 216–17, 221; George Lardner Jr., " '50s Memos Illustrate Rehnquist Consistency," *Washington Post,* July 20, 1986.

71 **Scalia was confirmed:** David Savage, "Scalia Takes Oath and Rehnquist Sworn In as Chief Justice," *Los Angeles Times,* September 27, 1986; Stuart Taylor, "Scalia Returns Soft Answers to Senators," *New York Times,* August 6, 1986.

72 **As a result, the energy:** Savage, "Scalia Takes Oath"; Greenhouse, "Senate, 65 to 33"; Jenkins, *The Partisan,* 221–22.

72 **Liberals were surprised:** "Justices 1789 to Present," Supreme Court of the United States, supremecourt.gov/about/members_text.aspx; Linda Greenhouse, "Lewis Powell, Crucial Centrist Justice, Dies at 90," *New York Times,* April 26, 1998; Richard Berke, "Senate Confirms Souter, 90 to 9, as Supreme Court's 105th Justice," *New York Times,* October 3, 1990; Greenhouse, "William H. Rehnquist."

73 **More than two decades:** "Justices 1789 to Present," Supreme Court; R. W. Apple Jr., "The Thomas Confirmation: Senate Confirms Thomas, 52–48, Ending Week of Bitter

Battle; 'Time for Healing,' Judge Says," *New York Times,* October 16, 1991; Linda Greenhouse, "Senate, 96–3, Easily Affirms Judge Ginsburg as a Justice," *New York Times,* August 4, 1993; Gwen Ifill, "President Chooses Breyer, an Appeal Judge in Boston, for Blackmun's Court Seat," *New York Times,* May 14, 1994; David Margolick, "Man in the News: The Supreme Court: Scholarly Consensus Builder: Stephen Gerald Breyer," *New York Times,* May 14, 1994.

73 **President Clinton, who had promised:** Alana Semuels, "The End of Welfare as We Know It," *Atlantic,* April 1, 2016; Jeffrey Volle, *Clinton/Gore: Victory from a Shadow Box* (New York: Palgrave Macmillan, 2012), 107.

73 **When Clinton signed:** Semuels, "End of Welfare as We Know It"; Alison Mitchell, "Two Clinton Aides Resign to Protest New Welfare Law," *New York Times,* September 12, 1996; Chris McGreal, "Clinton-Era Welfare Reforms Haunt America's Poorest Families, Critics Say," *Guardian,* March 7, 2016; Richard Fording and Sanford Schram, "The Welfare Reform Disaster," *Jacobin,* August 28, 2016; Edelman, "Dandridge v. Williams Redux," 981, 984–85.

74 **A national study found that:** Semuels, "End of Welfare as We Know It"; Liz Schott, "TANF at 20, Part 3: States Not Investing in Core Welfare Reform Areas," Center on Budget and Policy Priorities, August 17, 2016, cbpp.org/blog/tanf-at-20-part-3-states-not-investing-in-core-welfare-reform-areas; Ladonna Pavetti and Liz Schott, "TANF at 20: Time to Create a Program That Supports Work and Helps Families Meet Their Basic Needs," Center on Budget and Policy Priorities, August 15, 2016, cbpp.org/research/family-income-support/tanf-at-20-time-to-create-a-program-that-supports-work-and-helps; Jordan Weissmann, "The Failure of Welfare Reform," *Slate,* June 1, 2016; H. Luke Shaefer, "The Magnitude of the Change in $2-a-Day Poverty Since 1996 Is Even Larger After Reducing Survey Bias," *$2 a Day* blog, March 20, 2017, twodollarsaday.com/blog/2017/3/20/the-magnitude-of-the-change-in-2-a-day-poverty-since-1996-is-even-larger-after-reducing-survey-bias; Fording and Schram, "Welfare Reform Disaster"; Zach Parolin, "Welfare Money Is Paying for a Lot of Things Besides Welfare," *Atlantic,* June 13, 2019.

74 **The Center on Budget:** Pavetti and Schott, "TANF at 20: Time to Create"; Parolin, "Welfare Money Is Paying for a Lot"; "What Is 'Deep Poverty'?," Center for Poverty Research, University of California, Davis, poverty.ucdavis.edu/faq/what-deep-poverty.

75 **Government should have leeway:** Edelman, "Dandridge v. Williams Redux," 985–86.

75 **Benefit levels are also:** Edelman, "Dandridge v. Williams Redux," 985–86, 988; Semuels, "End of Welfare as We Know It."

75 **One study of Maine families:** Sandra Butler, "What Happens to Poor Families When They Hit Welfare Time Limits and Cash Benefits Disappear," Scholars Strategy Network, May 1, 2013, scholars.org/contribution/what-happens-poor-families-when-they-hit-welfare-time-limits-and-cash-benefits; Ife Floyd, "Arizona Cuts TANF Time Limit to Shortest Nationwide," Center on Budget and Policy Priorities, July 5, 2016, cbpp.org/blog/arizona-cuts-tanf-time-limit-to-shortest-nationwide.

75 **Congressional Republicans and President Clinton:** *James*, 402 U.S. at 145 (Marshall, J., dissenting); *United States v. Carolene Products Co.*, 304 U.S. 144, 152n4 (1938).

76 **The most centrist of the conservatives:** "Justices 1789 to Present," Supreme Court; William Branigin, Fred Barbash, and Daniela Deane, "Supreme Court Justice O'Connor Resigns," *Washington Post*, July 1, 2005.

76 **The plans were changed:** Coyle, *Roberts Court*, 60–61; Stevenson, "O'Connor to Retire"; David Stout and Elisabeth Bumiller, "President's Choice of Roberts Ends a Day of Speculation," *New York Times*, July 19, 2005; Branigin, Barbash, and Deane, "Supreme Court Justice O'Connor Resigns"; "John J. O'Connor, Ex-Justice's Husband, Dies," UPI, November 11, 2009.

76 **The ideological gatekeepers:** Richard Stevenson, "President Names Roberts as Choice for Chief Justice," *New York Times*, September 6, 2005; Jeffrey Toobin, "The Conservative Pipeline to the Supreme Court," *New Yorker*, April 17, 2017; Todd Purdum, Jodi Wilgoren, and Pam Belluck, "Court Nominee's Life Is Rooted in Faith and Respect for Law," *New York Times*, July 21, 2005.

77 **Roberts and his wife:** Purdum, Wilgoren, and Belluck, "Court Nominee's Life Is Rooted"; Coyle, *Roberts Court*, 61; Joan Biskupic, *The Chief: The Life and Turbulent Times of Chief Justice John Roberts* (New York: Basic Books, 2018), 18, 24, 72, 96, 115, 125.

77 **Roberts was confirmed:** David Stout, "Roberts Is Sworn In as Chief Justice of U.S.," *New York Times*, September 29, 2005.

77 **In the face of this:** Karl Rove, *Courage and Consequence: My Life as a Conservative in the Fight* (New York: Threshold Editions, 2010), 421–24; Elizabeth Bumiller and Carl Hulse, "Bush's Court Choice Ends Bid; Conservative Attacked Miers," *New York Times*, October 28, 2005; Toobin, "Conservative Pipeline"; "Roberts: 'My Job Is to Call Balls and Strikes and Not to Pitch or Bat,'" CNN, September 12, 2005.

77 **One of Alito's first political inspirations:** David Kirkpatrick, "From Alito's Past, a Window on Conservatives at Princeton," *New York Times*, November 27, 2005; Coyle, *Roberts Court*, 69; Rove, *Courage and Consequence*, 423.

78 **He was sometimes called:** Edward Kennedy, "Alito's Credibility Problem," *Washington Post*, January 7. 2006; Tom Donnelly and Brianne Gorod, "None to the Right of Samuel Alito," *Atlantic*, January 30, 2016; Biskupic, *The Chief*, 142.

78 **O'Connor and Kennedy:** Coyle, *Roberts Court*, 60–61; Stevenson, "O'Connor to Retire"; Stout and Bumiller, "President's Choice of Roberts"; Purdum, Wilgoren, and Belluck, "Court Nominee's Life Is Rooted"; Coyle, *Roberts Court*, 61; Marcia Coyle, "Column: Why Replacing the 'Swing' Justice Ignites Warring Passions of Special Interest Groups," PBS.com, July 11, 2018.

78 **As a result:** "Justices 1789 to Present," Supreme Court; "Obama Nominated Sonia Sotomayor," CNN, May 26, 2009; Carl Hulse, "Senate Confirms Kagan in Partisan Vote," *New York Times*, August 5, 2010.

79 **He had already served:** *Turner v. Rogers*, 564 U.S. 431 (2011); Kelly Terry, "The Movement for a Right to Counsel in Civil Cases: *Turner v. Rogers* (2011)," in *The Poverty*

Law Canon: Exploring the Major Cases, ed. Marie Failinger and Ezra Rosser (Ann Arbor: University of Michigan Press, 2016), 256–58.

79 **Turner was sentenced:** *Turner*, 564 U.S. 431; Terry, "The Movement for a Right," 259.

79 **Turner contended that:** *Turner*, 564 U.S. 431; Terry, "The Movement for a Right," 266.

79 **Advocates for the poor:** Terry, "The Movement for a Right," 266.

80 **In considering whether:** *Turner*, 564 U.S. 431; Terry, "The Movement for a Right," 269; *Turner*, 564 U.S. 431.

80 **On the third prong:** Terry, "The Movement for a Right," 269; *Turner*, 564 U.S. 431.

80 **The four dissenters:** Terry, "The Movement for a Right," 269; *Turner*, 564 U.S. 431.

81 **The executive director:** Terry, "The Movement for a Right," 269.

81 ***The New York Times* hailed:** *National Federation of Independent Business v. Sebelius*, 567 U.S. 519 (2012); Adam Liptak, "Supreme Court Upholds Health Care Law, 5–4, in Victory for Obama," *New York Times*, June 28, 2012.

81 **Legal analysts debated:** Tushnet, *In the Balance: Law and Politics on the Roberts Court* (New York: Norton, 2013), 1–2; Biskupic, *The Chief*.

82 **If a state did not expand:** Sara Rosenbaum and Timothy Westmoreland, "The Supreme Court's Surprising Decision on the Medicaid Expansion: How Will the Federal Government and States Proceed?," *Health Affairs* 31, no. 8 (August 2012): 1664; Nicole Huberfeld, Elizabeth Weeks Leonard, and Kevin Outterson, "Plunging into Endless Difficulties: Medicaid and Coercion in *National Federation of Independent Business v. Sebelius*," *Boston University Law Review* 93 (2013): 25, 41–42.

82 **Roberts had the five votes:** Huberfeld et al., "Plunging into Endless Difficulties," 21; Scott Lemieux, "Should Liberals Be Mad at Kagan and Breyer?," *American Prospect*, July 9, 2012; Biskupic, *The Chief*, 239–40; Joan Biskupic, interview by Dave Davies, *Fresh Air*, NPR, April 1, 2019.

82 **The pressure to accept Medicaid expansion:** *National Federation of Independent Business v. Sebelius*, 132 S. Ct. 2566, 2604–5 (2012).

83 **There was another reason:** *Sebelius*, 567 U.S. 519 (Ginsburg, J., concurring); *South Dakota v. Dole*, 483 U.S. 203 (1987).

83 **more than any justice:** *Sebelius*, 567 U.S. 519 (Ginsburg, J., concurring).

83 **"We came to know more":** Tushnet, *A Court Divided*, 104–5; *Jewish Women's Archive Encyclopedia*, s.v. "Ruth Bader Ginsburg," by Malvina Halberstam, jwa.org/encyclopedia/article/ginsburg-ruth-bader; Jane Eisner, "Jane Eisner Interviews Ruth Bader Ginsburg: Transcript," *The Forward*, February 5, 2018.

84 **One of her greatest victories:** Tushnet, *A Court Divided*, 104–5; 109–10.

84 **They made her, she said:** Tushnet, *A Court Divided*, 104–5; *Jewish Women's Archive Encyclopedia*, s.v. "Ruth Bader Ginsburg"; Eisner, "Jane Eisner Interviews Ruth Bader Ginsburg."

84 **Sotomayor was diagnosed:** Sheryl Gay Stolberg, "Sotomayor, a Trailblazer and a Dreamer," *New York Times*, May 26, 2009; Biography.com, s.v. "Sonia Sotomayor,"

biography.com/people/sonia-sotomayor-453906; Sonia Sotomayor, "Lecture: 'A Latina Judge's Voice,'" *New York Times*, May 14, 2009.

84 **Six years later:** Stolberg, "Sotomayor, a Trailblazer."

85 **Although she said she could:** Stolberg, "Sotomayor, a Trailblazer."

85 **One scholarly article said that:** Huberfeld et al., "Plunging into Endless Difficulties," 1, 87; *Sebelius*, 132 S. Ct. at 2641.

85 **Later, the nonpartisan:** Matthew Buettgens and Genevieve Kenney, "What If More States Expanded Medicaid in 2017? Changes in Eligibility, Enrollment, and the Uninsured," Urban Institute, July 20, 2016; Carter Price and Christine Eibner, "The Math of State Medicaid Expansion" (Santa Monica, Calif.: RAND Corp., 2013); *Sebelius*, 567 U.S. 519 (Ginsburg, J., concurring).

86 **He was striking down:** K. K. Rebecca Lai and Alicia Parlapiano, "Millions Pay the Obamacare Penalty Instead of Buying Insurance. Who Are They?" *New York Times*, November 28, 2017.

86 **The Court no longer saw:** Lai and Parlapiano, "Millions Pay the Obamacare Penalty."

86 **On a practical level:** Lyndon Johnson, Annual Message to Congress on the State of the Union (January 8, 1964, Washington, D.C.), Lyndon Baines Johnson Presidential Library, lbjlibrary.net/collections/selected-speeches/november-1963-1964/01-08-1964.html.

87 **In the aggregate:** Mark A. Graber, "The Clintonification of American Law: Abortion, Welfare, and Liberal Constitutional Theory," *Ohio State Law Journal* 58, no. 3 (1997): 787–88; *King*, 392 U.S. 327–333 (1968); Henry Freedman, "Sylvester Smith, Unlikely Heroine: *King v. Smith* (1968)," in *The Poverty Law Canon: Exploring the Major Cases*, ed. Marie Failinger and Ezra Rosser (Ann Arbor: University of Michigan Press, 2016), 65.

87 **In a recent year, nearly one million:** Carmen Solomon-Fears, Alison Smith, and Carla Berry, "Child Support Enforcement: Incarceration as the Last Resort Penalty for Nonpayment of Support," Congressional Research Service (2012), ncsea.org/documents/CRS-Report-on-CSE-and-Incarceration-for-Non-Payment-March-6-2012.pdf; Emily Badger and Quoctrung Bui, "In 83 Million Eviction Records, a Sweeping and Intimate New Look at Housing in America," *New York Times*, April 7, 2018.

88 **As with the beneficiaries:** Signe-Mary McKernan, "The Effect of Specific Welfare Policies on Poverty," Urban Institute (April 2006), 19; Ife Floyd, "States Should Repeal Racist Policies Denying Benefits to Children Born to TANF Families," Center for Budget and Policy Priorities, April 30, 2019.

88 **If the Court had not struck down:** Huberfeld et al., "Plunging into Endless Difficulties," 6; Buettgens and Kenney, "What If More States Expanded Medicaid"; Matthew Buettgens, "The Implications of Medicaid Expansion in the Remaining States: 2018 Update," Robert Wood Johnson Foundation, May 2018; Tara Golshan, "Study: The

US Could Have Averted About 15,600 Deaths if Every State Expanded Medicaid," *Vox*, July 23, 2019.

88 **That suggested that:** Melissa Majerol, Jennifer Tolbert, and Anthony Damico, "Health Care Spending Among Log-Income Households with and Without Medicaid," Kaiser Family Foundation, February 4, 2016.

88 **A study published:** Pam Belluck, "Medicaid Expansion May Lower Death Rates, Study Says," *New York Times*, July 25, 2012.

89 **It might have invalidated:** *Dandridge*, 397 U.S. at 487.

89 **There have been questions:** Kathryn Edin and H. Luke Shaefer, "20 Years Since Welfare 'Reform,'" *Atlantic*, August 22, 2016; Arloc Sherman, "Under $2 a Day in America Part 1," Center for Budget and Policy Priorities, *Off the Charts*, March 5, 2012; Dylan Matthews, "How Many Americans Live on $2 a Day? The Biggest Debate in Poverty Research, Explained," *Vox*, June 5, 2019.

89 **The Court's rulings:** Jeffrey Mondak, "Policy Legitimacy and the Supreme Court: The Sources and Contexts of Legitimation," *Political Science Quarterly* 47, no. 3 (1994): 675.

90 **It found, among other things:** Michael Karpman et al., "Material Hardship Among Nonelderly Adults and Their Families in 2017," Urban Institute (August 2018), 6; "Statement on Visit to the USA by Professor Philip Alston, United Nations Special Rapporteur on Extreme Poverty and Human Rights," Office of the High Commissioner for Human Rights, United Nations, December 15, 2017.

Chapter Three: Education

91 **The plaintiffs argued:** *San Antonio Independent School District v. Rodriguez*, 411 U.S. 1 (1973).

92 **The district's median:** Michael Heise, "The Story of San Antonio Independent School Dist. v. Rodriguez: School Finance, Local Control, and Constitutional Limits" (research paper, Cornell Law School, 2007); Mark G. Yudof and Daniel C. Morgan, "Rodriguez v. San Antonio Independent School District: Gathering the Ayes of Texas—The Politics of School Finance Reform," *Law and Contemporary Problems* 38 (1974): 391; Christine Drennon, "Social Relations Spatially Fixed: Construction and Maintenance of School Districts in San Antonio, Texas," *Geographical Review* 96 (October 2006): 584.

92 **"That would be as much":** Yudof and Morgan, "Rodriguez v. San Antonio," 383, 391; Cynthia E. Orozco, "Rodriguez v. San Antonio ISD," *Handbook of Texas Online*, June 15, 2010, tshaonline.org/handbook/online/articles/jrrht; Peter Irons, *The Courage of Their Convictions: Sixteen Americans Who Fought Their Way to the Supreme Court* (New York: Penguin, 1990); J. Steven Farr and Mark Trachtenberg, "The Edgewood Drama: An Epic Quest for Education Equity," *Yale Law & Policy Review* 7 (1999): 607; "Edgewood Ponders Situation," *Austin Statesman*, March 28, 1973.

93 **Property values in Alamo Heights:** Heise, "Story of San Antonio," 2; Jeffrey Sutton, "San Antonio Independent School District v. Rodriguez and Its Aftermath," *Virginia Law Review* 94 (2008): 1963, 1964.

93 **The facilities were also far superior:** Farr and Trachtenberg, "The Edgewood Drama," 607–8; *Rodriguez v. San Antonio School District*, 85–86.

93 **Taking all revenue into account:** *Rodriguez v. San Antonio Independent School District*, 337 F. Supp. 280, 282–83 (W.D. Tex. 1971); Yudof and Morgan, "Rodriguez v. San Antonio," 387–90; James E. Ryan, *Five Miles Away, A World Apart: One City, Two Schools and the Story of Educational Opportunity in Modern America* (New York: Oxford University Press, 2010).

93 **The poorest districts:** Yudof and Morgan, "Rodriguez v. San Antonio," 392–3.

93 **The state imposed a limit:** *Rodriguez v. San Antonio*, 411 U.S. 66.

94 **Connally, however, would soon leave:** Yudof and Morgan, "Rodriguez v. San Antonio," 390–91; Heise, "Story of San Antonio," 3.

94 **At the time, the Supreme Court:** Laura Isensee, "How a Dad Helped Start the Fight for Better Public School Funds in Texas," Houston Public Media, September 7, 2015; Yudof and Morgan, "Rodriguez v. San Antonio," 391; *Hobson v. Hansen*, 269 F. Supp. 401 (D.D.C. 1967), *aff'd sub nom., Smuck v. Hobson*, 408 F.2d 175 (D.C. Cir. 1969); *Griffin v. Illinois*, 351 U.S. 12 (1956); *Harper v. Virginia Board of Election Commissioners*, 383 U.S. 663 (1966); Arthur Gotchman obituary, *Austin American-Statesman*, October 27, 2010.

94 **Wise believed that school funding:** Heise, "Story of San Antonio," 15–16.

94 **The Equal Protection Clause did not permit:** *Hobson*, 269 F. Supp. 401.

95 **He wanted a better future:** Heise, "Story of San Antonio," 1–2; Yudof and Morgan, "Rodriguez v. San Antonio," 391; Isensee, "How a Dad Helped Start the Fight"; William Stevens, "U.S. Court Upsets Texas School Tax Tied to Property," *New York Times*, December 31, 1971; "Civil Service Worker Sure of Supreme Court Victory," Associated Press, October 15, 1972; Wayne Jackson, "Edgewood Depressed by Ruling," *Austin Statesman*, March 21, 1973; Melvin Urofsky, *One Hundred Americans Making Constitutional History* (Washington, D.C.: CQ Press, 2004), 173–74.

95 **At the time, when the Warren Court:** Laurence Tribe, *American Constitutional Law* (Mineola, N.Y.: Foundation Press, 1988), 1455–63; *Brown v. Board of Education*, 347 U.S. 483, 493 (1954); *United States v. Carolene Products*, 304 U.S. 144, 152n4 (1938); Gerald Gunther, "Foreword: In Search of Evolving Doctrine on a Changing Court: A Model for a Newer Equal Protection," *Harvard Law Review* 86, no. 1 (1972): 1, 8; Yudof and Morgan, "Rodriguez v. San Antonio," 391–92; Heise, "Story of San Antonio," 6.

95 **In *Brown v. Board of Education*:** Tribe, *American Constitutional Law*, 1455–63; *Brown*, 347 U.S. at 493; *Carolene Products*, 304 U.S. at 152n4; Gunther, "Foreword: In Search of Evolving Doctrine," 1, 8.

95 **It would be extremely difficult:** *Wex Legal Dictionary*, s.v. "Strict Scrutiny," Legal Information Institute, law.cornell.edu/wex/strict_scrutiny.

96 **That separate state constitutional claim:** William Greider, "Challenger to School Tax Saw Court Sink His Theory," *Austin Statesman*, March 28, 1973; Valerie Nelson, "John Serrano Jr., 69; His Lawsuit Changed the Way State's Schools Are Funded," *Los Angeles Times*, December 6, 2006; Richard Valencia, *Chicano Students and the Courts: The Mexican American Legal Struggle for Educational Equality* (New York: New York University Press, 2010), 85.

96 **In *Private Wealth and Public Education*:** Stephen Goldstein, "Interdistrict Inequalities in School Financing: A Critical Analysis of Serrano v. Priest and Its Progeny," *University of Pennsylvania Law Review* 120 (1972): 512; John Coons, Stephen Sugarman, and William Clune III, *Private Wealth and Public Education* (Cambridge, Mass.: Harvard University Press, 1970), 2, 435, 443 461–62; Linda Mathews, "School Funds Ruling to Have Broad Impact," *Los Angeles Times*, June 29, 1973; William Greider, "'Novel Theory' of School Spending Cashiered by Court," *Washington Post*, March 22, 1973; Richard Valencia, *Chicano Students and the Courts: The Mexican American Legal Struggle for Educational Equality* (New York: New York University Press, 2008), 85.

96 **When it was clear:** Yudof and Morgan, "Rodriguez v. San Antonio," 392.

96 **"By our holding today":** *Serrano v. Priest*, 5 Cal. 3d 584, 594, 614–15, 619 (1971).

97 **It also decided that the state's:** *Van Dusartz v. Hatfield*, 334 F. Supp. 870, 875–77 (D. Minn. 1971); Minnesota Department of Education Division of School Finance, "Minnesota School Finance History 1849–2016," December 2016.

97 **"At issue is the whole structure":** Greider, "'Novel Theory' of School Spending"; Joanne Leedom, "Upheaval in School Funding," *Christian Science Monitor*, September 2, 1971.

97 **As support, it quoted:** *Rodriguez*, 337. F. Supp. at 282–83; Heise, "Story of San Antonio," 5; Ryan, *Five Miles Away*.

98 **The court noted, however, that the system:** *Rodriguez*, 337 F. Supp. at 284.

98 **It simply ordered the legislature:** *Rodriguez*, 337 F. Supp. at 284–85.

98 **The *Rodriguez* plaintiffs wanted:** Frederick Andrews, "School Ruling Is Seen Changing the Nature of U.S. Cities, Suburbs," *Wall Street Journal*, March 13, 1972; Stevens, "U.S. Court Upsets Texas School Tax."

98 **Beverly Hills spent more than twice:** Andrews, "School Ruling Is Seen Changing the Nature."

99 **It quoted one lawyer:** Andrews, "School Ruling Is Seen Changing the Nature."

99 **The days after the *Rodriguez* decision:** Goldstein, "Interdistrict Inequalities in School Financing," 504, 506; Stevens, "U.S. Court Upsets Texas School Tax."

99 **A New Jersey superior court:** *Robinson v. Cahill*, 118 N.J. Super. 223 (1972); *Milliken v. Green*, 203 N.W.2d 457 (Mich. 1972); *Hollins v. Shofstall*, Civ. No. C-253652 (Super. Ct. Ariz., July 7, 1972); *Sweetwater Planning Committee v. Hinkle*, 491 P. 2d 1234 (Wyo. 1971).

100 **"We now have enough evidence":** Greider, "'Novel Theory' of School Spending"; Leedom, "Upheaval in School Funding"; Justin Driver, *The Schoolhouse Gate: Public*

Education, the Supreme Court, and the Battle for the American Mind (New York: Pantheon, 2018), 319.

100 **"Unlike many other societal problems":** Goldstein, "Interdistrict Inequalities in School Financing," 506; Driver, *Schoolhouse Gate*, 318.

100 **Wright was an outspoken conservative:** Yudof and Morgan, "Rodriguez v. San Antonio," 399; Christopher Lydon, "The Man Who Said 'No' for Nixon: Charles Alan Wright," *New York Times*, July 24, 1973.

101 **By the time the *Rodriguez* case:** *Ortwein v. Schwab*, 410 U.S. 656, 660 (1973).

101 **It would have been hard:** *King v. Smith*, 392 U.S. 309 (1968).

102 **He urged big business:** Lewis F. Powell Jr., "Powell Memorandum: Attack on American Free Enterprise System," August 23, 1971, 1, 7–8, Powell Papers, Lewis F. Powell Jr. Archives, Washington and Lee University School of Law, law2.wlu.edu/powellarchives/page.asp?pageid=1251 (portal for all materials on Powell Memorandum); Michael Graetz and Linda Greenhouse, *The Burger Court and the Rise of the Judicial Right* (New York: Simon & Schuster, 2016), 237–39, 407.

102 **It was "so militant":** Memorandum from Lewis F. Powell Jr. to Messrs. Buckley, Jeffries, and Owens, November 12, 1973, Powell Papers; Letter from Lewis F. Powell Jr. to Ross L. Malone, Sept. 13, 1971, Powell Papers; Graetz and Greenhouse, *The Burger Court*, 239; Fred P. Graham, "Powell Proposed Business Defense," *New York Times*, September 29, 1972; Alliance for Justice, *Justice for Sale: Shortchanging the Public Interest for Private Gain* (Washington, D.C.: Alliance for Justice, 1993).

102 **"This setting of the 'rich'":** "Powell Memorandum," 7–8, Powell Papers.

102 **It was "preservative of other rights":** Oral Argument, *San Antonio Independent School District v. Rodriguez*, 411 U.S. 1 (1973), oyez.org/cases/1972/71-1332; Yudof and Morgan, "Rodriguez v. San Antonio," 400.

103 **"They are fair men":** Yudof and Morgan, "Rodriguez v. San Antonio," 401; "Civil Service Worker Sure of Supreme Court Victory"; *Rodriguez*, 411 U.S. at 33.

103 **Powell wrote the majority opinion:** *Rodriguez*, 411 U.S. at 33; *Rodriguez*, 411 U.S. at 28.

103 **The plaintiff class was:** *Rodriguez*, 411 U.S. at 33–35.

103 **It was, he said:** *Rodriguez*, 411 U.S. 1, 33–35.

104 **Texas's school finance system:** *Rodriguez*, 411 U.S. at 49–50; *San Antonio Independent School District v. Rodriguez*, Supreme Court Case Files Collection, Box 8, Powell Papers.

104 **Powell said his opinion:** *Rodriguez*, 411 U.S. at 58–59.

104 **His sympathetic words:** *Rodriguez*, 411 U.S. at 59–62; Graetz and Greenhouse, *The Burger Court*, 91–92.

104 **It did not allow for true local control:** *Rodriguez*, 411 U.S. at 63–70.

105 **President Johnson appointed:** Linda Greenhouse, "Thurgood Marshall, Civil Rights Hero, Dies at 84," *New York Times*, January 25, 1993.

105 **Some of Marshall's most important cases:** *Shelley v. Kraemer*, 334 U.S. 1 (1948); *Smith v. Allwright*, 321 U.S. 649 (1944); *Sweatt v. Painter*, 339 U.S. 629 (1950); *McLaurin v.*

Oklahoma State Regents, 339 U.S. 637 (1950); Greenhouse, "Thurgood Marshall, Civil Rights Hero."

105 **He also argued:** *Rodriguez*, 411 U.S. at 111–16.

105 **The Court's decision:** *Rodriguez*, 411 U.S. at 71–72, 84–85; *Sweatt*, 339 U.S. 629; *McLaurin*, 339 U.S. 637; Charles J. Ogletree, "The Legacy of San Antonio Independent School District v. Rodriguez," *Richmond Journal of the Law and the Public Interest* XVII (2014): 515, 524–25; Sutton, "San Antonio Independent School District," 1963, 1970.

106 **If the Court would not provide:** *Rodriguez*, 411 U.S. at 98.

106 **"If a single Justice":** Warren Weaver Jr., "Court, 5–4, Backs Schools in Texas on Property Tax," *New York Times*, March 22, 1973.

106 **"It hurts," John Coons said:** Greider, "'Novel Theory' of School Spending"; Mathews, "School Funds Ruling to Have Broad Impact."

106 **Texas governor Dolph Briscoe said:** Weaver, "Court, 5–4, Backs Schools in Texas."

106 **"We're left holding the empty bag":** John MacKenzie, "Court Puts Reform Up to States," *Washington Post*, March 22, 1973; Jackson, "Edgewood Depressed by Ruling"; "Plaintiff Is Bitter," *New York Times*, March 22, 1973.

107 **The *Times* ran the report:** "Plaintiff Is Bitter," *New York Times*.

107 **These state claims were generally stronger:** *Rodriguez*, 411 U.S. at 133n100.

108 **Each would have to be brought:** Stephen Gard, 'San Antonio Independent School District v. Rodriguez: On Our Way to Where?," *Valparaiso University Law Review* 8 (Fall 1973): 1.

108 **The Louisiana Supreme Court:** "Overview of Litigation History," SchoolFundingInfo .org, schoolfunding.info/litigation-map/; William N. Evans, Sheila E. Murray, and Robert M. Schwab, "The Impact of Court-Mandated School Finance Reform," in *Equity and Adequacy in Education Finance: Issues and Perspectives*, by National Research Council (Washington, D.C.: National Academies Press, 1999).

108 **A lawyer who represented:** Jonathan Kozol, *Savage Inequalities: Children in America's Schools* (New York: Harper Perennial, 1991), 223–29; Bill Peterson, "Kentucky Public Schools Ruled Unconstitutional," *Washington Post*, June 9, 1989; Claudio Sanchez, "Kentucky's Unprecedented Success in School Funding Is on the Line," *All Things Considered*, NPR, April 26, 2016, npr.org/sections/ed/2016/04/26/475305022 /kentuckys-unprecedented-success-in-school-funding-is-on-the-line; Robert Garrett, "Texas School Funding Flawed but Legal, Justices Rule; First Win for State on Issue in Decades," *Dallas Morning News*, May 13, 2016.

109 **The fight to equalize school funding:** Monica Disare, "Here's the Education Lawsuit That Helped Motivate Cynthia Nixon's Run for Governor," Chalkbeat, March 29, 2018; "The History of Abbott v. Burke," Education Law Center, edlawcenter.org/litigation /abbott-v-burke/abbott-history.html.

109 **The Court could have recognized:** "Equity," *The Glossary of Education Reform*, available at edglossary.org/equity/.

110 Unlike other rulings, the Kentucky decision: Richard Day and Jo Ann Ewalt, "Education Reform in Kentucky: Just What the Court Ordered" (Curriculum and Instruction Faculty and Staff Scholarship paper, Eastern Kentucky University, 2013), 265.

110 After the reforms took effect: Day and Ewalt, *Education Reform in Kentucky,* 267.

111 The *Milliken* lawsuit: *Milliken v. Bradley,* 418 U.S. 717 (1974).

111 To members of the black community: Joyce Baugh, *The Detroit School Busing Case:* Milliken v. Bradley *and the Controversy over Desegregation* (Lawrence: University of Kansas Press, 2011), 68–70; "Bus Ruling Jars Detroit Suburbs," *New York Times,* October 3, 1971.

111 In the decade after the law passed: Erwin Chemerinsky, *The Case Against the Supreme Court* (New York: Penguin, 2014), 139; Frank Brown, "The First Serious Implementation of Brown: The 1964 Civil Rights Act and Beyond," *Journal of Negro Education* 73, no 3 (2004): 182–90.

112 White flight was helped: Myron Orfield, "Milliken, Meredith, and Metropolitan Segregation," *UCLA Law Review* 62 (2015): 376–77; Richard Rothstein, *The Color of Law: A Forgotten History of How Our Government Segregated America* (New York: Liveright, 2017); Baugh, *Detroit School Busing,* 21, 29–31.

112 The most well known of those: George Gagster, *Driving Detroit: The Quest for Respect in the Motor City* (Philadelphia: University of Pennsylvania Press, 2014), 139; Thomas J. Sugrue, *Origins of the Urban Crisis: Race and Inequality in Postwar Detroit* (Princeton, N.J.: Princeton University Press, 2014), 63–66; Orfield, "Milliken, Meredith," 397; Baugh, *Detroit School Busing Case,* 33.

112 By 1970, the black population: Susan Welch, *Race and Place: Race Relations in an American City* (Cambridge, England: Cambridge University Press, 2001), 27; Kurt Metzger and Jason Booza, *African Americans in the United States, Michigan and Metropolitan Detroit* (working paper, Center for Urban Studies, Wayne State University, Detroit, 2002), 10; *1970 Census of Population and Housing* (U.S. Department of Commerce, Bureau of the Census, 1970), 6, table 1; Orfield, "Milliken, Meredith," 397–8; Huff, "Only Feasible Desegregation Plan."

113 Some of the school districts: *Bradley v. Milliken,* 338 F. Supp. 582, 585 (E.D. Mich. 1971); *Bradley v. Milliken,* 484 F.2d 215 (6th Cir. 1973).

113 In early 1968, the Detroit: Baugh, *Detroit School Busing Case,* 70–74.

113 The commission declared: Martin Ginsburg, "Integration: The Gap Is Widening," *Annual Education Review,* 1968; National Advisory Commission on Civil Disorders, *Report of the National Advisory Commission on Civil Disorders* (1968), 11–12, 50; U.S. Commission on Civil Rights, *Racial Isolation in the Public Schools,* vol. 1 (1967), 1, 109–10, 219–10; Baugh, *Detroit School Busing Case,* 19.

114 Despite strong white opposition: Baugh, *Detroit School Busing Case,* 77–80.

114 None of the new board members: Baugh, *Detroit School Busing Case,* 81–86.

114 Since the city and state had rejected: Baugh, *Detroit School Busing Case,* 86; *Bradley v. Milliken,* 338 F.Supp. 582.

115 **Unless the courts changed the law:** Gordon, "Rights Lawyers Gird for Battle"; Berry, "South Leads in Integration"; Driver, *Schoolhouse Gate*, 284

115 **It was not as straightforward a case:** Huff, "Only Feasible Desegregation Plan"; Robert Sedler, "The Profound Impact of Milliken v. Bradley," *Wayne Law Review* 33 (1987): 1698–99; Baugh, *Detroit School Busing Case*, 108; *Bradley v. Milliken*, 338 F.Supp. 582.

115 **Such an order would also:** Baugh, *Detroit School Busing Case*, 124.

116 **A "metropolitan area" remedy:** Baugh, *Detroit School Busing Case*, 117, 125; Carrie Sharlow, "Michigan Lawyers in History: Stephen J. Roth," *Michigan Bar Journal* 91 (October 2012): 44–45.

116 **It made a strong impression:** "Judge Stephen Roth, 66, Dies; Ordered Detroit School Busing," *New York Times*, July 12, 1974; Baugh, *Detroit School Busing Case*, 92, 113.

116 **In an array of ways:** Baugh, *Detroit School Busing Case*, 116.

117 **That, he insisted, required:** *Bradley*, 338 F. Supp. at 585; *Bradley v. Milliken*, 345 F.Supp. 914 (E.D. Mich. 1972); Orfield, "Milliken, Meredith," 364, 402; Baugh, *Detroit School Busing Case*, 127.

117 **Roth appointed a committee:** *Bradley*, 345 F. Supp. at 918–19; Baugh, *Detroit School Busing Case*, 127–30; Orfield, "Milliken, Meredith," 401.

117 **In the state's May 1972 Democratic primary:** "Judge Stephen Roth, 66, Dies; Ordered Detroit School Busing," *New York Times*, July 12, 1974; Louis Masur, *The Soiling of Old Glory: The Story of a Photograph That Shocked America* (New York: Bloomsbury USA, 2009), 38; "Michigan Governor Fights Mass Busing," *Atlanta Journal-Constitution*, June 16, 1972; "Bombs Fail to Halt Busing," *Atlanta Constitution*, September 1, 1971; Orfield, "Milliken, Meredith," 404–5; William Jones, "Michigan Primary Keyed to Busing Issue," *Chicago Tribune*, May 13, 1972; Tom Gilchrist, "A Little History of Michigan Primary," *Politics & Elections* blog, Michigan Live, January 12, 2008.

117 **Given the demographics:** *Bradley v. Milliken*, 484 F.2d 215 (6th Circuit 1973).

118 **In 1971, in a case:** *Alexander v. Holmes County Board of Education*, 396 U.S. 19 (1969); *Swann v. Charlotte-Mecklenburg Board of Education*, 402 U.S. 1 (1971).

118 **That decision, which came:** *Keyes v. School District No. 1, Denver*, 413 U.S. 189 (1973); Driver, *Schoolhouse Gate*, 274; Orfield, "Milliken, Meredith," 411.

119 **The real question, however, was:** *Keyes*, 413 U.S. 189.

119 ***Milliken*, which was almost:** *Milliken*, 418 U.S. at 741–45, 745, 803 (1974). Justice Potter Stewart wrote a separate concurring opinion that, because his vote was necessary for the majority, must also be considered part of the Court's holding. He emphasized the fact that, on the record in the case, there was no evidence of any interdistrict violations. *Milliken*, 418 U.S. at 755–56.

119 **Upholding Roth's order:** *Milliken*, 418 U.S. at 741; Allen Katz (law clerk to Thurgood Marshall, 1973–1974), interview with the author, September 29, 2018.

119 **Unless Michigan "drew the district lines":** *Milliken*, 418 U.S. at 746–47.

120 **It was a more elaborate way:** *Milliken*, 418 U.S. at 753–62.

120 **Since the state was partly responsible:** *Milliken*, 418 U.S. at 799.
120 **That is, he said, "in the final analysis":** *Milliken*, 418 U.S. at 783–84.
121 **"In the short run":** *Milliken*, 418 U.S. at 781–815; Sedler, "Profound Impact of Milliken v. Bradley," 1693, 1699.
121 ***The Wall Street Journal*:** William Stevens, "Many White Parents Now See Their Children as Safe," *New York Times*, July 27, 1924; Agis Salpukas, "Joy Is Expressed in the Suburbs; Reactions in Detroit Divided," *New York Times*, July 26, 1974; Driver, *Schoolhouse Gate*, 287; Baugh, *Detroit School Busing Case*, 174.
122 **Judge J. Skelly Wright, in Washington:** John C. Jeffries, *Justice Lewis F. Powell, Jr.*, (New York: Charles Scribner's Sons, 1994), 314; "Wrong Without Remedy," *New York Times*, July 28, 1974.
122 **"Thus it will be of little concern":** Baugh, *Detroit School Busing Case*, 177–8. "'Detroit, Where Life Is Worth Living,'" *New York Times*, August 1, 1974.
122 **The Court, however, had now declared:** *Brown*, 347 U.S. at 495.
123 **The increase in actual busing:** Matthew Delmont, *Why Busing Failed: Race, Media, and the National Resistance to School Desegregation* (Berkeley: University of California Press, 2016), 172; *Milliken*, 418 U.S. at 812–13; Thomas Sugrue, "It's Not the Bus; It's Us," *London Review of Books*, November 20, 2008.
123 **"And yet, those whose children":** Louis Harris, "Majority of Parents Report School Busing Has Been Satisfactory Experience," Harris Survey no. 25, March 26, 1981; Erica Frankenberg and Rebecca Jacobsen, "School Integration Polls," *Public Opinion Quarterly* 75 (2011): 788, 801; Jonathan Zimmerman, "Joe Biden's Not Alone in Spreading Myths About Busing and Segregation," *Philadelphia Inquirer*, March 12, 2019.
123 **When it was done, the Court:** John A. Powell, "A Minority-Majority Nation: Racing the Population in the Twenty-First Century," *Fordham Urban Law Journal* 29 (2002): 1395, 1410.
124 **Powell cited Harvard College's admissions policy:** *University of California v. Bakke*, 438 U.S. 265 (1978).
124 **As a result of the decision:** Adam Harris, "What Happens When a College's Affirmative Action Policy Is Found Illegal," *Atlantic*, October 26, 2018; *Bakke*, 438 U.S. 265.
124 **As a result of the law:** Diane I. Osifchok, "Case Note: The Utilization of Intermediate Scrutiny in Establishing the Right to Education for Undocumented Alien Children: Plyler v. Doe," *Pepperdine Law Review* 10, no. 1 (1982): 140–41.
124 **Brennan also noted the harm:** *Plyler v. Doe*, 457 U.S. 202, 230 (1982); Osifchok, "Case Note: The Utilization of Intermediate Scrutiny," 139; Linda Greenhouse, "Danger Zone," *New York Times*, October 29, 2014; Driver, *Schoolhouse Gate*, 351–52.
125 ***Plyler* was also:** Driver, *Schoolhouse Gate*, 353–54; *Plyler*, 457 U.S. 202.
125 **When the bus no longer stopped:** *Kadrmas v. Dickinson*, 487 U.S. 450, 450–56 (1988).
125 **The majority opinion rejecting:** *Kadrmas*, 487 U.S. 450.
125 **She was elected:** Mark Tushnet, *A Court Divided: The Rehnquist Court and the Future of Constitutional Law* (New York: Norton, 2006), 49–51; Judith Olans Brown,

Wendy Parmet, and Mary O'Connell, "The Rugged Feminism of Sandra Day O'Connor," *Indiana Law Review* 32 (1999): 1219; B. Drummond Ayres Jr., "Woman in the News: 'A Reputation for Excelling,'" *New York Times,* July 8, 1981.

126 **He announced her nomination:** Lou Cannon, "When Ronnie Met Sandy," *New York Times,* July 7, 2005; Steven Weisman, "Stewart Will Quit High Court July 3; Reasons Not Given," *New York Times,* June 19, 1981; John MacKenzie, "Potter Stewart Is Dead at 70; Was on High Court 23 Years," *New York Times,* December 8, 1985; Kathleen Sullivan, "Chief Justice Rehnquist '52 and Justice O'Connor '52: A Tribute by Kathleen M. Sullivan, Stanley Morrison Professor of Law and Former Dean," *Stanford Lawyer* no. 73 (Fall 2005); Linda Greenhouse, "Senate Confirms Judge O'Connor; She Will Join High Court Friday," *New York Times,* September 22, 1981.

126 **Drawing on the writings:** Suzanna Sherry, "Civic Virtue and the Feminine Voice in Constitutional Adjudication," *Virginia Law Review* 72, no. 3 (April 1986): 543, 596.

126 **There was therefore:** *Kadrmas,* 487 U.S. at 458–59.

127 **It was still "difficult to imagine":** *Kadrmas,* 487 U.S. at 461–62; Bureau of Labor Statistics, "Family Poverty Status and Family Poverty Level Historical Variables" (National Longitudinal Surveys, 2016).

127 **A law that erects barriers:** *Kadrmas,* 487 U.S. at 466–71; Jeffrey Jenkins, "No Free Ride to the Schoolhouse Gate: Equal Protection Analysis in Kadrmas v. Dickinson Public Schools," *New Mexico Law Review* 20 (1990): 161, 171–72.

127 **"Now they have stated some conclusions":** Mary McGrory, "The Court Missed the Bus," *Washington Post,* June 28, 1988.

128 **One single father in San Diego:** Driver, *Schoolhouse Gate,* 361; Mario Koran, "San Diego Unified Sends Parents Who Can't Pay for School Bus Rides to a Collections Agency," *Voice of San Diego,* November 8, 2017; Kathleen Conti, "Most School Districts Can't Put Brakes on Bus Fees," *Boston Globe,* August 20, 2015; "Some States Allow School Districts to Charge Parents for School Bus Transportation or to Advertise in or on School Buses to Raise Additional Revenue" (report, Florida Legislature Office of Program Policy Analysis & Government Accountability, December 2011).

128 **After the orders were lifted:** National Advisory Commission on Civil Disorders, *Report,* 11–12, 50; *Board of Education of Oklahoma City v. Dowell,* 498 U.S. 237, 247 (1991); Linda Greenhouse, "Justices Rule Mandatory Busing May Go, Even If Races Stay Apart," *New York Times,* January 16, 1991; Sean F. Reardon et al., "Brown Fades: The End of Court-Ordered School Desegregation and the Resegregation of American Public Schools," *Journal of Policy Analysis and Management* 31, no. 4 (2012): 12, 34; Gary Orfield et al., "Brown at 60: Great Progress, a Long Retreat and an Uncertain Future" (UCLA Civil Rights Project, Los Angeles, May 2014), 10, 12, 36.

129 **It was communities choosing diversity:** Marcia Coyle, *The Roberts Court: The Struggle for the Constitution* (New York: Simon & Schuster, 2013), 31; *Parents Involved in Community Schools v. Seattle School District No. 1,* 551 U.S. 701 (2007); Chemerinsky, *Case Against the Supreme Court,* 48.

129 **Still, even with Kennedy's qualification:** Chemerinsky, *Case Against the Supreme Court,* 47–48; *Parents Involved in Community Schools,* 551 U.S. 701.

129 **Now that localities were using:** *Parents Involved in Community Schools,* 551 U.S. 701; Joan Biskupic, *The Chief: The Life and Turbulent Times of Chief Justice John Roberts* (New York: Basic Books, 2018), 190.

130 **It was a striking statement:** Linda Greenhouse, "Justices Limit the Use of Race in School Plans for Integration," *New York Times,* June 19, 2007; *Parents Involved in Community Schools,* 551 U.S. 701; Coyle, *Roberts Court,* 114–15; *Milliken,* 418 U.S. at 741; Chemerinsky, *Case Against the Supreme Court,* 48, 145–46.

130 **If it had, American education:** Driver, *Schoolhouse Gate,* 326.

130 **There are also profound:** Emma Brown, "In 23 States, Richer School Districts Get More Local Funding Than Poorer Districts," *Washington Post,* March 12, 2015; Rebecca Klein, "School Funding Inequality Makes Education 'Separate and Unequal,' Arne Duncan Says," *Huffington Post,* March 16, 2015; National Center for Education Statistics, Table A-1: "Current Expenditures Minus Federal Revenue and Other Than Impact Aid Per Pupil in Membership, by Poverty Quartile and State," nces.ed.gov/edfin/Fy11_12_tables.asp; Natasha Ushomirsky and David Williams, "Funding Gaps: Too Many States Still Spend Less on Educating Students Who Need the Most" (Washington, D.C.: Education Trust, 2015); Sarah Mervosh, "How Much Wealthier Are White School Districts Than Nonwhite Ones? $23 Billion, Report Says," *New York Times,* February 27, 2019.

130 **In Pennsylvania, Bryn Athyn:** Natasha Bertrand, "This Connecticut Metro Area Is the Most Unequal Place in America," *Business Insider,* December 9, 2014; "Spending Per Student," Connecticut School Finance Project, ctschoolfinance.org/spending/per-student; *Connecticut Coalition for Justice in Education Funding v. Rell,* 2, 36 (Conn. Super. Ct. Sept. 7, 2016); Emma Brown, "Pa. Schools Are the Nation's Most Inequitable. The New Governor Wants to Fix That," *Washington Post,* April 22, 2015.

131 **If school district funding levels:** Brian Jacob and Jens Ludwig, "Improving Educational Outcomes for Poor Children," *Focus,* Fall 2009, 56; Julia B. Isaacs, "Starting School at a Disadvantage: The School Readiness of Poor Children," Brookings Institution, March 2012; Marguerite Spencer and Rebecca Reno, "The Benefits of Racial and Economic Integration in Our Education System: Why This Matters for Our Democracy" (Kirwan Institute for the Study of Race and Ethnicity, Ohio State University, 2009), 11; Evans et al., "Impact of Court-Mandated School Finance Reform"; Andrew Reschovsky and Jennifer Imazeki, "The Development of School Finance Formulas to Guarantee the Provision of Adequate Education to Low-Income Students," in *Developments in School Finance, 1997: Does Money Matter?,* ed. W. J. Fowler Jr. (Washington, D.C.: U.S. Department of Education, National Center for Educational Statistics, 1998).

131 **Lower Merion also had a social worker:** Brown, "Pa. Schools are the Nation's Most Inequitable."

132 **One study found that for students:** C. Kirabo Jackson, Rucker Johnson, and Claudia Persico, "The Effects of School Spending on Educational and Economic Outcomes: Evidence from School Finance Reforms," *Quarterly Journal of Economics* 131, no. 1 (2016): 157, 160, 201–3, 212–13; C. Kirabo Jackson, Rucker Johnson, and Claudia Persico, "The Effect of School Finance Reforms on the Distribution of Spending, Academic Achievement, and Adult Outcomes" (working paper, National Bureau of Economic Research, Cambridge, Mass., May 2014), 5, 8, 38, 44; Julien Lafortune et al., School Finance Reform and the Distribution of Student Achievement, *American Economic Journal: Applied Economics* 10, no 2 (2018): 1–26; Kevin Carey and Elizabeth Harris, "It Turns Out Spending More Probably Does Improve Education," *New York Times,* December 12, 2016.

132 **In the new urban-suburban school district:** Orfield, "Milliken, Meredith," 416–19.

132 **From 1975 to 1977:** Orfield, "Milliken, Meredith," 416–19.

133 **By 2009–10:** Richard Rothstein, "For Public Schools, Segregation Then, Segregation Since," Economic Policy Institute, 2013, 13; Orfield et al., "Brown at 60," 10, 12, 36.

133 **The study found that:** Orfield, "Milliken, Meredith," 425; Geoffrey Borman and Maritza Dowling, "School and Inequality: A Multilevel Analysis of Coleman's Equality of Educational Opportunity Data," *Teachers College Record* 112 (2010): 1201; Rucker Johnson, "Long-Run Impacts of School Desegregation and School Quality on Adult Attainments" (working paper, National Bureau of Economic Research, Cambridge, Mass., September 2015), 18–19.

133 **American education today:** *Rodriguez,* 411 U.S. at 71.

134 **They are also doing considerably better:** Ronald Brownstein, "The Challenge of Educational Inequality," *Atlantic,* May 19, 2016; National Center for Education Statistics, "Status and Trends in the Education of Racial and Ethnic Groups 2017" (U.S. Department of Education, July 2017); Young Invincibles, "Race & Ethnicity as a Barrier to Opportunity: A Blueprint for Higher Education Equity" (Washington, D.C.: Young Invincibles, February 2017), 24; Mitchell Wellman, "Report: The Race Gap in Higher Education Is Very Real," *USA Today,* March 7, 2017.

134 **There are also large gaps:** Reardon, "Widening Academic Achievement Gap," 1, 5; Sean Reardon, "The Geography of Racial/Ethnic Test Score Gaps" (working paper, Stanford Center for Education Policy Analysis, April 2016), 24; Pell Institute, Indicators of Higher Education Equity in the United States, 2018 Historical Trend Report; Annie Waldman, "New Data Reveals Stark Gaps in Graduation Rates Between Poor and Wealthy Students," ProPublica, September 24, 2015.

134 **"As the children of the rich":** Reardon, "Widening Academic Achievement Gap," 27; Facundo Alvaredo, *World Inequality Report 2018,* World Inequality Lab, 6, wir2018.wid.world/files/download/wir2018-full-report-english.pdf.

CHAPTER FOUR: CAMPAIGN FINANCE

135 **The reforms included:** *Buckley v. Valeo,* 424 U.S. 1 (1976).

136 **"The first is money":** Michael Kazin, "The Nation; One Political Constant," *New York Times,* April 1, 2001.

136 **Many of the rules:** Rick Hasen, "The Nine Lives of Buckley v. Valeo" (Legal Studies Paper No. 2010–15, Loyola Law School, Los Angeles, 2010), 3–4; Bradley Smith, "Faulty Assumptions and Undemocratic Consequences of Campaign Finance Reform," *Yale Law Journal* 105 (1996): 1049, 1054–55; Anthony Johnstone, "Recalibrating Campaign Finance Law," *Yale Law & Policy Review* 32 (2013): 217, 220–21.

136 **There was no central office:** Hasen, "Nine Lives of Buckley," 5–6; U.S. Federal Election Commission, *The Presidential Public Funding Program* (April 1993), 76–78 (appendix 4).

137 **The Committee for the Re-election:** Adam Lioz, "Buckley v. Valeo at 40" (New York: Dēmos, 2016); Ciara Torres-Spelliscy, "How Much Is an Ambassadorship? And the Tale of How Watergate Led to a Strong Foreign Corrupt Practices Act and a Weak Federal Election Campaign Act," *Chapman Law Review* 16 (2012): 71; Michael Graetz and Linda Greenhouse, *The Burger Court and the Rise of the Judicial Right* (New York: Simon & Schuster, 2016), 256; Anthony Gaughan, "The Forty-Year War on Money in Politics: Watergate, FECA, and the Future of Campaign Finance Reform," *Ohio State Law Journal* 77 (2016): 791, 795–96.

137 **Much of the money:** Lioz, "Buckley v. Valeo at 40"; Richard Hasen, *Plutocrats United* (New Haven, Conn.: Yale University Press, 2016), 19–20; Brian Mooney, "Post-Watergate Campaign Funding Reforms Fade Away," *Boston Globe,* June 21, 2012; Torres-Spelliscy, "How Much Is an Ambassadorship?"; Graetz and Greenhouse, *The Burger Court,* 256; Gaughan, "Forty-Year War on Money in Politics," 796.

137 **In a September 1973 Gallup poll:** *Buckley,* 424 U.S. 1; Torres-Spelliscy, "How Much Is an Ambassadorship?"; United States Senate, "Final Report of the Select Committee on Presidential Campaign Activities" (Washington, D.C.: U.S. Government Printing Office, 1974), 569; Gaughan, "Forty-Year War on Money in Politics," 800; Hasen, "Nine Lives of Buckley," 7; Robert E. Mutch, *Buying the Vote: A History of Campaign Finance Reform* (New York: Oxford University Press, 2014), 137.

138 **To ensure that the regulations:** Hasen, *Plutocrats United,* 19; Lioz, "Buckley v. Valeo at 40."

138 **The most important challenges:** Lioz, "Buckley v. Valeo at 40"; *Buckley v. Valeo,* 519 F.2d 821 (D.C. Cir. 1975).

138 **The liberals and civil libertarians:** Lioz, "Buckley v. Valeo at 40"; *Buckley,* 519 F.2d 821.

139 **Since it was not:** *Buckley,* 519 F.2d 821.

139 **In the same way, the D.C. Circuit held:** Jessica Levinson, "The Original Sin of Campaign Finance Law: Why Buckley v. Valeo Is Wrong," *University of Richmond Law Review* 47 (2013): 881, 891–92; *Buckley,* 519 F.2d 821; *United States v. O'Brien,* 391 U.S. 367 (1968).

139 **"It would be strange indeed":** *Buckley*, 519 F.2d 821; *Harper v. Virginia Board of Elections*, 383 U.S. 663 (1966).

140 **Ford needed to nominate:** Lesley Oelsner, "Douglas Quits Supreme Court; Ford Hails 36½-Year Service," *New York Times*, November 13, 1975; Bob Woodward and Scott Armstrong, *The Brethren: Inside the Supreme Court* (New York: Simon & Schuster, 1979), 472–76; Robert McFadden, "The President's Choice: John Paul Stevens," *New York Times*, November 29, 1975, FindLaw, s.v. "John Paul Stevens," supreme.findlaw.com/supreme_court/justices/stevens.html.

140 **Stevens was sworn in:** Oelsner, "Douglas Quits Supreme Court"; Woodward and Armstrong, *The Brethren*, 472–76; McFadden, "President's Choice: John Paul Stevens"; "John Paul Stevens," FindLaw; Joan Biskupic, *The Chief: The Life and Turbulent Times of Chief Justice John Roberts* (New York: Basic Books, 2018), 41.

140 **In less than three months:** *Buckley*, 424 U.S. 1.

140 **At the same time:** *Buckley*, 424 U.S. 1 at 5; Levinson, "Original Sin of Campaign Finance Law," 902–4; *Buckley*, 424 U.S. at 20–21.

141 **Therefore, it insisted:** Richard Hasen, "The Untold Drafting History of *Buckley v. Valeo*," *Election Law Journal* 2 (2003): 241; Heather Gerken, "The Real Problem with Citizens United: Campaign Finance, Dark Money, and Shadow Parties," *Marquette Law Review* 97 (2013): 903, 908; *Buckley*, 424 U.S. 48–49; Graetz and Greenhouse, *The Burger Court*, 259; Lioz, "Buckley v. Valeo at 40," 6, 10.

141 **It gave wealthy individuals:** *Buckley*, 424 U.S. 1; Levinson, "Original Sin of Campaign Finance Law," 902–4.

141 **In this first major campaign finance ruling:** Burt Neuborne, "Campaign Finance Reform & the Constitution: A Critical Look at Buckley v. Valeo" (New York: Brennan Center for Justice, 1998), 12; Richard Hasen, "Untold Drafting History," 241.

142 **The Court's equation of money:** *Buckley*, 424 U.S. at 16; Levinson, "Original Sin of Campaign Finance Law," 892–93; *Sorrell v. Randall*, 126 S. Ct. 2479, 2508–9 (2006); *International Society for Krishna Consciousness, Inc. v. Lee*, 505 U.S. 672 (1992); David Kairys, "Money Isn't Speech and Corporations Aren't People," *Slate*, January 22, 2010.

142 **One commentator has said:** Lioz, "Buckley v. Valeo at 40."

143 **"I thought that was a disaster":** Hasen, "Nine Lives of Buckley," 23.

143 ***Buckley* adopted, according to this critique:** Hasen, "Untold Drafting History," 244; Lioz, "Buckley v. Valeo at 40," 5; Graetz and Greenhouse, *The Burger Court*, 258; David Schultz, "The Case for a Democratic Theory of American Election Law," *University of Pennsylvania Law Review* 164 (2016): 259, 260–62.

143 **If the trend of money:** J. Skelly Wright, "Money and the Pollution of Politics: Is the First Amendment an Obstacle to Political Equality?," *Columbia Law Review* 82 (1982): 609, 645.

144 **The vote was 5–4:** *First National Bank of Boston v. Bellotti*, 435 U.S. 765, 776–77 (1978).

144 **That would come:** *Bellotti*, 435 U.S. at 776–77; Graetz and Greenhouse, *The Burger Court*, 262–63.

144 **He warned, in a memorable phrase:** *Bellotti,* 435 U.S. at 809; Graetz and Greenhouse, *The Burger Court,* 264–65; *Bellotti,* 435 U.S. at 804–5, 821.

145 **"By traveling door to door":** *United States Postal Service v. Greenburgh Civic Association,* 453 U.S. 114, 144 (1981); "Justice Upholds Law Prohibiting Unstamped Matter in Mailboxes," *New York Times,* June 26, 1981.

145 **Posters on public property:** *City Council v. Taxpayers for Vincent,* 466 U.S. 789, 803–7, 820 (1984); Stephen Loffredo, "Poverty, Democracy, and Constitutional Law," *University of Pennsylvania Law Review* 141 (1993): 1364–65.

146 **It is hard to avoid:** Loffredo, "Poverty, Democracy, and Constitutional Law," 1277, 1364.

146 **The Court in *Austin*:** Miriam Valverde, "Sen. John McCain Fought to Clean Up Money in Politics. Are We Better Off Today?" PolitiFact, August 31, 2018.

146 **It was enacted not long after:** Valverde, "Sen. John McCain Fought to Clean Up Money."

147 **The soft-money loophole allowed:** Deborah Goldberg and Ciara Torres-Spelliscy, "Pandora's Box of Corporate Money in Federal Elections Is Open Again," *Huffington Post,* June 6, 2007; Seth Waxman, "Free Speech and Campaign Reform Don't Conflict," *New York Times,* July 10, 2002.

147 **A group of plaintiffs:** *Federal Election Commission v. McConnell,* 540 U.S. 93, 205 (2003); Linda Greenhouse, "A Court Infused with Pragmatism," *New York Times,* December 12, 2003; Hasen, *Plutocrats United,* 28; Matt Ford, "Elizabeth Warren vs. the Roberts Court," *New Republic,* August 27, 2018.

147 **The main majority opinion:** *McConnell v. Federal Election Commission,* 540 U.S. 93, 205 (2003); Greenhouse, "A Court Infused"; Hasen, *Plutocrats United,* 28; Ford, "Elizabeth Warren vs. the Roberts Court."

148 **Once he arrived:** *McConnell,* 540 U.S. at 205; Greenhouse, "A Court Infused."

148 **Writing for the four liberal dissenters:** *Federal Election Commission v. Wisconsin Right to Life,* 551 U.S. 449 (2007); Marcia Coyle, *The Roberts Court: The Struggle for the Constitution* (New York: Simon & Schuster, 2013), 213–15.

149 **The lawsuit had the potential:** Phillip Rucker, "Citizens United Used 'Hillary: The Movie' to Take On McCain-Feingold," *Washington Post,* January 22, 2010; Dahlia Lithwick, "The Supreme Court Reviews Hillary: The Movie," *Slate,* March 24, 2009; Hasen, *Plutocrats United,* 18; Coyle, *Roberts Court,* 225; Michael Kang, "The End of Campaign Finance Law," *Virginia Law Review* 98 (2012): 2, 8.

149 **He told *The New York Times:*** David Kirkpatrick, "A Quest to End Spending Rules for Campaigns," *New York Times,* January 24, 2010; Jane Mayer, *Dark Money: The Hidden History of the Billionaires Behind the Rise of the Radical Right* (New York: Doubleday, 2016), 237.

149 **It was a cursory argument:** Coyle, *Roberts Court,* 224–28.

150 **It was a lot of law:** Hasen, *Plutocrats United,* 18.

150 **The justices had an intense debate:** Coyle, *Roberts Court,* 251–52.

150 **After everything that had occurred:** Coyle, *Roberts Court*, 249–50; Adam Liptak, "Justices Are Pressed for a Broad Ruling in Campaign Case," *New York Times*, September 9, 2009.

151 **As was increasingly becoming the norm:** Adam Liptak, "Justices, 5–4, Reject Corporate Spending Limit," *New York Times*, 21, 2010.

151 **He had strong corporate sympathies:** *Lawrence v. Texas*, 539 U.S. 558 (2003); *Obergefell v. Hodges*, 135 S. Ct. 2584 (2015); *Roper v. Simmons*, 543 U.S. 551 (2005); *Fisher v. University of Texas*, 36 S. Ct. 2198 (2016).

151 **Kennedy also helped:** Sam Stanton and Darrell Smith, "Justice Kennedy Loves Sacramento, but Friends Doubt He'll Retire in His Hometown," *Sacramento Bee*, June 27, 2018; Cynthia Gorney, "A Cautious Conservatism," *Washington Post*, December 14, 1987.

152 **He was right:** John A. Jenkins, *The Partisan: The Life of William Rehnquist* (New York: PublicAffairs, 2012), 232–33; Kenneth Noble, "Bork Irked by Emphasis on His Role in Watergate," *New York Times*, July 2, 1987; John C. Jeffries, *Justice Lewis F. Powell, Jr.* (New York: Charles Scribner's Sons, 1994), 555; Gorney, "A Cautious Conservatism."

152 **Political speech is:** *Citizens United v. Federal Election Commission, 558* U.S. 310 (2010); Erwin Chemerinsky, *The Case Against the Supreme Court* (New York: Penguin, 2014), 252; Coyle, *Roberts Court*, 270; Stanton and Smith, "Justice Kennedy Loves Sacramento."

152 **They "blaze[d] through our precedents":** *Citizens United*, 558 U.S. 310 (Stevens, J., dissenting); Liptak, "Justices, 5–4, Reject Corporate Spending Limit"; Coyle, *Roberts Court*, 273.

152 **Corporate "personhood" can be:** *Citizens United*, 558 U.S. 310 (Stevens, J., dissenting).

153 **With the Court's decision:** *Bellotti*, 435 U.S. at 809.

153 **It was, he said:** Robert Barnes and Dan Eggen, "Supreme Court Rejects Limits on Corporate Spending on Political Campaigns," *Washington Post*, January 22, 2010; Coyle, *Roberts Court*, 273.

153 **Unlike the Court:** Dan Eggen, "Poll: Large Majority Opposes Supreme Court's Decision on Campaign Financing," *Washington Post*, February 17, 2010; Elizabeth Hartfield, "Stephen Colbert: Thank You, God Bless You and God Bless Citizens United," ABC News, January 13, 2012.

153 **The same call went out:** Kang, "End of Campaign Finance Law," 1, 3–4; Ari Berman, "Citizens Unite Against 'Citizens United,'" *Nation*, August 16, 2010; Daniel Weiner, "*Citizens United*: Five Years Later" (New York: Brennan Center for Justice, 2015), 1; "Progress Report: Amend the Constitution," Reclaim the American Dream, reclaimtheamericandream.org/progress-amend/.

154 **There was strong support for this:** Kang, "End of Campaign Finance Law," 2; *SpeechNow.org v. Federal Election Commission*, 599 F.3d 686 (D.C. Cir. 2010); "Nine Things You Need to Know About Super PACs," Sunlight Foundation, January 31, 2012, sunlightfoundation.com/2012/01/31/nine-things-you-need-know-about-super-pacs/;

Gerken, "The Real Problem with Citizens United," 909; Mayer, *Dark Money*, 237–38; Hasen, *Plutocrats United*, 33; Coyle, *Roberts Court*, 276.

155 **On the fifth anniversary:** Karl Evers-Hillstrom, Raymond Arke, and Luke Robinson, "A Look at the Impact of Citizens United on Its 9th Anniversary" (Open Secrets, January 21, 2019); Philip Bump, "How Citizens United Is—and Isn't—to Blame for the Dark Money President Obama Hates So Much," *Washington Post*, January 21, 2015.

155 **Kagan, in dissent:** *Arizona Free Enterprise Club's Freedom Club PAC v. Bennett*, 564 U.S. 721 (2011); Nina Totenberg, "High Court Takes Another Stab at Campaign Finance," *Morning Edition*, NPR, March 28, 2011; Scott Lemieux, "The Five Worst Roberts Court Rulings," *American Prospect*, August 1, 2016; Ganesh Sitaraman, *The Crisis of the Middle Class Constitution: Why Economic Inequality Threatens Our Republic* (New York: Alfred A. Knopf, 2017), 265.

155 **The Court was raising the overall:** *McCutcheon v. Federal Election Commission*, 572 U.S. 185 (2014); Hasen, *Plutocrats United*, 35; Adam Liptak, "Supreme Court Strikes Down Overall Political Donation Cap," *New York Times*, April 2, 2014; "What Is McCutcheon v. FEC?" (New York: Dēmos, April 8, 2014).

156 **Candidates are now:** Kenneth Vogel, "Big Money Breaks Out," *Politico*, December 29, 2014; Mark McKinnon, "The 100 Rich People Who Run America," *Daily Beast*, January 5, 2015; Dan Balz, "'Sheldon Primary' Is One Reason Americans Distrust the Political System," *Washington Post*, March 28, 2014; Blair Bowie and Adam Lioz, "Billion Dollar Democracy: The Unprecedented Role of Money in the 2012 Elections" (New York: Dēmos, 2013), 10; Thomas Edsall, "Why Is It So Hard for Democracy to Deal with Inequality?," *New York Times*, February 15, 2018; Carrie Levine and Dave Levinthal, "GOP Megadonor Miriam Adelson Is Winning a Medal. But Are Republicans Losing the Political Money War?" (Center for Public Integrity, November 16, 2018).

156 **The impact the largest corporations:** "Billionaires: The Richest People in the World," *Forbes*, March 5, 2019; Sarah Hansen, "America's Largest Public Companies in 2019," *Forbes*, May 15, 2019.

157 **There were similar increases:** Weiner, "*Citizens United*: Five Years Later," 1–4.

157 **In 2018, according to the Center:** Evers-Hillstrom et al., "A Look at the Impact of Citizens United"; Weiner, "*Citizens United*: Five Years Later," 7.

157 **"I just know":** Ronald Dworkin, "The Decision That Threatens Democracy," *New York Review of Books*, May 13, 2010; Hasen, *Plutocrats United*, 47–48; Daniel Tokaji and Renata Strause, "The New Soft Money: Outside Spending in Congressional Elections" (Columbus, Ohio: Ohio State University Michael E. Moritz College of Law, 2014), moritzlaw.osu.edu/thenewsoftmoney/; Adele Stan, "Who's Behind Friedrichs?," *American Prospect*, October 29, 2015; "Billionaires: The Richest People in the World."

158 **The candidates came to pledge:** Molly Ball, "The Sheldon Adelson Suck-up Fest," *Atlantic*, April 2, 2014; Hasen, *Plutocrats United*, 1–2; Bowie and Lioz, "Billion Dollar Democracy," 10.

158 **Jolly considered the Republican:** Norah O'Donnell, "Are Members of Congress Becoming Telemarketers?," *60 Minutes*, April 24, 2016, cbsnews.com/news/60-minutes

-are-members-of-congress-becoming-telemarketers/; Cyra Master, "'60 Minutes': Fundraising Demands Turning Lawmakers into Telemarketers," *The Hill*, April 24, 2016.

158 **"It seems like I took a nap"**: O'Donnell, "Are Members of Congress"; Master, "'60 Minutes': Fundraising Demands."

159 **Minimum-wage employees**: "Top Interest Groups Giving Members of Congress, 2016 Cycle" (Open Secrets, 2019), opensecrets.org/industries/mems.php.

159 **"When a majority of citizens"**: Martin Gilens and Benjamin Page, "Testing Theories of American Politics: Elites, Interest Groups, and Average Citizens," *Perspectives on Politics* 12 (September 2014): 564, 576. For critiques of the Gilens and Page study, see Dylan Matthews, "Remember That Study Saying America Is an Oligarchy? 3 Rebuttals Say It's Wrong," *Vox*, May 9, 2016.

159 **Even President Trump has said**: Matthew Goldstein and Ben Protess, "Trump Tax Plan Silent on Carried Interest, a Boon for the Very Rich," *New York Times*, April 27, 2017; Jeff Guo, "Trump Said Hedge Funders Were 'Getting Away with Murder.' Now He Wants One to Help Run the Economy," *Washington Post*, November 30, 2016.

160 **The Legal Services Corporation**: Alec MacGillis, "The Billionaires' Loophole," *New Yorker*, March 14, 2016; Aviva Aron-Dine, "An Analysis of the 'Carried Interest' Controversy" (Center on Budget and Policy Priorities, 2007); Victor Fleischer, "How a Carried Interest Tax Could Raise $180 Billion," *New York Times*, June 5, 2015; "LSC Receives $25 Million Spending Boost from Congress," Legal Services Corporation, March 23, 2018.

160 **The bill died quietly**: MacGillis, "Billionaires' Loophole"; Michael J. de la Merced, "Schwarzman's Unfortunate War Analogy," *New York Times*, August 16, 2010; "Top Interest Groups Giving to Members of Congress, 2018 Cycle" (Open Secrets, 2019), opensecrets.org/industries/mems.php.

160 **The Center for Responsive Politics**: "Hedge Funds" (Open Secrets, 2019), opensecrets.org/industries/indus.php?ind=F2700.

160 ***Mother Jones* ran an exposé**: Stuart Silverstein, "This Is Why Your Drug Prescriptions Cost So Damn Much," *Mother Jones*, October 21, 2016.

161 **It calculated that if Part D**: Marc-André Gagnon and Sidney Wolfe, "Mirror, Mirror on the Wall: Medicare Part D Pays Needlessly High Brand-Name Drug Prices Compared with Other OECD Countries and with Government Programs" (policy brief, Carleton University School of Public Policy and Administration, Ottawa, Ontario, and Public Citizen, Washington, D.C., July 23, 2015), 2.

161 **One survey found that**: Gagnon and Wolfe, "Mirror, Mirror on the Wall," 6.

161 **In 2015, the pharmaceutical industry**: Stuart Silverstein, "Lobbyists, Campaign Cash Help Drug Industry Stymie Bid to Restrain Medicare Prescription Costs" (Open Secrets, October 16, 2016); "Top Interest Groups Giving Members of Congress, 2016 Cycle."

161 **According to an analysis**: David Kamin et al., "The Games They Will Play: Tax Games, Roadblocks, and Glitches Under the 2017 Tax Legislation," *Minnesota Law Review* 103 (2018); Noah Bierman and Brian Bennett, "Trump Notches First Big

Legislative Win with Tax-Cut Bill—But It's Far from His Populist Promises," *Los Angeles Times,* December 20, 2017; Justin Fox, "Tax Bill Will Deliver a Corporate Earnings Gusher," *Bloomberg,* December 27, 2017.

162 **General Motors had $4.3 billion:** Fox, "Tax Bill Will Deliver"; "60 Profitable Fortune 500 Companies Avoided All Federal Income Taxes in 2018" (Washington, D.C.: Institute on Taxation and Economic Policy, April 11, 2019).

162 **Of the 11,078 lobbyists registered:** Geoff West, "Tax Lobbyists Donated Millions to Members of Congress" (Open Secrets, December 22, 2017).

162 **Senator Lindsey Graham:** Cristina Marcus, "GOP Lawmaker: Donors Are Pushing Me to Get Tax Reform Done," *The Hill,* November 11, 2017; Geoff West, "Tax Lobbyists Donated Millions to Members of Congress" (Open Secrets, December 22, 2017); Rebecca Savransky, "Graham: 'Financial Contributions Will Stop' If GOP Doesn't Pass Tax Reform," *The Hill,* November 9, 2017.

163 **The high levels of opposition:** Jennifer Agiesta, "Public Opposition to Tax Bill Grows as Vote Approaches," CNN, December 19, 2017; Gilens and Page, "Testing Theories of American Politics," 564, 576; Lawrence Norden, Shyamala Ramakrishna, and Sidni Frederick, "How Citizens United Changed Politics and Shaped the Tax Bill" (New York: Brennan Center for Justice, November 14, 2017).

163 **The month after President Trump:** Jacob Pramuk and Brian Schwartz, "Sheldon Adelson Gives $30 Million in Bid to Save House GOP Majority—and Could Give More This Year," CNBC, May 10, 2018.

163 **With the role that large campaign contributions:** Historical Highest Marginal Income Tax Rates, Tax Policy Center (2018), taxpolicycenter.org/statistics/historical-highest-marginal-income-tax-rates; Amanda Becker, "Three Quarters of Americans Favor Higher Taxes for Wealthy—Reuters/Ipsos Poll," Reuters, October 11, 2017.

164 **"The result," says Nobel Prize–winning economist:** Paul Krugman, "Challenging the Oligarchy," *New York Review of Books,* December 17, 2015; "Historical Highest Marginal Income Tax Rates," Tax Policy Center.

164 **Progressive tax systems:** Facundo Alvaredo, *World Inequality Report 2018, Executive Summary* (World Inequality Lab), 6, 15, wir2018.wid.world/executive-summary.html.

165 **Support for limits:** Bradley Jones, "Most Americans Want to Limit Campaign Spending, Say Big Donors Have Greater Political Influence," Pew Research Center, May 8, 2018, pewresearch.org/fact-tank/2018/05/08/most-americans-want-to-limit-campaign-spending-say-big-donors-have-greater-political-influence/.

165 **By 2016, only 7 percent said:** "Voter Anger with Government and the 2016 Election" (Voice of the People, November 2016), 5, vop.org/wp-content/uploads/2016/11/Dissatisfaction_Report.pdf; American National Election Studies, "Is the Government Run for the Benefit of All, 1964–2012," *ANES Guide to Public Opinion and Electoral Behavior,* electionstudies.org/resources/anes-guide/top-tables/?id=59.

165 **Fully 91 percent:** Jennifer Finney Boylan, "The Year of the Angry Voter," *New York Times,* February 10, 2016; "Why Are 2016 Voters So Angry," CBS News, May 27, 2016;

Patty Culhane, "U.S. Election: The Year of the Angry Voter," Al Jazeera, April 27, 2016; "Voter Anger with Government and the 2016 Election," Voice of the People, 5, 17.

CHAPTER FIVE: DEMOCRACY

167 **The election contest:** David Margolick, "The Path to Florida," *Vanity Fair,* March 19, 2014; *Encyclopædia Britannica,* s.v. "Bush v. Gore."

167 **The Supreme Court halted the recount:** Margolick, "Path to Florida"; *Encyclopædia Britannica,* s.v. "Bush v. Gore."

168 **If anyone was going to break:** *Brown v. Board of Education,* 347 U.S. 483 (1954); *United States v. Nixon,* 418 U.S. 683 (1974).

168 **"I mean, it couldn't be clearer":** Lani Guinier, "Supreme Democracy: Bush v. Gore Redux," *Loyola University Chicago Law Journal* 34 (2002): 45; Lorraine Minnite, *The Myth of Voter Fraud* (Ithaca, N.Y.: Cornell University Press, 2017) 92.

168 **The decision handed Bush:** Guinier, "Supreme Democracy," 45; Minnite, *Myth of Voter Fraud,* 92; Linda Greenhouse, "Bush Prevails; by Single Vote, Justices End Recount, Blocking Gore After 5-Week Struggle," *New York Times,* December 13, 2000; Joan Biskupic, *The Chief: The Life and Turbulent Times of Chief Justice John Roberts* (New York: Basic Books, 2018), 127–28.

168 **There was another point of continuity:** Jack Balkin, "Bush v. Gore and the Boundary Between Law and Politics," *Yale Law Journal* 110 (2001): 1407, 1410.

169 **That disparate treatment:** Greenhouse, "Bush Prevails"; Mark Brodin, "Bush v. Gore: The Worst (or at Least Second-to-the-Worst) Supreme Court Decision Ever," *Nevada Law Journal* 12 (2012): 563, 565–66.

169 **The right to uniform:** Jed Rubenfeld, "Not as Bad as Plessy. Worse," in *Bush v. Gore: The Question of Legitimacy,* ed. Bruce Ackerman (New Haven, Conn.: Yale Scholarship Online, 2013), 21; Owen Fiss, "The Fallibility of Reason," in *Bush v. Gore: The Question of Legitimacy,* ed. Bruce Ackerman (New Haven, Conn.: Yale Scholarship Online, 2013), 89.

170 **One Harvard law professor:** John A. Jenkins, *The Partisan: The Life of William Rehnquist* (New York: PublicAffairs, 2012), 250; Alan Dershowitz, *Supreme Injustice: How the High Court Hijacked Election 2000* (New York: Oxford University Press, 2001), 81–82.

170 **To the decision's critics:** *Bush v. Gore,* 531 U.S. 98, 109 (2000); Chad Flanders, "Bush v. Gore as Precedent" (Student Scholarship Papers, Yale Law School, March 2007), digitalcommons.law.yale.edu/student_papers/36; *United States v. Virginia,* 518 U.S. 515 (1996) (Scalia, J., dissenting).

170 **Souter and Breyer agreed:** Greenhouse, "Bush Prevails."

171 **While the other dissenters:** *Bush,* 531 U.S. at 128–29, 144, 158; Greenhouse, "Bush Prevails."

171 **"When I was faced with a gross":** Rubenfeld, "Not as Bad as Plessy," 36; Margaret Jane Radin, "Can the Rule of Law Survive Bush v. Gore?," in *Bush v. Gore: The*

Question of Legitimacy, ed. Bruce Ackerman (New Haven, Conn.: Yale Scholarship Online, 2013), 125; Jonathan Schell, "Letter from Ground Zero," *Nation*, July 15, 2004.

171 **Gore, speaking from his vice presidential:** David Sanger, "The 43rd President: The Texas Governor; Bush Pledges to Be President for 'One Nation,' Not One Party; Gore, Conceding, Urges Unity," *New York Times*, December 14, 2000.

172 **When Warren was asked:** *Baker v. Carr*, 369 U.S. 186 (1962); *Reynolds v. Sims*, 377 U.S. 533 (1964); Robert McKay, "Mr. Justice Brennan, Baker v. Carr, and the Judicial Function," *Rutgers-Camden Law Journal* 4 (1972).

173 **In the same year:** *South Carolina v. Katzenbach*, 383 U.S. 301 (1966); *Harper v. Virginia Board of Elections*, 383 U.S. 663 (1966); Joshua Houston, "A Right to Preserve All Others: Reflections on the Poll Tax," Texas Interfaith Center for Public Policy, 2015.

173 **"It has asserted":** Samuel Issacharoff, "The Court in the Crossfire," *New York Times*, December 14, 2000; Richard Hasen, "Bush v. Gore and the Future of Equal Protection Law in Elections," *Florida State University Law Review* 29 (2001): 377, 380–81, 381n17.

174 ***Bush v. Gore* cannot be taken seriously:** Matt Vasilogambros, "Voting Lines Are Shorter—But Mostly for Whites," *Stateline*, Pew Charitable Trusts, February 15, 2018; Hasen, "Bush v. Gore and the Future of Equal Protection," 386–90; Fatima Hussein, "Republicans Limiting Early Voting in Marion County, Letting It Bloom in Suburbs," *Indianapolis Star*, August 10, 2017.

174 **Lower federal courts:** Josh Blackmun, "Justice Thomas Cites the Bush v. Gore 'Unprecedent' in Arizona Dissent," *Josh Blackmun's Blog*, June 17, 2013; Adam Liptak, "Bush v. Gore Set to Outlast Its Beneficiary," *New York Times*, December 22, 2008.

174 **Its real message, she said:** Guinier, "Supreme Democracy," 23–26, 32, 45, 48; Lani Guinier biography, Harvard Law School, hls.harvard.edu/faculty/directory/10344/Guinier.

175 **Under pressure from Karl Rove:** Justin Driver, "Rules, the New Standards: Partisan Gerrymandering and Judicial Manageability After Vieth v. Jubelirer," *George Washington Law Review* 73 (2005): 1166, 1170; J. Gerald Herbert and Marina Jenkins, "The Need for State Redistricting Reform to Rein in Partisan Gerrymandering," *Yale Law & Policy Review* 29 (2010): 543, 550n39.

175 **Although there were more:** Driver, "Rules, the New Standards," 1166, 1170; Herbert and Jenkins, "Need for State Redistricting Reform," 543, 550n39.

176 **Kennedy, who provided:** *Vieth v. Jubelirer*, 541 U.S. 267 (2004).

176 **Stevens did not invoke:** *Bush*, 531 U.S. 98 (2000).

176 **As voting data became:** Laura Royden, Michael Li, and Yurij Rudensky, *Extreme Gerrymandering & the 2018 Midterm* (New York: Brennan Center for Justice, 2018).

176 **After all the buildup:** Ariane de Vogue, "Anthony Kennedy Doesn't Tip Hand in Gerrymandering Case," CNN, October 4, 2017; *Gill v. Whitford*, 138 S. Ct. 1916 (2018), and *Benisek v. Lamone*, 138 S. Ct. 1942 (2018).

177 **His confirmation fulfilled:** Michael Shear, "Supreme Court Justice Anthony Kennedy Will Retire," *New York Times*, June 27, 2018; Mark Landler and Maggie Haberman, "Brett Kavanaugh Is Trump's Pick for Supreme Court," *New York Times*, July

9, 2018; Sheryl Gay Stolberg, "Kavanaugh Is Sworn In After Close Confirmation Vote in Senate," *New York Times*, October 6, 2018.

177 **In Maryland, Democrats:** Adam Liptak, "Supreme Court Bars Challenges to Partisan Gerrymandering," *New York Times*, June 27, 2019; *Rucho v. Common Cause*, No. 18-422 (U.S. June 27, 2019); Matt Ford, "A Partisan Supreme Court Upholds Partisan Power," *New Republic*, June 27, 2019.

177 **"There are no legal standards":** Liptak, "Supreme Court Bars Challenges"; *Rucho*, No. 18-422 (U.S. June 27, 2019).

178 **Once again, the Court:** *Rucho*, No. 18-422 (U.S. June 27, 2019); Adam Liptak, "Supreme Court Avoids an Answer on Partisan Gerrymandering," *New York Times*, June 18, 2018; *Gill*, 138 S. Ct. 1916 (2018); *Benisek*, 138 S. Ct. 1942 (2018); *Gill v. Whitford*, No. 16-1161 (U.S. Supreme Court, June 18, 2018); Guinier, "Supreme Democracy," 26–27.

178 **Once again, the "robust and engaged citizens":** *Crawford v. Marion County Election Board*, 553 U.S. 181 (2008).

179 **According to the same study:** "Citizens Without Proof: A Survey of Americans' Possession of Documentary Proof of Citizenship and Photo Identification" (New York: Brennan Center for Justice, 2006).

179 **One aide to a Republican state legislator:** John Nichols, "ALEC Exposed: Rigging Elections," *Nation*, August 1–8, 2011; Edward Foley, "Crawford v. Marion County Election Board: Voter ID, 5–4? If So, So What?," *Election Law Journal* 7 (2008): 63, 64; Michael Wines, "Some Republicans Acknowledge Leveraging Voter ID Laws for Political Gain," *New York Times*, September 16, 2016.

180 **Fees for birth certificates:** Foley, "Crawford v. Marion County Election Board," 64–67; Linda Greenhouse, "In a 6-to-3 Vote, Justices Uphold a Voter ID Law," *New York Times*, April 29, 2008; Brief for Petitioner, *Crawford v. Marion County Election Board*, No. 07-21, April 28, 2008.

180 **One study released:** David Schultz, "Less Than Fundamental: The Myth of Voter Fraud and the Coming of the Second Great Disenfranchisement," *William Mitchell Law Review* 34 (2008): 483, 486; Justin Levitt, "The Truth About Voter Fraud" (New York: Brennan Center for Justice, 2007); John Ahlquist, Kenneth Mayer, and Simon Jackman, "Alien Abduction and Voter Impersonation in the 2012 U.S. General Election: Evidence from a Survey List Experiment," *Election Law Journal* 13 (2014): 460.

180 **Stevens left open the possibility:** *Crawford v. Marion County Election Board*, 553 U.S. 181 (2008); *Encyclopædia Britannica*, s.v. "John Paul Stevens," britannica.com/biography/John-Paul-Stevens.

180 **In both circumstances:** *Crawford*, 553 U.S. 181.

181 **"From all accounts":** Associated Press, "Nuns with Dated ID Turned Away at Ind. Polls," NBCNews.com, May 6, 2008.

181 **Some of the laws are stricter:** Manny Fernandez, "Texas' Voter ID Law Does Not Discriminate and Can Stand, Appeals Panel Rules," *New York Times*, April 27, 2018; "Voter ID History," National Conference of State Legislatures, ncsl.org/research/elections-and-campaigns/voter-id-history.aspx.

181 **These studies confirm:** Michael Wines, "Wisconsin Strict ID Law Discouraged Voters, Study Finds," *New York Times,* September 25, 2017.

182 **Indiana's voter ID law:** *Crawford,* 553 U.S. 181; John Schwartz, "Judge in Landmark Case Disavows Support for Voter ID," *New York Times,* October 15, 2013; Robert Barnes, "Stevens Says Supreme Court Decision on Voter ID Was Correct, but Maybe Not Right," *Washington Post,* May 15, 2016.

182 **President Johnson signed it:** E. W. Kenworthy, "Johnson Signs Voting Rights Bill, Orders Immediate Enforcement; 4 Suits Will Challenge Poll Tax," *New York Times,* August 7, 1965.

182 **It brought most of the South:** Jon Greenbaum, Alan Martinson, and Sonia Gill, "*Shelby County v. Holder*: When the Rational Becomes Irrational," *Howard Law Journal* 57, no. 3 (2014): 811, 818–19.

183 **President Reagan signed:** Greenbaum, Martinson, and Gill, "*Shelby County v. Holder,*" 813, 823, 835, 867.

183 **The reauthorization passed:** Greenbaum, Martinson, and Gill, "*Shelby County v. Holder,*" 813; Associated Press, "Bush Signs Voting Rights Act Extension," July 27, 2006.

183 **If the Court struck down:** *Shelby County v. Holder,* 570 U.S. 529 (2013).

183 **Section 4 failed to meet:** *Shelby County,* 570 U.S. 529; Martha McCluskey, "Toward a Fundamental Right to Evade Law? The Rule of Power in Shelby County and State Farm," *Berkeley Journal of African-American Law & Policy* 16 (2015): 216, 217; "How Did We Get the Principle of Equal State Sovereignty (in the Shelby County Case)?," *Constitutional Law Prof Blog,* June 28, 2013.

184 **He was not impressed:** *Shelby County,* 570 U.S. 529; Greenbaum, Martinson, and Gill, "*Shelby County v. Holder,*" 855, 865; Nicole Flatow and Ian Millhiser, "Scalia: Voting Rights Act Is 'Perpetuation of Racial Entitlement,'" *ThinkProgress,* February 27, 2013.

184 **The senators who heard Roberts:** U.S. Constitution, amendment XV; Greenbaum, Martinson, and Gill, "*Shelby County v. Holder,*" 844; *Blodgett v. Holden,* 275 U.S. 142 (1927).

185 **Posner, a Reagan nominee:** Greenbaum, Martinson, and Gill, "*Shelby County v. Holder,*" 852–54; *Shelby County,* 570 U.S. 529; Eric Posner, "Supreme Court 2013: The Year in Review," *Slate,* June 26, 2013.

185 **"Throwing out preclearance":** *Shelby County,* 570 U.S. 529.

185 **The Department of Justice ordered Kilmichael:** *Shelby County,* 570 U.S. 529.

186 **He promised that his administration:** "John Lewis and Others React to the Supreme Court's Voting Rights Act Ruling," *Washington Post,* June 25, 2013.

186 **There was a clear racial pattern:** Maggie Astor, "Seven Ways Alabama Has Made It Harder to Vote," *New York Times,* June 23, 2018.

186 **Reducing the number of polling places:** Matt Vasilogambros, "Polling Places Remain a Target Ahead of November Elections," Pew Charitable Trusts Stateline, September 4, 2018.

187 **The U.S. Commission on Civil Rights:** Ari Berman, "How the 2000 Election in Florida Led to a New Wave of Voter Disenfranchisement," *Nation,* July 28, 2015; Katie Sanders, "Florida Voters Mistakenly Purged in 2000," *Tampa Bay Times,* June 15, 2012.

187 **It later turned out:** Jonathan Brater, "Voter Purges: The Risks in 2018" (New York: Brennan Center for Justice, 2018).

187 **It also reported that:** Brater, "Voter Purges: The Risks in 2018"; Andy Sullivan and Grant Smith, "Use It or Lose It: Occasional Ohio Voters May Be Shut Out in November," Reuters, June 2, 2016; Kevin Morris, "Voter Purge Rates Remain High, Analysis Finds," Brennan Center for Justice, August 1, 2019.

188 **If they did not respond:** Adam Liptak, "Supreme Court Upholds Health Care Law, 5–4, in Victory for Obama," *New York Times,* June 28, 2012; *Husted v. A. Philip Randolph Institute,* No. 16-980 (U.S. June 11, 2018); Amelia Thomson-DeVeaux, "This Ohio Case Could Change Who Gets Purged from the Rolls," FiveThirtyEight, January 10, 2018.

188 **Election officials said they sent:** Adam Liptak, "Supreme Court Upholds Ohio's Purge of Voting Rolls," *New York Times,* June 11, 2018; *Husted,* No. 16-980 (U.S. June 11, 2018); Thomson-DeVeaux, "This Ohio Case Could Change Who Gets Purged"; Pete Williams, "Purged from Ohio's Voter Rolls, This Navy Vet Has His Day at the Supreme Court," NBC.com, January 10, 2018.

188 **The Sixth Circuit said Ohio's:** Liptak, "Supreme Court Upholds Ohio's Purge"; *Husted,* No. 16-680 (U.S. June 11, 2018).

188 **It did not apply to the Ohio purge:** Liptak, "Supreme Court Upholds Ohio's Purge"; *Husted,* No. 16-680 (U.S. June 11, 2018).

188 **Sotomayor, in a solo dissent:** Richard Hasen, "Sonia Sotomayor's Dissent in the Big Voter-Purge Case Points to How the Law Might Still Be Struck Down," *Slate,* June 11, 2018; *Husted,* No. 16-680 (U.S. June 11, 2018); Liptak, "Supreme Court Upholds Ohio's Purge"; *Husted,* No. 16-680 (U.S. June 11, 2018).

189 **A head of the Justice Department:** Veronica Stracqualursi, "Battleground Breakdown: Where Ohio Stands in the 2016 Presidential Race," ABC News, October 17, 2016; Judicial Watch, "Judicial Watch Statement on Supreme Court Decision Upholding Ohio Efforts to Maintain Voter Rolls," June 11, 2018; Public Interest Legal Foundation, "J. Christian Adams Praises SCOTUS Decision on Ohio Voter List Maintenance Procedures," June 11, 2018; Ari Berman, "Trump Administration on the Right to Vote: Use It Or Lose It," *Mother Jones,* August 8, 2017; Eliza Newlin Carney, "The GOP's Weapon of Suppression: Voter Purges," *American Prospect,* December 15, 2017.

189 **In her concession speech:** Sullivan and Smith, "Use It or Lose It"; Brooke Seipel, "Trump's Victory Margin Smaller Than Total Stein Votes in Key Swing States," *The Hill,* December 1, 2016; Richard Fausset, "How Voting Became a Central Issue in the Georgia Governor's Race," *New York Times,* November 3, 2018; Jessica Taylor, "Georgia's Stacey Abrams Admits Defeat, Says Kemp Used 'Deliberate' Suppression to

Win," NPR, November 16, 2018; Johnny Kauffmann, "Georgia Law Allows Tens of Thousands to Be Wiped from Voter Rolls," NPR, October 22, 2018.

190 **"They went after minority counties":** Jonathan Brater et al., "Purges: A Growing Threat to the Right to Vote" (New York: Brennan Center for Justice, 2018); Morris, "Voter Purge Rates."

190 **It was the right advice:** Kevin Morris and Myrna Perez, "Florida, Georgia, North Carolina Still Purging Voters at High Rates" (New York: Brennan Center for Justice, October 1, 2018.)

191 **When voting does not matter:** Thomas Wolf and Peter Miller, "How Gerrymandering Kept Democrats from Winning Even More Seats Tuesday," *Washington Post*, November 8, 2018; Alan Blinder, "New Election Ordered in North Carolina Race at Center of Fraud Inquiry," *New York Times*, February 21, 2019.

191 **Not all of that structural:** David Lieb, "GOP Won More Seats in 2018 Than Suggested by Vote Share," Associated Press, March 21, 2019.

191 **Weakening the Voting Rights Act:** Vann R. Newkirk II, "How Voter ID Laws Discriminate," *Atlantic*, February 18, 2017.

192 **There is every reason to believe:** Michele E. Gilman, "A Court for the One Percent, *Utah Law Review* 2 (2014): 434, citing Larry Bartels, *Unequal Democracy* (Princeton, N.J.: Princeton University Press, 2018), 3–4, 37.

CHAPTER SIX: WORKERS

194 **Ledbetter, who was concerned:** Lilly Ledbetter, *Grace and Grit: My Fight for Equal Pay and Fairness at Goodyear and Beyond* (New York: Three Rivers Press, 2012), 15, 18, 22–3, 25, 82; Don Noble, "'Grace and Grit' Details Lilly Ledbetter's Fight for Equality," *Tuscaloosa News*, March 11, 2012; "Lilly Ledbetter's Fight for Equal Pay Brings Her Back to Supreme Court," *Birmingham News*, September 1, 2018; *Ledbetter v. Goodyear Tire & Rubber Co.*, 550 U.S. 618 (2007).

194 **When the going got rough:** Ledbetter, *Grace and Grit*, 15, 22–23, 25, 41–42, 44, 91, 96, 98, 110, 117, 154; Noble, "'Grace and Grit.'"

194 **"The way she said it":** Ledbetter, *Grace and Grit*, 14–16, 222; Noble, "'Grace and Grit'"; "Lilly Ledbetter's Fight for Equal Pay," *Birmingham News; Ledbetter*, 550 U.S. 618.

195 **"It was clear that Goodyear":** Ledbetter, *Grace and Grit*, 222; Noble, "'Grace and Grit'"; "Lilly Ledbetter's Fight for Equal Pay," *Birmingham News; Ledbetter*, 550 U.S. 618.

195 **When the case went to trial:** *Ledbetter*, 550 U.S. 618; Linda Greenhouse, "Justices' Ruling Limits Lawsuits on Pay Disparity," *New York Times*, May 30, 2007; Steven Greenhouse, "Experts Say Decision on Pay Reorders Legal Landscape," *New York Times*, May 30, 2007; Tessa Stuart, "Meet the Woman Trying to Smash the Gender Pay Gap," *Rolling Stone*, February 1, 2016.

195 **It did not matter:** *Ledbetter*, 550 U.S. 618; Erwin Chemerinsky, *The Case Against the Supreme Court* (New York: Penguin, 2014), 186.

195 **She also complained:** *Ledbetter*, 550 U.S. 618 (Ginsburg, J., dissenting).

196 **Ledbetter had no way to know:** *Ledbetter,* 550 U.S. 618 (Ginsburg, J., dissenting).
196 **"Once again," she wrote:** *Ledbetter,* 550 U.S. 618 (Ginsburg, J., dissenting).
196 **Hillary Clinton, who was beginning:** Patrick Healy, "Campaign as Trailblazer, by Proxy and Association," *New York Times,* June 12, 2007; Caroline Frederickson, "In Favor of Ledbetter Fair Pay Act," *The Hill,* June 27, 2007; Noble, "'Grace and Grit.'"
196 **Judges would go on:** Robert Pear, "Justices' Ruling in Discrimination Case May Draw Quick Action by Obama," *New York Times,* January 4, 2009; Greenhouse, "Experts Say Decision on Pay."
197 **With Ledbetter looking on:** Robert Pear, "Congress Relaxes Rules on Suits over Pay Inequity," *New York Times,* January 27, 2009; Sheryl Gay Stolberg, "Obama Signs Equal-Pay Legislation," *New York Times,* January 29, 2009.
197 **Congress had used:** David J. Garrow, "Toward a Definitive History of Griggs v. Duke Power Co.," *Vanderbilt Law Review* 67 (2014): 197, 200–1; Robert Belton, "Title VII at Forty: A Brief Look at the Birth, Death, and Resurrection of the Disparate Impact Theory of Discrimination," *Hofstra Labor & Employment Law Journal* 22 (2005): 431, 433.
198 **Although they were formally:** Garrow, "Toward a Definitive History of Griggs," 209–13, 18; Deborah Widiss, "Griggs at Midlife," *Michigan Law Review* 113 (2015): 993, 998; *Griggs v. Duke Power Co.,* 401 U.S. 424 (1971).
198 **the civil rights lawyers:** Belton, "Title VII at Forty," 438–40.
198 **The ruling was a clear message:** *Griggs,* 401 U.S. 424; Linda Greenhouse, "Job Ruling Makes It Clear: Court Has Shifted to the Right," *New York Times,* June 7, 1989.
199 **"If an employment practice":** *Griggs,* 401 U.S. 424; Greenhouse, "Job Ruling Makes It Clear."
199 ***Griggs* was quickly recognized:** Garrow, "Toward a Definitive History of Griggs," 199, 234; Widiss, "Griggs at Midlife," 993.
199 ***The New York Times* called *Griggs*:** Melissa Hart, "From Wards Cove to Ricci: Struggling Against the 'Built-In Headwinds' of a Skeptical Court," *Wake Forest Law Review* 46 (2011): 261, 263; Greenhouse, "Job Ruling Makes It Clear."
199 **Even as the Court:** Linda Greenhouse, "The 'Quota' Dispute," *New York Times,* July 21, 1990.
200 **With its holding, the Court gave women:** *Meritor Savings Bank v. Vinson,* 477 U.S. 57 (1986).
200 **They pointed to practices:** *Wards Cove Packing Co. v. Atonio,* 490 U.S. 642 (1989).
201 **It was difficult:** Hart, "From Wards Cove to Ricci," 267–68.
201 **"One wonders," he concluded:** Hart, "From Wards Cove to Ricci," 268; *Wards Cove,* 490 U.S. 642 (1989).
201 **In a third case:** Linda Greenhouse, "A Changed Court Revises Rules on Civil Rights," *New York Times,* June 18, 1989.
201 **The paper noted:** Greenhouse, "A Changed Court Revises Rules."
202 **The Court, which had once:** Adam Clymer, "Civil Rights Bill Is Passed by House," *New York Times,* November 8, 1991; Adam Clymer, "Senate Approves Civil Rights

Bill, 95–5," *New York Times*, October 31, 1991; Donald R. Livingston, "The Civil Rights Act of 1991 and EEOC Enforcement," *Stetson Law Review* 23 (1993): 53–54.

202 **One of the most prominent:** Michael Selmi, "The Evolution of Employment Discrimination Law: Changed Doctrine for Changed Social Conditions," *Wisconsin Law Review* 2014, no. 5: 953; Stolberg, "Obama Signs Equal-Pay Legislation."

202 **He married his high school sweetheart:** *Workplace Fairness: Has the Supreme Court Misinterpreted Laws Designed to Protect American Workers? Hearing Before the Senate Committee on the Judiciary,* 111th Cong. (2009) (statement of Jack Gross), judiciary.senate.gov/download/testimony-of-grosspdf.

203 **"They claimed that this":** *Workplace Fairness* (statement of Jack Gross); Yuki Noguchi, "Age Discrimination Suits Jump, but Wins Are Elusive," *Morning Edition*, NPR, February 16, 2012.

203 **The St. Louis–based:** *Gross v. FBL Financial Services,* Inc., 557 U.S. 167.

203 **One barred negative employment actions:** *Gross*, 557 U.S. 167; Brian Noonan, "The Impact of Gross v. FBL Financial Services, Inc. and the Meaning of the But-For Requirement," *Suffolk University Law Review* 43 (2010): 921, 923.

203 **The Court had engaged:** *Gross*, 557 U.S. 167 (Stevens, J., dissenting) (internal quotation omitted).

204 **Gross said his friends:** *Workplace Fairness* (statement of Jack Gross); Arthur Delaney, "Chuck Grassley, Tom Harkin Strike Back Against Supreme Court on Age Discrimination," *Huffington Post*, March 13, 2012.

204 **Congress has still not enacted:** *Workplace Fairness* (statement of Jack Gross); Robert Weiner and Daniel Khan, "Iowa Case Shows Age Discrimination Persists, Despite Law," *Des Moines Register*, May 11, 2016.

204 **They could also see:** *Wal-Mart Stores, Inc. v. Dukes*, 564 U.S. 338 (2011).

205 **Kwapnoski was finally promoted:** Jami Floyd, "Women Accuse Wal-Mart of Bias," ABC News, June 19, 2019; "Christine Kwapnoski," Wal-Mart Class Website, March 29, 2011, walmartclass.com/staticdata/mar29brief/11Christine%20Kwapnoski.329.pdf; Michael Corkery, "Betty Dukes, Greeter Whose Walmart Lawsuit Went to Supreme Court, Dies at 67," *New York Times*, July 18, 2017; First Amended Complaint, *Dukes v. Wal-Mart Stores*, No. C-01-2252 (N.D. Cal. 2001).

205 **The Court made it clear:** *Wal-Mart*, 564 U.S. 338; Suzette Malveaux, "How Goliath Won: The Future Implications of Dukes v. Wal-Mart," *Northwestern University Law Review Colloquy* 106 (2011): 34, 38–39.

205 **The dissenters would have:** *Wal-Mart*, 564 U.S. 338; Adam Liptak, "Justices Rule for Wal-Mart in Class-Action Bias Case," *New York Times*, June 20, 2011.

206 **Vance also complained:** *Vance v. Ball State University*, 570 U.S. 421 (2013); Brief for Petitioner at 6–7, *Vance*, 570 U.S. 421 (2013) (No. 11-556); "Title VII—Employer Liability for Supervisor Harassment—Vance v. Ball State University," *Harvard Law Review* 127 (2013): 398–99.

206 **In her lawsuit, Vance:** *Vance*, 570 U.S. 421.

206 **Controlling a subordinate's:** *Vance*, 570 U.S. 421.

207 **It was a striking thing:** *Vance*, 570 U.S. 421.

207 **Much of this early suppression:** Elisabeth Israels Perry and Karen Manners Smith, *The Gilded Age and Progressive Era: A Student Companion* (New York: Oxford University Press, 2006), 138; *Encyclopaedia Britannica*, s.v. "Ludlow Massacre."

207 **In the protective environment:** Julia Wolfe and John Schmitt, "A Profile of Union Workers in State and Local Government," Economic Policy Institute, June 7, 2018; Kate Andrias, "The New Labor Law," *Yale Law Journal* 126 (2016): 1; "Union Members—2018," Bureau of Labor Statistics, January 18, 2019, bls.gov/news.release/union2.nro.htm.

208 **As one commenter said:** Jake Rosenfeld, Patrick Denice, and Jennifer Laird, "Union Decline Lowers Wages of Non-Union Workers," Economic Policy Institute, August 30, 2016; Andrias, "New Labor Law," 1; Robert Gebelhoff, "Why Are Unions in the U.S. So Weak," *Washington Post*, August 1, 2016.

208 **The labor market has changed:** Drew DeSilver, "Job Categories Where Union Membership Has Fallen Off Most," Pew Research Center, April 27, 2015; Dan Kopf, "Union Membership in the US Keeps On Falling, Like Almost Everywhere Else."

208 **The firings killed off:** "Right to Work States," National Right to Work Legal Defense Foundation, 2018, nrtw.org/right-to-work-states/; Joseph McCartin, "The Strike That Busted Unions," *New York Times*, August 2, 2011; Andrew Glass, "Reagan Fires 11,000 Striking Air Traffic Controllers Aug. 5, 1981," *Politico*, August 5, 2008; Michael Graetz and Linda Greenhouse, *The Burger Court and the Rise of the Judicial Right* (New York: Simon & Schuster, 2016), 271–72.

209 **The Mackay decision was a "judicial de-radicalization":** *NLRB v. Mackay Radio & Telegraph Co.*, 304 U.S. 333 (1938); Julius Getman and Thomas Kohler, "The Story of NLRB v. Mackay Radio & Telegraph Co.: The High Cost of Solidarity," in *Labor Law Stories*, ed. Laura J. Cooper and Catherine L. Fisk (New York: Foundation Press, 2005), 13; Julius Getman, "The National Labor Relations Act: What Went Wrong; Can We Fix It?," *Boston College Law Review* 45 (2003): 125, 128.

209 **Congress had put language:** James Gray Pope, "How Americans Lost the Right to Strike, and Other Tales," *Michigan Law Review* 103 (2004): 518, 527–28, 528n51; Eileen Silverstein, "If You Can't Beat 'Em, Learn to Lose, but Never Join Them," *Connecticut Law Review* 30 (1998): 1371, 1373.

209 **The Mackay doctrine has:** Pope, "How Americans Lost the Right."

209 **In a case pitting a union:** *NLRB v. Gissel Packing Co.*, 395 U.S. 575 (1969); *NLRB v. Allis-Chalmers Manufacturing Co.*, 338 U.S. 175, 180 (1967); Lee Modjeska, "Labor and the Warren Court," *Industrial Relations Law Journal* 8 (1986): 479, 480, 485–87.

210 **The Court held:** *Lechmere, Inc. v. NLRB*, 502 U.S. 527 (1992); Ellen Dannin, *Taking Back the Workers' Law: How to Fight the Assault on Labor Rights* (Ithaca, N.Y.: Cornell University Press, 2008), 12; Pope, "How Americans Lost the Right," 518, 540, 541.

210 **He was confirmed:** William Welch, "Thomas Presided over Shift in Policy at EEOC, Records Show," Associated Press, July 25, 1991; Joel Handler, letter to the editor, *New York Times*, July 23, 1991.

210 **Thomas served briefly:** Welch, "Thomas Presided over Shift."

211 **In speaking to a group:** Handler, letter to the editor, *New York Times.*

211 **Organized labor came out:** Jagan Ranjan, "The Politicization of Clarence Thomas," *Michigan Law Review* 101 (2003): 2084, 2091; Steven Holmes, "N.A.A.C.P. and Top Labor Unite to Oppose Thomas," *New York Times,* August 1, 1991.

211 **In an editorial:** "The Youngest, Cruelest Justice," *New York Times,* February 27, 1992.

212 **If they could not reach:** *Lechmere, Inc.*, 502 U.S. 527.

212 **A critic writing:** Katherine Van Wezel Stone, "The Feeble Strength of One," *American Prospect,* Summer 1993.

212 **He was, however:** Julius Getman, "The NLRB: What Went Wrong and Should We Try to Fix It?," *Emory Law Journal* 64 (2015): 1495, 1500.

213 **For the government to force:** *Abood v. Detroit Board of Education,* 431 U.S. 209 (1977).

213 **If enough workers:** Benjamin Sachs, "Agency Fees and the First Amendment," *Harvard Law Review* 131 (2018): 1046.

214 **Since *Abood* was:** *Abood,* 431 U.S. at 211, 222 (1977); *Chicago Teachers Union v. Hudson,* 475 U.S. 292 (1986).

214 **By 2017, public-sector unions:** Wolfe and Schmitt, "A Profile of Union Workers."

214 **"Now there's a bull's-eye":** Steven Greenhouse, "Strained States Turning to Laws to Curb Labor Unions," *New York Times,* January 3, 2011; Steven Greenhouse, "Wisconsin's Legacy for Unions," *New York Times,* February 22, 2014; Susan Guyett, "Indiana Becomes 23rd 'Right to Work' State," Reuters, February 1, 2012.

214 **All five of the conservative justices:** *Knox v. Service Employees,* 567 U.S. 298 (2012); Adam Liptak, "Unions Come into the Justices' Cross Hairs, Again," *New York Times,* June 12, 2017; A. G. Sulzberger, "Union Bill Is Law, but Debate Is Far from Over," *New York Times,* March 11, 2011; "Leading Cases: Constitutional Law—Freedom of Speech—Compelled Subsidization," *Harvard Law Review* 126 (2012): 186.

215 **The Economic Policy Institute, which:** Celine McNicholas et al., "Janus and Fair Share Feed," Economic Policy Institute, February 21, 2018.

215 **It appeared that Alito:** Harold Meyerson, "Supreme Court Rules Disadvantaged Workers Should Be Disadvantaged Some More," *American Prospect,* June 30, 2014; *Harris v. Quinn,* 573 U.S. 616 (2014).

216 **In a few years, an essay:** *Harris,* 573 U.S. 616; "Supreme Court Strikes Blow Against Government Bullies," National Right to Work Committee, July 3, 2014, nrtwc.org/supreme-court-strikes-blow-government-bullies; Brianne Gorod, "Sam Alito: The Court's Most Consistent Conservative," *Yale Law Journal* 126 (January 24, 2017).

216 **Public-sector agency fees:** Adam Liptak, "Issues and Implications in Supreme Court's Public Union Case," *New York Times,* January 11, 2016; Adam Liptak, "Victory for Unions as Supreme Court, Scalia Gone, Ties 4–4," *New York Times,* March 29, 2016; Adele Stan, "Who's Behind Friedrichs?," *American Prospect,* October 29, 2015; Meyerson, "Supreme Court Rules Disadvantaged Workers."

216 **He was a liberal:** Sheryl Gay Stolberg and Adam Liptak, "Merrick Garland's Path to Nomination Marked by Deference, with Limits," *New York Times,* March 16, 2016.

216 **Much of the money:** Stolberg and Liptak, "Merrick Garland's Path to Nomination"; Burgess Everett, "Conservative Group Launches SCOTUS Ad to Pressure Dems," *Politico,* June 27, 2018; Margaret Sessa-Hawkins and Andrew Perez, "Dark Money Group Received Massive Donations in Fight Against Obama's Supreme Court Nominee," Maplight, October 24, 2017.

217 **In 2019, McConnell made it clear:** Lauren Carroll, "Mitch McConnell Exaggerates 'Tradition' of Not Confirming Election Year Supreme Court Nominees," PolitiFact, March 22, 2016; Daniel Victor, "McConnell Says Republicans Would Fill a Supreme Court Vacancy in 2020, Drawing Claims of Hypocrisy," *New York Times,* May 29, 2019.

217 **It would be Gorsuch, not Garland:** Adam Liptak and Matt Flegenheimer, "Neil Gorsuch Confirmed by Senate as Supreme Court Justice," *New York Times,* April 7, 2017; Douglas Martin, "Anne Gorsuch Burford, 62, Reagan E.P.A. Chief, Dies," *New York Times,* July 22, 2004; Adam Liptak et al., "In Fall of Gorsuch's Mother, a Painful Lesson in Politicking," *New York Times,* February 4, 2017; Audrey Carlsen and Wilson Andrews, "How Senators Voted on the Gorsuch Confirmation," *New York Times,* April 7, 2017.

218 **Maddin said that Gorsuch:** David Savage, "What We Learned About Neil Gorsuch During His Confirmation Hearing," *Los Angeles Times,* March 24, 2017; Ariane de Vogue and Dan Berman, "Neil Gorsuch Confirmed to the Supreme Court," CNN, April 7, 2017; Teresa Baldas, "Detroit Man: I Almost Froze to Death, and Gorsuch Didn't Care," *Detroit Free Press,* March 24, 2017.

218 **Janus had chosen not:** Adam Liptak, "Supreme Court Ruling Delivers a Sharp Blow to Labor Unions," *New York Times,* June 27, 2018.

218 **Even requiring fees:** Liptak, "Supreme Court Ruling Delivers."

219 **Kagan was a liberal:** Lisa Foderaro and Christine Haughey, "The Kagan Family: Left-Leaning and Outspoken," *New York Times,* June 18, 2010; Peter Baker and Jeff Zeleny, "Obama Picks Kagan as Justice Nominee," *New York Times,* May 9, 2010; *Janus v. AFSCME,* 138 S. Ct. 2448 (2018).

219 **The First Amendment, she insisted:** Liptak, "Supreme Court Ruling Delivers."

219 **It was widely predicted:** Amelia Thomas-DeVeaux, "Could the Supreme Court Really Bust Public-Sector Unions?," FiveThirtyEight, February 26, 2018; Patrick Wright, "Symposium: Evidence Shows Unions Will Survive Without Agency Fees," *SCOTUSblog,* December 22, 2017.

219 **When *Janus* was decided:** John Bowden, "Teachers Union Expects to Lose 300K Members If High Court Overturns Fees," *The Hill,* May 22, 2018; Noam Scheiber, "Labor Unions Will Be Smaller After Supreme Court Decision, but Maybe Not Weaker," *New York Times,* June 27, 2018; Liptak, "Issues and Implications in Supreme Court's"; Patrick Wright, "Symposium, Evidence Shows Unions Will Survive Without Agency Fees," *SCOTUSblog,* December 22, 2017, scotusblog.com/2017/12/symposium-evidence-shows-unions-will-survive-without-agency-fees/.

220 **The Freedom Foundation, another anti-union:** Brief of the National Education Association et al. as Amici Curiae in Support of Respondents at 29–31, *Janus v. AFSCME*, No. 16-1466 (January 19, 2018).

220 **After Michigan adopted:** Michael Watson, "Teachers Unions Report First Effects from Janus Decision," Capital Research Center, December 5, 2018; Tom Gantert, "32,000 Flee Teachers Union Under Michigan Right-to-Work Law," *Michigan Capitol Confidential*, December 14, 2018.

220 **One study of the effect:** James Feigenbaum, Alexander Hertel-Fernandez, and Vanessa Williamson, "From the Bargaining Table to the Ballot Box: Political Effects of Right to Work Laws" (working paper, National Bureau of Economic Research, Cambridge, Mass., January 20, 2018); Kevin Drum, "What the Union Fight Is Really About: Defunding the Left," *Mother Jones*, March 25, 2011; "Top Organization Contributors" (2016 election cycle), Open Secrets (2017); Sean McElwee, "How the Right's War on Unions Is Killing the Democratic Party," *Nation*, January 22, 2018.

221 **In a tweet the morning:** Drum, "What the Union Fight Is Really About"; Sean McElwee, "How the Right's War on Unions"; Donald Trump (@realDonaldTrump), "Supreme Court rules in favor of non-union workers," Twitter, June 27, 2018, 10:11 a.m., twitter.com/realdonaldtrump/status/1011975204778729474.

221 **In that same cycle, OpenSecrets.org:** Curtlyn Kramer, "Vital Stats: The Widening Gap Between Corporate and Labor PAC Spending," Brookings Institution, March 31, 2017; "Business-Labor-Ideology Split in PAC & Individual Donations to Candidates, Parties, Super PACs and Outside Spending Groups," (2018 election cycle), OpenSecrets.org.

222 **The Ed Uihlein Family Foundation:** "Sheldon Adelson Lost His First Fight with a Union. Will It Have a Domino Effect?," *Guardian*, February 23, 2017; Ryan Erickson and Karla Walter, "Right to Work Would Harm All Americans," *American Prospect*, May 18, 2017; "About Us," AFL-CIO, aflcio.org/about-us; "Top Individual Contributors: All Federal Contributions" (2018 election cycle), Open Secrets (2019); Celine McNicholas, "Janus and Fair Share Fees."

222 **"Donations can open the door":** Geoff Mulvihill, "Political Money in State-Level Campaigns Exceeds $2B," Associated Press, November 1, 2018; Sanya Mansoor, Liz Essley Whyte, and Joe Yerardi, "Why Are Corporations Pouring Millions into Shoo-in Governor Races," *USA Today*, September 21, 2018.

222 **The large amount:** Jody Knauss and Jonas Persson, "Cookie-Cutter ALEC Right-to-Work Bills Pop in Multiple States," *PR Watch*, Center for Media and Democracy, March 11, 2015; Nancy Scola, "Exposing ALEC: How Conservative-Backed States Laws Are All Connected," *Atlantic*, April 14, 2012.

223 **In 2018, Missouri voters:** "Right-to-Work States," National Conference of State Legislatures, ncsl.org/research/labor-and-employment/right-to-work-laws-and-bills.aspx; Jeff Stein, "Missouri Voters Defeat GOP-Backed 'Right to Work' Law, in Victory for Unions, Associated Press Projects," *Washington Post*, August 7, 2018.

223 **These declines hurt workers:** Laura Malugade, "Union Membership Plummets in Most Right-to-Work States," *Labor Relations Law Insider* (blog), January 26, 2018; Jonathan Berlin and Kyle Bentle, "Data: What Wisconsin Says About What Could Happen to Illinois After Janus," *Chicago Tribune*, June 29, 2018.

223 **In the United States:** David Cooper, "Raising the Minimum Wage to $15 by 2024 Would Lift Wages for 41 Million American Workers," Economic Policy Institute, April 26, 2017; Lawrence Mishel, Elise Gould, and Josh Bivens, "Wage Stagnation in Nine Charts," Economic Policy Institute, January 6, 2015; Christopher Ingraham, "The U.S. Has One of the Stingiest Minimum Wage Policies of Any Wealthy Nation," *Washington Post*, December 29, 2017; Lawrence Mishel, "Causes of Wage Stagnation," Economic Policy Institute, January 6, 2015.

223 **The groups behind the letter:** Robbie Feinberg, "The Money Against the Minimum Wage," Open Secrets, April 4, 2014; Dave Jamieson, "Senate Republicans Block Minimum Wage Bill," *Huffington Post*, April 30, 2014.

224 **In a Gallup poll shortly:** Andrew Dugan, "Most Americans for Raising Minimum Wage," Gallup, November 11, 2013.

224 **In the end, the minimum-wage bill:** "The Case for a Higher Minimum Wage," editorial, *New York Times*, February 8, 2014; "Raise the Minimum Wage," editorial, *Los Angeles Times*, September 13, 2013; "U.S. Economy Needs a Higher Minimum Wage," editorial, *Salt Lake Tribune*, December 11, 2013; Thomas Ferraro, "Senate Republicans Block Bid to Hike Minimum Wage," Reuters, April 30, 2014; U.S. Conference of Catholic Bishops and Catholic Charities USA to Senators, January 8, 2014, usccb.org/issues-and-action/human-life-and-dignity/labor-employment/upload/joint-minimum-wage-letter-2014-01-08.pdf.

224 **No one thought to blame:** Thomas Ferraro, "Senate Republicans Block Obama Bid to Hike Minimum Wage," *Chicago Tribune*, April 30, 2014; "Minimum Wage Boost Blocked in Senate," NBC.com, April 30, 2014.

225 **The report called for stronger:** Philip Mattera, "Grand Theft Paycheck: The Large Corporations Shortchanging Their Workers' Wages," Good Jobs First, June 2018; Jessica Corbett, "'Jaw-Dropping' Report Reveals Rampant Wage Theft Among Top US Corporations," Common Dreams, June 6, 2018.

225 **The National Employment Law Project:** Michael Lax and Rosemary Klein, "More Than Meets the Eye: Social, Economic, and Emotional Impacts of Work-Related Injury and Illness," *New Solutions* 18 (2008).

225 **Those funds have created:** Jamie Smith Hopkins, "The Campaign to Weaken Worker Protections," Center for Public Integrity, June 29, 2015.

226 **Taken as a whole:** David Neumark and Wendy Stock, "The Effects of Race and Sex Discrimination Laws" (working paper, National Bureau of Economic Research, Cambridge, Mass., April 2001); M. V. Lee Badgett, "The Wage Effects of Sexual Orientation Discrimination," *Industrial and Labor Relations Review* 48 (1995): 726; Scott J. Adams, "Age Discrimination Legislation and the Employment of Older Workers," *Labour Economics* 11 (2004): 219; Stewart Schwab, "Employment Discrimination," in

Encyclopedia of Law and Economics, ed. Boudewijn Bouckaert and Gerrit De Geest (Cheltenham, England: Edward Elgar, 2000).

226 **In some cases, ProPublica found:** Victoria Lipnic, "The State of Age Discrimination and Older Workers in the U.S. 50 Years After the Age Discrimination in Employment Act," U.S. Equal Employment Opportunity Commission, June 2018; "Age Discrimination in Employment Act (Charges Filed with EEOC) FY 1997–FY 2018," U.S. Equal Employment Opportunity Commission, eeoc.gov/eeoc/statistics/enforcement/adea.cfm; Peter Gosselin and Ariana Tobin, "Cutting 'Old Heads' at IBM," ProPublica, March 22, 2018.

226 **A lawyer with the AARP:** Robert Weiner and Daniel Khan, "Iowa Case Shows Age Discrimination Persists, Despite Law," *Des Moines Register*, May 11, 2016; Michael Winerip, "Three Men, Three Ages. Which Do You Like?," *New York Times*, July 22, 2013; Noguchi, "Age Discrimination Suits Jump, but Wins Are Elusive."

226 **They also are often left unemployed:** Bob Sullivan, "For Older Workers, Getting a New Job Can Be a Gamble," CNBC, July 10, 2016.

227 **In addition to the immediate loss of income:** *Missed by the Recovery: Solving the Long-Term Unemployment Crisis for Older Workers: Hearing Before the U.S. Senate Special Committee on Aging*, 112 Cong. (May 15, 2012) (statement of Charles Jeszeck, U.S. Government Accountability Office); Ann Brenoff, "Older Workers Stay Unemployed Much Longer Than Younger Ones, Study Says," *Huffington Post*, December 6, 2017.

227 **Now, many of these cases:** Bryce Covert, "Exclusive: 43 Sexual Harassment Cases That Were Thrown Out Because of One Supreme Court Decision," ThinkProgress, November 24, 2014.

227 **Other forms of harassment:** Amy Blackstone, Heather McLaughlin, and Christopher Uggen, "Workplace Sexual Harassment," Stanford Center on Poverty and Inequality (2018).

228 **There is already evidence:** Sarah Kellogg, "Wal-Mart v. Dukes," *Washington Lawyer*, September 2011; Nina Martin, "The Impact and Echoes of the Wal-Mart Discrimination Case," ProPublica, September 27, 2013.

228 **Workers fired late:** Judith D. Fischer, "Public Policy and the Tyranny of the Bottom Line in the Termination of Older Workers," *South Carolina Law Review* 53 (2002): 227; Elena Andreeva, "Depressive Symptoms as a Cause and Effect of Job Loss in Men and Women," *BMC Public Health* 15 (2015); "Health Impact Assessments of the Layoff and Bumping Process," Cincinnati Health Department Health Impact Assessment Committee (October 2011), 5; Sidra Goldman-Mellor et al., "Economic Contraction and Mental Health," *International Journal of Mental Health* 39 (Summer 2010): 6; Yin Paradies et al., "Racism as a Determinant of Health: A Systematic Review and Meta-Analysis," *PLOS One*, September 23, 2015; Jason Silverstein, "How Racism Is Bad for Our Bodies," *Atlantic*, March 12, 2013; Tene Lewis, "Chronic Exposure to Everyday Discrimination and Coronary Artery Calcification in African-American Women: The SWAN Heart Study," *Psychosomatic Medicine* 68 (2006): 362.

228 **As a result of these new incentives:** Adaku Onyeka-Crawford, "Vance v. BSU Anniversary: A Case of the Terrible Twos," National Women's Law Center, June 24, 2015.

229 **Barry Hirsch, a Georgia State University economist:** Barry Hirsh, "Reconsidering Union Wage Effects: Surveying New Evidence on an Old Topic," *Journal of Labor Research* 25 (2004): 233, 260; Matthew Walters and Lawrence Mishel, "How Unions Help All Workers," Economic Policy Institute, August 26, 2003; Susan Dynarski, "Fresh Proof That Strong Unions Help Reduce Income Inequality," *New York Times*, July 6, 2018.

229 **When benefits are taken:** Walters and Mishel, "How Unions Help All Workers."

229 **As unions lost members:** Bruce Western and Jake Rosenfeld, "Unions, Norms, and the Rise of U.S. Wage Inequality," *American Sociological Review* 76 (2011): 513.

229 **The Economic Policy Institute:** Elise Gould and Will Kimball, "'Right-to-Work' States Still Have Lower Wages," Economic Policy Institute, April 22, 2015; Lisa Nagele-Piazza, "The Resurgence of Right-to-Work Laws," Society for Human Resource Management, July 21, 2017; "Right-to-Work States," National Conference of State Legislatures.

230 **In twenty-nine states:** David Cooper et al. "We Can Afford a $12.00 Federal Minimum Wage in 2020," Economic Policy Institute, April 30, 2015; "The Pennsylvania Minimum Wage 2018," Keystone Research Center, January 2, 2018; "State Minimum Wages 2019, Minimum Wage by State," National Conference of State Legislatures, January 7, 2019.

230 **It found that a $1:** Arindrajit Dube, "Minimum Wages and the Distribution of Family Incomes" (discussion paper, IZA Institute of Labor Economics, Bonn, Germany, February 2017); Alex Gertner et al., "Association Between State Minimum Wages and Suicide Rates in the U.S.," *American Journal of Preventive Medicine* 56 (2019): 658; Robert Hahn, "Poverty and Death in the United States," *International Journal of Health Services* 26 (1996).

230 **The report noted that:** David Cooper and Teresa Kroeger, "Employers Steal Billions from Workers' Paychecks Each Year," Economic Policy Institute, May 10, 2017.

231 **"Many respondents reported":** Deborah Berkowitz, "Workplace Safety Enforcement Continues to Decline in Trump Administration," National Employment Law Project, March 14, 2019; Lax and Klein, "More Than Meets the Eye."

CHAPTER SEVEN: CORPORATIONS

233 **The resulting oil spill:** *Exxon Shipping Co. v. Baker*, 554 U.S. 471 (2008); Alan Taylor, "The Exxon Valdez Oil Spill: 25 Years Ago Today," *Atlantic*, March 24, 2014; Jeff Kerr, "*Exxon Shipping Co v. Baker*: The Perils of Judicial Punitive Damages Reform," *Emory Law Journal* 59 (2010): 731.

233 **It was not clear why:** *Exxon Shipping Co.*, 554 U.S. 471; Taylor, "Exxon Valdez Oil Spill"; Kerr, "*Exxon Shipping Co v. Baker*," 731.

234 **The jury awarded compensatory damages:** *Exxon Shipping Co.*, 554 U.S. 471; Keith Schneider, "Jury Finds Exxon Acted Recklessly in Valdez Oil Spill," *New York Times*,

June 14, 1994; Keith Schneider, "Exxon Is Ordered to Pay $5 Billion for Alaska Spill," *New York Times*, September 17, 1994.

234 **Even after that:** Schneider, "Exxon Is Ordered to Pay $5 Billion for Alaska Spill"; *Exxon Shipping Co. v. Baker*, 554 U.S. 471.

234 **In an 1851 dispute:** Emily Gottlieb, "What You Need to Know About . . . Punitive Damages," Center for Justice & Democracy, September 2011; *Day v. Woodworth*, 54 U.S. 363 (1851).

235 **Nor did the history:** Robert Riggs, "Constitutionalizing Punitive Damages: The Limits of Due Process," *Ohio State Law Journal* 52 (1991): 859.

235 **They wanted Congress:** F. Patrick Hubbard, "The Nature and Impact of the 'Tort Reform' Movement," *Hofstra Law Review* 35 (2006): 437, 469–70.

236 **Tort reformers put up billboards:** Hubbard, "Nature and Impact of the 'Tort Reform' Movement," 437, 469–73; Gerald Shargel, "'Hot Coffee' Documentary Skewers Tort Reformers: A New Documentary Calls the McDonald's 'Hot Coffee' Lawsuit Frivolous," *Daily Beast*, June 24, 2011; Ralph Nader, "Suing for Justice," *Harper's*, April 2016.

236 **The truth was:** Caroline Forell, "McTorts: The Social and Legal Impact of McDonald's Role in Tort Suits," *Loyola Consumer Law Review* 24 (2011): 105, 134–35.

236 **Tort reformers also made:** Nader, "Suing for Justice"; Stephen Burbank and Sean Farhang, "Litigation Reform: An Institutional Approach," *University of Pennsylvania Law Review* 162 (2014): 1544, 1545; "Fact Sheet: Caps on Compensatory Damages: A State Law Summary," Center for Justice and Democracy at New York Law School, centerjd.org/content/fact-sheet-caps-compensatory-damages-state-law-summary.

236 **It was a case:** Myriam Gilles, "The Day Doctrine Died," *University of Illinois Law Review* 2016, no. 2 (2016): 111, 119; David Schwartz, "Do-It-Yourself Tort Reform: How the Supreme Court Quietly Killed the Class Action," *SCOTUSblog*, September 16, 2011; Edward A. Purcell Jr., "The Class Action Fairness Act in Perspective: The Old and the New in Federal Jurisdictional Reform," *University of Pennsylvania Law Review* 156, no. 6 (June 2008): 1823.

237 **BMW had a policy:** *BMW of North America, Inc. v. Gore*, 517 U.S. 559, 563–64 (1996).

237 **BMW thought the award:** *BMW*, 517 U.S. at 564–67.

237 **The Court ruled:** *BMW*, 517 U.S. 559.

238 **Campbell ended up:** *State Farm Mutual Automobile Insurance Co. v. Campbell*, 538 U.S. 408 (2003).

238 **State Farm took the case:** *State Farm*, 538 U.S. 408.

238 **In this case:** *State Farm*, 538 U.S. 408.

239 **A jury might well:** *State Farm*, 538 U.S. 408.

239 **It found that Philip Morris's:** *Philip Morris USA v. Williams*, 549 U.S. 346 (2007); Kristin Younger and Sara Rosenbaum, "Philip Morris USA v. Williams: Implications for Public Health Policy and Practice," *Public Health Reports* 122, no. 5 (September–October 2007), 702–4.

239 **He worried that Philip Morris:** Robert Barnes, "Supreme Court Ends Philip Morris's Challenge of Punitive Award," *Washington Post*, April 1, 2009.

240 **It was properly considering:** *Philip Morris*, 549 U.S. 346.

240 **A case note:** "The Supreme Court—Leading Cases: Punitive Damages," *Harvard Law Review* 121 (2007): 278.

240 **Although the Court:** *Exxon Shipping*, 554 U.S. 471; Jeffrey Fisher, "The *Exxon Valdez* Case and Regularizing Punishment," *Alaska Law Review* 26 (2009): 1, 15, 18.

241 **Therefore, he said:** *Exxon Shipping*, 554 U.S. 471.

241 **She also worried:** *Exxon Shipping*, 554 U.S. 471.

242 **The Court's decisions made it:** "Fortune 500, 2003," *Fortune*, archive.fortune.com/magazines/fortune/fortune500_archive/full/2003/.

242 **The Court did not explain:** *State Farm*, 538 U.S. 408.

242 **Poor people never were:** Martha McCluskey, "Constitutionalizing Inequality: Due Process in State Farm," *Buffalo Law Review* 56 (2008): 1036, 1055; *State Farm*, 538 U.S. at 417, 426 (quoting *Honda Motor Co. v. Oberg*, 512 U.S. 415, 432 [1994]).

243 **A month later:** *BMW*, 517 U.S. 559.

244 **That same year:** Erwin Chemerinsky, "The Roberts Court at Age Three," *Wayne Law Review* 54 (2008): 22; Jeffrey Rosen, "Supreme Court Inc.," *New York Times*, March 16, 2008; Adam Liptak, "Pro-Business Rulings Are Defining This Supreme Court," *New York Times*, May 4, 2013.

244 **The study, which was published:** J. Mitchell Pickering, "Something Old, Something New—Something Borrowed, Something Blue," *Santa Clara Law Review* 49 (2009): 1063, 1072, 1098.

244 **Agreeing with the *Santa Clara* study:** Lee Epstein, William Landes, and Richard Posner, "How Business Fares in the Supreme Court," *Minnesota Law Review* 97 (2013): 1450, 1471.

245 **It was such a priority:** Public Citizen, "The Chamber of Litigation," October 26, 2016, 7–8, chamberofcommercewatch.org/wp-content/uploads/2016/10/Chamber-litigation-report-part-1.pdf.

245 **The drafters of the federal class action:** Jed S. Rakoff, "The Cure for Corporate Wrongdoing: Class Actions vs. Individual Prosecutions," *New York Review of Books*, November 19, 2015; Owen Fiss, "The Political Theory of the Class Action," *Washington and Lee Law Review* 53 (1996): 21, 25; Robert Klonoff, "The Decline of Class Actions," *Washington University Law Review* 90 (2013): 729, 731, 736; Caroline Bressman, "The Future of Class Actions," *Minnesota Law Review*, March 30, 2017; Linda Mullenix, "Rethinking the American Class Action," *Emory Law Journal* 64 (2014): 399.

246 **The changes would, he said:** Benjamin Kaplan, "A Prefatory Note," *Boston College Law Review* 10 (1969): 497; David Marcus, "The History of the Modern Class Action, Part I: *Sturm und Drang*, 1953–1980," *Washington University Law Review* 3 (2013): 587, 600n52.

246 ***Rodriguez v. San Antonio*:** Margo Schlanger, "Beyond the Hero Judge: Institutional Reform Litigation as Litigation," *Michigan Law Review* 97 (1999): 1994, 2003–4; David Marcus, "The History of the Modern Class Action, Part II: Litigation and Legitimacy, 1981–1994," *Fordham Law Review* 86 (2018): 1785, 1807.

247 **They reached $6.1 billion:** Ralph Blumenthal, "Veterans Accept $180 Million Pact on Agent Orange," *New York Times,* May 8, 1984; Harvey Berman, "The Agent Orange Veteran Payment Program," *Law and Contemporary Problems* 53 (1990): 49; Katrina Frayter, "Enron Investors to Split Billions from Lawsuit," CNN, September 9, 2008; "Judge Approves $3.56 Billion Settlement for WorldCom Investors," *Bloomberg,* September 22, 2005.

247 **Fitzpatrick concluded that:** Daniel Fisher, "Study Shows Consumer Class-Action Lawyers Earn Millions, Clients Little," *Forbes,* December 11, 2013; Brian Fitzpatrick, "Do Class Action Lawyers Make Too Little?," *University of Pennsylvania Law Review* 158 (2010): 2043–46.

247 **Tort reform advocates:** Marcus, "Modern Class Action, Part II," 1812–13, 1828.

248 **Ed Markey, who was then:** Klonoff, "Decline of Class Actions," 729, 732–33; "Bush Signs Limits on Class Actions," Associated Press, February 18, 2005.

248 **Erwin Chemerinsky, dean of the University:** Suzette Malveaux, "How Goliath Won: The Future Implications of Dukes v. Wal-Mart," *Northwestern University Law Review Colloquy* 106 (2011): 52; Catherine L. Fisk and Erwin Chemerinsky, "The Failing Faith in Class Actions: Dukes v. Wal-Mart and AT&T Mobility v. Concepcion," *Duke Journal of Constitutional Law & Public Policy* 7, Special Issue (2011): 79–80, dx.doi.org/10.2139/ssrn.1966624.

248 **Its new standards:** Nina Martin, "The Impact and Echoes of the Wal-Mart Discrimination Case," ProPublica, September 27, 2013; Michael Selmi and Sylvia Tsakos, "Employment Discrimination Class Actions After Wal-Mart v. Dukes," *Akron Law Review* 48 (2015): 803, 804, 804n5.

249 **Behrend and several other:** *Comcast Corp. v. Behrend,* 569 U.S. 27 (2013).

249 **The liberal dissenters:** *Comcast,* 569 U.S. 27.

249 **In "The End of Class Actions?":** Fisk and Chemerinsky, "Failing Faith in Class Actions," 73; Malveaux, "How Goliath Won," 52; Klonoff, "Decline of Class Actions," 729; Wataru Aikawa, "A Bleak Future for Class Actions," *Regulatory Review,* May 7, 2015; Brian Fitzpatrick, "The End of Class Actions?," *Arizona Law Review* 57 (2015): 162, 199.

250 **The Court has been a strong supporter:** Elizabeth Colman, "How America's Wealthiest, Most Powerful Companies Use Fine Print to Subvert Employee Rights," Employee Rights Advocacy Institute for Law & Policy, June 2018.

250 **Before long, a movement:** Michael Moffitt, "Before the Big Bang: The Making of an ADR Pioneer," *Negotiation Journal,* October 2006, 437–39.

250 **In his 1976 speech:** Moffitt, "Before the Big Bang," 437–39; Deborah Hensler, "Our Courts Ourselves: How Alternative Dispute Resolution Movement Is Re-shaping Our Legal System," *Pennsylvania State Law Review* 108 (2003): 165, 174.

251 **Much of the arbitration:** Hensler, "Our Courts, Ourselves," 176–177.

251 **As one arbitration firm:** Hensler, "Our Courts, Ourselves," 184; Kerri Anne Renzulli, "Workers at Google, Facebook, eBay and Airbnb Can Now Sue over Sexual Harassment—Here's What That Means for Employees," CNBC, November 19, 2018;

Jessica Silver-Greenberg and Michael Corkery, "In Arbitration, a 'Privatization of the Justice System,'" *New York Times,* November 1, 2015; "Arbitration," National Association of Consumer Advocates, consumeradvocates.org/for-consumers/arbitration.

252 **She resigned, and publicly:** *The Arbitration Trap: How Credit Card Companies Ensnare Consumers* (Washington, D.C.: Public Citizen, September 2007), 2, 17, citizen.org/article/the-arbitration-trap-how-credit-card-companies-ensnare-consumers-2/30.

252 **The prediction proved:** Eric Berkowitz, "Is Justice Served?," *Los Angeles Times,* October 22, 2006.

252 **A California appellate justice:** "Judicial Salary Tracker," National Center for State Courts, ncsc.org/microsites/judicial-salaries-data-tool/home/Explore-the-Data.aspx; *Arbitration Trap,* 31; Berkowitz, "Is Justice Served?"; National Center for State Courts, "Judicial Salary Tracker."

253 **It reported, under the bullet point:** *Arbitration Trap,* 2, 17, 30; Berkowitz, "Is Justice Served?"

253 **Public Citizen concluded:** Laurence Tribe, *Uncertain Justice: The Roberts Court and the Constitution* (New York: Macmillan, 2014), 295; *Arbitration Trap,* 3, 7.

253 **In 1983, Brennan:** *Moses H. Cone Memorial Hospital v. Mercury Construction Corp.,* 460 U.S. 1 (1983); Gilles, "The Day Doctrine Died," 124; Martin Malin, "The Three Phases of the Supreme Court's Arbitration Jurisprudence: Empowering the Already-Empowered," *Nevada Law Journal* 17 (2016): 23, 39–40.

254 **Gilmer wanted to bring:** *Gilmer v. Interstate/Johnson Lane Corp.,* 500 U.S. 20 (1991).

254 **"Unfortunately, the Supreme Court":** *Epic Systems Corp. v. Lewis,* 138 S. Ct. 1612 (2018); David Savage, "How the Supreme Court Is Invoking a 1925 Law to Restrict Workers' Rights Today," *Los Angeles Times,* May 23, 2018; Matthew Finkin, "'Workers' Contracts' Under the United States Arbitration Act: An Essay in Historical Clarification," *Berkeley Journal of Employment and Labor Law* 17 (1996): 282.

255 **She did not believe:** *Green Tree Financial Corp.-Alabama v. Randolph,* 531 U.S. 79 (2000); Katherine Stone, "Will Workers and Consumers Get Their Day in Court?," *American Prospect,* May 5, 2016.

255 **The Court did not seem to care:** *Green Tree Financial,* 531 U.S. 79 (2000).

256 **It was around this time:** *Green Tree Financial,* 531 U.S. 79; Stone, "Will Workers and Consumers Get Their Day"; Gilles, "The Day Doctrine Died," 124.

256 **The Concepcions filed:** *AT&T Mobility v. Concepcion,* 131 S. Ct. 1740 (2011); Peter Rutledge and Christopher Drahozal, "'Sticky' Arbitration Clauses? The Use of Arbitration Clauses After *Concepcion* and *Amex,*" *Vanderbilt Law Review* 67 (2014): 955, 957–58, 957n4; Adam Liptak, "Supreme Court Allows Contracts That Prohibit Class-Action Arbitration," *New York Times,* April 27, 2011.

257 **It would not be worth:** *AT&T Mobility, LLC v. Concepcion,* 563 U.S. 333 (2011).

257 **The San Francisco–based U.S. Court:** *AT&T Mobility,* 563 U.S. 333; Myriam Gilles and Gary Friedman, "After Class: Aggregate Litigation in the Wake of AT&T Mobility v. Concepcion," *University of Chicago Law Review* 79 (2012): 623, 637.

257 **As a result, Scalia said:** *AT&T Mobility*, 563 U.S. 333; Erwin Chemerinsky, *The Case Against the Supreme Court* (New York: Penguin, 2014), 175.

257 **"What rational lawyer":** *AT&T Mobility*, 563 U.S. 333.

258 **The Court's ruling, one class action expert said:** Liptak, "Supreme Court Allows Contracts."

258 **To prove its case:** *American Express Co. v. Italian Colors Restaurant*, 570 U.S. 228 (2013).

258 **The Federal Arbitration Act:** *American Express*, 570 U.S. 228.

259 **Kagan provided what:** *American Express*, 570 U.S. 228; Sheldon Whitehouse, "Conservative Judicial Activism: The Politicization of the Supreme Court Under Chief Justice Roberts," *Harvard Law & Policy Review* 9 (2015): 195, 199.

259 **As Lewis pointed out:** *Epic Systems*, 138 S. Ct. 1612 (2018); Brief for the Respondent at 3–4, *Epic Systems*, 138 S. Ct. 1612 (2018).

259 **That included, he said:** *Epic Systems*, 138 S. Ct. 1612 (2018).

260 **The Court's conservatives:** *Epic Systems*, No. 16-285 (U.S. May 21, 2018).

260 **The permit that Coeur Alaska:** *Coeur Alaska, Inc. v. Southeast Alaska Conservation Council*, 557 U.S. 261 (2009).

261 **"If a mining company":** *Coeur Alaska*, 557 U.S. 261; "Supreme Court Clears Way for Mining Company to Destroy Alaskan Lake," Earthjustice, June 22, 2009, earthjustice.org/news/press/2009/supreme-court-clears-way-for-mining-company-to-destroy-alaskan-lake; People for the American Way Foundation, "Rise of the Corporate Court: How the Supreme Court Is Putting Businesses First," September 2010, pfaw.org/report/rise-of-the-corporate-court-how-the-supreme-court-is-putting-businesses-first/.

261 **In a 2004 decision:** "Key Judge Warns of Political Danger of Monopoly, Calls for Revival of Antitrust Tools," *Monopoly Matters* (blog), Open Markets Institute, May 3, 2019; *Verizon Communications, Inc. v. Trinko*, 540 U.S. 398 (2004); *United States v. Terminal Railroad Association of St. Louis*, 224 U.S. 383 (1912).

261 **Wood, who taught:** "Key Judge Warns of Political Danger," *Monopoly Matters*.

262 **It is unlikely:** *Hearings on Competition and Consumer Protection in the 21st Century, Before the Federal Trade Commission*, November 15, 2018 (Comments of the Electronic Frontier Foundation).

262 **After the Court:** John Y. Gotanda, "Punitive Damages: A Comparative Analysis" (Working Paper Series 8, Villanova University Charles Widger School of Law, August 2003), digitalcommons.law.villanova.edu/wps/art8/.

263 **The problem of regulatory capture:** Lawrence Tribe and Joshua Matz, *Uncertain Justice: The Roberts Court and the Constitution* (New York: Macmillan, 2014), 293; Emily Stewart, "Mick Mulvaney Once Called the CFPB a 'Sick, Sad' Joke. Now He Might Be in Charge of It," *Vox*, November 16, 2017.

263 **Public Citizen said that:** Public Citizen and National Association of Consumer Advocates, "Report: In Wake of Supreme Court's AT&T v. Concepcion Decision, Consumers Are Worse Off," April 25, 2012, citizen.org/news/report-in-wake-of-supreme

-courts-att-v-concepcion-decision-consumers-are-worse-off/; Public Citizen, "Cases That Would Have Been: Three Years After AT&T Mobility v. Concepcion, Claims of Corporate Wrongdoing Continue to Pile Up," May 2014.

264 **The author of the report:** Seyfarth Shaw LLP, "Seyfarth Shaw's Jerry Maatman Presents on 2018 Class Action Trend," *Workplace Class Action Blog*, February 13, 2019.

264 **"The ability to access":** Imre Stephen Szalai, "The Prevalence of Consumer Arbitration Agreements by America's Top Companies," *UC Davis Law Review* 52 (2019): 233–35; Silver-Greenberg and Gebeloff, "Arbitration Everywhere."

264 **After *Epic Systems:*** Adam Liptak, "Supreme Court Upholds Workplace Arbitration Contracts Barring Class Actions," *New York Times*, May 21, 2018.

265 **The new policy:** Szalai, "Prevalence of Consumer Arbitration Agreements," 234–35; "Fact Sheet: Cases Tossed Out of Court," Center for Justice and Democracy at New York Law School; Emily Flitter, "JPMorgan Chase Seeks to Prohibit Card Customers from Suing," *New York Times*, June 4, 2019; Cale Guthrie Weissman, "Chase Bank Is Quietly Adding a Forced Arbitration Clause to Some Credit Cards," *Fast Company*, May 30, 2019; Silver-Greenberg and Gebeloff, "Arbitration Everywhere."

265 **"For employers looking":** Stephanie Russell-Kraft, "The Supreme Court's War Against Workers," *New Republic*, May 21, 2018; Adam Liptak, "Supreme Court Upholds Workplace Arbitration Contracts Barring Class Actions," *New York Times*, May 21, 2018; Szalai, "Prevalence of Consumer Arbitration Agreements," 234–35; "Fact Sheet: Cases Tossed Out of Court," Center for Justice and Democracy at New York Law School; Michael E. Brewer, Michael Leggieri, and Robin Samuel, "You Had Me at 'Class Action Waiver,'" *Employer Report*, Baker McKenzie, November 29, 2018, theemployerreport.com/2018/11/you-had-me-at-class-action-waiver/.

265 **Although these cases:** David Weinberg, "Supreme Court Strongly Pro-Business in Roberts Years," *Marketplace*, Minnesota Public Radio, June 24, 2013.

266 **The Court's anti-environmental rulings:** John Tozzi, "Pollution's Annual Price Tag? $4.6 Trillion and 9 Million Dead," *Bloomberg*, October 19, 2017; David Cooper and Teresa Kroeger, "Employers Steal Billions from Workers' Paychecks Each Year," Economic Policy Institute, May 10, 2017; Seyfarth Shaw LLP, "Seyfarth Shaw's Jerry Maatman Presents."

Chapter Eight: Criminal Justice

267 **King was tried:** *Maryland v. King*, 569 U.S. 435 (2013).

268 **The Court of Appeals of Maryland:** *King*, 569 U.S. 435; U.S. Department of Justice, "Fingerprinting—Search and Seizure," *Justice Manual*, § 251, justice.gov/jm/criminal-resource-manual-251-fingerprinting-search-and-seizure.

268 **At oral argument:** Barry Friedman, "The Supreme Court Fails the Fourth Amendment Test," *Slate*, June 5, 2013; *King*, 569 U.S. 435; Erin Murphy, "License, Registration, Cheek Swab: DNA Testing and the Divided Court," *Harvard Law Review* 127 (2013): 161; Stephen Mercer and Jessica Gabel, "Shadow Dwellers: The Unregulated

World of State and Local DNA Databases," *NYU Annual Survey of American Law* 69 (2014): 639, 649.

268 **A DNA database:** Brief of Amici Curiae Electronic Privacy Information Center and Twenty-Six Technical Experts and Legal Scholars in Support of Respondent, *Maryland v. King*, 569 U.S. 435 (2013) (No. 12-207).

268 **The Electronic Privacy Information Center:** Brief of Amici Curiae Electronic Privacy Information Center.

269 **Federal law allowed DNA:** Brief of Amici Curiae of American Civil Liberties Union, ACLU of Maryland, and ACLU of Northern California in Support of Respondent, *Maryland v. King*, 569 U.S. 435 (2013) (No. 12-207); "DNA Sample Collection from Arrestees," National Institute of Justice, nij.gov/topics/forensics/evidence/dna/pages/collection-from-arrestees.aspx.

269 **Even though the law:** Brief for the Howard University School of Law Civil Rights Clinic as Amicus Curiae in Support of Respondent, *Maryland v. King*, 569 U.S. 435 (2013) (No. 12-207).

269 **Scalia dissented, along with:** *King*, 569 U.S. 435.

269 **He also emphasized:** *King*, 569 U.S. 435.

270 **The government is prohibited:** *King*, 569 U.S. 435; "ACLU Comment on Supreme Court DNA Swab Ruling (Maryland v. King)," ACLU, June 3, 2013, aclu.org/press-releases/aclu-comment-supreme-court-dna-swab-ruling-maryland-v-king; Andrea Roth, "Maryland v. King and the Wonderful, Horrible DNA Revolution in Law Enforcement," *Ohio State Journal of Criminal Law* 11 (2013): 295, 299.

270 **Scalia suggested that:** *King*, 569 U.S. 435.

270 **Senator Ted Cruz:** Hannah Jeffrey, "Ted Cruz, Randy Weber Condemn Supreme Court DNA Ruling," *Houston Chronicle*, June 4, 2013; Norman Reimer, "The Scalia Dissent in *Maryland v. King*: Exposing a Contrived Rationale Today and a Dangerous Precedent for Tomorrow," *Engage* 14, no. 3 (October 2013).

271 **If the police obtained:** Corinna Barrett Lain, "Countermajoritarian Hero or Zero? Rethinking the Warren Court's Role in the Criminal Procedure Revolution," *University of Pennsylvania Law Review* 152 (2004): 1370–71, 1373, 1379.

271 **The state never produced:** *Mapp v. Ohio*, 367 U.S. 643 (1961); William Yardley, "Dollree Mapp, Who Defied Police Search in Landmark Case, Is Dead," *New York Times*, December 9, 2014; Lain, "Countermajoritarian Hero," 1375.

272 **At the time of Mapp's arrest:** Lain, "Countermajoritarian Hero," 1373; "High Court Bars Evidence States Seize Illegally," *New York Times*, June 20, 1961; *Weeks v. United States*, 232 U.S. 383 (1914); Lucas A. Powe Jr., *The Warren Court and American Politics* (Cambridge, Mass.: Belknap Press, 2000), 195.

272 ***The New York Times*, in a front-page story:** Lain, "Countermajoritarian Hero," 1373; "High Court Bars Evidence," *New York Times*; *Weeks*, 232 U.S. 383; Powe, *The Warren Court*, 195.

272 **The result was a Court:** "Justices 1789 to Present," Supreme Court of the United States, supremecourt.gov/about/members_text.aspx.

273 **"If you examine the criminal law decisions":** Lain, "Countermajoritarian Hero," 1379, 1383–84, 1386–87, 1398; Michael Klarman, "Rethinking the Civil Rights and Civil Liberties Revolutions," *Virginia Law Review* 82, no. 1 (February 1996): 1, 65; Morton Horwitz, "The Warren Court and the Pursuit of Justice," *Washington and Lee Law Review* 50 (1993): 5, 9.

273 **The Warren Court was:** Powe, *The Warren Court,* 199; Horwitz, "Warren Court and the Pursuit of Justice," 1, 9.

273 **In 1966, the Court issued a second:** *Miranda v. Arizona,* 384 U.S. 436 (1966).

274 **After Miranda was questioned:** Bernard Schwartz, "Chief Justice Earl Warren: Super Chief in Action," *Tulsa Law Journal* 33 (1977): 477, 493, 495 (1997).

274 **The Court's rules:** *Miranda v. Arizona,* 384 U.S. 436 (1966); Michael Graetz and Linda Greenhouse, *The Burger Court and the Rise of the Judicial Right* (New York: Simon & Schuster, 2016), 74–75; Erwin Chemerinsky, *The Case Against the Supreme Court* (New York: Penguin, 2014), 136; Powe, *The Warren Court,* 394–95.

274 **"I guess now":** Lain, "Countermajoritarian Hero," 1361, 1421, 1421n307; David Courtwright, *No Right Turn: Conservative Politics in a Liberal America* (Cambridge, Mass.: Harvard University Press, 2010), 53; Alden Whitman, "Earl Warren, 83, Who Led High Court in Time of Vast Social Change, Is Dead," *New York Times,* July 10, 1974.

274 **With Nixon's quick nomination:** Yale Kamisar, "The Warren Court and Criminal Justice: A Quarter-Century Retrospective," *Tulsa Law Journal* 31 (1995): 1, 3; "Justices 1789 to Present," Supreme Court; Bernard Schwartz, *A History of the Supreme Court* (New York: Oxford University Press, 1993), 329; Robert B. Semple Jr., "Warren E. Burger Named Chief Justice by Nixon; Now on Appeals Bench," *New York Times,* May 22, 1969.

274 **It was less than two years:** *Harris v. New York,* 401 U.S. 222 (1971); Graetz and Greenhouse, *Burger Court,* 45, 369.

275 **Marshall, in dissent:** *Oregon v. Mathiason,* 429 U.S. 492 (1977); *California v. Beheler,* 463 U.S. 1121 (1983); John C. Jeffries, *Justice Lewis F. Powell, Jr.* (New York: Charles Scribner's Sons, 1994), 399; Graetz and Greenhouse, *Burger Court,* 45, 369.

275 **The holding that the police:** *New York v. Quarles,* 467 U.S. 649 (1984).

275 **"A majority of the Court":** *Dickerson v. United States,* 530 U.S. 428 (2000); Graetz and Greenhouse, *Burger Court,* 45, 369; Chemerinsky, *Case Against the Supreme Court,* 137.

275 **In dissent, Brennan:** *Schneckloth v. Bustamonte,* 412 U.S. 218, 277 (1973).

276 **White, writing for the majority:** *United States v. Leon,* 486 U.S. 897 (1984); *Massachusetts v. Sheppard,* 468 U.S. 981 (1984).

276 **"It now appears":** *Leon,* 486 U.S. 897; *Sheppard,* 468 U.S. 981; Graetz and Greenhouse, *Burger Court,* 49.

276 **Bostick consented, and the police:** *Florida v. Bostick,* 501 U.S. 429 (1991); David Cole, *No Equal Justice: Race and Class in the American Criminal Justice System* (New York: New Press, 1999), 16.

277 **He warned that:** *Bostick,* 501 U.S. 429.

277 **Searches of the kind:** *Bostick*, 501 U.S. 429.

277 ***Terry* was, however:** John G. Miles Jr., "Decline of the Fourth Amendment: Time to Overrule Mapp v. Ohio," *Catholic University Law Review* 27 (1978): 9, 16; David Rudovsky and David Harris, "*Terry* Stops-and-Frisks: The Troubling Use of Common Sense in a World of Empirical Data," *Ohio State Law Journal* 79 (2018): 1, 3.

278 **The ruling greatly increased:** Rudovsky and Harris, "*Terry* Stops-and-Frisks," 6–8.

278 **Few law enforcement tactics:** Al Baker and Colin Moynihan, "Paterson Signs Bill Limiting Stop-and-Frisk Data," *New York Times*, July 16, 2010; "Policing the Police on Stop-and-Frisk," editorial, *New York Times*, June 23, 2016.

278 **The Court accepted Gideon's case:** Stephen Bright and Sia Sanneh, "Fifty Years of Defiance and Resistance After *Gideon v. Wainwright*," *Yale Law Journal* 122 (2013): 2106; Anthony Lewis, "The Silencing of Gideon's Trumpet," *New York Times*, April 20, 2003.

279 **The same day, in *Douglas v. California*:** *Gideon v. Wainwright*, 372 U.S. 335; *Douglas v. California*, 372 U.S. 353 (1963).

279 **Anthony Lewis, a *New York Times* journalist:** Bright and Sanneh, "Fifty Years of Defiance and Resistance," 2106; Richard Posner, *Cardozo: A Study in Reputation* (Chicago: University of Chicago Press, 1993), 55–56; Powe, *The Warren Court*, 379; IMDb, s.v. "Gideon's Trumpet," imdb.com/title/tt0080789/.

280 **The ruling was clearly at odds:** *Kirby v. Illinois*, 406 U.S. 682 (1972); *United States v. Ash*, 413 U.S. 300 (1973).

280 **In dissent, Douglas:** *Ross v. Moffitt*, 417 U.S. 600, 616 (1974).

281 **He also testified:** *Washington v. Strickland*, 693 F.2d 1243.

281 **Even if it had not been:** *Strickland v. Washington*, 466 U.S. at 700.

281 **He insisted that there was no way:** Graetz and Greenhouse, *Burger Court*, 52–53; *Strickland*, 466 U.S. at 694, 710.

282 **It led one exasperated legal commentator:** *Muniz v. Smith*, 647 F.3d 619 (6th Cir. 2011); "Recent Cases, Muniz v. Smith," *Harvard Law Review* 125 (2012): 1498, 1505, 1505n73; Kimberly Sachs, "You Snooze, You Lose, and Your Client Gets a Retrial: United States v. Ragin and Ineffective Assistance of Counsel in Sleeping Lawyer Cases," *Villanova Law Review* 62 (2017): 427, 429, 429n11.

282 **Although the lawyer failed:** *Holsey v. Warden, Georgia Diagnostic Prison*, 694 F.3d 1230 (11th Cir. 2012); *Holsey v. Humphrey*, 133 S. Ct. 2804 (2013); Erik Eckholm, "After Delay, Inmate Is Executed in Georgia," *New York Times*, December 9, 2014.

282 **The New York State appellate court:** Ken Armstrong, "What Can You Do with a Drunken Lawyer?," Marshall Project, December 10, 2014.

283 **Many jurisdictions had extremely:** American Bar Association, *Gideon's Broken Promise: America's Continuing Quest for Equal Justice* (Chicago: American Bar Association Standing Committee on Legal Aid and Indigent Defendants, 2005), iv, 41, 46; Stephanos Bibas, "Shrinking *Gideon* and Expanding Alternatives to Lawyers," *Washington and Lee Law Review* 70 (2013): 1287, 1288; Thomas Giovanni and Roopal Patel, "Gideon at 50: Three Reforms to Revive the Right to Counsel" (New York: Brennan Center for Justice, 2013).

283 **"The court reporter":** Sixth Amendment Center, *The Right to Counsel in Mississippi: Evaluation of Adult Felony Trial Level Indigent Defense Services* (Boston: Sixth Amendment Center, 2018); Cole, *No Equal Justice*, 112–13.

283 **As one critic said:** Sixth Amendment Center, *Right to Counsel;* Cole, *No Equal Justice*, 84–85; Chemerinsky, *Case Against the Supreme Court*, 149–50 (quoting Douglas Vick, "Poorhouse Justice: Underfunded Indigent Defense Services and Arbitrary Death Sentences," 43 [1995]: 329, 398); Sara Mayeux, "What *Gideon* Did," *Columbia Law Review* 116 (2016): 15, 86, 86n352.

284 **"Pack mules can carry a lot":** American Bar Association, *Gideon's Broken Promise*, 17–18; Oliver Laugland, "The Human Toll of America's Public Defender Crisis," *Guardian*, September 7, 2016.

284 **The report cited a survey:** American Bar Association, *Gideon's Broken Promise*, 19.

284 **It does not, however:** Giovanni and Patel, "Gideon at 50," 6; *Missouri v. Frye*, 566 U.S. 134 (2012); Emily Yoffe, "Innocence Is Irrelevant," *Atlantic*, September 2017; Jed S. Rakoff, "Why Innocent People Plead Guilty," *New York Review of Books*, November 20, 2014.

285 **The report had a name:** American Bar Association, *Gideon's Broken Promise*, 19

285 **The Cincinnati-based U.S. Court of Appeals:** *Bordenkircher v. Hayes*, 434 U.S. 357, 359–60 (1978).

286 **He went on to praise:** Graetz and Greenhouse, *Burger Court*, 57–58; *Bordenkircher*, 434 U.S. at 364.

286 **That is "a tremendous amount":** *Bordenkircher*, 434 U.S. at 368; John Pfaff, *Locked In: The True Causes of Mass Incarceration—and How to Achieve Real Reform* (New York: Basic Books, 2017), 131–32.

286 **In his *Bordenkircher* dissent:** Yoffe, "Innocence Is Irrelevant"; *Bordenkircher*, 434 U.S. at 368.

287 **Defendants move through the system:** "Inside NOLA Public Defenders' Decision to Refuse Felony Cases," *60 Minutes*, CBS, available at cbsnews.com/news/inside-new-orleans-public-defenders-decision-to-refuse-felony-cases/; Emily Lane, "Orleans Public Defenders on '60 Minutes': Innocent Imprisoned Because We're Overworked," *New Orleans Times-Picayune*, April 16, 2017; American Bar Association, *The Louisiana Project: A Study of the Louisiana Defender System and Attorney Workload Standards* (New York: Postlethwaite & Netterville and the American Bar Association Standing Committee on Legal Aid and Indigent Defendants, 2017); Debbie Elliott, "Public Defenders Hard to Come By in Louisiana," *All Things Considered*, NPR, March 10, 2017.

287 **As it was, Gamble:** "Inside NOLA Public Defenders' Decision"; Lane, "Orleans Public Defenders on '60 Minutes.'"

287 **The National Registry of Exonerations:** Rakoff, "Why Innocent People Plead Guilty"; Innocence Project, "DNA Exonerations in the United States," available at innocenceproject.org/dna-exonerations-in-the-united-states/; "% Exonerations by

Contributing Factor," National Registry of Exonerations," law.umich.edu/special/exoneration/Pages/ExonerationsContribFactorsByCrime.aspx.

288 **"If his lawyer":** Rakoff, "Why Innocent People Plead Guilty."

288 **In 1984, 1986, and 1994:** Tanya Golash-Boza, "America's Mass Incarceration Problem in 5 Charts—Or Why Sessions Shouldn't Bring Back Mandatory Minimums," *The Conversation,* May 29, 2017, theconversation.com/americas-mass-incarceration-problem-in-5-charts-or-why-sessions-shouldnt-bring-back-mandatory-minimums-78019; Inimai Chettiar and Lauren-Brooke Eisen, "The Complex History of the Controversial 1994 Crime Bill" (New York: Brennan Center for Justice, April 14, 2016); Office of the President, "Economic Perspectives on Incarceration and the Criminal Justice System" (April 2016), 18–19; Mirko Bagaric, Sandeep Gopalan, and Marissa Florio, "A Principled Strategy for Addressing the Incarceration Crisis: Redefining Excessive Imprisonment as a Human Rights Abuse," *Cardozo Law Review* 38 (2017): 1663, 1680–81; Pfaff, *Locked In,* 54; American Bar Association Justice Kennedy Commission, *Reports with Recommendations to the ABA House of Delegates* (August 2004), iii; "Mandatory Minimum Sentences Decline, Sentencing Commission Says," United States Courts, July 25, 2017, uscourts.gov/news/2017/07/25/mandatory-minimum-sentences-decline-sentencing-commission-says.

289 **In 2002, one of those inmates:** Jed Rakoff, "Mass Incarceration: The Silence of the Judges," *New York Review of Books,* May 21, 2015; Office of the President, "Economic Perspectives on Incarceration"; Michael Mueller-Smith, "The Criminal and Labor Market Impacts of Incarceration" (unpublished working paper, University of Michigan, Ann Arbor, August 18, 2015); Peter Wagner and Wendy Sawyer, "Mass Incarceration: The Whole Pie 2018," Prison Policy Initiative, March 14, 2018, prisonpolicy.org/reports/pie2018.html; Erwin Chemerinsky, "Cruel and Unusual: The Story of Leandro Andrade," *Drake Law Review* 52 (2003).

289 **Andrade was thirty-seven:** *Lockyer v. Andrade,* 538 U.S. 63, 63–68 (2003); Chemerinsky, "Cruel and Unusual," 1, 1–3.

289 **The San Francisco–based U.S. Court of Appeals:** *Andrade v. Attorney General of California,* 270 F.3d 743 (9th Cir. 2001); *Lockyer,* 538 U.S. at 77; Chemerinsky, "Cruel and Unusual," 3–4; *Andrade,* 270 F.3d 743.

290 **Souter, writing for the four liberal justices:** *Lockyer,* 538 U.S. at 77; Chemerinsky, "Cruel and Unusual," 3–4.

290 **The Eighth Amendment did:** *State Farm Mutual Automobile Insurance Co. v. Campbell,* 538 U.S. 408 (2003).

291 **The United States has about 4.3 percent:** Wendy Sawyer and Peter Wagner, "Mass Incarceration: The Whole Pie 2019," Prison Policy Initiative, March 19, 2019, prisonpolicy.org/reports/pie2019.html; "World Prison Populations," BBC News, news.bbc.co.uk/2/shared/spl/hi/uk/06/prisons/html/nn1page1.stm.

291 **The incarceration rate has dipped:** Office of the President, "Economic Perspectives on Incarceration"; Pfaff, *Locked In,* 4–5; Golash-Boza, "America's Mass Incarceration

Problem in 5 Charts"; John Gramlich, "America's Incarceration Rate Is at a Two-Decade Low," Pew Research Center Fact Tank, May 2, 2018, pewresearch.org/fact-tank/2018/05/02/americas-incarceration-rate-is-at-a-two-decade-low/.

291 **Another leading criminology expert:** Lauren-Brooke "L.B." Eisen et al., "How Many Americans Are Unnecessarily Incarcerated?" (New York: Brennan Center for Justice, December 9, 2016); Adam Gopnik, "How We Misunderstand Mass Incarceration," *New Yorker,* April 10, 2017; Adam Liptak, "U.S. Prison Population Dwarfs That of Other Nations," *New York Times,* April 23, 2008.

292 **"I think it's a miscarriage":** Mallory Simon and Sara Sidner, "The Judge Who Says He's Part of the Gravest Injustice in America," CNN, June 3, 2017.

293 **He noted, however:** Richard A. Oppel Jr., "Sentencing Shift Gives New Leverage to Prosecutors," *New York Times,* September 25, 2011.

293 **Many more, however, are:** Patrick Liu et al., "The Economics of Bail and Pretrial Detention," Brookings Institution, 2018, 3.

293 **The cash bail system:** Liu, "Economics of Bail and Pretrial Detention," 3–6; Samuel Wiseman, "Pretrial Detention and the Right to Be Monitored," *Yale Law Journal* 123 (2014): 1118.

294 **The crime he was accused of:** *United States v. Salerno,* 481 U.S. 739 (1987); Associated Press, "Supreme Court Won't Consider Georgia City's Cash Bail Policy," *U.S. News & World Report,* April 1, 2019; Scott Shackford, "Supreme Court Turns Away Georgia Cash Bail Challenge," *Reason,* April 2, 2019.

294 **Celebrities have weighed in:** Udi Ofer, "We Can't End Mass Incarceration Without Ending Money Bail," ACLU, December 11, 2017; Shawn Carter, "Jay Z: For Father's Day, I'm Taking On the Exploitative Bail Industry," *Time,* June 16, 2017; Brief for the American Bar Association as Amicus Curiae in Support of Petitioner, *Walker v. Calhoun* (Supreme Court, No. 18-814, 2019).

295 **It also reported that:** Kia Makarechi, "What the Data Really Says About Police and Racial Bias," *Vanity Fair,* July 14, 2016; Sharon LaFraniere and Andrew Lehren, "The Disproportionate Risks of Driving While Black," *New York Times,* October 24, 2015.

295 **Whites searched without:** Makarechi, "What the Data Really Says About Police and Racial Bias"; *Report of the Blue Ribbon Panel of Transparency, Accountability, and Fairness in Law Enforcement* (City of San Francisco, July 2016), SFBlueRibbonPanel.com.

295 **It found that when:** "Research Finds Racial Disparities in Prison Sentences," *Weekend Morning Edition,* NPR, November 25, 2017; Christopher Ingraham, "Black Men Sentenced to More Time for Committing the Exact Same Crime as a White Person, Study Finds," *Washington Post,* November 16, 2017; German Lopez, "Report: Black Men Get Longer Sentences for the Same Federal Crime as White Men," *Vox,* November 17, 2017; Glenn R. Schmitt, Louis Reedt, and Kevin Blackwell, "Demographic Differences in Sentencing: An Update to the 2012 *Booker* Report" (Washington, D.C.: U.S. Sentencing Commission, November 14, 2017); Josh Salman, Emily Le Coz, and Elizabeth Johnson, "Florida's Broken Sentencing System," *Sarasota Herald-Tribune,* December 12, 2016.

296 **McCleskey argued that:** *McCleskey v. Kemp,* 481 U.S. 279 (1987).

296 **He argued that Georgia's death penalty:** *McCleskey,* 481 U.S. 279; Chemerinsky, *Case Against the Supreme Court,* 43; Jeffries, *Justice Lewis F. Powell, Jr.,* 438.

296 **"If we accepted McCleskey's claim":** *McCleskey,* 481 U.S. 279; Chemerinsky, *Case Against the Supreme Court,* 45.

296 **If McCleskey "asked his lawyer":** *McCleskey,* 481 U.S. at 292–93, 322–23; Samuel Gross, "David Baldus and the Legacy of McCleskey v. Kemp," *Iowa Law Review* 97 (2012): 1906, 1915–16.

297 **The majority had made clear:** *McCleskey,* 481 U.S. at 292–93, 322–23.

297 **Anthony Amsterdam, a professor:** Adam Liptak, "New Look at an Old Memo Casts More Doubt on Rehnquist," *New York Times,* March 19, 2012.

297 **The result would not only:** Douglas Berman, "Introduction: McCleskey at 25: Reexamining the 'Fear of Too Much Justice,'" *Ohio State Journal of Criminal Law* 10 (2012): 1.

298 **The reason, she said:** Transcript, *Bill Moyers Journal,* PBS, April 2, 2010, pbs.org/moyers/journal/04022010/transcript1.html; Michelle Alexander, *The New Jim Crow: Mass Incarceration in the Age of Colorblindness* (New York: New Press, 2010), 114.

298 **The Securities and Exchange Commission:** *Dirks v. Securities and Exchange Commission,* 463 U.S. 646 (1983).

299 **The majority then used this "innovation":** *Dirks,* 463 U.S. 646.

299 **He challenged his conviction:** *Cheek v. United States,* 498 U.S. 192 (1991); Nicholas A. Mirkay III, "The Supreme Court's Decision in *Cheek*: Does It Encourage Willful Tax Evasion?," *Missouri Law Review* 56, no. 4 (Fall 1991): 1119–22.

299 **White said Cheek:** *Cheek,* 498 U.S. at 192; Mirkay, "Supreme Court's Decision in *Cheek,*" 1119–22.

299 **The decision, Blackmun said:** Bruce Grace, "Ignorance of the Law as an Excuse," *Columbia Law Review* 86 (1986): 1392, 1395; Linda Greenhouse, "Supreme Court Ruling Supports Tax Protester," *New York Times,* January 9, 2009.

300 **The dissenters, Blackmun and Marshall:** *Cheek,* 498 U.S. at 199; "Pilot Convicted of Income Tax Fraud," *Chicago Tribune,* January 28, 1992.

300 **The Court's overall message:** Peter Henning, "Narrowing the Definition of White Collar Crimes," *New York Times,* March 3, 2015; *Ratzlaf v. United States,* 510 U.S. 135 (1994).

300 **The Court had become:** J. Kelly Strader, "The Judicial Politics of White Collar Crime," *Hastings Law Journal* 50 (1999): 1199, 1201–2, 1246; *Evans v. United States,* 504 U.S. 255, 289 (1992).

301 **Rehnquist voted for the defendant:** Strader, "Judicial Politics of White Collar Crime," 1199, 1229–30.

301 **For years now, the only justices:** Strader, "Judicial Politics of White Collar Crime," 1250; Thomas Byrne Edsall, "Studies: Conservatives Are from Mars, Liberals Are from Venus," *Atlantic,* February 6, 2016.

302 **This statistic supports:** Bernadette Rabuy and Daniel Kopf, "Prisons of Poverty," Prison Policy Initiative, July 9, 2015, prisonpolicy.org/reports/income.html; Nathaniel

Lewis, "Mass Incarceration: New Jim Crow, Class War, or Both?," People's Policy Project, January 30, 2018.

302 **In a sample of prisoners:** Economic Mobility Project and the Public Safety Performance Project of the Pew Charitable Trusts, "Collateral Costs: Incarceration's Effect on Economic Mobility" (Washington, D.C.: Pew Charitable Trusts, 2010), 3–4; Rabuy and Kopf, "Prisons of Poverty"; Melissa Kearney and Benjamin Harris, "Ten Economic Facts About Crime and Incarceration in the United States," Brookings Institution, May 1, 2014; Adam Looney and Nicholas Turner, "Work and Opportunity Before and After Incarceration," Brookings Institution, March 14, 2018; Dylan Matthews, "Want to Stay Out of Prison? Choose Rich Parents," *Vox*, March 14, 2018; Christopher Ingraham, "Where America's Future Prisoners Are Born," *Washington, Post*, March 14, 2018.

302 **While 6 percent of white men:** Hedwig Lee et al., "Racial Inequalities in Connectedness to Imprisoned Individuals in the United States," *Du Bois Review: Social Science Research on Race* 12 (Fall 2015): 269–82; Wagner and Sawyer, "Mass Incarceration: The Whole Pie 2018"; John Gramlich, "The Gap Between the Number of Blacks and Whites in Prison Is Shrinking," Pew Research Center, April 30, 2019; Rakoff, "Mass Incarceration."

302 **Much of that gap is due:** Pew Charitable Trusts, "Collateral Costs," 3–4; Rabuy and Kopf, "Prisons of Poverty"; Kearney and Harris, "Ten Economic Facts About Crime and Incarceration"; Looney and Turner, "Work and Opportunity Before and After Incarceration"; Matthews, "Want to Stay Out of Prison?"; Ingraham, "Where America's Future Prisoners Are Born."

303 **When a father is imprisoned:** Pew Charitable Trusts, "Collateral Costs," 3–4.

303 **The Pew Charitable Trusts study concluded:** Pew Charitable Trusts, "Collateral Costs," 20; Valerie Strauss, "Mass Incarceration of African Americans Affects the Racial Achievement Gap—Report," *Washington Post*, March 15, 2017.

303 **The detective arrested:** *Utah v. Strieff*, 136 S. Ct. 2056 (2016); "Leading Case, Utah v. Strieff," *Harvard Law Review* 130 (2016): 337.

304 **When he appealed:** *Strieff*, 136 S. Ct. 2056; "Leading Case, Utah v. Strieff," *Harvard Law Review*.

304 **Thomas said, however:** *Strieff*, 136 S. Ct. 2056.

305 **In many cases, warrants:** Randall Guynes and Russell Wolff, "Un-served Arrest Warrants: An Exploratory Study," National Institute of Justice/Department of Justice, April 22, 2004; "How NYC Is Tackling 1.4 Million Open Arrest Warrants for 'Quality-of-Life' Crimes," *PBS NewsHour*, January 19, 2016; *Utah v. Strieff*, 136 S. Ct. 2056 (2016); "U.S. Finds Pattern of Biased Policing in Ferguson," NBC News, March 3, 2015.

305 **As a result, Kagan said:** *Strieff*, 136 S. Ct. 2056.

305 **As a result, anything the officer:** *Strieff*, 136 S. Ct. 2056.

305 **At jail, the officer can:** *Strieff*, 136 S. Ct. 2056.

306 **The system the Court was establishing:** *Strieff*, 136 S. Ct. 2056.

306 **As the sociologists explain:** David Jacobs, "Inequality and Police Strength: Conflict Theory and Coercive Control in Metropolitan Areas," *American Sociological Review* 44 (1979): 913, 914.

307 **"I doubt that the proud men":** *Strieff*, 136 S. Ct. 2056; *King*, 569 U.S. 435 (2013).

CONCLUSION

309 **Majority Leader Mitch McConnell:** Alan Fram, Lisa Mascaro, and Matthew Daly, "Kavanaugh Sworn to High Court After Confirmation," Associated Press, October 6, 2018; Clare Foran, "Brett Kavanaugh Sworn In as Supreme Court Justice," CNN, October 6, 2018.

310 **Many Court watchers believed:** Jess Braven, "Conservative-Dominated Supreme Court Fulfills Nixon-Era Dream," *Wall Street Journal*, October 9, 2018.

313 **Now that O'Connor was gone:** Louise Melling, "Will the Supreme Court Overturn Roe v. Wade After All?," *New York Times*, December 11, 2018.

313 **In a big case:** Erwin Chemerinsky, *The Case Against the Supreme Court* (New York: Penguin, 2014), 47–48; *Parents Involved in Community Schools v. Seattle School District No. 1*, 551 U.S. 701 (2007); *Fisher v. University of Texas*, 36 S. Ct. 2198 (2016); Adam Harris, "The Era of Affirmative Action May Not Last Much Longer," *Atlantic*, July 3, 2018.

313 **It was possible that:** Dylan Matthews, "America Under Brett Kavanaugh," *Vox*, October 5, 2018.

314 **Millions of Americans:** Melling, "Will the Supreme Court Overturn"; Harris, "Era of Affirmative Action May Not Last."

315 **In the "switch in time":** *A.L.A. Schechter Poultry Corp. v. United States*, 295 U.S. 495 (1935); *United States v. Butler*, 297 U.S. 1 (1936).

315 **It included a presentation:** Peter Montgomery, "'Rome Wasn't Burned in a Day': Right Wing Plans for SCOTUS to Dismantle the Safety Net," *Right Wing Watch*, People for the American Way, July 24, 2018.

315 **"Don't be cowed":** Andrew C. McCarthy, "Limiting the General Welfare Clause," *National Review*, June 30, 2012; Montgomery, "'Rome Wasn't Burned in a Day.'"

316 **In 1995 and 2000:** *United States v. Lopez*, 514 U.S. 549 (1995); *United States v. Morrison*, 529 U.S. 598 (2000).

316 **In his opinion:** *National Federation of Independent Business v. Sebelius*, 567 U.S. 519 (2012).

316 **When Barack Obama:** James Stewart, "In Obama's Victory, a Loss for Congress," *New York Times*, June 29, 2012; Brad Plumer, "Supreme Court Puts New Limits on Commerce Clause. But Will It Matter?," *Washington Post*, June 28, 2012; Tom Scocca, "Obama Wins the Battle, Roberts Wins the War," *Slate*, June 28, 2012.

317 **At the oral argument:** Eliot Mincberg, "Edit Memo: Inside Trump's Plan to Pack Our Courts and Repeal the New Deal," People for the American Way, 2018; Amy Howe, "Argument Analysis: An Epic Day for Employers in Arbitration Case," *SCOTUSblog*, October 2, 2017.

317 **A survey by an employment website:** Kevin Kelleher, "Gilded Age 2.0: U.S. Income Inequality Increases to Pre–Great Depression Levels," *Fortune*, February 13, 2019; "The Shrinking Middle Class," *Fortune*, December 20, 2018; Emmie Martin, "The Government Shutdown Spotlights a Bigger Issue: 78 Percent of U.S. Workers Live Paycheck to Paycheck," CNBC, January 9, 2019.

318 **Dalio called on the nation's leaders:** Erik Schatzker, "Ray Dalio Sounds a New Alarm on Capitalism's Flaws, Warns of Revolution," *Bloomberg*, April 4, 2019; Eduardo Porter, "Income Inequality and the Ills Behind It," *New York Times*, July 29, 2014; Catherine Clifford, "Warren Buffett on Income Inequality: 'A Family' Takes Care of Its Own and the US Should Too," CNBC, February 26, 2019.

PHOTOGRAPH CREDITS

Insert page 1, top: Jacobus tenBroek Library, National Federation of the Blind. **Bottom:** Earl Warren, 1891– . LC-USZ62-41653. Prints and Photographs Division, Library of Congress.

Page 2: Petition for a Writ of Certiorari from Clarence Gideon to the Supreme Court of the United States. Appellate Jurisdiction Case File *Gideon v. Wainwright*, 1/8/1962–4/12/1963. Record Group 267: Records of the Supreme Court of the United States, 1772–2007. National Archives Catalog.

Page 3, top: LBJ Library photo by Yoichi Okamoto, 08/06/1965. Serial number A1030-17a. LBJ Presidential Library. **Bottom left:** Thurgood Marshall by Yoichi Okamoto, 06/13/1967. White House Photo Office Collection, 11/22/1963–1/20/1969. National Archives Catalog. **Bottom right:** Official portrait of United States Supreme Court Justice Abe Fortas. From the Collection of the Supreme Court of the United States.

Page 4, top: President Nixon and Warren Burger. White House Photo Office Collection (Nixon Administration), 1/20/1969–8/9/1974. **Bottom left:** Justice William H. Rehnquist, 1972. LC-USZ62-60141. Prints and Photographs Division, Library of Congress. **Bottom right:** Justice Lewis F. Powell Jr., January 26, 1976. LC-USZ62-60140. Prints and Photographs Division, Library of Congress.

Page 5, top: U.S. Supreme Court, 1976. LC-USZ62-60135. Prints and Photographs Division, Library of Congress. **Bottom:** Supreme Court justices by Karl H. Schumacher, 9/30/1977. White House Staff Photographer's Collection, 1/20/1977–1/20/1981. National Archives Catalog.

Page 6, top: President Ronald Reagan meeting with Supreme Court nominee Sandra Day O'Connor and William French Smith, 7/15/1981. White House Photographic Collection, 1/20/1981–1/20/1989. National Archives Catalog. **Middle:** President Ronald Reagan announcing nomination of Judge Anthony Kennedy, 11/11/1987. White House Photographic Collection, 1/20/1981–1/20/1989. National Archives Catalog. **Bottom:** President Reagan with Supreme Court justices, 9/25/1981. White House Photographic Collection, 1/20/1981–1/20/1989. National Archives Catalog.

Page 7, top: Appointment of Ruth Bader Ginsburg, 6/14/1993. Photographs of the White House Photograph Office (Clinton Administration), 1/20/1993–1/20/2001. National Archives Catalog. **Bottom left:** President George W. Bush and Supreme Court justice nominee John Roberts, by Eric Draper, 7/19/2005. **Bottom right:** President George W. Bush announces his nomination of Judge Samuel A. Alito Jr., by Paul Morse, 10/31/2005. Records of the White House Photo Office (George W. Bush Administration), 1/20/2001–1/20/2009. National Archives Catalog.

Page 8, top: President Barack Obama signs into law the Lilly Ledbetter Fair Pay Act in the East Room of the White House, January 29, 2009. Official White House Photo by Joyce Boghosian. **Bottom:** President Donald J. Trump and Supreme Court Justice Brett Kavanaugh, November 8, 2018. Official White House Photo by Shealah Craighead.

INDEX

ALSO AVAILABLE

Imbeciles

The Supreme Court, American Eugenics, and the Sterilization of Carrie Buck

In 1927, the Supreme Court handed down a ruling so disturbing, ignorant, and cruel that it stands as one of the great injustices in American history. In *Imbeciles*, bestselling author Adam Cohen exposes the court's decision to allow the sterilization of a young woman it wrongly thought to be "feebleminded" and to champion the mass eugenic sterilization of undesirable citizens. With the intellectual force of a legal brief and the passion of a front-page exposé, *Imbeciles* is an ardent indictment of our champions of justice.

"Combines an investigative journalist's instinct for the misuse of power . . . and a historian's eye for detail to tell this compelling and emotional story." –*Los Angeles Review of Books*

PENGUIN BOOKS